On the Ego and on God

Further Cartesian Questions

John D. Caputo, *series editor*

PERSPECTIVES IN
CONTINENTAL
PHILOSOPHY

JEAN-LUC MARION

On the Ego and on God
Further Cartesian Questions

TRANSLATED BY CHRISTINA M. GSCHWANDTNER

FORDHAM UNIVERSITY PRESS
New York ▪ 2007

All of the essays selected by Jean-Luc Marion for *On the Ego and on God: Further Cartesian Questions* were published in French in 1996 under the title *Questions cartésiennes II: Sur l'ego et sur Dieu* © Presses Universitaires de France, 1996.

This book has been published with the assistance of the National Center for the Book—French Ministry of Culture.

Ouvrage publié avec le soutien du Centre national du livre—ministère français chargé de la culture.

Library of Congress Cataloging-in-Publication Data

Marion, Jean-Luc, 1946–
[Sur l'ego et sur Dieu. English]
On the ego and on God : further Cartesian questions / Jean-Luc Marion ; translated by Christina M. Gschwandtner.—1st ed.
    p. cm.
Includes bibliographical references (p.   ) and index.
ISBN-13: 978-0-8232-2754-9 (cloth : alk. paper)
ISBN-13: 978-0-8232-2755-6 (pbk. : alk. paper)
1. Descartes, René 1596–1650. 2. Self. 3. God. I. Title
B1875.M336513 2007
194—dc22

                                                      2007039799

Printed in the United States of America
09 08 07 5 4 3 2 1
First edition

For Cécile and Marie

Contents

Translator's Introduction

Jean-Luc Marion has written extensively on the work of René Descartes. In order to appreciate the present study more fully, it is useful to set it in the context of Marion's other writings and to see its place in his thought. Marion's early publications are all close studies of various topics in Descartes, especially concerning metaphysics, God, and the human ego. Marion's first major book, *Sur l'ontologie grise de Descartes* (Paris: Vrin, 1975; translated by Sarah Donohue as *Descartes's Grey Ontology* [South Bend, IN: St. Augustine's Press, 2007]) focused on Descartes' "gray ontology" in his early treatise *Regulae ad directionem ingenii* (*Rules for the Direction of the Mind*), in which Descartes responds to and subverts Aristotelian theses and arguments. Throughout this first work Marion shows how Descartes transforms the concept of metaphysics into an epistemological endeavor, namely, a study of first principles. Ontology hence becomes dependent on the knowledge of the ego, which grounds all being.

Marion followed this early engagement with Descartes' metaphysics with a detailed and careful study: *Sur la théologie blanche de Descartes* (Paris: Presses Universitaires de France, 1981). As the title indicates, Marion is here more concerned with Descartes' theology, which he argues is a "refused" endeavor; Descartes explicitly leaves the place of theology "blank" or "erased" in his work. He does so through his objection to the practice of making God subject to human language, which is particularly evident in his insistence on the creation of the eternal truths. Descartes refuses to employ univocal language for the divine in the way in which most thinkers of his day do, especially when they apply the language of being and of human geometry or logic to God. Throughout this important work Marion shows how the rise of this univocal language is linked to the demise of the medieval doctrines of analogy.

Marion concluded what he called his triptych on Descartes with a third work on the "metaphysical prism" of Descartes: *Sur le prisme métaphysique de Descartes* (Paris: Presses Universitaires de France, 1986; translated by Jeffrey L. Kosky as *On Descartes' Metaphysical Prism* [Chicago: University of Chicago Press, 1999]). Here he analyzes Descartes' metaphysics beyond the *Regulae* in the Cartesian corpus as a whole and argues that it not only displays an onto-theological structure (in Heidegger's sense of the term) but does so in a doubled fashion. Descartes, in Marion's reading, develops two onto-theo-logical metaphysical systems. One is based on the ego and is a metaphysics of thought. (This refers to what Marion calls in his earlier work a "gray ontology" because it subverts traditional ontology into an epistemological register.) The ego makes all other beings possible by thinking them as their source and center. A second metaphysical system crosses and supplements the first, in which God (and no longer the ego) functions as ground of the system that sustains all other beings (including the ego), especially through divine causality. Marion assumes familiarity with this argument in several of the chapters included in this book, especially those on Descartes' concepts of substance and of the *causa sui* (both notions closely linked to the two metaphysical systems).

Although Marion's interest after these early writings has seemed increasingly turned toward more theological and phenomenological work, he has never stopped analyzing and interpreting Descartes. A first collection of papers on Descartes, especially concerned again with the topic of metaphysics, was published in 1991 as *Questions cartésiennes* (Paris: Presses Universitaires de France; translated by Daniel Garber as *Cartesian Questions* [Chicago: University of Chicago Press, 1999]). The present work followed in 1996 as *Questions cartésiennes II: Sur l'ego et sur Dieu*. As its subtitle makes clear, the book deals with two great themes in the work of Descartes: the human ego and God. In it Marion brings together papers and articles on these topics that were written between 1985 and 1996. Although the first *Cartesian Questions* focused primarily on metaphysics (e.g., exploring the metaphysical situation of the *Discourse* or the development of metaphysics in the *Meditations*), the topic of metaphysics is not absent from this present work, since this theme is always closely linked to the other two (God and ego) for Marion (and indeed, for Descartes himself).

In fact, some insights into Marion's assertions about metaphysics (and specifically Cartesian metaphysics) are necessary for understanding many of his claims in this work. Marion obviously presupposes familiarity with the arguments of his earlier writings. Let me summarize briefly a couple of the arguments particularly important (or perhaps less familiar to the English reader). First, in chapter 2 of *Cartesian Questions* Marion outlines the development of Descartes' metaphysics from the *Discourse* to the *Meditations* in terms of the proofs for God's existence. He suggests that the *Discourse* contains a robust theory of the ego (and therefore a fully developed onto-theology of thought) but is still missing the notion of the *causa sui* and the definition of and proof for God that is dependent upon it (and therefore also lacks the second onto-theo-logy of causality based on God). The need for the *causa sui* in order to establish a full metaphysical system is presupposed and more fully developed here (in Chapter 8). In this context, Marion makes an interesting argument. He suggests that the development of the Cartesian metaphysical system (and especially his use of the notion of the *causa sui*) might lead to a reevaluation of the metaphysical status of the thinkers prior to Descartes. Since the medieval scholars (and Marion cites many of them) consistently refused any notion of a *causa sui* or any submission of God to efficient causality, one might suggest that their thinking is precisely not "metaphysical"—at least not in the "onto-theo-logical" sense of that term. It is therefore important to read Marion's claims about metaphysics in light of his reading of both Descartes and Heidegger.

Second, in chapter 3 of *Cartesian Questions* and the second part of *Théologie blanche* Marion reconstructs a "code" in Descartes' work and explains the notion of the "simple natures" that make this code possible. "Simple nature" refers to the most basic notion to which a thing can be reduced as an idea in the mind. (It does not refer to the objects directly but to the mind's construction.) In the article in *Cartesian Questions*, he examines the status of the simple natures in the *Meditations*, while he argues in *Théologie blanche* that Descartes' notion of "simple natures" develops from something the mind discovers in nature to something it must construct and organize into an order (which constitutes the code). So while at first it seems that the

code can be discovered in nature by deconstructing it into simple natures, increasingly the code becomes the logic the human mind constructs and imposes on nature. Marion also suggests in both places
that Descartes envisions the idea of a super- or hyper-code (which
helps make sense of the confusing demon at the beginning of the *Meditations*). This would be the acknowledgment by the human ego that
it cannot have direct access to the divine order but must discover
the particular code that God has actually employed in creating this
particular world (and that might well have been otherwise). It is
therefore not deceived by God but really deceives itself. Marion refers to this argument and to the simple natures repeatedly in the present study.

Finally, chapters 5 and 6 of *Cartesian Questions* already deal with
the topic of the ego. While chapter 6 primarily outlines the traditional
view of the Cartesian self as solitary, closed in upon itself, and incapable of encountering any true alter ego, Marion does suggest at the
end of this chapter that the ego might encounter a true other in the
divine (130). Chapter 5 of *Cartesian Questions* takes a further step in
this direction by exploring the idea that in some places the Cartesian
ego might affect itself. He employs Michel Henry in order to show
that the ego is not pure intentionality directed outward toward objects, but also exercises a kind of "auto-affection" that is a "receptiv-
ity," an experience of absolute immanence (104–5). Marion proceeds
to develop the notion of a kind of generosity of the ego that would
allow for an other to affect the ego and that would begin to challenge
the traditional autistic view of the subject. Marion presumes familiarity with these arguments in Chapters 1 and 2 of *On the Ego and on
God*, where he will carry these suggestions much further.

Since I have already alluded to several of the arguments Marion
sustains in the present work, let me introduce them a bit more, before
concluding by outlining some of the ways in which these discussions
are significant for Marion's work overall. First, a brief word regarding the organization of the chapters. The order of the chapters in the
French original has been slightly modified to accommodate the omission of two chapters in the French version, one on Kant and one on
Mersenne. The French version has three sections: I. Ego, II. God,
III. Contexts. Since the original chapters 8 (on Kant) and 9 (on
Mersenne) are not included here, the chapter on the dialogue structure of the *Meditations*, originally chapter 9, has been included as
Chapter 2 in Part I, on the ego (where it fits well, since it supple-
ments the argument Marion outlines in Chapter 1). The chapter on

Pascal, originally chapter 10, to some extent fits into both sections, since it connects not only to the topic of the ego but also to that of God. It follows Chapter 2, which examines the "general rule of evidence/truth" in Descartes, particularly well, however, since it shows how Pascal used and departed from this rule and its evidence. Chapters 5 and 6 in the original have also been switched, so that the two chapters dealing with the topic of the eternal truths immediately follow each other. My comments below refer, of course, to the order of the chapters in this translation.

In Chapter 1, Marion examines what he calls the "inherent alterity" of the ego. He argues that Descartes moves from a solipsistic view of the ego as *ego cogito, ergo sum* in his earlier writings to a nonsolipsistic definition of the ego as *ego sum, ego existo* in the *Meditations*. In the later text, the ego does not establish its existence in a tautology, but rather is engaged in a primordial dialogue. Although the dialogue partner is not definitively identified (it might be God or the evil genius or even the ego itself as a sort of alter ego), this interpretation challenges, in Marion's view, the traditional view of Descartes' theory of the self as enclosed in itself and without connection to the outside world or to any other. Marion also shows how Descartes goes beyond Augustine's formulation of a proof for the self's existence through its doubt or deception (which Descartes rejects as a simplistic tautology) to a new formulation of the self as being in dialogue with another who addresses it first: the ego "does not have the first word. It hears it." Marion therefore contends that there is not a simple inconsistency (of different formulations) but rather a significant development in Descartes' work from the *Discourse* to the *Meditations*.

He carries this interpretation further in Chapter 2 (chapter 9 in the original) by showing that especially the *Meditations*, but in fact all Descartes' works, are written in a dialogue form. He insists that Descartes always expected objections to his initial theses and then consistently responded to these objections with replies. This responsorial schema, as Marion calls it, becomes more and more explicit as Descartes' work evolves. While it is mostly implicit in the early works (the *Regulae*, e.g., constitutes a sort of implied dialogue with Aristotle), it becomes more obvious after the *Discourse*, where Descartes responded to the objections made to his work in personal letters. Even more explicitly, the *Meditations*, Marion argues, are to a great extent a direct response to the objections posed to the metaphysical aspects (part 4) of the *Discourse on Method*. The *Replies*, which follow the *Meditations* and were printed with it, therefore constitute an integral part of the text and are not merely an insignificant and superfluous appendix. Descartes fully expected and actively solicited these objections and planned the replies to them as necessary for fully understanding his argument. This structure suggests, moreover, that Descartes conceived of his philosophy as generated through and in dialogue, not as the isolated exercise of a solitary and solipsistic thinker: "Cartesian reason is communicative, precisely because truth manifests itself by a display of evidence; indissolubly, at one and the same time, it is to one's own reason and to the community of those looking on that the thing appears." Chapter 2 therefore confirms and deepens the insights of Chapter 1 by showing that both in content (definition of the ego) and in style (organization of the work) Descartes is far from the solipsistic thinker as whom he has often been portrayed.

Chapters 3 and 4 (chapters 2 and 10, respectively, in the original) focus on the "general rule of truth," first in Descartes and then in Pascal. Descartes establishes as a "general rule" what he sees by the "light of nature," namely, that whatever is completely clear and evident is absolutely true. Marion argues that Descartes does not engage in a circular argument here, as has often been claimed. In fact, most canonical interpretations of this passage miss the point altogether and ignore what constitutes the real problem for Descartes. In Marion's reading, Descartes is worried not that the establishment of evidence might be uncertain and would need divine confirmation but rather that the ego might not sustain the attentive perception necessary for establishing something as clearly evident. Descartes makes the rule dependent entirely upon the ego; the two go together and imply each other. It is thus less a matter of finding external confirmation of this rule (e.g., by grounding it in divine veracity) than it is a matter of the ego's perceiving clearly. (Thus, as Marion concludes, it is an epistemological and not a theological difficulty.) Evidence is established by being based on the ego. The equivalence between self-thinking and the thinker's existence not only is never challenged and must not be verified by an outside truth, but becomes "extended to God and, in a weaker sense, to the essences of material things." Marion concludes that not only is the general rule never really in doubt, but it "does not cease to be deployed, to the point where it appears as the speculative heart of the whole *Meditations*, since it sustains its very ambition—that evidence always show the truth."

In Chapter 4, Marion suggests that Pascal challenges this conception that sees truth as based on evidence and instead makes a distinction between two different kinds of truth or evidence, namely, those of the mind and of the heart. He traces Pascal's development of this second kind of evidence or knowledge through several works, showing how Pascal first seems entirely Cartesian in his scientific investigations and repeats Descartes' "rule of truth." Yet Pascal quickly begins to set aside cases in which evidence dazzles us and is so evident that rules cannot be applied to it; it is grasped in a different fashion. Pascal goes on to speak of the evidence of the heart, of a method of persuasion or pleasure that is not about knowledge or proof but about a kind of charm or agreeableness. To know this kind of truth, we must not think it but love it, since it appeals primarily not to our mind but to our will or desire. Marion insists that Pascal does not merely employ this method (albeit in an undeveloped fashion) for theological matters (e.g., to relate to God) but uses it in a more generally philosophical fashion. Pascal therefore challenges Descartes and maybe even suggests "a new definition of the essence of truth."

In Chapter 5, Marion examines the concept of substance in Descartes. In a close comparison with Suárez' use of this term, Marion shows how Descartes subverts Suárez' definition of substance in terms of perseity, nonindigence, and subsistence in order to apply the concept of substance primarily (if not solely) to the ego (instead of to God). Marion points out how substance, in its meaning of subsistence and when applied to the ego, ends up defining being in terms of "permanent presence" (as Heidegger will later contend). He claims that for Descartes there is no "relation of analogy between the total substantiality of God and the conditional substantiality of the created"; God becomes merely a way of supporting the substantiality of the ego. The internal contradictions in Descartes' use of the term *substance* are united in his focus on the principal attribute that allows substance to be known to the mind. In Marion's view, Descartes therefore effectively empties the term of its content. His ambivalent use of the concept accounts for its disappearance from the subsequent history of metaphysics.

In Part II, Marion moves to the topic of God in Descartes. Chapters 6 and 7 (chapters 4 and 6 in the original) are devoted to the question of the creation of the eternal truths. Much of Marion's argument in both chapters is grounded in his thorough treatment of this problematic in *Théologie blanche*, where he shows that Descartes' thesis that the eternal truths are created by God and dependent upon the divine is not only unique to Descartes but at the very heart of Descartes' thought about God. By insisting that mathematical truths are not superior to God and that they could have been otherwise if God had so chosen (and are therefore dependent upon the divine will), Descartes opposes most of the scientific (and even theological) thinking of his time, represented especially by Kepler, Galileo, and Mersenne (a brief summary of this argument is found in section 3 of the final chapter).

In Chapter 6 Marion examines the second part of Descartes' statement to Mersenne that the eternal truths are created: "The mathematical truths which you call eternal have been laid down by God and depend on him entirely no less than the rest of his creatures. *Indeed to say that these truths are independent of God is to talk of him as if he were Jupiter or Saturn and to subject him to the Styx and the Fates*" (AT I:145; CSMK III:23; my emphasis).[1] Marion shows how Descartes not only rejects a purely mathematical univocity, which would apply the same reason and logic to God as it does to human beings, or an ontological univocity, which would apply the terminology of being to God in the same way as to human beings, but is wary of any thinking that would make God subject to fate or chance. According to Marion, Descartes suggests that this is exactly what his contemporaries are doing by emphasizing the eternity and immutability of the eternal truths, which consequently become imposed upon God and the divine becomes subject to them. Descartes insists that to interpret the eternal truths as equal or superior to God is to submit God to the fates or to Jupiter. Marion does not see this poetic reference (to Jupiter and Saturn) as merely a superfluous repetition of the first part of Descartes' statement. Instead he shows that Descartes is using his knowledge of poetry to oppose himself explicitly to an argument that can be identified as part of a long history, both in thinkers who do submit the divine to chance (from Homer to Seneca) and in theologians who reject this submission (from Luther to Mersenne) or who suggest a reconciliation of God's providence and fate (e.g., Justus Lipsius). Descartes is therefore not only part of a larger conversation, but he is making explicit choices supported with resources drawn from a variety of disciplines (philosophy, theology, poetry, etc.).

In Chapter 7, Marion takes up the same question of the eternal truths, but now focuses on Descartes' successors, especially Spinoza,

Malebranche, and Leibniz. He shows that all three considered Descartes' thesis and rejected it. In the history of the development of the principle of reason, a dependency of reason on the divine has no place. Instead, these three thinkers clearly subject God to the eternal truths and insist not only that these truths could not have been otherwise, but that God must follow them in the creation of the world. Descartes is therefore unique in rejecting as blasphemous the idea that logic might be superior to God. Metaphysics reaches its definitive formulations (especially in Leibniz) as the notion of the creation of the eternal truths is rejected and suppressed in conjunction with the *ego sum, ego existo* (thus connecting to the argument of the first chapter). While Descartes refuses any absolute human knowledge, Spinoza establishes a parallel or adequation between divine and human knowing, especially in emphasizing that rational causality is absolute and could not be otherwise. Malebranche is insistent "to the point of obsession" that God is subject to the eternal truths because the divine would otherwise not be immutable but irrational (and rationality must be univocal). Leibniz goes beyond both Spinoza and Malebranche in the establishment of the principle of sufficient reason that assumes that God is absolutely subject to reason (conjoined with this he limits human freedom radically). In Leibniz the metaphysics prepared by Descartes becomes fully achieved in enclosing God within it as its founding principle.

Yet Descartes does not always speak of God in such ineffable fashion. In Chapter 8 (chapter 5 in the original) Marion examines the idea of the *causa sui* more closely. He had already argued in *Théologie blanche* and *Metaphysical Prism* that the *causa sui* is not only Descartes' invention but Descartes' most definitively metaphysical statement about God. Marion deepens his analysis in this chapter by defending Descartes again as making the first conscious employment of what was recognized as a contradiction in terms by all prior thinkers (especially the medieval theologians) and by showing how Descartes rethinks causality in terms of efficacy. Marion claims that Descartes sustains the risk of an apparently self-contradictory statement (something being the cause of itself) for the sake of his metaphysical system, which requires the *causa sui* for its full formulation. He suggests simultaneously that this constitutes the first real ontological proof for God's existence (picking up on an argument he had made in *Cartesian Questions* in regard to Anselm) and that the need for an ontological proof (and a fully elaborated metaphysics) is the main reason why Descartes risks the contradiction of this notion of *causa sui*. Marion therefore confirms here his earlier interpretation (especially in *Metaphysical Prism* but also in *Cartesian Questions*) of Descartes' metaphysics as onto-theo-logically constituted in a doubled fashion. Descartes develops not only an onto-theo-logy of the ego based on thought (Chapters 3 and 5 illustrate this particularly well), but also an onto-theo-logy of God based on causality, which requires the *causa sui* and God's efficacious causality.[2] One might suggest that this is also why the terminology of substance becomes so problematic for Descartes. In some sense one could say that "substance" is primarily concerned with the first version of metaphysics (that of the ego, which is why—as Marion argues—the term *substance* for Descartes designates primarily the ego, and the divine only derivatively or not at all), whereas *causa sui* refers to the second version of metaphysics, in which God becomes the ground of all being.

Finally, Chapter 9 (chapter 7 in the original) provides an outline of the idea of God as it is developed during this period. This chapter not only serves as a marvelous introduction to philosophical thought about God in the seventeenth century, it also summarizes many of Marion's essential arguments (especially in sections 5 and 6 on Descartes). Marion shows in detail (although he calls it "in outline") how Descartes is part of a long history of thinkers whose thought he parallels or rejects, by whom he is influenced, and whom he influences in turn. Marion insists again that Descartes is unique in rejecting the submission of God to mathematical truths and in resisting the move to univocal language about God, but at the same time Descartes also inaugurates a confusion of the traditional divine names and God's submission to causality (and maybe even materiality). The idea of God's essence as infinite and incomprehensible, although maintained by Descartes, becomes lost in the subsequent tradition, with the exception of Blaise Pascal's transcendence of charity. Since the final chapter is an overview of both Marion's conclusions and philosophical discussions of God during this historical period, those unfamiliar with the thinkers in question might consider reading this chapter first.

This book, maybe more so than any of Marion's other writings, shows the profound connections between his primarily historical work on Descartes and his more recent writings on theology and phenomenology. It does so especially because it highlights the connection in both directions: on the one hand, it makes very clear how

Marion's work on Descartes influences his later theological and phe-nomenological concerns and interests; on the other hand, since it is his most recent work on Descartes, contemporaneous with much of his theological work and even some of his more explicitly phenome-nological writings, it actually also reveals how his readings of Hus-serl and Heidegger and his theological concerns influence his work on Descartes. It therefore makes very evident that Marion's impor-tant phenomenological and theological writings cannot be separated from his work on Descartes and that these writings cannot be ig-nored if one does not want to misinterpret Marion's phenomenologi-cal claims. In conclusion, I will briefly explore one example for each of the two directions of influence, although many more could be explicated.

The first chapter is a particularly clear example of the way in which Marion's phenomenological work influences his reading of Descartes. As indicated above, Marion argues that the Cartesian ego is addressed by an other and that this dialogue is prior to any per-ceived solipsism. Marion suggests that much of what has been said about the solitary and solipsistic nature of the Cartesian ego revolves around a lack of recognition of Descartes' development as a thinker. While the *ego cogito, ergo sum* of the *Discourse on Method* and other ear-lier writings is indeed the basis of all knowledge and reality, which it perceives (and controls) as mere objects, Descartes arrives at a radi-cally new insight in the *Meditations*, where he recognizes that the self is essentially addressed by an other. Much of this interpretation arises out of Marion's phenomenological criticism of traditional views of the subject and his reconception of a self displaced and ad-dressed by an other who would be prior to it (developed most thor-oughly in the final section of *Being Given*). Ruud Welten has therefore argued that Marion is merely reading his phenomenology back into his interpretation of Descartes.[3] Géry Prouvost is more worried about the theological traces in Marion's interpretation. He suggests that "Marion has assigned himself the impossible task of reuniting Dionysius and Descartes, apophaticism and transcendental affirmation."[4]

It is indeed quite evident that Marion's reading of Descartes is deeply influenced by Levinas's concern with the need for alterity in the constitution of the self (it is less evident that the reading therefore constitutes a misinterpretation of Descartes). This is a concern in-forming many of Marion's writings in phenomenology, in which he develops a view of the self that would neither be solipsistic nor describe the ego as self-sufficient subject. He suggests that the self must be addressed by or even devoted to the inbreaking phenomenon of an anonymous other. Similarly, in the present study he seeks the primordial address of such an anonymous other in Descartes' dialogue, which precedes (and makes possible) any constitution of the ego (at least in its most mature version in the *Meditations*). Marion's reading of the Third Meditation is certainly provocative and joins other creative rereadings of Descartes by recent French thinkers (Michel Henry primary among them). Marion's deepening of this analysis in Chapter 2 (where he argues that Descartes' work as a whole displays an essentially dialogic structure) is in similar ways grounded in his own analyses of the importance of dialogue in any reconception of the self, as he conducts it, for example, in his recent work on the erotic phenomenon (which is explicitly set up as a collection of six meditations and a challenge to a search for certainty with a desire for affirmation—the parallel to Descartes is obvious).

In fact, much of what Marion claims in his theological and phenomenological writings is carefully prepared for in his work on Descartes. It is obvious that Marion's assertions that certain ways of speaking about God are idolatrous (as developed in *The Idol and Distance*) and that we require safeguards for preserving the divine ineffability (e.g., by not limiting it with the philosophical language of being, as he argues in *God Without Being*) are firmly grounded in his exploration of Descartes' thesis of the creation of the eternal truths.[5] What might be less evident is the way in which his talk about the phenomenological excess or saturation of phenomena of revelation, and his insistence on charity or love as more appropriate ways of speaking about the divine, also arise out of insights gained this time not primarily from Descartes but from Descartes' contemporary Blaise Pascal. While the studies that focus primarily on other thinkers, like Kant and Mersenne, have been left out in this English edition, it seemed important to retain the chapter on Pascal. The reason may not be immediately obvious, so I will briefly justify this decision by illustrating how this particular chapter makes possible and supports Marion's thesis on the excess of givenness. It focuses—as indicated above—on the "general rule" (*regula generalis*), a rule of evidence or truth. In Descartes, this rule deals with things that are clear and distinct, what the "light of nature" has shown, and posits that such clearly evident things are true. Pascal acknowledges and challenges this rule, as Marion shows in detail in his essay. In this discussion of Pascal's use of Descartes' rule of truth, Marion develops philosophically what he has said in other places in a more theological register. Pascal attempts to overcome Descartes with an order of charity that goes beyond the order of understanding and reason to which Descartes subscribes. Marion shows that Pascal does not merely simplistically invalidate or reject Cartesian philosophy for a purely theological option. Rather, Pascal clearly practices philosophy by applying the rule of truth (or evidence) to the heart and the will (claiming that it is not merely a reflection of faith but an explicit philosophical claim: the heart and the will have access to a kind of evidence that does not reason but persuades by pleasure or agreeableness, by our liking and desiring it). This new kind of evidence is a clear challenge to Descartes and maybe even an attempt to move beyond the metaphysical confines of Cartesian philosophy.

Yet this challenge is significant beyond its immediate content. Already in *Metaphysical Prism* Marion had included a major final section on Pascal, in which he outlines how Pascal overcomes the Cartesian metaphysical system by retaining the divine name of God as infinite and ineffable and by displacing Cartesian knowledge (as "useless and uncertain") with a new kind of insight, that of charity. Similarly, Marion concludes his outline and conception of God in the Cartesian epoch (the final chapter in this volume) with Pascal. In fact, Pascal is mentioned in crucial places in Marion's work and often it is Pascal's notion of the three orders (especially the second order of the mind and the third order of charity) to which Marion refers or on which he relies.[6] While Marion does not deal with the orders in detail in this book (a summary can be found in *Metaphysical Prism*, §23, 106–22) and also does not emphasize the theological implications nearly as much as he does in other places (e.g., *Prolegomena to Charity*, chapter 3, 53–70), he does develop the idea of a distinction between two kinds of evidences or truths explicitly in this final chapter, and in the most strictly philosophical fashion of any of his treatments of Pascal.

This distinction informs Marion's work significantly, even when Pascal is not mentioned at all. One might argue that his by now well-known concept of the supremely saturated phenomenon is grounded in this distinction. Marion argues (in *Being Given* and *In Excess*) that saturated phenomena are paradoxes of a certain kind that overwhelm us with their bedazzling evidence.[7] They are thus not grasped by our minds, which are unable to supply signification for the excess of their givenness. Similarly, Pascal delineates certain truths that come to us with an excess of evidence and dazzle us with their brilliance. We cannot apprehend them in the traditional way, but they impose themselves immediately. Marion's most recent work on the erotic phenomenon relies on this distinction even more fully.[8] The contrast he draws between knowledge and love (the search for certainty and the search for affirmation) arise directly out of the insights explicated in this chapter on evidence in Pascal. Marion clearly shows (especially in the first chapters of that book) how the message of the heart, concerned with love and being loved, subverts all traditional ways of dealing with evidence and allows access to truth via the will and the heart instead of the certainty of the mind.

Marion expresses much regret in the final section of the chapter that Pascal found himself unable to develop further the method of pleasing (knowledge of the heart or will), especially in a strictly philosophical fashion. One might suggest that much of Marion's work in phenomenology is precisely an attempt to succeed where Pascal failed or at least to continue where he hesitated. Pascal challenges metaphysics by moving from evidence to charity: that is the move that Marion wants to make in much of his work. Although these studies on Descartes may not make this move as explicit as much of his work in contemporary phenomenology, the same thesis is here, illustrated in a particular historical context (Pascal's challenge) or by specific philosophical questions (creation of the eternal truths). When we read Marion on Descartes, we come to a similar conclusion as when we read Marion on Husserl or Heidegger or Marion on his own: metaphysics restricts the ego and confines God; the self is described more authentically in dialogue with other(s) and God can only be spoken of as ineffable, never confined within philosophical definitions (as, for example, the *causa sui*). Whether Marion commends or condemns Descartes, that message is clear throughout.

Chapters 1, 2, and 9 have previously appeared in translation.[9] These translations have been followed, except where Marion introduced changes in the book publication, and they have been slightly modified to fit the style of the rest of the book. Significant divergences from the French book publication (or the English articles) are indicated in the notes.

Marion consistently quotes Descartes and his late medieval interlocutors (or predecessors) in the original Latin, often without providing a French translation. These Latin quotations have been translated for the English reader, and any quotes longer than a few words have been placed into the endnotes, even when Marion includes them in the main body of the text, so as to make the reading less cumbersome. Where available, existing English translations of French and Latin works have been employed. When confusion would result from the title (i.e., where English and French/Latin titles are identical or too similar), the translation has been referred to by the translator's or editor's name in later references. Where no English edition exists, the translations are my own, except for texts in Latin, which were prepared with significant assistance from Dr. Antonio Calcagno. I am particularly grateful to him for not merely correcting my translations from the Latin but in most cases retranslating the texts completely. Without his generous help Suárez especially would have made little sense.

Throughout I have attempted to supply publishing information, even when it was not fully provided in the French text (especially first names of authors and names of publishers). I am very grateful to Katie S. Duke, librarian at the University of Scranton, for her assistance in tracking down particularly obscure references. Although I generally follow Marion's practice of giving bibliographical information only upon first mention of the work, when these instances are separated by several chapters I repeat the full citation to ease finding the reference. Marion cites Descartes according to the Adam/Tannery edition, abbreviated by AT. I list Marion's references to the AT edition first, followed by references to the standard English translation of Descartes' works: *The Philosophical Writings of Descartes*, translated by John Cottingham, Robert Stoothoff, and Dugald Murdoch (and Anthony Kenny for volume 3), 3 vols. (Cambridge: Cambridge University Press, 1984–91). They are abbreviated by the customary CSM or CSMK, respectively. (For clarity's sake, I have often included the abbreviation AT and the volume number, even when Marion does not do so, in order to distinguish it from CSM/CSMK.) All other English translations used are indicated when they are first cited. Although I have attempted to use inclusive language wherever possible, I have not altered direct quotations and have not changed Marion's masculine references to God.

Finally, I want to thank Helen Tartar for entrusting me with this translation and for her support throughout the project and Jean-Luc Marion for his willingness to respond to my questions about various French expressions and references. My gratitude also goes to Eleanore Harrington and Dr. Ann Pang-White for their aid in finding certain references and Dr. David Pellauer for helpful translation suggestions (especially regarding Chapter 5). Special thanks to Dr. Joyce Hanks and Dr. Antonio Calcagno for their tremendous assistance with the French and Latin, respectively. Any remaining mistakes are, of course, entirely my own. I would like to dedicate this translation to my foster children, Jasmine and Kasey. Thank you for the joy you have brought to my life. May you know yourselves loved and valuable, wherever your paths may take you.

Preface to the French Edition

After systematic research into the gray ontology (1975), the white theology (1981), and the concept of metaphysics in Descartes (1986), I assembled some more independent essays into a first collection, entitled *Cartesian Questions*.[1] Both before and after the products that emerge polished and presentable, the workshop of the historian of philosophy is full of fragmented research that is dedicated, sometimes relentlessly, to resolving this or that difficulty, whether classic or unforeseen. Even when what these efforts have achieved seems very solid, not always should they (or can they) be integrated into one complete interpretation; sometimes they even contradict one or another earlier articulation or hypothesis.[2] But that matters little, provided that each throws new light on the Cartesian text.

Once more the welcome of P.-L. Assoun and the Presses Universitaires de France has given me the opportunity to bring together a number of new essays, in a volume entitled *Questions cartésiennes II*, published during the quadricentennial of Descartes' birth. I owe them profound gratitude for this mark of confidence. Likewise, I want to thank those responsible for the journals or collective works that have given permission for the use of previously published essays, in a publication anticipated in what they have sustained or welcomed: M. M. Olivetti (*Archivio di Filosofia*, Rome); M. Meyer (*Revue internationale de philosophie*, Brussels); J. Gayon (Université de Bourgogne, Dijon); M. Fumaroli and G. Molinié (*Revue XVIIe siècle*); D.

Garber (*The Cambridge History of Seventeenth-Century Philosophy*) and M. Fattori (*Nouvelles de la République des lettres*); J.-F. Courtine, L. Millet, and P. Aubenque (*Les Études philosophiques*); and O. Depré (Université Catholique de Louvain–La-Neuve). But I also owe more than I can say to those who, with their invitations and their objections, have supported me in the honest job of the historian of philosophy: first, J.-M. Beyssade, who knows my esteem and my gratitude; then T. Gregory (Rome), Richard A. Watson (St. Louis), D. Garber (Chicago), R. Specht (Mannheim), G. Belgioioso (Lecce), E. Balibar (Paris-Nanterre), and V. Carraud (Caen), the erudite master of the work of the *Bulletin cartésien*. I also owe much to my students, especially to those of a magnificent seminar held with Paris X–Nanterre at the ENS [École Normale Supérieur] in 1990–94 (particularly J.-C. Bardout, T. Bedouelle, C. Bouriau, G. Olivo, and L. Renault), as well as to those at the University of Chicago (T. Carlson, Z. Janowski, and J. Kosky). No one can achieve anything without such professional communities, both visible and invisible — they constitute the sole stable reality of the university.

The studies brought together here concern three foci in the debate concerning Descartes. The first is the ego, with respect to which I uphold three paradoxes, which I began to examine elsewhere but clarify here. In Chapter 1, I show that the ego is not primarily a thought of the self by itself, even in figures of the performative or of auto-affection, but a thought of the self by an other, however undetermined this other may be. If, from the beginning, the ego thus escapes ontic solipsism, a fortiori it also escapes the epistemic solipsism that one calls "circular," for evidence does not demand any other guarantee than its absence as presupposition, as I argue in Chapter 3 [chapter 2 of the French volume]. Finally, although Descartes never gives the ego the title of "subject," should one understand it as a substance? Or, rather, as I show in Chapter 5 [chapter 3 of the French], is not this concept of substance, so heavy with tradition, subjected to such redevelopment and aporias that it becomes highly problematic to apply it univocally to the ego?

The second concerns God. I first attempt to complete a description of the backdrop of the history of ideas against which the polemic concerning the creation of eternal truths emerges: in fact, much as the criticism of Jupiter submitted to the Fates returns to a largely ignored topic, attesting to an attack that is very conscious of its aim, so in Chapter 6 [chapter 4 of the French] we see that Descartes' position remains more ambiguous, at least in its literary formulation, than one might have expected. By contrast, the concept of the creation of eternal truths was unanimously rejected, above all by those of Descartes' successors who otherwise maintain many of his fundamental concepts, as is discussed in Chapter 7 [chapter 6 of the French]. The Cartesian definitions of the divine essence, otherwise complex and perhaps subject to strong tensions, are inscribed in a continuous and structured debate that, from Suárez (indeed, Thomas Aquinas) to Hume (indeed, Kant), opposes univocity to equivocity, the act of being to causality. I have retraced them in outline in Chapter 9 [chapter 7 of the French].

Finally, it is a matter of contexts, insofar as the debates surrounding the Cartesian theses and their points of departure are an integral part of those theses. I have first traced, albeit in broad brushstrokes, the parallel between Descartes and Kant, since it seems to fix for me a fundamental architectonic of the epochs that they, respectively, define. This concerns a truly essential question, still young and harboring within it the future of the history of classical metaphysics; others will doubtless prove it definitively (chapter 8 in the French [not included in this volume, at Marion's request], referring back to Chapter 9 [of this volume]). I have illuminated the structure that governs not only the writings of 1641 but their relationship to the *Discourse* of 1637, indeed, to the ensemble of the Cartesian oeuvre: a thesis, objections, replies, and a new thesis. Here I barely so much as open the debate on a hypothesis that might appear strange. As I ask in Chapter 2 [chapter 9 of the French], referring back to Chapter 1, would Descartes have written and thought only in an uninterrupted dialogue? Pascal also seems Cartesian to me, playing Descartes against and beyond Descartes, in ways different from those treated recently by V. Carraud; in Chapter 4 [chapter 10 of the French] I focus on the *regula generalis* (*veritatis*), harking back to Chapter 3. Finally, I have systematized Mersenne's concept of *metaphysica*, before testing whether Descartes' ignoring of *ontologia*, or at least his lack of interest in the question of the *ens in quantum ens*, had a parallel at a time and in an academic environment that emphasized them; the response is clearly positive, as I show in chapter 9 [of the French; not included here]).[3]

Always and still Descartes, as if this work, so sober and unpretentious, multiplies itself to the degree that one progresses within it. Like all my predecessors on this site, I am surprised by this. And the explication of this paradox may not be easy: indeed, Descartes does not offer first or only one philosophy among others. As is proven by the worldwide expansion of Cartesian studies in the last quarter century and above all by the constancy of all the great philosophers without exception, from Spinoza all the way to Heidegger (and beyond), who discuss the figure of the *ego sum* at the center of their own work, one must recognize in Descartes not only one of the rare founding moments of genius in the entire history of metaphysics, but also one of the privileged locations of the exercise, today and tomorrow, of philosophy as such—whatever form it may take. Descartes does not belong to France (or to Holland, or to Bavaria) or to anyone; he belongs only to his own sudden emergence. Indeed, it is possible that philosophy does not cease to go back to it and to be subject to it, if only to dismantle it; in short, it may be that contemporary philosophy is entering into a Cartesian age [*aetas cartesiana*] without any Cartesianism whatsoever.[4]

On the Ego and on God

Further Cartesian Questions

PART I

Questions about the Ego

The Originary Otherness of the Ego

A Rereading of Descartes' Second Meditation

§1. The Scission and the Closure

The question of the subject always comes back into play, reinforced even by condemnations that persistently attempt to exile it. Too quickly convinced each time by the charge of "metaphysics," subjectivity persists all the same, at least as a place for interrogation. This obstinacy is easily explained: any discourse requires, if not always a point of origin, at least a point of impact, toward which to orient itself and on which to operate. Even if I do not speak in terms of an origin, even if I do not think with a transcendental status, even if I am not in the posture of a substance [*substantia*], it is still necessary to speak of an "I" that at least hears, at least empirically experiences the world, at least notices a beingness [*étanité*], albeit a derived and relative one. If the figure of the "I" must pass away, it will do so only for the benefit of and before that which will still say "I." Announcing the disappearance of the subject thus comes down to a self-destructive enunciation, if, in this crisis, it concerns no more than the fact of the "I," of an "I" in fact: because, in fact, the "I" is there by definition.

The real difficulty, however, plays itself out elsewhere or otherwise—not with regard to the "I" itself, but with regard to the status of the one who speaks this "I." Modern metaphysics, that is to say, what Descartes inaugurates and what does not cease to develop its possibilities, even and above all when it believes itself to pass beyond him, commences when the existence of the finite thinking thing receives the dignity of "the basis on which it seems to me that all human certainty can be founded."[1] Fundamentally, the "I" does not become worthy of being put into question until it pretends to attain or to posit [itself as] a foundation. Only this pretension institutes subjectivity as the "first principle of the philosophy I was seeking" (AT VI:32, 23; CSM I:127). Yet in coming about, by the same gesture this pretension exposes the "I," which henceforth is inasmuch as it thinks, to two aporias—a scission and a closure.

The scission follows directly and in principle from the function of founding. The foundation cannot emerge as such except in the capacity of principle—as that which implies the rest (ontically and epistemologically) and therefore makes it possible. Thus, the "I" has a transcendental function as foundation: it defines the conditions of possibility of experience, which it opens because it precedes experience. Certainly, such a transcendental priority decidedly confirms the exceptional singularity of the "I," but it also imposes a restriction on the "I": if the "I" determines the conditions of possibility of experience and of the objects of experience, it hence does not belong to this experience and does not count among its objects. Strictly speaking, it excludes itself from experience, precisely because it makes experience possible: a nonobject of experience, it will never appear in experience, held this side of all categorical determinations of the object; it eludes even space and time, since it opens the field of the one and the flux of the other. As transcendental, the "I" remains invisible, undetermined, and universally abstract. It would thus enter into visibility only in determining and individualizing itself according to experience, thus by way of the object. From here on, the transcendental "I" is doubled by an empirical "me," definable and individualized because visible, but deprived of all function and anteriority in principle. If the ego pretends to the rank of principle, it must thereby endure a scission with itself, into a first transcendental (hence abstract) "I" and an empirical (real, but second) "me." Does this scission, which reigns explicitly from Kant to Husserl, already affect the Cartesian ego? Must it already choose between its phenomenological visibility and its primacy in principle? This is the first question.

Yet this intimate scission of the ego from itself is accompanied paradoxically by a closure: the character of the first principle, which makes [rend] experience possible precisely because it does not surrender [rend] to it, pushes the ego back into an absolute phenomenological singularity—that of a condition of possibility of experience without the possibility of being itself experienced there. This empty sufficiency leads to the solution of a continuity between it and all thinkable phenomena—the heterogeneous relation between the gaze and its object, known only by objectifying. It follows that, knowing only the object that it produces, the ego would not be able to access any other ego as such, but only that which it objectifies in itself, an altered ego, a simple other "me." Altering[2] the other [*autrui*] into an other [*autre*] object, the ego is hence closed in on itself, without door or window, in the aporia of solipsism. Consequently, it compromises all access to an originary ethics: the provisional morality remains definitive and definitively insufficient. Does the ego instituted by Descartes remain stuck in this sterile grip of solipsism?[3] This is the second question. And the majority of arguments against Descartes' institution of the ego can be led back to one of the following: either an objection of transcendentality (Hume, Nietzsche, Wittgenstein) or an objection in the name of ethics (Pascal, Levinas).

Can one describe or even surmount this scission and this solipsism? One will not be able to do so except by going back to the emergence of this "I" that precedes, provokes, and exploits them. According to this hypothesis, one would have to go back from the transcendental "I" to what makes it possible—the ego, understood in general (and in particular by Kant and Husserl) as essentially an *ego cogito*, that is to say, all the way back to Descartes. We will therefore examine two "trouble spots" in this unique stake. (a) Did Descartes assume and privilege the figure of such an *ego cogito*? Although this question seems to call forth an obviously positive response, we should not presuppose that it admits of a univocal signification. (b) Above all, does Descartes' enterprise imply by itself the ego's scission into a transcendental "I" and an empirical "me," hence a solipsistic closure without ethics?

§2. The *Ego Cogito, Ergo Sum* According to the Canonical Interpretation of Metaphysics

The history of the interpretation of the *ego cogito, ergo sum* remains to be written, and we will not claim to do so here. But it is at least possible to follow the emergence of a dominant and continually corroborated tradition that thinks the ego by equating it with the self through the intermediary of its thoughts, thus identifying the ego with its own being.

(a) Malebranche posits this double equivalence clearly: "Of all our knowledge, the first is the existence of our soul: all our thoughts make incontestable demonstrations of it, because there is nothing more evident than that what actually thinks is actually something."[4] The soul (the ego) identifies itself with its thoughts by an act of thought, thus in the act identifying itself with its existence. Without a doubt, Malebranche does not grant us the clear and distinct idea of this equivalence, but only a simple internal sensation. Yet this denial makes it even more visible that in a normal case (to know, without the theological disturbance of the laws of knowledge), the self's transparency to its own existence through its ideas would remain the rule and by right would remain their paradigm.

(b) Spinoza also radicalizes this double equivalence when he transcribes the Cartesian formula into another, which is apparently non-Cartesian: "Man thinks" (*Homo cogitat*). In fact, this axiom of *Ethics* 2 resumes a clearer transposition, fulfilling the *Principles of Cartesian Philosophy* (*Principia Philosophiae Cartesianae*): "So *I think, therefore I am* is a unique proposition which is equivalent to this, *I am thinking*."[5] By "unique proposition" one must understand here not only a proposition that is not divided (contrary to that of Descartes, which turns on an *ergo*) but even a unified proposition, whose terms all pass into each other by the mediation of a third, following a restless equivalence: *ego* implies *sum*, inasmuch as it implies *cogitans*, and so on, according to all the dispositions of the three terms. With a remarkable economy of means, Spinoza extends the Cartesian formula to the simple statement of these three terms. Thus he opens the road to a system of crossing confirmations: where *cogitans* mediates *ego* and *sum*, then *sum* mediates *ego* and *cogitans*, and finally *cogitans* mediates *ego* and *sum*.

(c) Kant undertakes a radical critique of the paralogisms of pure reason according to rational psychology, to which he assimilates the *ego cogito, ergo sum*. However, even this critique finally only accuses this argument of not sufficiently consolidating the equivalence between being and thought with which the dominant interpretation credits Descartes. Let us consider the Kantian argument: the *I think* remains a simple empirical proposition, containing in itself *I am*; but as I cannot affirm that all that which thinks exists (a statement that far surpasses the field of possible experience), one must conclude more modestly that "my existence then can no longer be considered, as Descartes had believed, to be deduced from the proposition *I think* (since otherwise it would be necessary to have it proceed from this major premise: *all that which thinks exists*), but rather is identical with it [*mit ihm identisch*]."[6] But even if it does not attain an existence verifiable by intuition (which, moreover, would furnish only an *a posteriori* existence, conforming to the perceptible status of all intuition),[7] the Cartesian proposition remains understood [by Kant] as a proposition of identity (in Leibniz's sense, but also that of Spinoza): *I think* amounts to *I am*, according to a strict tautology: "The Cartesian reasoning *cogito ergo sum* is, in fact, tautological in that the *cogito* (*sum cogitans*) [already] names the effective force."[8] Put simply, this tautology remains a logical one. It is thus intuitively empty and does not result in positing any individual existence as an effect. Thus, Kant does not separate himself from the Spinozist interpretation of the *ego cogito, ergo sum* as a tautology of identity concerning existence and thought in the ego—he only stigmatizes its impossibility. Far from putting the common model in question, his critique reproaches it only for not having the means to assert itself; that is to say, it leads only to an indeterminate principle, open to a simple dilemma: whether to remain a transcendental principle, but one that as noumena is unknowable, or to determine itself empirically and lose the rank of principle.[9] But the tautology remains unchallenged.[10]

(d) It falls to Hegel to fix this tautology clearly. Starting in 1807, he posits that it goes "back to the concept of Cartesian metaphysics, that being and thought are in themselves the same."[11] This thesis, in fact the thesis par excellence of the common interpretation, accentuates the entire account, otherwise absolutely brilliant, in the *Lectures on the History of Modern Philosophy*: "The determination of being is immediately connected to the I, the pure I, this *cogito* to which it is immediately connected. . . . Such is the celebrated *cogito, ergo sum*, thought and being are there inseparably connected."[12] Thus understood, the Cartesian ego does not end up only with its own existence, one among others, even though exemplary or primary, but in an equivalence (which Kant rejects straightaway) between all thought, at least that which is elevated to the concept, and being. The tautology becomes universal, and the being of all beings is settled in and according to the determination of thought. The ego is not in play only for itself and its existence, but for all existence, insofar as that ought, at one moment or another in logic, to pass through the concept.[13]

(e) Not until Nietzsche, paradoxically, was the canonical interpretation put in question. Without a doubt, at first his challenge seemed more radical in that his critique was not directed—unlike all his predecessors—at the immediate identity of *cogito ergo* and *sum*, but rather at the connection between the *ego* and the *cogito*: the simple fact that thoughts loom up and impose themselves on the conscious subject does not imply that it falls to the subject to think them. These thoughts prove that "it thinks," but not that *I* think these thoughts, choose them and produce them. " 'It thinks, consequently there is a thinker': It is there that Descartes' whole argumentation rests." Thus, this concerns only a grammatical habit, a metaphysical idol supposing a cause where one can imagine an effect. On the contrary, an exact description of the process of thought establishes what it deploys without or despite the acts (or illusions of acts) of a pretended thinking subject. One knows the fortunes of this critique, taken up by psychoanalysis and the Marxist theory of ideology. It must not, however, conceal what is essential for our purpose: Nietzsche does not doubt for an instant that Descartes did not at bottom conceive his *ego cogito, ergo sum* as the immediate and tautological identity of the ego and its *cogitationes*: "In that one reduces the proposition to 'That thinks, consequently there is thought by it' one obtains then a pure and simple tautology [*blosse Tautologie*]."[14] By this he is content to repeat negatively the positive assumption of previous criticisms that Descartes saw a tautological identity between *cogito* and *sum*. A single difference remains: Kant contests the passage from thought to existence, while Nietzsche contests the passage from the *ego* to thought; but both criticisms are addressed to a tautology that is presupposed.

What we will call the canonical interpretation thus obstinately deploys these two decisions: (a) to privilege the formulation *ego cogito, ergo sum* in preference to all others; (b) to read it as a tautology. It remains all the more in place because even the attacks on it are organized around its way of presenting the issue.

§3. *Ego Cogito, Ergo Sum* as a Formulation Privileged by the Commentaries

It would seem necessary, then, to conclude with Husserl that the *ego cogito, ergo sum* defines itself as "a resolutely solipsistic philosophizing [*ein ernstlich solipsistisches Philosophieren*]."[15] It would be all the more necessary since the most scrupulous historians of philosophy confirm the interpretation followed by the metaphysicians. Let us give two examples.[16]

(a) Heidegger, whose *coups de force* often throw great light on the texts that he examines, remains here strangely imprecise. Not only does he privilege the formula *ego cogito, ergo sum*, but he glosses it in the direction of a representational interpretation: "the *cogito me cogitare rem* of Descartes"; "Descartes says: all *ego cogito* is *cogito me cogitare*, all 'I represent something to myself' represents at the same time 'me,' me representing it."[17] He does not seem to have any suspicion of the plurality of Cartesian formulae, or that the *cogitatio* could exceed the representation, or, above all, that the *cogitatio* of a thing could not serve as the norm of the *cogitatio sui*. Here research into a genealogy of nihilism through the emergence of the principle of reason, hence of thought as foundation, obfuscates patent textual facts.

(b) One would scarcely suspect M. Gueroult, whose claims long remained absolutely uncontested, of speculative fantasy, and yet he maintains that with the ego "one reaches something which in certain respects already resembles the Kantian 'I think' or the Fichtean Myself."[18] On what ground does he ratify the canonical interpretation? In fact, Gueroult finds so few texts to justify this that he makes them up unconsciously, sliding from slip to slip. Descartes certainly never describes the *cogito* as reflexive awareness, nor does he admit a "reflexive awareness of the *cogito*"; on the contrary, he explicitly rejects this interpretation: "It is further required that it should think that it is thinking, by means of a reflexive act, or that it should have awareness of its own thought. This is deluded."[19] Furthermore, Descartes does not set aside the reflexive repetition of the *ego cogito, ergo sum*, only because he refuses from the start to make it a representation. Even the term *repraesentare*, although often used to define *idea* in general,[20] to my knowledge never appears in connection with the *ego cogito*. This fact does not restrain Gueroult, who does not hesitate to introduce here "a representation: that of a 'spiritual thing' by which 'I represent myself to myself.'"[21] What textual support justifies this resistance by the interpreter to what he is interpreting? For his whole argument Gueroult refers to only one text, a passage from the Third Meditation in de Luynes' translation: "among my ideas, besides that which presents me or makes me manifest to myself."[22] But one notices immediately that he quotes only a snippet of text, in a context that no longer concerns the *ego cogito* (which has been explicitly left behind). One might then point out that Gueroult doubles the simple formula "me représenter moi-même" to "me répresente[r] moi-même *à moi-même*"; that is to say, he substitutes for one representation of myself a reflexive representation of myself by myself. But this way of making the French citation doubly awkward is added onto an earlier modification of this same French translation — "me ré-presente à moi-même" from the original Latin "Ex his autem meis ideis, praeter illam quae me ipsum mihi exhibet," which one could better translate as "besides that which presents me or makes me manifest to myself."[23] The original Latin is then wholly unaware of a representation and *a fortiori* of a reflexive representation of self to self. These derivative additions result in transforming what Descartes understands as an exhibition of the ego, and thus as a pure eruption into appearance, into a reflection of self on self and so an equation I = I. A pure phenomenological manifestation becomes an abstract logical identity, a factual happening falls back into an atemporal principle. This textual inexactness by one of the most authoritative interpreters attests to the fragility of every hermeneutic of the *ego cogito, ergo sum* as a guiding thread for the "reflection enveloped by the constituting process of the cogito,"[24] thus for the equality of self to self and, in short, for the canonical interpretation.

But we should emphasize that, to avoid a metaphysical, reflexive, and representational interpretation of the *ego cogito, ergo sum*, it is not enough to return to a purely logical or pragmatic analysis. Indeed, to interpret it as a syllogism (or an *intuitus*), as an inference (strict or not), as an existential affirmation (or not), as a performative linguistic act (or not) — these interpretations all suppose that it serves to pass from an *ego* to a *sum* by means of logic alone in its deductive (or inductive) or even pragmatic form.[25] But, precisely, regarding the self, must one deploy, whether analytically or synthetically, a unity that first off swathes together subjectivity and existence to validate (or invalidate) a logically legitimate self-positing? Is it simply a matter of a self-positing of the ego in existence justified by formal operations? Clearly we do not deny that the formulation *ego cogito, ergo sum* can be interpreted in these terms, even ought to be so interpreted. That has been done brilliantly, and it will happen again. This is not the issue. We ask only whether this formula (and so also the privileged position that it induces in favor of reflexivity) exhausts the Cartesian concept of the *cogito*; in short, whether the canonical interpretation remains the only acceptable one.

Let us consider here a curious remark, otherwise left without consequences, by an excellent commentator [Edwin Curley]: "The Second Meditation is notoriously an exception."[26] A notable exception in respect to what? In that, by contrast to the *Discourse on Method* ("this truth: *I think, therefore I am*"; "cette vérité: *je pense, donc je suis*"), to the Second Replies ("*I think, therefore I am, or I exist*"; "*ego cogito, ergo sum, sive existo"*), to the *Principles of Philosophy* ("this piece of knowledge—*I am thinking, therefore I exist*—is first and most certain of all"; "haec cognitio, *ego cogito, ergo sum* est omnium prima et certissima"), to the *Conversation with Burman* ("cogito ergo sum"), even to the Third Rule ("everyone can mentally intuit that he exists, that he is thinking"; "uniusquisque animo potest intueri, se existere, se cogitare"), the Second Meditation introduces a different formula: "must finally conclude that this proposition, *I am, I exist*, is necessarily true whenever it is put forward by me or conceived in my mind," or again: "this [thought] alone is inseparable from me. I am, I exist."[27] What difference does this other formulation imply? We have shown elsewhere, following J. Hintikka, that it takes us from a passage of reasoning (of whatever sort it may be) to a performative.[28] This point remains incontestable: I am certain insofar as I say that I am because the thought does not occur in the statement but outside of it—it precedes it inasmuch as it brings it about. The *cogitatio* does not "speak" itself in the statement, since it "speaks" the statement: thus it remains absent from the statement precisely because it verifies it. All the other statements—those that favor the canonical interpretation—remain within reasoning, constatives of an act that they do not "speak" or perform. Only the statement in act of the Second Meditation does what it says. It is appropriate, then, to admit the statement privileged by the canonical interpretation only on the basis of and under the condition of the performative statement of the Second Meditation, which alone justifies it.

But one other point remains to be worked out: How and why can Descartes abandon, in 1641 and only in the Second Meditation, the statement *ego cogito, ergo sum*, which all the canonical interpretation has validated as brilliantly sufficient, in favor of a statement that is at once more performed (since performative) and more enigmatic: *ego sum, ego existo*? And by what right might one privilege the formulation of 1641, rather than the canonical formulation, which is employed more often? In short, how could one justify that, precisely in the text of reference, the *Meditations on First Philosophy*, the formulation that has always been privileged by the canonical interpretation disappears? Is it a matter of an inexact stylistic variant? Is it not more likely a matter of the irruption of an essentially different argument? And, since the canonical interpretation results in solipsism, could one not envisage that the formulation of 1641 goes beyond a solipsism of the ego?

§4. *Ego Sum, Ego Existo* as the Formulation Privileged by Descartes

We offer the hypothesis that the formulation *ego sum, ego existo* reveals an acceptance of the first principle of philosophy radically different from that permitted by the canonical formula *ego cogito, ergo sum*. In other words, we accept without reservation one of Husserl's extraordinarily pertinent remarks: "Behind the apparent triviality of the celebrated proposition *ego cogito, ergo sum* there lies, in effect, a dark yawning chasm."[29] What abyss is this? Our hypothesis will be the following: while the formula privileged by the canonical interpretation leads necessarily to solipsism, the second brings out an originary otherness of the ego.

We are not unaware of the paradox of this hypothesis, especially since a recent critique, which also underlines the privileged formula of the Second Meditation, leads to the confirmation of solipsism—in contrast to our approach. Indeed, as Etienne Balibar astutely notes, this formula is finally clarified in the phrase "But I do not yet have a sufficient understanding of what this 'I' is, that now necessarily exists." Now, this phrase is easily reduced to *sum ego ille, qui sum*, or to *I am that I am*; that is to say, it imitates closely the *sum qui sum* of Exodus 3:14.[30] And in this divine name—the Name—the identity of the self with itself is fulfilled at the highest level. This is the only identity that could justify a solipsism.

Appearing in this brute form, the interpretation is, literally, unacceptable. We oppose it for two reasons. First, for a philological reason: the privileged passage that we have just cited does not contain the formula *ego sum, ego existo*; on the contrary, it points out its limits, since the performative fact of my existence is not sufficient to establish what (or who) I am: in short, the inference from existence to essence is not valid. One would indeed be able to comment only on what the formula covers (my existence, my being), leaving out what it acknowledges is not covered (what I am, my essence). Second, at no time does the text cited assert the identity of the ego with the ego, or of the ego with its being; on the contrary, it explicitly demands that one distinguish the certain knowledge of the fact that I am from the "rash" [literally "imprudent"] assumption of the "quid aliud . . . in locum mei," of something else taken in the place and instead of what I am.[31] Thus, nothing permits us to talk about solipsism where "the space of the ego" is missing. If there is, then, an interpretive model for the formula of the Second Meditation, the assumed identity of Exodus 3:14 does not exactly capture it, since it leads back to the equivalence of the ego with the ego, and then to solipsism, establishing again the canonical interpretation. This new interpretation offers less first aid than final distraction.

It remains, then, to read the *ego sum, ego existo* proper to the Second Meditation in an altogether different way—to read it for and from itself. This means reading it neither from a later sequence of lines (Balibar), nor from parallel passages (the canonical interpretation), but from the text that precedes and leads up to it.[32] This sequence unfolds a complex argument whose subtitle is sometimes misleading. We will attempt to follow it in four stages.

The first sequence (AT VII:24, 19–26 = IXA:19, 17–22; CSM II:16) tries to contest the preceding conclusion, namely, knowing that all that I see is false, that "nothing is certain [*nihil esse certi*]" (24, 18). To this end, one asks whether there might not be "another different thing [*quelque autre chose différente/diversum*]" AT IXA:19, 17 = AT VII:24, 19) that I absolutely could not doubt. What does "different" signify here? Certainly, it concerns all that cannot fall into doubt, such as bodies and simple material natures (24, 16–17), and then other *things*; but there is more: it concerns not only an other, but, more radically, an other as little identifiable as the rest: "Some God, or whatever I may call him."[33] Hence this first surprising result: the other emerges as hypothesis *before* the ego, from the first attempt at overcoming doubt. It is indeed a question of an other [*autrui*] (and not of another [*autre*] in general) since one accepts for it the name of "God." Certainly, this interlocutor remains masked by its indeterminacy; the French translation thus makes it equivalent to "some other power [*quelque autre puissance*]" (AT IXA:19–20), and the subsequent development of the argument underlines the anonymity ("I know not who"; *nescio quis*; AT VII:25, 6; CSM II:16–17) and later "some one" (*aliquis*; 26, 24). God also advances masked—"enchanted before God [*larvatus pro Deo*]" becomes an "enchanted God [*Deus larvatus*]."[34] But this anonymity does not eliminate completely the essential character of such an other, reinforced by its very indeterminacy. On the one hand, I indeed name it as an other (*nomine illum voco*; 24, 22); on the other hand, in return it "puts into me the thoughts I am now having."[35] It sends them to me (*immittit*; AT VII:24, 23; CSM II:16). God, or what here takes his place (as one might name it), is from the beginning imposed as the interlocutor of the ego; without existing, without showing any essence, without name, it suffices to deceive me and to interrogate me—unconditioned because perfectly abstract, it has no need of reality in order to place into doubt reality by and for me. Far from doubt deploying itself in the solipsism of an abstract and doubled thought (in the sense that the skeptic finds nothing certain besides the absence of certainty; 24, 12–13), it thus deploys itself in a space of interlocution—the ego and the indeterminate other. No doubt the reasoning immediately reverses itself: if the other sends me these thoughts, why not consider that it is myself, directly, who produces them ("maybe that I am capable of producing them myself"; AT IXA:19, 21–22; *ipsemet author*, 24, 24)? But this substitution changes nothing in the space of interlocution, since the ego, in becoming the cause of the ideas that reach it, only pretends to assume, over and above its own role, that of the other. It is a matter of the first use of a hypothesis; Descartes never shrinks from the contradiction implicit in it—to be the cause in me, unknown by me, of the idea of an other than me.[36] Here I would be both ego and its other. Moreover, the first rough sketch of my existence—"In that case am not I, at least, something?"—opens itself to a simple and powerful objection: if I have neither senses nor body, that is to say, I cannot access what is other than myself through the sensible, which has been put in doubt as not being a (sensible) other than me, then I am not able, in place of the other, to cause my own ideas.[37] In consequence, I am not the other and, by the same movement, I am not myself and not even me. Astonishingly, I have not accessed being at the very moment in which the indeterminate other no longer gets through—to this extent the horizon of the first coincides precisely with the second.

The second sequence (AT VII:24, 26 – 25, 5 = IXA:19, 30; CSM II:16) seems, on first reading, to weaken the hypothesis of an interlocutory space for the ego, since it inquires about the ego's identity alone and attempts only to object to (*haereo tamen*; 24, 26) (i) the objection that I am not *aliquid*, since there is no body and nothing that can be sensed. The counterargument validly runs: (ii) Am I at this point reducible to my body and to the senses, so that I cannot exist without them? But this counterargument immediately produces its own counter: (iii) I am convinced that there is in the world neither earth nor heavens nor bodies nor spirits. This echoes nearly literally the argument from hyperbolic doubt in the First Meditation. The Second Meditation omits the simple material natures (extension, shape, size, place, etc.). Their putting in doubt alone makes possible doubt about the "heavens and the earth," but the text adds *minds*, which do not fall under hyperbolic doubt. This change has only one goal—to include in the doubt even the *cogitationes* and the *ego*.[38] Controversial though it may be, this argument is thus able to claim to challenge whether "I am something" (*ego aliquid sum*; 24, 25). Spirits, like bodies, give rise to doubt, so that even I (*etiam me*; 25, 4) am not.

One expects here the theoretically best reply, that the argument is invalid because it enlarges doubt from bodies to spirits without any justification. Descartes prefers another reply. He recalls that argument (iii) rests on my conviction of the (controversial) universality of hyperbolic doubt—"I have convinced myself" or "I am persuaded" (*je me suis persuadé*; *mihi persuasi*; AT IXA:19, 25–26 = VII:25, 2; CSM II:16)—and instead of replying with regard to the content (improperly enlarged) or the propriety of this conviction, he examines its form. Whatever may be the content of which I am persuaded, at least I am myself persuaded of this content, thus (iv) "No: if I am persuaded of something, then I certainly existed" (25, 5),[39] which the French glosses: "Non certes: j'étais sans doute, si je me suis persuadé" (or only if I have thought something; IXA:19, 28–30). In short, the conclusion of argument (iii), "I do not exist" (*me non esse*; 25, 4–5), "I was not" (*je n'étais point*; IXA:19, 28), contradicts itself like an inverted performative. If I think (or say) that I am not, I am, because the act producing my nonexistence (content) establishes my existence/being (performance). One finds oneself already before a performative like the one that is explicitly achieved some lines later.

Nevertheless, before we consider the motives for this anticipation (or this delay), we ought to confront another difficulty, argument (iv): "I certainly am, if I am persuaded."[40] Does this not illustrate perfectly, contrary to our thesis, the solipsism of the canonical interpretation? Does not the sequence "*je me* suis persuadé"[41] bring to full visibility the identity with self implied by the formula *ego cogito, ergo sum*? The contrary seems immediately true for two basic reasons. (a) First, because the persuasion received by the ego, at least in the First Meditation, which sets the horizon of the whole argument, at this point in the Second Meditation precisely does not come from the ego, but from a "*long-standing opinion in my mind*" (*meae mentis vetus opinio*; AT VII:21, 1–2; CSM II:14), which suggests an omnipotent God. This opinion imposes itself—whether culturally, historically, or religiously, matters little—on the mind, which discovers it has always (*vetus*) been fixed (*infixa*) on itself. It thus determines the ego by virtue of its facticity ("preconceived . . . opinion," *praeconcepta . . . opinio*, as one can read at AT VII:36, 8–9; CSM II:25). The ego thus enters into doubt only according to its facticity (its "already there" [*déjà là*], which is originarily nonoriginary). It finds itself early on situated before a fait accompli, however indeterminate. One can identify this fact [this "fait"] as the opinion itself, or as God who can do all, or as an indefinite deceiver—it matters little, since in any case the ego finds itself preceded, on the road to a solipsism that should identify it with itself alone, by a certain other. It does not access itself in a monologue but in an originary dialogue. One must then conclude that argument (iv) simplifies to a self-persuasion of the ego, the persuasion that, according to the order of reasons, the other first exerts on it.[42] We will see that Descartes quickly rejects this simplification.

Let us suppose that argument (iv) does reach existence by pure self-persuasion. Is it a matter of a solipsistic identity with the self? Clearly not, because if *ego* and *mihi* identify themselves empirically, they distinguish themselves radically by their illocutionary functions. Descartes follows the following schema: the existence of that which remains in the position of subject (*ego eram*) depends here essentially (*si*) on the persuasion exercised on it (*mihi*; 25, 5) by something indeterminate, whatever it may be, provided that it persuades me. This implies: (a) that the existence follows from the persuasion, and so from the rational discursiveness; without a self-positioning in existence; (b) that the *ego* existing in the nominative itself results from a *mihi* in the dative, whose privilege consists only in yielding passively to the persuasion, thus to a *quid* distinct from itself without solipsism; (g) that the *mihi* does not then play the same character as the *ego*, which effaces itself before it, but that two voices play two roles in real dialogue: *I* am in response to the fact that it brings to me a persuasion. This persuasion does not identify itself to me or in itself identify the ego with *mihi*, because it is at play in the irreducibility of a *quid* that is done and contained.[43] In short, at this point the persuasion opens a dialogical space, both constraining and originary, in which the *ego* must, in order to maintain its character, change itself into a *mihi*. Argument (iv), "if I convinced myself of something then I certainly existed" (*imo certe eram, si quid mihi persuasi*), confirms, then, not the solipsistic identity of the ego but, on the contrary, its unfolding under the double billing of *ego* and of *mihi*, according to an originary dialogical space in which it doubles itself to receive a guarantee of existence.

The third sequence (AT VII:25, 5–10 = IXA:19, 30–34; CSM II:17) confirms this dialogical arrangement by replacing the formula "if I convinced myself of something then I certainly existed" (*certes ego eram, si quid mihi persuasi—si je me suis persuadé*) by another that is equivalent but explicitly dialogical: "In that case I too undoubtedly exist, if he is deceiving me" (*haud dubie igitur ego etiam sum, si me fallit,* AT VII:25, 7–8; CSM II:17; *point de doute que je suis, s'il me trompe,* 19, 32). Certainly "I am persuaded" [*je me suis persuadé*] is opposed to "I am deceived" [*je suis trompé*] as the certainly true to the false. In fact, the inversion of truth value in no way changes the formal identity of the two syntagma (to persuade *me*, to deceive *me*) and, especially, one and the same result holds for the one (positive) as well as for the other (negative): I am ("I was," *ego eram*; "I also am," *ego etiam, sum*). What signifies my existence follows indifferently from my self-persuasion and my error.

How can we explain this paradox? By admitting that the contents do not matter but that only the permanence of the unique structure counts. What structure if not that of a dialogue? This dialogue supposes an other speaker who challenges the ego and precedes it. In fact, when the ego admits that it is, it admits first that it is only second, that it comes after an other (*ego etiam sum*). If it is only an *also*, what then is the first?[44] The answer is obvious—that which deceives me with great cunning and power but of whose identity I am ignorant (*deceptor nescio quis,* AT VII:25, 6; *je ne sais quel trompeur,* IXA:19, 30; "I know not what deceiver," CSM II:17, trans. mod.). No doubt its existence has not yet been demonstrated, no doubt also when another existence is demonstrated it will involve only a supreme power purified of all deception. It still remains the case that only this interlocutor, with an existence uncertain but anterior to my own, can allow me to prove my own existence and put it to the test. Perhaps it is necessary that he deceive me for me to know with certainty that I am. I am if he deceives me; this implies that I am only if he deceives me, thus he addresses me, challenges me, and assists me. Certain existence results from my challenge by what, although uncertain, nevertheless precedes it. Whether what deceives me exists or not, so long as it addresses me (or assaults me), I am. I am to the exact degree and at the very time that I am challenged. Existence does not follow from a syllogism, from an intuition, from an autonomous performance, or from a self-*affection*, but from my being acted on (from "my affection") by an other than me.

Descartes goes further. In supposing that his deception is not able "ever to bring it about" (*jamais faire,* AT IXA:19, 33; *numquam tamen efficiet,* VII:25, 9) that I am not, does he not suggest that this other even "provokes" my existence *efficiently*? One can do no more than underline that I am not by (means of) myself but, paradoxically, by (means of) this other who deceives me (maybe even in not deceiving me) and who, possibly, is not. Cartesian argumentation inscribes itself in an originarily dialogical space, where the ego finds itself caught before it even exists, brought about from the outset by an other, of whom it knows only this: that the other assaults it and so addresses it. I am an other, certainly—but because it is by an other. [*Je est un autre, certes—mais parce qu'il est par un autrui.*]

The fourth sequence (AT VII:25, 10–13 = IXA:19, 34–38; CSM II:17) at first seems to contradict this conclusion. Indeed, it reestablishes the shortcircuit of the ego without mentioning "I know not what deceiver." *Ego sum, ego existo* is put forward and performed by me, exclusively *a me* (AT VII:25, 12). Is it a matter of a reprise of argument (iv) of the second sequence, *ego eram, si quid mihi persuasi* (25, 5)? Without a doubt. In both cases the other is relegated to the second level to shorten the argument and make it more forceful. But we have already established that in this case the dialogical situation, far from disappearing, is displaced and is in play between the *ego* (*mihi*, me) as interpellated and the ego as interpellating (like the other [*autrui*] of itself). We have then shown, with respect to persuasion, that it is in play as an illocutionary act. Can we now extract a plausible interlocution by which the ego would carry out an interpellation of the ego? No doubt, since Descartes uses here the characteristic vocabulary of the performative. It is a matter of a linguistic act ("proclaimed," "put forward"; *pronuntiatum, profertur*) given a temporal dimension as such ("wherever," "as often as"; *quoties*) in a dialogue in which the ego is born out of its own interpellation. This dialogue between self and self ought not only to be understood as a reflection on the self—"mind turning around on itself" (*mens in se conversa*), "I withdraw alone" (*solus secedo*), "mind, while it understands, in a way turns around upon itself" (*mens, dum intelligit, se ad ipsum quoddammodo convertat*),[45] in short, as a representation of the self. One must, rather, recognize here an address to the self, an act of speech toward (even against) the self. "And conversing only with myself" (*meque solum adloquendo*; 34, 16; CSM II:24, trans. mod.), me taking the side of myself challenging myself. I, who am not, make the me foreign to myself, in order, by the me preceding myself, to speak and put forth this other existence (nevertheless my own) and in the act to guarantee it. In this hypothesis, auto-affection and ecstasy no longer contradict each other: I affect myself (and experience myself as being) in the exact measure to which I allow myself to be addressed, interlocuted, and finally thought by a still undecided alterity, either the illusion of a deceiver, or the opinion of an omnipotence, or my own thought remaining other than me. Alterity would thus be in play before the distinction between auto-affection and hetero-affection, between the same and ecstasy, is even established.

We conclude, then, that the formulation *ego sum, ego existo* achieves, in the Second Meditation, and only there, an argument that is absolutely original and irreducible to the canonical interpretation, which privileges the formulation *ego cogito, ergo sum*. Here the ego guarantees its existence by its originary inscription (before which it does not exist), in a dialogical space in which an illocutionary act—to be deceived—by an other who is first, indeterminate, and anonymous recognizes it as such and assigns it being. Solipsism and a sealed identity of self with self do not, then, define either necessarily or always the Cartesian *ego sum*, even if they can do so on occasion (in the canonical interpretation). This *ego sum* can (and on occasion should) receive itself from an originary interlocution, which operates first on an other. That this other remains empty and problematic makes the constitutive function that it performs for the ego all the more emblematic. Before being a thinking thing, the ego exists as deceived and persuaded, thus as a thought thing (*res cogitans cogitata*), hence the first truth, *ego sum, ego existo*, does not have the first word. It hears it.[46]

§5. The Ego as *Finitus* or the Reestablishment of an Originary Alterity

This noncanonical interpretation can deal with such arguments as have been brought against it. It remains then only to present, albeit summarily, some other arguments that confirm it. The first concerns the formulation of the ego's existence in other statements. Thus the *Discourse on Method* reaches the canonical formulation without any reference to an interlocutor whatever, but in so doing it puts the weight of the argument exclusively on the I, which becomes redundant to the point of excess: "But immediately I noticed that while I was trying thus to think everything false, it was necessary that I, who was thinking this, was something. And observing that this truth '*I am thinking, therefore I exist*' was so firm and sure that all the most extravagant suppositions of the sceptics were incapable of shaking it, I decided that I could accept it without scruple as the first principle of the philosophy I was seeking."[47] It has been correctly emphasized that the *Discourse* is still unaware of hyperbolic doubt due to omnipotence (F. Alquié). It should be added that consequently it is also unaware of the illocutionary relation between, on the one hand, the ego, deceived, interrogated, and hence thought before thinking, and, on the other hand, the originary interlocutor, who is indefinite and anonymous but the first to speak and to think [it]. The intervention of the canonical formulation is here marked by the absence of the originary interlocution—there occurs only the communication of I with itself, which sees itself existing for its own reasoning. The *Principles of Philosophy*, which equally privileges the canonical formulation, also ignores the interlocution, which is replaced, at lesser cost, by a logical contradiction: "For it is a contradiction to suppose that what one thinks does not, at the very same time when it is thinking, exist. Accordingly, this piece of knowledge—*I am thinking, therefore I exist*—is the first and most certain of all to occur to anyone who philosophizes in an orderly way."[48] An "I know not who" (*nescio quis*) no longer intervenes, and the ego owes its existence only to the logical contradiction that would be there if that which thinks was not at the moment in which it thinks: thus the text does not envisage the essential point—Am I then certain that I think?—and does not mobilize the only argument that establishes it: I think because, more originarily, I am thought by a *nescio quis*. And if the canonical formula excludes interlocution, it confirms thus, *a contrario*, that the formula of the Third Meditation itself has to rest on an originary interlocution.

But such an access to the *ego sum, ego existo* from an other different from the ego finds further confirmation in the Third Meditation. (a) When at the beginning of this Meditation Descartes reviews the truths already acquired,[49] he repeats explicitly the first truth to proceed from an originary interlocution: "Yet when I turn to the things themselves which I think I perceive very clearly, I am so convinced by them that I spontaneously declare: "Let *whoever* can do so *deceive me, he* will never bring it about that I am nothing, so long as I continue to think I am something."[50] Remarkable here is the coordination within the same sequence of two formulations that can be distinguished. Certainly one finds the thought of the self by itself ("to think I am something"),[51] following the canonical formulation, but it occurs only in the second place, preceded by and subordinate to the formulation of the originary interlocution "deceive me who will,"[52] and here the ego does not occur first in the nominative but in an oblique case (*me*, "me"), subordinate to whoever or whatever thinks and determines it. I am thought by the other before I think myself as first existing.

(b) The conclusion of the Third Meditation radicalizes this dependence by articulating explicitly the dependence of the knowledge of self on the knowledge of the other who thinks me not only before I think it but even before I think *me*. This other is here finally recognized as God. Descartes extracts an argument from the similitude and likeness of God that I carry in myself, insofar as I am his creature. It does not reduce to a real image, hence to a limited "part" of my substance, which could be detached from it or at least distinguished by reason. On the contrary, the similitude with God determines me according to the totality of the thinking thing (*res cogitans*) that I am. I have, then, the idea of God (by image and likeness) by the very fact that I think not necessarily God but first and solely myself. It is not that I have the idea of God, among other ideas: I am radically and exclusively this idea itself. The ego *is* the idea of the infinite. Put otherwise, "I perceive that likeness, which includes the idea of God, by the same faculty which enables me to perceive myself."[53] The Latin further emphasizes this paradox: "illamque similitudinem . . . a me percipi per eandem facultatem per quam ego ipse a me percipior."[54] Put otherwise: the faculty by which I myself perceive myself, that is to say, the canonical formulation of my existence resulting from the thought of myself by myself (and the Latin does not shrink from a nearly incorrect redundancy of *egoité—ego ipse a me*—which the French does not succeed in rendering), is also equivalent in the same stroke and "at the same time" (*en même temps*, AT IXA:41, 18; *simul etiam*, AT VII:51, 27) to the knowledge of the idea of God. The convertibility of the one into the other rests on a principle evident to Descartes—the positive infinity of God is conceived immediately from the awareness of its finitude by the created (in the circumstance of the ego that doubts): "but I also understand at the same time that he on whom I depend has within him all those greater things [to which I aspire]."[55] In discovering itself "a thing which is incomplete and dependent on another" (*rem incompletam et ab alio dependentem*; AT VII:51, 24–25; CSM II:35) the ego does not merely repeat the perception of its existence in reflective doubt, it founds it in its dependence and its aspiration toward the infinite that it thinks. That is to say, it recognizes that its existence results from an interlocutionary intrigue, from an interior dialogue, and this time no longer with *nescio quis*, the eventual deceiver, but with "actually God" (*revera Deus*; 52, 2), who is not "subject to any faults" (*sujet à aucuns défauts*;

AT IXA:41, 29). The originary dialogical situation of the *ego sum, ego existo* disengages itself at last from the fiction of a God supposed to be a deceiver (because truly all-powerful) to play in the full light of the connection between the infinite, first thinker and speaker, and the finite, first existent but earlier thought because even earlier spoken to. And it is in this framework, finally reestablished as such, that the following Meditations are situated.[56]

(c) In this context, one could even interpret the Letters of 1630 on the creation of the eternal truths as a first example of the original interlocution of the mind thinking the finite by the infinite. Indeed, if the "eternal truths" (AT I:149, 21, 152, 5; CSMK III:24, 25) "depend" (145, 9; 150, 7, 17; CSMK III:23, 25) on God in the same way as the "other creatures" (152, 25–26; CSMK III:25) and "the rest of creatures" (145, 9–10; CSMK III:23) that he has "established" (145, 14, 29; CSMK III:23), then they are imposed on the finite spirit as an accomplished fact, other and from the outside. Yet, precisely because they come to it as "eternal truths," as henceforth immovable and fundamental, they do not remain exterior or extrinsic to it, as one object among others; rather, they define nothing less than the finite conditions of rationality; thus they are identified with the thinking, or more exactly calculating, ego: "There is no single one that we cannot grasp if our mind turns to consider it. They are all inborn in our minds" (*mentibus nostris ingenitae*; 145, 18–19; CSMK III:23). The innateness of these truths implies that they are confused with the very conditions of finite rationality, hence with the ego. In consequence, one must conclude that "our soul being finite" (152, 12; CSMK III:25), it receives an infinite institution of the conditions of rationality and of itself. The institution and exercise of the ego thus results from a more original interlocution — "of which the power surpasses the limits of human understanding" (150, 18–19; CSMK III:25).

These texts offer, finally, a last teaching: the two formulations that we have separated — on the one hand, *ego cogito, ergo sum*, on the other, *ego sum, ego existo* — are not opposed so directly that the canonical interpretation of solipsism (which is based on the first) contradicts the dialogical interpretation (which follows the intrigue where the second appears). On the contrary, the two interpretations, the two formulations articulate each other perfectly: the ego's return upon itself actually becomes in effect always possible and legitimate (even pedagogically preferable) as a result of the more radical interpellation of this ego (under the title of "me," *mihi*) by whatever interlocutor in a space of originary interlocution. Provided that the common formula remains subordinate to and dependent on the formulation proper to the Second Meditation, there is no serious incentive to declare a tension, even an inconsistency, between the Cartesian texts. It is sufficient to maintain a hierarchy and so, primarily, not to mask the difference between them.

§6. Augustinian and Cartesian Formulations

There is a final problem: it would be premature to remark that Descartes' argument against the skeptics concerning the immaterial existence of the ego can be authorized by Saint Augustine. Of course, Descartes knew and recognized Augustine as someone who would have been included among the greatest authorities for his readers and for his possible adversaries: "I am grateful to you for pointing out the places in Saint Augustine which can be used to give authority to my views. Some other friends of mine had already done so, and I am pleased that my thoughts agree with those of such a great and holy man."[57] Why, therefore, did he decline such a profitable alliance? Formally, because he preferred the bare force of his own arguments to those of external authorities, even those of Augustine: "I shall not waste time here by thanking my distinguished critic [Arnauld] for bringing in the authority of Saint Augustine to support me, and for setting out my arguments so vigorously that he seems to fear that their strength may not be sufficiently apparent to anyone else."[58] Nevertheless, the question appears more complex.

(a) In fact, Mersenne, having read a manuscript of the *Discourse on Method*, drew Descartes' attention to "a passage of St. Augustine."[59] But to what "passage"? In all likelihood, it was *De civitate Dei* 11.26: "So far as these truths are concerned, I do not at all fear the arguments of the Academics when they say, What if you are mistaken? For if I am mistaken, I exist. For he who does not exist surely cannot be mistaken; and so, if I am mistaken, then, through this, I exist. And since, I exist if I am mistaken, how can I be mistaken that I exist, when it is certain that I exist if I am mistaken?"[60] From this parallel (25 May 1637), one may conclude, first, that even before the appearance of the *Discourse on Method* (licensed on 8 June 1637), Descartes knew that his first principle could be read in the light of Augustine, and second, that he distanced himself from the "passage in Saint Augustine, because he did not seem to have put it to the same use as I have."[61] But no explication is given here to illuminate this apparently evident difference in usage.

(b) By contrast, in a later commentary, dating from the time of the completion of the *Meditations*, Descartes clarifies this distancing: "I am obliged to you for drawing my attention to the passage of Saint Augustine relevant to my *I am thinking, therefore I exist*. I went today to the library of this town to read it, and I do indeed find that he does use it to prove the certainty of our existence. He goes on to show that there is a certain likeness of the Trinity in us in that we exist, we know that we exist, and we love the existence and the knowledge we have. I, on the other hand, use the argument to show that this *I* which is thinking is *an immaterial substance* with no bodily element. These are two very different things."[62] The argumentation should surprise us. In fact, (i) the Second Meditation never employs *substance* or *immaterial* with regard to the ego[63]; (ii) nor does it use the formulation *ego cogito, ergo sum*; (iii) as for the image (and resemblance) of God (if not the Trinity), that is indeed the concern of the conclusion of the Third Meditation. The differences that Descartes invokes to distinguish himself from Augustine rest, in fact, only on inaccurate citations of his own text: however, to avoid the risk of a hermeneutic of dissimulation or—worse—of erroneous auto-interpretation, we shall draw the minimal conclusion that, here at least, Descartes does not rationally justify the difference between his *ego sum* and Augustine's.

The story is otherwise after the *Meditations*. (c) At the beginning of his objections, Arnauld suggests another comparison, this time explicit, with *De libero arbitrio* 2.3.7: "And to begin from those things which are most evident, I ask you first of all if you yourself exist. But perhaps you are afraid of deceiving yourself in this matter, and yet you absolutely could not deceive yourself if you did not exist at all."[64] To justify this comparison, Arnauld links this text with the central passage (for our purposes) of the Second Meditation: "But there is I know not what deceiver, of supreme power and cunning, who is deliberately and constantly deceiving me. In that case I too undoubtedly exist, if he is deceiving me."[65] Yet, although thanking Arnauld for the support of this authority, Descartes declines under the pretext (as we have seen) that an appeal to any authority would suggest that his own arguments could not support themselves.[66] This is a strange response: for if appealing to an external authority never reinforces a weak argument, it cannot weaken a strong one. Yet is not another reason concealed behind this polite refusal, this time a profound reason for Descartes' refusal to align himself with the sympathies of a professed Augustinian? Such appears to be the case, if one even rapidly compares these two texts. Augustine deduces existence directly from self-deception (*fallaris* has parimarily this sense), hence from self-reflection, by the simple identity of oneself with oneself [*soi à soi*]: to be mistaken presupposes existence and, here, these are tautologously equivalent; the Augustinian argument accepts, therefore, the identity of the mind with the self. By contrast, the text of Descartes' argument begins with a deceiver-as-interlocutor, one who deceives *me* inasmuch as he presents himself as different from me and persuades me as something external to my being (*fallaris* is radicalized here into *me fallit*). So, contrary to Arnauld's claim (*similia . . . verba*),[67] the issue involves very different kinds of reasoning: in one case a tautology, in the other an interlocutor—an identity or, better yet, a dialogue.

Descartes, therefore, had a profound reason for challenging the authority of Saint Augustine, even if he preferred to offer a diplomatic dodge: it is nothing less than the distinction between the two formulations, where *ego sum, ergo cogito* harkens back to Augustine's tautology (noncontradiction, logical identity) *si non esses, falli omnino non posses*, while *ego sum, ego existo* rests on Descartes' own 1641 interlocution *sum, si me fallit*. When one looks at it this way, one can finally understand how Descartes secures the originality of his thesis *against* Augustine's (and *against* his own expositions of 1637 and 1644). One understands in a flash why he did not stop insisting, almost with contempt, "In itself it is such a simple and natural thing to infer that one exists from the fact that one is doubting that it could have occurred to any writer," to the point of posing the equivalence "this cliché: I think, [therefore] I am [*hoc tritum: Cogito, sum*]."[68] How can we explain that Descartes himself considered *cogito sum* such a truism (and found an indefinite number of precedents in addition to Augustine), if not by accepting that this formulation of his first principle does *not* correspond precisely to the one he favors: *ego sum, ego existo*?[69]

In short, if Descartes challenges the patronage of Saint Augustine, it is because the latter maintained the canonical formulation and—rather strangely—ignored the illocutionary formulation: the otherness that originarily makes possible the ego, which is insofar as it is thought. Not only does comparison between the Cartesian texts and the possible Augustinian sources of the *ego sum* not contradict the distinction (or the hierarchy) that we have established between the two Cartesian formulations, it permits a better reconstruction of Descartes' progression. He commenced by adopting from the tradition (Augustinian or otherwise) a formulation relatively common, if not already banal—*ego cogito, ergo sum*. Next, he substituted the non-canonical formulation, well suited for his more speculative writing (the *Meditations*) and placed it in the context of an interlocution, no longer as a tautology—*ego sum, ego existo*. Saint Augustine (and the Augustinians in Descartes' entourage) played, without a doubt, an essential role in this evolution, but not at all the role one might have expected: the interlocution did not replace the tautology because of the influence of the most authoritative theologian of the seventeenth century (who, precisely, remains caught up in the identity of thought with being and of the ego with itself, fastened to the canonical interpretation, just like later metaphysicians), but in spite of it. Descartes did not accede to the originary interlocution of *ego sum* in yielding to theology; instead, he resisted it with a polemic as stubborn as it was diplomatic. It remains to be seen if, in the end, the best theologian will be the one who is opposed to the greatest theologian.

§7. The Otherness of the Ego

I hope to have shown, if not completely to have proven, that one ought to question the exclusive priority of the canonical formulation *ego cogito, ergo sum*. Descartes distances himself from it in a very explicit way: *hoc tritum: Cogito, sum*. The ego does not attain itself except by the interlocution whereby an other than itself establishes it prior to every self-positing. This other is exercised first under the mask of an omnipotent God, at one time confused (against all coherence) with the evil genius who deceives, and, in any case, maintained in anonymity with a *nescio quis*. He proclaims himself finally in the idea of the infinite, the first Cartesian divine name, which cancels the first phantasm. Between the two instances there is only one common point—an unconditional otherness that precedes the *ego* of the *cogito* first chronologically and finally by right to the point where this *ego* reveals itself first as a *cogitatum*, persuaded, deceived, brought about. I am thought by another, then I am: *res cogitans cogitata*. An important consequence follows upon this. I have shown elsewhere that the *ego sum* displays itself as supreme being only insofar as it extends the onto-theo-logy of the *cogitatio* (under the heading of *cogitatio sui*—"thought of itself") but it becomes again a second being (created, derived) since the onto-theo-logy of the *causa* imposes God as supreme being (under the head of *causa sui*—"cause of itself"). This thesis can be confirmed by a new argument here: while the *causa sui* exercises its primacy by a pure tautology—effect and cause, existence and essence make only one, in the same "superabundance of power" (*exuperentia potestatis*; AT VII:112, 10) —the *ego sum, ego existo* does not attain itself by a simple tautology (and here our syntagma *cogitatio sui* could induce an error) but rather in exposing itself to an originary other (who deceives and persuades), hence in a space of interlocution. The *causa sui* would then only be able to assume rightfully the tautological circularity that would privilege the canonical interpretation of the *ego sum* by the whole modern metaphysic, and that is doubtlessly why this last has not ceased to assimilate the *ego* to *causa sui* (positively with Spinoza and Hegel, negatively with Kant and Nietzsche). On the contrary, the properly Cartesian formulation —*ego sum, ego existo*—not only confines itself to the onto-theology of the *cogitatio* and thus admits its finitude but grounds itself in an originary otherness: challenged by an other, the ego is itself only by an other than itself. The distinction of these two onto-theo-logies within Cartesian metaphysics then strengthens itself by the strict assignment of the tautology to God and the otherness to (the) finite mind.

This subversion of the canonical interpretation to the profit of the illocutionary interpretation, if it is an innovation in the history of philosophy, is otherwise nothing novel in philosophy. It was already perfectly described by Levinas: "The I in the negativity manifested by doubt breaks with participation, but does not find in the *cogito* itself a stopping-place. It is not I—it is the other that can say *yes*. From him comes affirmation; he is at the commencement of experience. . . . to possess the idea of infinity is to have already welcomed the Other."[70] Even and especially the ego, first being, has its existence from the call of an other, whoever that may be, even if anonymous. Transcendental idealism does nothing but simplify and mask this originary dialogical intrigue.

Let us risk a conclusion in the form of an answer to the two initial questions. (a) Descartes has posited the ego in its indubitable existence, but not univocally: alongside the identitary model A = A, let us say, *ego cogito, ergo sum*, which has always been privileged by the canonical interpretation of modern metaphysics, he has constructed another, illocutionary model in which the ego accedes to its primordial existence only by virtue of a thought that first thinks itself—a *res cogitans cogitata*.

(b) The aporia of solipsism, in which the very conditions for thought would deny to the ego on principle the least access to the other, hence does not result from the canonical formulation of an auto-referential and tautological ego identical to itself. (In this precise case, our previous analyses on the alteration of the other by the ego remain valid.) Descartes hence really does anticipate the impasses of Husserl's "Fifth Cartesian Meditation," which is thus even more Cartesian than Husserl supposed. But this aporia is found surpassed, or at least displaced, if one considers the original formulation of the Second Meditation (and the connected texts), for the *ego sum, ego existo* here presupposes that an original interlocution by the other alone posits the ego in the existence of its thought, hence in the thought of its existence. Henceforth, the other thinks me before I think myself—or causes me not to think myself except on the condition that at the same instant he himself thinks me more originarily. Even more essentially than as *res cogitans*, the ego is experienced as *res cogitans cogitata*. The ego appears always already taken and instituted in an alterity with itself, which, before the encounter of any finite or intramundane other, identifies the ego as different from itself, or rather as deferring the appeal by the delay even of its response. In this sense, Descartes anticipates what one can call the self-alterity of subjectivity according to Husserl.[71]

(c) A final hypothesis emerges from this: Could not the originarily interpellated ego of Descartes conceal a figure of subjectivity other than the transcendental one and allow us to surmount the scission between the transcendental "I" and the empirical "me"? Indeed, the "first principle" itself arises insofar as it always is first behind the origin that thinks it—and it does not remain first despite this being behind, but, on the contrary, by it and in virtue of the evocation that it receives from it. In this way the ego only accedes to the rank of first thinking, hence of "first principle," to the extent to which it discovers itself as first thought, interpellated, interlocuted. It is not a matter of a primacy of second rank, conditional or delegated, but of a primacy instituted by the event itself of experiencing itself originarily thought. The distinction between I and "me" would then lose all pertinence, since in a sense the I takes its possibility from what (who or what that might be) thinks me (*me*), "me" [*moi*]. The "me" no longer consigns, afterward, the empiricity that would posit the "I," but the "I" arises in the original facticity where it experiences itself as a "me" thought. The "me" and the "I" exchange their functions only in not confusing them—they are organized following another logic, that of the originary interlocution.

In this hypothesis, far from having only instituted the metaphysical era of objectifying and objectified subjectivity, whose traces fade before our very eyes, might Descartes also—and throughout—have anticipated without knowing it, or at least without having signified it explicitly to us, that which comes after the [transcendental] subject and which we have not ceased to sketch and to await?

The Responsorial Status of the *Meditations*

§1. A Question of the Corpus

One question imposes itself even in a simple consideration of the corpus of the *Meditations on First Philosophy*: Given that we cannot refrain from taking the six meditations as the body of the work, should we add the *Objections* and *Replies* merely as related pieces (*integumenta*, Descartes would have said) or recognize them as inseparable members of the central body? In other words, do we have in the volume of 1641 a short work burdened with a confused apparatus of academic and far from methodical discussions, sometimes tedious and often useless, or is it an organic whole, in which the *Replies* plays an essential, albeit secondary, role in relation to the six meditations?

To a large extent this question determines the whole interpretation of the *Meditations*. It does so for an obvious reason: certain decisive doctrines appear only in the *Replies*, while the *Meditations* overlooks them—doctrines such as the *causa sui*, the understanding of the divine essence as power, the physical explanation of the Eucharist, the positive indifference of God, and so on. It goes without saying that the status of these doctrines will be entirely different depending on whether the *Replies* is taken as a facultative annex to or as an essential consequence of the *Meditations*. The reply to this question must begin from an obvious fact: from the time he planned to publish his first philosophy, Descartes envisaged joining objections and replies indissolubly to the body of his demonstration itself. Nevertheless, this very fact remains problematic: we still need to understand why Descartes intended this joint publication.

§2. The Responsive Structure of the *Meditations* in Relation to the *Discourse on Method*

The first explicit indication of the role of objections in the *Meditations* is found in the "Preface to the Reader." There, Descartes specifies that in the *Discourse* he had asked that his readers not hesitate to present to him all possible objections: "In the *Discourse* I asked anyone who found anything worth criticizing in what I had written to be kind enough to point it out to me. In the case of my remarks concerning God and the soul, only two objections worth mentioning were put to me, which I shall now briefly answer before embarking on a more precise elucidation of these topics."[1]

This declaration calls for two comments. First, there are two objections that precede the *Meditations:* one based on the claim that when the mind turns to itself it perceives only the *res cogitans*, the other based on the claim that the existence of a thing more perfect than myself can be deduced from my idea of it. Furthermore, each of these objections receives a brief reply as early as this preface. The first: "To this objection I reply" that I do not know a thinking thing except according to the "order of perception" without claiming to achieve "the order that follows the truth of the thing."[2] The second: "But I reply" (*sed respondeo*) that the idea must be taken objectively and not materially. In a word, the *Meditations* is not followed but positively preceded by objections and replies.

Second, these objections (and replies) follow from a request made as early as the *Discourse* (*ibi rogassem*); in other words, the objections that precede the *Meditations* also proceed directly from the *Discourse*, as the conclusion of the *Discourse* confirms: "I cannot tell if I have succeeded in this, and I do not wish to anticipate anyone's judgements about my writings by speaking about them myself. But I shall be very glad if they are examined. In order to provide more opportunity for this, I beg all who have any objections to take the trouble to send them to my publisher, and when he informs me about them I shall attempt to append my reply at the same time, so that readers can see both sides together, and decide the truth all the more easily. I do not promise to make very long replies, but only to acknowledge my errors very frankly if I recognize them; and where I cannot see them I shall simply say what I consider is required for defending what I have written, without introducing any new material, so as to avoid getting endlessly caught up in one topic after another."[3]

This solemn declaration amounts further, in Descartes' mind, to a commitment for him and for his eventual objectors to give reasons for their positions and nothing but reasons—in short, to do nothing but argue rationally. He also refers to this in a letter to Mersenne, in which he is in fact addressing the rector of Clermont College, Father J. Hayneuve, on the subject of the attacks by Father Pierre Bourdin: "For I have indeed, in the *Discourse on Method*, asked all those who should find errors in my writings, to be so kind as to warn me of them; thus I have given assurance that I was ready to correct them, and I did not believe there would be anyone who prefers to condemn me before others in my absence rather than to show my errors to me in person, especially any one professing the religious life, whose charity toward his neighbor one would not venture to call into doubt."[4]

Remarkably, Descartes cites the same passage of this letter when, at the close of the *Meditations*, in a letter to Father Jacques Dinet, provincial of the Jesuits in France, he again complains about the intrigues of the same Father Bourdin: "Being warned of this, I at once wrote to the Reverend Father of the College, and begged that 'since my opinions had been judged worthy of public refutation, he would not also judge me unworthy—I who might still be counted among his disciples—to see the arguments which had been used to refute them.' . . . Further, in the *Discourse on Method*, p. 75, I asked all those who may read my writings to take the trouble of making me acquainted with any errors into which they may have seen me slide."[5] So, with a citation of a citation, his declaration in the *Discourse* in which he calls for objections in order to be able to reply to them rationally, Descartes closes the whole of the *Meditations* through the letter to Dinet. He had already used the same citation, as we have seen, in the address to the reader that opens the *Meditations*. It must be concluded, therefore, that the complete text of 1641 is framed by the call for possible objections and the promise of responding arguments that Descartes had already made at the close of the *Discourse on Method*.

This textual fact calls for several remarks. First, Descartes does not envisage publishing his own theses without the prospect of a contradictory debate that confirms them (or possibly refutes them). In his mind publication necessarily gives rise to public discussion, and that is without a doubt why he preferred to remain semi-anonymous in 1637. But in 1641, in the *Meditations*, he radicalized that demand by appending the record of the debate to the first publication of the theses, something he had not done in the *Discourse*; thus it is through the inclusion of the *Objections* and *Replies* in the *Meditations* that Descartes consciously accomplished what in 1637 still remained a mere intention. Consequently, and contrary to a widespread legend, Descartes is neither here nor elsewhere anything like a solitary, or even autistic, thinker, soliloquizing, in the manner perhaps of Spinoza. On the contrary, in every one of his works he offers to convince his readers that he has demonstrated results. Demonstration here constantly retains the double function of evidence: to make a thing manifest and to give proof (evidence) of it to another. Cartesian reason is communicative, precisely because truth manifests itself as a display of evidence; indissolubly, at one and the same time, it is to one's own reason and to the community of those looking on that the thing appears.

In short, it appears that Descartes proceeded in this way for each work, following a schema that can be summarized as consisting in three installments: the plot develops in a text, then in objections, and finally in replies. For convenience, we shall call this plot the responsorial schema. Note that this schema is not limited to the writings of 1637 and 1641; in part it already governed the *Rules*, which, even though it remained unpublished, constitutes throughout objections to Aristotelianism. Descartes can also be seen, paradoxically, to bring this schema to its fulfillment in the *Principles*, in which the style of the objectors, their vocabulary, and their concepts are integrated into the very exposition of the text, so that at last argument, objections, and replies compose a single whole. Doubtless it is the same with *The Passions of the Soul*, where the objections and replies precede the text in the form of three exchanges of letters, so that the text acquires the appearance of a global reply. There remain the cases of 1637 [*Discourse on Method*] and 1641 [*Meditations*]. It is in 1641 that the schema is expressed in the clearest fashion, in three plainly distinct and chronologically ordered installments. Nevertheless, it is announced as such for the first time in 1637, even though at that point the objections and replies are not yet integrated into the text and remain pieces added in the correspondence.

From here on, the stages in my argument follow quite naturally. It will be appropriate to inquire first whether and to what extent the *Discourse* received objections—and what objections—and then whether and to what extent Descartes gave them correct replies.

Only then can one envisage a final question: What is the link between the responsorial schema of the *Discourse* and that of the *Meditations*? Is it only a question of a repetition (even though radicalized) or of a closer link with the responsorial schema of the *Discourse*?

§3. Objections and Replies to the *Discourse on Method*

No one denies that the *Essays* of 1637 received numerous objections. Descartes himself made a provisional catalogue of them in 1638: "As for the foreigners, Fromondus of Louvain made several fairly substantial objections, and another man called Plempius, a professor of medicine, sent me some objections concerning the movement of the heart, which, I think, covered all the points that could possibly be made against my views on this topic. There was another man, also from Louvain, who did not wish to give his name, but who, between us, is a Jesuit [Ciermans]; he sent me some objections concerning the colors of the rainbow. Lastly, someone else from The Hague sent me objections on several different topics. That is all I have received up till now."[6] To the objections of "foreigners" must be added those that came from France, principally those of Pierre de Fermat, Gilles Personne de Roberval, and Jean de Beaugrand dealing with the *Geometry* as well as those of the Jesuit Bourdin concerning such material as the *Optics* [*Dioptrics*].[7] Descartes replied to all these objections, not allowing for an instant any suspicion of the slightest remorse or the slightest hesitation. From his point of view at least, it was entirely clear that he had vanquished his adversary in each debate. Thus we have here the simplest schema of discussion: theses, objections, and replies.

But the situation is different for the objections that concern the metaphysics of the *Discourse*. It is more difficult to examine them, since we no longer have at our disposal the texts sent by Jean de Silhon, Guillaume Gibieuf, Antoine Vatier, and others. But by a rare chance we do have access to those that Pierre Petit presented to Descartes.[8] They are of special interest, since, bearing on the metaphysics (the fourth part of the *Discourse*), they evoke an ambiguous reaction from Descartes. The reaction is ambiguous because, despite two clear and plain condemnations transmitted to Mersenne, Descartes never formally replied to Petit (who, moreover, complained about this to Mersenne). It is also ambiguous because Descartes hesitates in this case between two kinds of defense. First, he claims to evade Petit's objections by saying that they consist only in "some poor platitudes, derived for the most part from the atheists, which he heaped up indiscriminately, confining himself mainly to what I wrote about God and the soul, not one word of which he understood."[9] Here the adversary would seem to be opposing Descartes' theses (moreover, badly understood) by maintaining the point of view of atheists; thus his harmfulness is due to his atheism, borrowed if not explicitly his own, in the face of Cartesian metaphysics, which would defend the cause of God. One can infer that this criticism of Descartes is directed at two of Petit's objections. In the first, Petit questions whether we have an idea of God at our disposal. He appeals to the hypothesis that "[a good person may be] father of an atheist or vice versa" and thus rejects the innateness of the (nontransmissable) idea of God. He also invokes the "stories that clerics themselves have told of the Canadians" and questions whether all the "thoughts of perfections" can and must be concentrated on "a single subject" and could not be dispersed among several "gods." Moreover, he attributes the presence of such an idea of God in us to the education that "makes us join our two hands together, . . . puts us on our knees, . . . makes us beat our breasts, in a word . . . imprints us and . . . stamps us so before a divinity in the mind, that it would be to strip us of our own nature or abandon our own characters to lose the idea of it."[10] These arguments can indeed seem to Descartes to be "borrowed . . . from atheists," since they anticipate the objections against the innateness of the idea of the infinite, to which he will reply in the Third Meditation.

Some months later Descartes' tactics changed completely: Petit is no longer said to be developing reasoning borrowed from atheists, but instead Descartes sees him as using "one [argument] that he has borrowed from me." The borrowing now stems, not from adversaries, that is, from the atheists, but from Descartes himself. But then how can he explain that Petit is still an adversary? Even though he never answered Petit, Descartes did explain to Mersenne that "the reasons he gives to prove the existence of God are so frivolous that he seems to have wanted to make game of God in writing them; and even though there is one that he has borrowed from me, he has nevertheless deprived it of all its force by putting it the way he has put it."[11] This time, Petit's fault consists in an inaccurate and caricature-like pastiche of the correct "arguments" of Cartesian metaphysics concerning the existence of God. We can reconstruct the double line of reasoning that Descartes thus invokes. The argument "borrowed from me" probably refers to the argument in which Descartes "compares the certainty of the existence of God with geometrical demonstrations," that is, the so-called ontological argument of the Fifth Meditation. Petit, according to Descartes, "has nevertheless deprived it of all its force" by declaring straightaway that "we must not say that *the existence of God is at least as certain as a demonstration of Geometry*, since it is incomparably more certain. *Ego sum qui sum:* there is no one but himself who properly exists."[12] But, Descartes adds, Petit understands poorly what he has borrowed. We may be astonished by such a reproach, since it is striking that Petit is here maintaining to the letter a Cartesian position. He cites—without knowing it—a formula from 1630: "to demonstrate metaphysical truths in a manner that is more evident than the demonstrations of geometry." Perhaps Petit is somehow putting what was in fact the Cartesian thesis of 1630 in opposition to the thesis of 1637, which Descartes expresses more modestly and ambiguously in the *Discourse*: "It is at least as certain that God, who is that perfect Being, is or exists, as any demonstration of Geometry could be."[13] As to the "frivolous" arguments, it is doubtless a question of the physical and cosmological proofs advanced by Petit—such as those from the "illumination of the whole Earth," the qualities of the sea, and the finitude of the elements of the world.[14]

Thus it is possible to treat Petit's objections, on the one hand, as strictly adversarial positions or, on the other, as deformations of Cartesian doctrine—in short, now as "borrowed from the atheists," now as "borrowed from me." Does this ambivalence rest solely and in the first instance on a lack of understanding on the part of Petit? This is doubtful when we consider that the Cartesian texts can be related to the two series of objections as if the definitive (printed) text had reproduced them in order to reply to them better thereafter. It also becomes doubtful when the suspicion is raised that the metaphysics of the *Discourse* itself is liable to contradictory interpretations. I have shown elsewhere that the metaphysics of 1637 was still inadequate, particularly with regard to the existence of God, since it fails to employ the concept of causality.[15] One may also suspect that Petit's objections play a part in exposing the faults of the Cartesian demonstration, which they would help to indicate. These three hypotheses have yet to be discussed. Only a serious conceptual study could properly establish the metaphysical importance of the objections put forward by Petit.

Nevertheless, in all cases and without waiting for other confirmations, it is patent that Descartes recognized several times that he could not reply definitively and immediately to objections made to the metaphysics of the *Discourse on Method*. In March 1637 he confesses to Mersenne: "Your second objection is that I have not explained at sufficient length how I know that the soul is a substance distinct from the body and that its nature is solely to think. This, you say, is the only thing that makes obscure the proof of the existence of God. I admit that what you say is very true and that this makes my proof of the existence of God difficult to understand." In the same month he admits the same weakness to Silhon: "I agree, as you observe, that there is a great defect in the work you have seen, and that I have not expounded, in a manner that everyone can easily grasp, the arguments by which I claim to prove that there is nothing at all more evident and certain than the existence of God and of the human soul." Finally, in February 1638 he admits to Father Vatier that "it is true that I have been too obscure in what I wrote about the existence of God in this treatise on Method, and I admit that although the most important, it is the least worked out section in the whole book."[16] Thus the objections (even if they are misinterpretations) of Pierre Petit do not lack a certain justice: they arose, doubtless in error but not without reason, from an inadequacy in the metaphysics expounded in the fourth part of the *Discourse on Method*. For want of the argument of hyperbolic doubt, the abstraction of mind from matter is there not adequate for the idea of God (the idea of the infinite) to be perceived clearly and distinctly. Furthermore, this is surely why in the period following 1637, Descartes never stops underlining the particular difficulty of metaphysics, "which is a science that hardly anyone understands," since "the imagination, which is the part of the mind that most helps mathematics, is more of a hindrance than a help in metaphysical speculation."[17]

From this multiple admission, one conclusion follows clearly enough: although Descartes replied in the text of the *Essays* to the objections that were addressed to it, the text of the *Discourse*, and particularly part 4 on metaphysics, received objections to which it was impossible to reply, according to the admission repeated by Descartes himself. Thus the responsorial schema was achieved completely in the scientific essays but remained incomplete, in anticipation of replies, in the metaphysical essay. In other words, in 1637 the request for rational and well-argued discussion permitted the validation of the scientific results but not of the metaphysical conclusions.

The question then becomes: Did Descartes ever reply to the objections left without reply in 1637?

§4. The Essentially Responsorial Function of the *Meditations*

I propose the following hypothesis: as a whole, the *Meditations* constitutes, with several years' delay, replies to the objections made to the "certain amount of metaphysics" inserted into the *Discourse on Method*.[18] In other words, we should not simply speak of objections made after the *Meditations*, in the *Objections* and *Replies*, but consider the *Meditations* itself as primarily and essentially replies given in 1641 to the objections formulated in 1637. Moreover, this hypothesis would confirm the view that the *Meditations* constitutes a repetition, with more powerful means and more radical concepts, of the fourth part of the *Discourse*, which remains only a mere sketch.

A first argument for this hypothesis is based on a letter to Mersenne of November 1639. Declaring mathematicians incapable of thinking by means of pure understanding and of liberating themselves from the imagination, which "is more of a hindrance than a help in metaphysical speculation," Descartes announces: "I am now working on a discourse in which I try to clarify what I have hitherto written on this topic. It will be only five or six printed sheets, but I hope it will contain a great part of my metaphysics."[19] What is this "discourse"? Its function is to clarify what has been written "hitherto" on "this topic," that is, on metaphysics: this appears to be the metaphysics of the *Discourse on Method*, which Descartes has admitted remained "difficult to understand" because it was too "obscure."[20] This cannot be a question of the "beginning of metaphysics" from 1629, since what is necessary is precisely to reply to the difficulties of the publication of 1637; besides, the fragment of 1629, of which in any case we know nothing, could not have been reemployed except at the price of radical modifications. The text in question here is thus very probably the first sketch of the *Meditations* of 1641, understood as a repetition and a deepening of the abstraction from sense, which permits making absolutely convincing the two demonstrations sought: that of the spirituality of the soul and that of the existence of God. It is the failure of the *Discourse* to meet the objections made to its metaphysics that, as a reply to these objections, evokes the *Meditations*.

There is more: from the start of the project of writing the *Medita-tions*, Descartes foresees submitting them for objections; that is to say, he presents them for a second time in a responsorial schema. In order to achieve full certitude and to convince completely this time, the replies made in 1641 to the objections of 1637 (first responsorial schema) had to be exposed to objections (second responsorial schema). Indeed, the November 1639 letter to Mersenne continues: "To make it as good as possible [that is, to clarify], I plan to have only twenty or thirty copies printed, and send them to the twenty or thirty most learned theologians I can find, in order to have their criti-cism and learn what should be changed, corrected or added before publication."[21] Thus the connection of the *Meditations* with its *Objec-tions* and *Replies* simply doubles, by inverting, the earlier connection of the *Meditations* as replies to objections made to the metaphysics of the *Discourse* and until then left pending.

A second argument in favor of this thesis comes from a letter to Constantijn Huygens in July 1640. Huygens had happened to hear about the new metaphysical work projected by Descartes. Descartes replies to him with a denial—"I have not yet delivered anything to the publisher, or indeed got anything ready that is not too slight to be worth mentioning"—and then admits the existence of this "some-thing on metaphysics." And it is here that he alludes again to the two determinations we have already encountered. It is a question of a reply to the objections made to the *Discourse* and of a request for ex-amination by other objectors: "In short, your information must be quite inaccurate—apart from the fact that I remember having told you last winter that I was proposing to clarify what I wrote in Part Four of the *Discourse on the Method*, not to publish it, but merely to have twelve or fifteen copies printed to send to our leading theolo-gians for their verdict."[22] Here again, more than six months after a similar declaration to Mersenne, Descartes promises first to "clarify" what the fourth part of the *Discourse* contains that is "too obscure," which amounts to furnishing at last the long-delayed reply to the ob-jections of 1637. Here again Descartes announces that he will submit his reply (of 1641) to the objections (of 1637) to a new round of ob-jections, those of "twelve or fifteen . . . theologians" (no longer twenty or thirty). Thus the responsorial schema is doubled, since the *Meditations* here plays the part, first, of replies to the objections made to the *Discourse*, in order then to take on the role of the text to which objections are to be made. There is even more: the copies of the new treatise on metaphysics sent for examination to the eventual objectors will not be sold or circulated to the public: "I intend . . . not to publish it, but merely to have twelve or fifteen copies printed." It must be understood that the exposition of the reply to the objections of 1637, that is, the *Meditations* itself, holds from the start so essential a relation to the future objections that its printing remains limited to a restricted circulation, exactly as if it were not supposed to be accessible, nor could be understood, without the dialogue to come through objections and replies. The printing limited to restricted circulation would even allow us to consider this a simple printing *pro manuscripto*, neither definitive nor public. The publication, strictly speaking, would not take place until the objections had been received and refuted by proper replies. In short, to do what he had left pending in the *Discourse*—to reply to the objections to the metaphysics—in the *Meditations* Descartes goes so far as to include the whole responsorial apparatus in the original text.

A third argument is furnished by a letter to Henricus Regius of 24 May 1640. It gives evidence of a reading of the *Meditations* and of objections made even before its appearance (and certainly before publication).[23] Descartes confirms the existence of this reading by thanking his correspondents for it: "I am much obliged to you and M. Emilius for examining and correcting the manuscript which I sent to you." Not only did they deign to "correct the punctuation and spelling," but they also presented "objections."[24] It is important to study the first of these objections: we have at our disposal something of the wisdom, the power, the goodness, the magnitude, and so on, starting from which we can form the idea of a wisdom that is infinite or at least indefinite, and so on. Descartes replies, obviously, that this formation (of the idea of infinite wisdom etc.) by the passage to the infinite of qualities that are finite in us would remain impossible if we did not have at our disposal, from the start and innately, the idea of the infinite and of the infinite in act. But it is remarkable that what is in question is, almost in the same terms, the objection put forth in 1637 by Pierre Petit and soon again to be repeated by Gassendi.[25] One can even conjecture that a development of the Third Meditation was directly inspired by Descartes' concern with replying to the objections of Petit in 1637 and Regius and Emilius in 1641.[26]

Let us then consider it as established that the composition of the *Meditations* was governed by two types of objections: those addressed to the fourth part of the *Discourse on Method* but, by Descartes' own admission, left without replies, and then in turn those of the readers of the manuscript (or of a limited edition). It remains to identify in the two cases what modifications of the initial text the objections provoked. This enterprise is easier for the readings of the manuscript of the *Meditations* before its definitive publication. One need only think of the numerous corrections of the text printed in 1641 that were provided by Descartes at the suggestion of Mersenne or in discussion with him.[27] As for the replies to the objections provoked by the *Discourse*, they cannot be found at all in the text of the *Meditations* except by a strict comparative examination of the conceptual situations of the two works. Note first that this investigation would give to the differences between the metaphysics of 1637 and of 1641 — indisputable in my view — a new status and a new interest: it would no longer be a question of fearing contradictions and incoherences between two equally Cartesian texts, but rather of reconstituting a deepening of Cartesian thought from one to the other, through integration, in the second exposition of metaphysics, of replies to the objections made to the first exposition and left without reply. In this hypothesis, the strict corpus of the six meditations ought to be read, indissolubly, as an ensemble of replies to the scattered objections made to the *Discourse on Method* and as a text itself destined from the first — even before its (regular) publication — to be submitted to objections, to which Descartes would reply.[28] Not only would it be illegitimate to read the *Meditations* in abstraction from the *Objections* and *Replies*, with which it intentionally forms an organic whole, but it would also be wholly illegitimate to read it otherwise than as replies to the objections provoked by the *Discourse on Method*. Far from being soliloquy or solipsism, Cartesian thought, insofar as it obeys a logic of argumentation, is inscribed at its very origin in the responsorial space of dialogue.

3

The General Rule of Truth in the Third Meditation

§1. The Aporia

Like all great texts, the *Meditations* contains passages that are almost unintelligible. In interpreting them, one must confront and test this difficulty, even when one cannot hope to resolve it. This is so for the opening of the Third Meditation, in how it erects as a "general rule" an equivalence between evidence ("that whatever I perceive very clearly and distinctly") and truth ("is true").[1] This is not only an encounter with an aporia, but there is even more.

This is so, first, in the sense in which the majority of critics agree in recognizing it: Descartes introduces a "general rule" of equivalence between (subjective) evidence and (objective) truth, such that an omnipotent God, although confused with the evil genius, can disqualify evidence. Hence the truth of this rule regarding truth must still be assured. Although it is due to divine veracity, this remains problematic. A second incoherence is joined to the first: the demonstration of the eventual existence of a true God is also grounded in the "general rule," which its veracity must guarantee. The "general rule" would lead to the existence of a true God, who, in turn, would establish the "general rule"—which is "taken as suspect as long as the divine veracity does not guarantee it."[2] In short, at issue is the aporia of the "circle." If this does not already refer to Arnauld's objection (AT VII:214, 7; CSM II:150), which Descartes examines (AT

VII:245, 25; CSM II:171), then it constitutes at least a rupture in the order of reasons comparable to how the principle of causality breaks forth in the middle of the same Third Meditation (AT VII:40, 21–41, 4; CSM II:28).

This famous (although rather tenuous) difficulty cannot mask other less visible but more serious aporias, in that they rely on indisputable textual facts. First, this "general rule" (*regula generalis*; 35, 14; CSM II:24) receives the definitive title of "rule of truth" (*regula veritatis*; 70, 26; CSM II:49) at the end of the Fifth Meditation. One wonders whether this refers already to a rule of truth in the Third Meditation or whether its status evolves from one text to the other. The response to this question seems obvious: divine veracity has been established in the meantime, in the sense that the rule has moved from being "general" (*generalis*) to being "true" (*veritatis*). Yet this is a rather awkward response: today we have evidence (*indices*) that the Latin text (and the French translation by the Duke of Luynes) never uses the term *veracitas* (or *veracité*),[3] or terms signifying "guarantee" (or a Latin equivalent, which is, moreover, difficult to identify). This absence throws both suspicion and light on this aporia of the *regula veritatis*: suspicion that the conflation of these terms in the most authoritative commentaries testifies uniquely to a logical phantasm of the interpreters, rather than to a problem recognized or experienced by Descartes; and light in that the correct reading might consist in not presupposing that he proceeds here in a "circle" that requires a "guarantee" of evidence by divine "veracity." In a word, it is possible that the epistemological overtheologization characteristic of modern commentary not only raises a difficulty where there is none, but above all hides the difficulties Descartes really faced.

Which difficulties? Literally and structurally the *Meditations* indicate at least one of these straightaway. The *regula generalis* (and not yet *veritatis*) in the order of reasons is first mentioned at the opening of the Third Meditation. This banal fact has not caught the attention of exegetes. This is definitely a mistake, because in the volume of 1641 the final (and most enlightening) pages Descartes wrote (without doubt already at the proof stage), namely those of the *Synopsis*, attribute this rule to the Fourth Meditation: "In the Fourth Meditation it is proved that everything that we clearly and distinctly perceive is true."[4] In fact, in conclusion the Fourth Meditation does mention the equivalence between what is evident and what is true: "every clear and distinct perception is undoubtedly something, and hence cannot come from nothing, but must necessarily have God for its author. Its author, I say, is God, who is supremely perfect, and who cannot be a deceiver on pain of contradiction; hence the perception is undoubtedly true."[5] Why this curious displacement of the Third Meditation to the Fourth Meditation?

Yet there is more: this displacement becomes intensified even further, since in the end the operative uses of this rule are encountered again in a third text, the Fifth Meditation. These are as follows: (1) "For it is obvious that whatever is true is something; and I have already amply demonstrated that everything of which I am clearly aware is true";[6] (2) "Admittedly my nature is such that so long as I perceive something very clearly and distinctly I cannot but believe it to be true";[7] (3) "But I now know that I am incapable of error in those cases where my understanding is transparently clear. . . . But none of these were things which I clearly and distinctly perceived: I was ignorant of this rule for establishing the truth, and believed these things for other reasons which I later discovered to be less reliable."[8] Before such a de-multiplication, one can really envision only two hypotheses. One can maintain that the *regula generalis* is partially linked to the "circle" and to divine "veracity" (despite the absence of the latter term and the ambiguity of the first). One must then admit that Descartes has not understood the order of reasons very well himself, in mentioning the same rule three times and in assigning it, in the *Synopsis*, first to the Fourth Meditation, to the detriment of the Third Meditation. In short, one would have to invent an aporia of "veracity" and discount the aporia of the multiple occurrences of the rule as simple carelessness. Or one could confront the possibility that the multiple occurrences of the *regula generalis/veritatis* constitute the true aporia, hence an essential responsibility of the order of reasons, whereas the classical difficulty of "veracity" resolves itself in the course of an internal reading that would be even more scrupulous or less charged. I will follow here, inasmuch as possible, the second hypothesis.

§2. Repetition of the Acquired: Reduction

The *regula generalis* (in fact, the *regula veritatis*) cannot be examined without taking seriously some lines preceding its formulation (AT VII:34, 12–35; CSM II:24). Often neglected, the passage signals less by an obvious repetition of the definition of the *res cogitans* (AT VII:28, 20–22; CSM II:19 = AT VII:34, 18–21; CSM II:24) than by its interpretation of manners of thinking (AT IXA:27, 16) as an ensemble of *modi cogitandi* (34, 23).[9] This syntagma appears here for the first time in the course of the *Meditations*. What does its intervention signify? Must one accord it some kind of importance? This question will serve as a guide. In effect, the introduction of the *cogitandi modi* results in a precise operation: closing one's eyes and one's ears, "destroying" (*delebo*; AT VII:34, 14; CSM II:24) the images of corporeal things. How should one understand this operation? One must ask this question, because Descartes no longer speaks of doubt here except as one of the functions of the *res cogitans* (it is one among others, but without preeminence; 34, 18; CSM II:24). This destruction also does not amount to an annihilation of the world (Hobbes), because at issue is only the matter of regarding sensible images *as vacuous* (AT IXA:27, 6 = *ut inanes . . . pendam*, AT VII:34, 15; CSM II:24), thus challenging these images by disqualifying, not by suppressing, them. In fact, it is a question of an ἐποχή, a putting in parenthesis, in short, of a phenomenological reduction. Husserl recognized this perfectly in Descartes: "Anything belonging to the world, any spatio-temporal being, exists for me—that is to say, is accepted by me—in that I experience it, remember it, think of it somehow, judge about it, value it, desire it, or the like. Descartes, as we know, indicated all that by the name *cogito*. The world is for me absolutely nothing else but the world existing for and accepted by me in such a conscious *cogito*. It gets its whole sense, universal and specific, and its acceptance as existing, exclusively from such *cogitationes*."[10] The disqualification of the thoughts of the world as vacuous (*ut inanes*) hence results in their requalification.[11] The world, then, does not reside in itself, in its proper *exteriority* and in its *existence*, but in its translation in and by thought. Thought does not reside in the world but the world in thought and as much as thought. This reversal of validities converts transcendence into immanence. Thus for the first time in the *Meditations* it is no longer a matter of doubting opinions in an epistemic, hence provisional, fashion but of suspending external transcendences for the benefit of absolute immanences. These remain definitive, following the affirmation that "I cannot have any knowledge of that which is outside of me except through the intervention of ideas that I have had in me."[12] In this way, the ἐποχή frees the truth of immanence under the appearance of transcendence (the world is external to me and I am in it): the world only appears in its ideas, only in the thoughts I think and receive; it is in me and not outside.

Placing transcendence in parentheses ("regarding . . . as vacuous" = *ut inanens . . . pendam*; AT VII:34, 15; CSM II:24) thus liberates, in turn, absolute immanence, hence pure subjectivity: "To maintain myself only with myself" (*meque solum alloquendo*; AT VII:34, 16; IXA:27, 7; CSM II:24). At stake here is not only a repetition of a "dialogue without words of the soul with itself,"[13] or a precept, "Do not wish to go out; go back into yourself. Truth dwells in the inner man,"[14] but what the French translation glosses as "my interior" (AT IXA:27, 8): the original interiority of immanence. Subjectivity is not valid as a being among others (even a more certain or more immediate being); it imposes itself as the condition of intelligibility and hence of the possibility of all beings, which are only in the strict measure in which they are here and are here thought. The ego of the *cogito* no longer counts among beings but opens the plane of immanence (Deleuze). Starting from here, beings could be inasmuch as they are thoughts (*ens ut cogitatum*). And hence, to undertake to make oneself "little and little more known and more familiar with oneself" (IXA:27, 8–9) is no longer a question of introspection but of an exploration of the plane of immanence and its ultimate possibilities.

From that moment on, the question closing this first sequence becomes intelligible: for once all the thoughts of the ego are inventoried *as* reduced thoughts—*quatenus* (AT VII:34, 1; CSM II:22) has the function of indicating reduction—one must inevitably ask "to see whether there may be *other* insights within me which I have not yet noticed."[15] What is surprising here consists not in research into new insights[16] thus far ignored but in the paradox that the others (*alia*) must in any case still be found in me (*in me*). The *me* then in no way indicates a region among other regions and situated in an exterior world, since in that case the new insights would either be *other* but no longer *in* me, or *in* me but then no longer *other*. They cannot appear at the same time *other* and nevertheless *in* me, inasmuch as this "me" is not numbered with the regions of the world, but makes them all possible by way of pure immanence, of the plane of immanence—in short of the transcendental field. The question hence asks: Has all pure immanence been erased with the discovery of the *res cogitans* and with its immediate *modi cogitandi*, or does this plane of immanence receive still other immanences ("other things within me"; *adhuc apud me alia*; AT VII:35, 5–6; CSM II:24)? In Husserlian terms: outside of real immanence (the immediate terms taken in the flow of consciousness) can one also (*adhuc*) admit cases of intentional immanence for other things (*alia res*; 36, 28–29; CSM II:25)?[17]

§3. The Enlargement of Immanence

Let it be the field of pure immanence that certifies my existence: "I am certain that I am a thinking thing."[18] This first certainty does not permit any doubt, but does it not "also" (AT IXA:27, 25; *etiam*, 35, 7; CSM II:24) allow access to another knowledge? In principle, no, seeing that to the degree that it is performative or auto-affected, the ego cannot, by definition, put into play anything except itself.[19] But Descartes turns the difficulty around more subtly: he does not literally demand another knowledge to have import for a new thing that would be different from the ego and hence inaccessible; he demands a new knowledge in the second degree, with reference to the ego and always to it alone: What formal condition of true knowing is then required, that I might be certain of the ego's existence (and that I am it)? And by beginning with this still unique example, which consists in a formal (though audacious) universalization of interrogation, one wonders what would be required for me to be certain of "anything" (*de aliqua re*; AT VII:35, 8; IXA:27, 26; CSM II:24) in general?

The question is doubly displaced here: (a) as regards new knowledge, one asks only about its formal conditions of truth with respect to the ego, and (b) one supposes that the formal conditions of truth valid for the ego (so far the only certain ones) are universally valid for any other true knowledge (whether there is any in fact or not). One sees already that all succeeding new knowledge can neither weaken nor be equivalent to the ego, since such knowledge not only results from the ego, but above all does not consist in another being, another "thing." It consists in a formal, not a real, truth (uniquely in the second degree); in short, an enunciated transcendental that does not make the conditions of the possibility (of truth) of the objects of experience a new object of this experience. On these conditions, the question becomes intelligible and legitimate and will therefore receive a response.

Indeed, one discovers in the "first knowledge" (*prima cognitio*; AT VII:35, 8–9; IXA:27, 26; CSM II:24) not one but *two* results: (a) really, the certain existence of the ego but also (*etiam*; 35, 7; CSM II:24) (b) formally, that, by right only a clear and distinct perception is necessary for obtaining that certain existence (and that I have in fact obtained it). I therefore affirm: "There is simply a clear and distinct perception of what I am asserting."[20] This shows itself in this way: if by any chance (*unquam contingere*; 35, 12; CSM II:24) such a clear and distinct perception can produce a falsehood, then it would never suffice (*sane*; 35, 10; CSM II:24) to make me certain of truth (that is to say, following the laws of hyperbolic doubt). Now, evidently the argument presupposes that the only case where, up until now, I had a clear and distinct perception (the existence of the ego) at my disposal, it furnished a truth. In order to place in doubt the equivalence between a clear and distinct perception and truth, one must therefore put in doubt the ego itself, which is definitely impossible. As a result (*ac proinde*; 35, 13), this equivalence is valid not only for the ego but for all that reproduces its formal conditions. Descartes fixes this universally in a general rule (*regula generalis*; 35, 14; CSM II:24), which he later calls rule of truth (*regula veritatis*; 70, 26; CSM II:48): "All these things which we conceive very clearly and distinctly are true."[21]

Yet the best interpreters hesitate before this lucid reasoning, namely, those most concerned to reconstitute the order of reasons.[22] One must hence insist on certain characteristics of the *regula veritatis*. (a) It is given like a certainty: the verb *statuere* introducing it (AT VII:35, 14; CSM II:24) had already introduced the existence of the ego with the same solemnity (25, 11; CSM II:17). (b) In the same way, *videor* (35, 14; CSM II:24) must not be weakened into a simple "it seems to me" (AT IXA:27, 30), since in other places it marks the nonecstatic and nonobjectifying evidence of the ego affecting itself (e.g., AT VII:29, 15; 53, 18, and 509, 17; CSM II:19, 37 and 347). (c) The universality of the equivalence between truth and clear and distinct perception is not restricted in any way: the rule is proposed as general (*generalis*; 35, 14; CSM II:24) and concerns all (*omne*; 35, 14; CSM II:24). From its intention one would not know to contrast certain evidences (the existence of the ego) to others (for example, mathematical evidence in atheist science). This is so first because no other is yet mentioned, but above all because the ego not only illustrates this rule and proceeds from it, but because it was the first (and so far the only one) to discover it by putting it to work. (d) Finally and above all, the institution of this rule does not mention the doubt, the supposed "trickery" of God, or divine veracity at all, except by overdetermining the text with terms not actually there. Hence one must admit that the validity of the *regula veritatis* is established within hyperbolic doubt itself and that it is deployed here parallel to the ego itself. What is surprising in this, since it [the establishment of the ego] results from it [hyperbolic doubt]?

The interpretation of the enlargement of real immanence by the conquest of a formal and transcendental statement admits of other confirmations, both internal and external. (a) A sequence in the *Discourse on Method* (AT VI:33, 12–22; CSM I:127) anticipates the Third Meditation—first by demanding "that which is required for a proposition for being true and certain; for since I just found one that I know to be such, I will think that I must *also* know in what this certainty consists." Courcelles translates this "also" by *posse etiam* (559, 6), corresponding to the same *etiam*, hence to *adhuc . . . alia* of 1641 (AT VII:35, 7 and 5–6; CSM II:24). In both cases, one must understand that, concerning the ego's certainty, it is more a matter of certainty than of the ego. A second, similar moment follows: since I remark also "that there is no more of that in this: *I think hence I am*, which assures me that I speak the truth, except that I see very clearly that, for thinking, being is required," I infer a transcendental enunciation from this first and perfect equivalence between evidence and truth: "I will judge that I can take as general rule, that the things which we conceive very clearly and distinctly are all true." The general rule is deduced only from the ego, since it alone is certain, by way of the transcendental condition (*a priori*) discovered after the fact (*a posteriori*).

One should not object that Descartes here grounds the ego's certainty on the principle still doubted here, that being is required for thinking (as is the object of an ancient and doubtless vain polemic). In fact, as the *Principles of Philosophy* 1, §7 explains, this principle itself is imposed by the ego, which does not depend on the principle. In seeing the ego's performance and auto-affection clearly and distinctly, one also discovers a possible contradiction (*Repugnat enim, ut putemus*) if what thinks (itself) in act does not exist. This principle, establishing the equivalence between (self-)thinking and being, results from the certain existence of the ego in exactly the same way as does the equivalence between evidence and truth in the *regula generalis*. Moreover, we can reunite them in a single formula: the clear and distinct perception (evidence) of thought thinking (itself) in act implies universally the truth of its existence. This is verified first by the ego, but it is extended to God and, in a weaker sense, to the essences of material things.

Another, stronger objection remains. (b) If one admits the unconditional validity of the *regula generalis*, would it not introduce a second principle that would rival the ego? Does this not weaken the order of reasons? Yet it is possible that this objection is based on a confusion: for the *regula generalis* has the rank of a transcendental principle (conditions of possibilities), hence remains unreal (no new existent thing is known to it), while the ego posits itself in principle existent and real. Now this distinction is not imposed from without. Descartes formulated it explicitly: "The word 'principle' can be taken in several senses. It is one thing to look for a *common notion* so clear and so general that it can serve as a principle for proving the existence of all the beings, or entities, to be discovered later; and another thing to look for a *being* whose existence is known to us better than that of any other, so that it can serve as a principle for discovering them."[23] These two meanings are perfectly applied in the present case. The second defines the real principle, "a being" whose existence is known to us before all others: the ego. In contrast, the first reproduces the characteristics of the *regula generalis*: a *common* notion that is *general*, serving for *all* the beings still to be known. The contradiction is hence dissolved: there are really two principles, but they do not play the same role, nor are they defined in a parallel manner. In fact, the real difficulty is found somewhere else. The *regula generalis* does not pretend only to the rank of (transcendental) principle in the Third Meditation; indeed, after the way toward God by ideas alone fails, Descartes doubles the equivalence between evidence and truth into a different "common notion," which would supposedly be manifest by natural light: that of the equality between effect and cause, applied not only to real being (*esse*) or to reality (*realitas*; AT VII:40, 21–26; CSM II:28) but "also to ideas" (*etiam de ideis*; 41, 3; CSM II:28). Is this a principle in a second sense? That seems to be the case. Yet does it manage to derive its certainty from that of the ego, as the *regula generalis* succeeded in doing so well? That can be doubted because, among other reasons, cause or causality never intervenes in the conquest of the ego's existence. If a rupture in the order of reasons is present, it would be found not in the beginning (AT VII:35; CSM II:24), but in the center (AT VII:40–41; CSM II:28) of the Third Meditation.[24] Regarding this objection, we will conclude that the difference established by Descartes between the two meanings of *principe* recover first the difference between real principle (ego) and transcendental principle (*regula generalis*), then that between real immanence (the ego) and intentional immanence (*regula generalis*).

Finally, two external confirmations can be added to this result. (c) When Spinoza, in this case a faithful commentator, takes up the course of the order of reasons in the *Principia Philosophiae Cartesianae*, he underlines to the extreme the link between the existence of the ego and the validity of the *regula generalis*: "Hence, because he had

50 ■ Questions about the Ego

laid bare this truth [I think, therefore I am] he had *at the same time also* discovered the foundation of all the sciences, and *also* the measure and rule of other truths: Whatever is perceived as clearly and distinctly as that [I think, therefore I am] is true."[25] Remarkably, here the insistence is placed not only—as already by Descartes—on the cardinal fact that with the ego follows also (*etiam*) the acquisition of the *regula generalis* but above all on the strict simultaneity of this acquisition with the ego. In this way, not only is the suspicion of a rivalry or of a contradiction between ego and *regula generalis* excluded straightaway but, to the contrary, it appears almost as two faces (one real, the other transcendental) of one and the same event of thought. Consequently, one understands better why Spinoza begins his exposition of Cartesian doctrine only after the *cogito* and the *regula generalis* are maintained together in a simple preamble: for him (as for Descartes), it is a matter of one and the same unique truth, even if for him alone (against Descartes) the order of reasons only begins authentically when it becomes synthetic.

(d) Clauberg, the most faithfully intelligible of Descartes' commentators, articulates the Cartesian argument even more clearly: if what makes the ego certainly true (namely, to know nothing more than its clear and distinct perception) cannot be extended to all similar cases (and hence each time convert evidence into truth), then the ego itself cannot become indubitable:[26] "And consequently it seems to me now that even by beginning with a single term so far known indubitably, but which, if its reason is not extended to all the other similar [cases], would not become then itself more indubitable, one can conclude surely this general rule: *All that I perceive* or understand *very clearly and distinctly is true and certain for me.*"[27] In this way the intimate link between the real certainty of the ego and the formal certainty of the *regula generalis* is decidedly confirmed, simultaneously distinguished and connected.

§4. The Real Difficulty

If the *regula generalis* really is sufficiently legitimized by the ego, how would one explain the reticence that its exercise provokes? We know the hypothesis of the majority of commentators: the *regula generalis* remains subject to hyperbolic doubt, hence inoperative as long as divine "veracity" does not come to "guarantee" it. We have already seen how feeble textual arguments are in favor of such an interpretation. But above all this hypothesis contradicts Descartes' thesis, which assigns a completely different difficulty to the *regula generalis*: not doubt that evidence is equivalent to truth but the rarity of clear and distinct perceptions, as indicated by one too-brief sequence: "Yet I previously accepted as wholly certain and evident many things which I afterwards realized were doubtful."[28] In no way is the issue here divine trickery or veracity, but only the fact that I can take perceptions as clear and evident that do not appear clear when used. The weight of the difficulty lies not on "God" or what takes the place of the divine, but on the human spirit in the exercise of its intellectual faculties. It is not a matter of "veracity" but of attention. A number of parallels confirm this.

(a) First the *Discourse*: "Only there is some difficulty in recognizing which are the things that we distinctly conceive" (AT VI:33, 22–24; CSM I:127). This illuminates another remark: "For it is not enough to have a good mind; the main thing is to apply it well" (2, 13; CSM I:111). The "difficulty" of the *regula generalis* consists not in its status facing "God," but in its application by the attentive mind; it is not a matter of theology, but of epistemology.

(b) A text from the Second Replies confirms this exemplarily. It reminds us first of the habitual doctrine: "as soon as we think that we correctly perceive something, we are spontaneously convinced that it is true."[29] Then it actually anticipates the objection of several modern commentators by contrasting this doctrine to the theological objection that an absolute falsity (from the point of view of God or of an angel) could disqualify this truth. He immediately refuses this firmly: "Why should this alleged 'absolute falsity' bother us? . . . For the supposition which we are making here is of a conviction so firm that it is quite incapable of being destroyed."[30] Indeed, absolute falsity would revolve around unsurpassable evidence. It could neither be discovered nor surpassed; hence it would not matter. In contrast, once the theological objection is refused, one must still specify the real difficulty, which is strictly epistemological: "But it may be doubted whether any such certainty, or firm and immutable conviction, is in fact to be had."[31] It is quite remarkable that, even in the context where the pretended illusion of evidence could seem conceivable (by "God" or an angel), Descartes maintains his habitual position: in the *regula generalis*, it is a matter of attention to evidence and not of a guarantee of truth.[32]

(c) The *Principles of Philosophy* only mentions the real difficulty, that of attention to authentically clear and distinct perceptions. First in §44: "the light of nature tells us that we should never make a judgment except about things we know. What does very often give rise to error is that there are many things which we think we perceived in the past; once these things are committed to memory, we give our assent to them just as we would if we had fully perceived them, whereas in reality we never perceived them at all."[33] Then in §45: "Indeed there are very many people who in their entire lives never perceive anything with sufficient accuracy to enable them to make a judgment about it with certainty."[34] The difficulty of the *regula generalis* hence essentially consists in the presumption of those—the majority—who imagine themselves to have conquered the clear and distinct ideas (and immediately apply to them the conversion into as many truths), although in fact their ideas are merely confused and/or obscure.

(d) A final commentary (even more significant because in 1647 it plays a part in the course of a rather harsh polemic with Regius) states definitively the only difficulty that Descartes recognizes in the application of the *regula generalis*: "We should note that even though the rule, 'Whatever we can conceive of can exist,' is my own, it is true only so long as we are dealing with a conception which is clear and distinct, a conception which embraces the possibility of the thing in question, since God can bring about whatever we clearly perceive to be possible. But we ought not to use this rule heedlessly, because it is easy for someone to imagine that he properly understands something when in fact he is blinded by some preconception and does not understand it at all."[35] Evidence can always be converted into truth provided that it really is evident. Otherwise, one must use the *regula generalis* carefully. The principal difficulty (one that is in fact unique to the *regula*) concerns its point of departure, not its point of arrival. Spinoza will retain this requirement and will essentially devote himself to distinguishing inadequate ideas from adequate ideas, although possibly with less prudence than Descartes, who confines himself to a simple *notio completa* and admits to remaining removed from "a fully adequate conception of things (and no one has this sort of conception either of the infinite or of anything else, however small it may be)."[36] This opens the formidable question of the univocity of the idea.[37] We therefore conclude that Descartes only admits an epistemological difficulty, namely, identifying clear and distinct perception, but never a theological one, namely, obtaining the divine "guarantee," for employing the *regula generalis*. Although the Third Meditation mentions it only briefly (VII:35, 16–18; CSM II:24), many other texts develop it unambiguously. We must hence base ourselves on these.

§5. Examination of the Supposed Evidences

Once the *regula generalis* is posited (§3) and its true difficulty of application recognized (§4), it remains to put it to work. Descartes proceeds in two steps. Before restoring it, at least programmatically, to evidences convertible into truths (§6), he eliminates perceptions that are not evident and hence not convertible into truths, although they had been taken as such (§5). The negative use of the *regula* hence precedes its positive employment, just as doubt precedes certainty. But in both cases, the decisive question will have import only for whether the character of the clear and distinct perceptions is authentic. God's eventual interventions will be inscribed in this uniquely epistemological problematic.

Once the problem of attention and of authenticity of evidence is recalled (AT VII:35, 16–18; CSM II:14), a question imposes itself: "What were these?" (*qualia ergo ista fuere?*; AT VII:35, 18 = IXA:27, 36–37; CSM II:24)—these things that are first taken as evident and "then" (*postea*) revealed as doubtful, confused, and/or obscure? Two cases can be drawn from the First Meditation's method of doubt.

First case: perception of the sensible origin of the sky, the earth, the stars, etc. At issue is the sensible inasmuch as sensible; this refers to the "no earth, no sky" (*nulla . . . terra, nullumque caelum*) in the First Meditation. Descartes does not mention, of course: "no shape, no size, no place" (*nulla figura, nulla magnitudo, nullus locus*). These all belong to simple material natures, which are purely intelligible.[38] Why is it correct to doubt these perceptions? Because I have confounded two elements in them. On the one hand, I perceive an undeniable clarity (*clare*) and distinction in them: for inasmuch as "the ideas or thoughts of such things" (*rerum ideas, sive cogitationes*) "appeared before my mind" (*menti meae obversari*; AT VII:35, 20–22; CSM II:24), they showed me what they no longer show, namely, to know the sensible as sensible lived experiences and as perceived in the pure immanence of the ego. They arise from a principle formulated in 1627: "the intellect can never be deceived by any experience, provided that when an object is presented to it, it intuits it in a fashion exactly corresponding to the way in which it possesses the object, either within itself or in the imagination."[39] Sensible ideas are undeniably "in me" (*in me*; AT VII:35, 22; CSM II:25), but precisely only in me, immanent, hence without transcendent validity.

On the other hand, in the natural attitude anterior to doubt, I do not limit myself to recognizing immanence in the *cogitatio* of the sensible as such (as lived experience); but I also defer it as a real attribute to the supposedly known exterior (transcendent) object, although I do not in fact have any clear and distinct idea not only of this attribute but also of the essence and even the existence of such an object. As much as the first perception can demand clarity, indeed certain distinction, to the same extent is the judgment attributing it to an unknown object totally missing from it. From 1627 on, the Twelfth Rule stigmatized this confusion in the same phrase that recognized the rights of perception as such, in adding: "Furthermore, it must not judge that the imagination faithfully represents the objects of the senses, or that the senses take on the true shapes of things, or in short that external things always are just as they appear to be."[40] In 1641, the Third Meditation takes up exactly this argument in denouncing the habit of believing to perceive clearly ("which through habitual belief I thought I perceived clearly")[41] what in fact I do not perceive not only not clearly, but not at all ("I did not in fact do so"; *revera non percipiebam*; 35, 25); snapping one's finger at this deficit of clarity and distinction, lacking evidence, I then commit the principal error already denounced in similar terms in 1627: I judge that "This was that there were things outside of me which were the sources of my ideas and which resembled them in all respects."[42] From the literal connection between the Third Meditation and the argument of the *Regulae*, one must hence conclude that, even in the regimen of hyperbolic doubt, the disqualification of sensible knowledge results from a strictly epistemological weakness (the absence of a clear and distinct perception permitting a judgment on the transcendent validity of immanent lived experiences). Perception reveals itself as intrinsically confused. It hence confirms the *regula generalis* negatively. Divine "guarantee" has no role at all to play here.[43]

Is the same thing true in the second case of "things Arithmetical or Geometrical" (*res Arithmeticae vel Geometricae*; AT VII:35, 30; CSM II:25)? Let us consider intrinsically: first, they offer "something very simple and straightforward" (*aliquid valde simplex et facile*; 36, 1; CSM II:25). According to the Second Rule, this mathematical "object so pure and simple" (*objectum purum et simplex*) is such that it does not suppose any "assumptions that experience might render uncertain" (*quod experientia reddiderit incertum*; AT X:365, 16–18; CSM I:12). Therefore the faculty that attains this object defines itself as an act of seeing (*intueri*; AT VII:36, 3; CSM II:25). This term, rare in 1641, goes back to the *intuitus*, which the Third Rule defined precisely as the propriety of forming "the conception of a clear and attentive mind, which is so easy and distinct that there can be no room for doubt about what we are understanding."[44] One must hence acknowledge that mathematics delivers a clear and distinct perception regarding its object, that is to say intrinsically. Yet can the *regula generalis* be applied here and be converted into an indubitable truth? No, because one must also consider the extrinsic status of mathematical perception. The example given — $2 + 3 = 5$ and similar ones (AT VII:36, 2; CSM II:25) — returns unequivocally to what is subject to hyperbolic doubt in the Second Meditation (21, 9–10; CSM II:14). Similarly, "my preconceived belief in the supreme power of God"[45] goes back to "firmly rooted in my mind is the long-standing opinion that there is an omnipotent God."[46] In the situation of hyperbolic doubt, which is literally reproduced from one Meditation to the other, this simple opinion offers a "reason" (*causa*; 36, 4; CSM II:25), a motive for doubting[47] truths, or rather (since they would actually not be true) of evaluating the truth of mathematical perceptions. Indeed, this God could have caused my nature to deceive me regarding what appears to me the most manifest, "could have given me a nature such that I was deceived even in matters which seemed most evident,"[48] hence regarding what I regard as most evident (*quam manifestissime intueri*; 36, 12). The clarity and intrinsic distinction of mathematical perception remain uncontested, but their status is placed into a situation of extrinsic lack: they operate in an extrinsic spirit (by virtue of its creation and of its finitude); the consequence of clear and distinct perception of truth is not worth much (more). Must one not conclude from this that here at least, and for the first time, the *regula generalis* is discovered to be subject to the preliminary condition of the divine "guarantee"? We do not think so, for several reasons.

(a) The argument here precedes that of the First Meditation. As we have attempted to show elsewhere,[49] it never says formally that God deceives me, but only that *I* deceive *myself* [*am deceived*]; and if God is not a deceiver, he must then neither become "true" nor "guarantee." Despite its tenacious use, one must not confuse the "God who can do all" (and does not deceive) with the "evil genius" (who does deceive and absolutely is not able to do all).

(b) Hyperbolic doubt then does not result from any trickery, but from what can be named an epistemological super-"encoding." Just as mathematical language codes sensible perceptions by assigning measurable and moving extended figures to them as cause (and truth), which the natural attitude can absolutely neither see nor understand because an epistemological gap separates it from them (21, 7–9; CSM II:14), in the same way, I too (*ita ego*; 21, 9; *etiam . . . me*; 36, 11), who follow in the posture of mathematical interpreter of nature, can rationally envisage the hypothesis of a system of axioms. These would be infinitely more powerful than those that regulate my proper evidences and can reinterpret them from top to bottom in statements that are definitively unintelligible to me. From this other point of view, which is rendered inaccessible by a new epistemological rupture, I deceive myself in holding my evidences as unsurpassable and convertible into absolute truths. Divine omnipotence certainly disqualifies mathematics, but it does so with an epistemological argument.

(c) Consequently, mathematical perceptions, while preserving their clarity and intrinsic distinction, do not allow the *regula veritatis* to function without falling under the blow of whatever kind of "trickery" or reclaiming the least "guarantee." Indeed, admittedly it is enough simply to state that mathematical evidences are not yet perfectly evident: they still lack extrinsic evidence of their status. In other words, they can exclude neither clearly nor distinctly that the finite mind operating them might be fallible by nature, nor assure that their system of axioms is unsurpassable. Regarding these two preliminary and extrinsic conditions, the shadow of divine omnipotence obfuscates all light, all clarity and distinction.

Sensible perceptions cannot put the *regula generalis* to work due to the intrinsic defect of clarity and of distinction; the mathematical evidences, models of clarity and of intrinsic distinction, cannot do so either, by extrinsic lack of clarity and of distinction. The *regula generalis* remains absolutely established, but without employment, due to the clear and distinct given and not because of a supposed "trickery."

§6. The Reconquest of Equivalence

Up to this point the analysis was conducted from the *regula generalis* and its conditions of application. Henceforth, Descartes will consider its eventual fields of application: return "to the things" (*ad ipsas res*; AT VII:36, 13; IXA:28, 16; CSM II:25) themselves, as I judge them to be perceived clearly and distinctly. It is not a matter of an opposition to the consideration of divine omnipotence, but of reconsidering the question regarding the convertibility of evidence into truth, this time from the point of view of authentic or apparent evidence. Indeed, spontaneously (*sponte*; AT VII:36, 14), evidences appear to us as evidences, and one must determine precisely, each time, whether they can reach truth under the authority of the *regula generalis*. Descartes distinguishes three cases. Let us look at them again.

(a) First, the ego of the *cogito*, reformulated in the terms of the Second Meditation: "Let whoever can do so deceive me, he will never bring it about that I am nothing, so long as I continue to think I am something."[50] Descartes here does not comment whether the conversion of this evidence into truth is valid. Would the *regula generalis* be suspended? So a number of commentators have suggested. We see no reason to admit this: rather, the whole sequence bursts with an almost irrepressible confidence in the truth of evidence.[51] And the silence on the *regula* marks less its absence than the excess of its work. Starting from the previous analyses, it becomes possible to confirm the hypothesis in this way: in the case of the existence of the ego, whose clarity and intrinsic distinction (in contrast to that of sensible perceptions) nothing contests, clarity and extrinsic distinction, far from disappearing before the "omnipotent God" (in contrast to mathematical evidences), reinforce each other paradoxically by the fact itself that it (he or some other) deceives me; for if I think myself deceived, I am inasmuch as thinking, even if I do not think (myself) inasmuch as deceived. Here the attack provoking the confusion of self-perception reinforces its clarity and distinction: so for me to confuse myself, it is still first necessary that I exist.[52] The ego permits the *regula generalis* to be put to work — it passes from evidence to the rank of truth. One must not forget that the ego's existence here is not taking an inventory of the number of falsifiable evidences (§5) and that there is hence no motive for establishing a parallel to mathematical evidences and sensible perceptions, nor the least reason for contesting its absolute privilege.[53] Moreover, the equivalent passage in the Second Replies puts the ego in the first rank of what we can think without believing it to be true — "believing them to be true" (*quin vera esse credamus*; 145, 24; CSM II:104).

In contrast, the other two cases appear more difficult, since they are introduced in a hypothetical mode respectively by *vel* ["or"] and *vel forte* (and prolonged by *vel similia* ["or anything of this kind"]; 36, 17, 18, and 20; CSM II:25): Would the ego occur again here and put to work the *regula generalis*? Yet do these adverbs not mark "the imperceptible hesitation of thought at the instant where it escapes the critical requirement"?[54] We will show that the critical requirement is perfectly respected here: Descartes only attempts to prolong the privilege of the ego's evidence as far as possible, in order to place under its aegis other evidences that would all be already intrinsically clear and distinct, but could still be marked by an extrinsic deficit of clarity and distinction.

(b) The second of the three cases concerns logical evidences: for example, the fact that if I am today, it will be impossible for it not to be true later that I existed in the past (AT VII:36, 17–18; CSM II:25). This parallel to the Second Replies confirms that this constitutes an example of the principle of contradiction, of the primary one in fact: "that I exist so long as I am thinking, or that what is done cannot be undone."[55] How could the truth of the ego make the statement tangentially valid, at least in part, although Descartes will never contest that divine omnipotence is able to accomplish (or not) what we do not understand: for example, not to divide the extended infinitely or cause not to have taken place what has already happened, and so on? The response depends on a more precise reading of the text: it is not a matter of an abstract contradiction—"it will be true one day that that which has been has never been"—but of a temporal variation of the ego's certainty. What is presently true,[56] namely, knowing the clarity and the extrinsic and intrinsic distinction of the auto-affected and illocutionary performance of the fact of my thought, both thought and thinking, will continue into the future and, later, it will remain in the past. Despite the appearance given by pure logic, the contradiction deploys the evidence only temporally, hence the truth of the ego's existence in the present. Descartes here vindicates only *one sole* contradiction, among all those logic will later give him to resolve, namely, what ensues from the temporality of the ego's existence and what can be reduced to a perfect immanence: it is enough to add temporality (by definition remaining immanent) to the totally immanent evidence of the ego. The second case hence does not add anything really new (no other *thing*) to the truth of the ego—it is limited to declining according to the decline even of immanent temporality. In fact, this temporalized perception of the ego is not affected by any confusion, and therefore the *regula generalis* proceeds correctly by converting it into a definitive truth.

The third and final case (c) inserts mathematical statements into the number of clear and distinct perceptions (AT VII:36, 18–21; CSM II:25). This last advance indisputably poses a difficult question: Can Descartes not remember that the (intrinsic) evidences of mathematics still suffer (extrinsic) obscurity in the face of an omnipotent God (35, 30–36, 12)? By what right does he then list them on the same level as the existence of the ego, which is clear and distinct both intrinsically and extrinsically? Must one not admit that he allows "the Cogito [to] re-descend now to the level of mathematical truths"?[57] In fact, there is none of that. "In no way has this text placed the cogito's evidence and that of mathematical truths on the same level, although the same divine veracity is required by both. Rather, one here finds the temptation expressed not to require the guarantee of divine veracity any more for the second than for the first."[58] For understanding Descartes' approach, one must first recognize his prudence: he is the first to understand that mathematical evidences can no longer benefit the *regula generalis*; thus, he introduces them only with the reservation of a "yet even" (*vel forte etiam*).[59] Yet why does he overstep the limits of prudence, if he sees them? He will persist in this transgression; the Second Replies will still confirm these limits, in leaving the field, after the ego and a contradiction, to that "regarding which we manifestly possess this kind of certainty."[60] But this supposedly continuous move from the ego to mathematical evidences, as surprising as it appears here, has in fact nothing incoherent about it; it goes back to the list of privileged (because clear and distinct) objects of the 1627 *intuitus*: "Thus everyone can mentally intuit that he exists, that he is thinking, that a triangle is bounded by just three lines, and a sphere by a single surface, and the like. Perceptions such as these are more numerous than most people realize, disdaining as they do to turn their minds to such simple matters."[61]

A remarkable sequence, in that it establishes: (i) the transition without dissolving continuity between the elements of the future *ego cogito, sum* and mathematical evidences; (ii) the motive of this continuity, namely, to know that a unique *intuitus* perceives their clarity and distinction; (iii) the goal of this common recension, establishing the group of simple natures, both intellectual and material; (iv) that the enumeration remains open without limits (*et similia*; 368, 24; CSM I:14), anticipating here the *vel similia* of the Third Meditation (AT VII:36, 20; CSM II:25) and the *alia sunt* of the Second Replies (146, 14; CSM II:104). Descartes' intention in 1641 is illuminated immediately: within the regimen of hyperbolic doubt, he has just regained the simple intellectual natures (thought, will, in short all modes of the *res cogitans* repeated in VII:34, 18–21) in assigning to them certain of the common simple natures (existence and time). He defines his next objective in referring to his 1627 epistemological project, which is never demolished: reestablishing the simple material natures. This ambition remains problematic (*vel forte etiam*), but not unthinkable. He actually already has at his disposal an argument that is real though fragile. Let us reconstitute it, all the more carefully as it has escaped all the commentators.

How does Descartes formulate mathematical evidences, which he is supposed to introduce here overwhelmingly? Does he take up again his habitual formula "2 + 3 = 5" (used still in 36, 2; CSM II:25)? Not at all. He utilizes a strange and unique formula: "That two or three together makes neither more nor less than five."[62] The argument does not lean directly on the mathematical evidence of addition, as had always been the case before, but on the fact that all other results (more or less than five) would provoke a *repugnatia manifesta*, a manifest contradiction.[63] Now this unthinkable contradiction goes back not only to the intrinsic identity of mathematical evidences, but to the ego's self-identity, namely, to the already unthinkable contradiction that I would be able not to have been although I am and have been. Admittedly, this identity is not deduced directly by the ego (in contrast to the ego's temporal deployment), but it shares an essential property with it: self-identity as intrinsic noncontradiction. Therefore there is really an epistemological noncontradiction (albeit a feeble one) between the evidence of the ego and that of mathematical statements. The project of reintegrating them into the field where the *regula generalis* applies hence has nothing absurd or impossible about it.

What is missing from mathematical evidences that would allow their conversion into truths? In virtue of common *intuitus* and of noncontradiction they already share the intrinsic evidence of the existing ego. Thus, the only thing lacking in them is the absence of an extrinsic questioning of their clarity and distinction. The ego alone succeeds in establishing its clarity and distinction intrinsically and extrinsically in the regimen of hyperbolic doubt. No other evidences can do so. For the *regula generalis* to be applied to other things (*ulla alia re*; 36, 29; CSM II:25), it is hence necessary that this first and absolute truth relieve the uncertainty that the "omnipotent God" had heavily imposed. For the first and final time, Descartes here dares to speak pedagogically of a deceiving God (*deceptor*; 36, 23, 28). To establish extrinsically the status of evidence other than that of the ego, it is necessary to demonstrate that omnipotence does not deceive. This will become the project of the Third Meditation.[64]

Let us conclude. (a) The *regula generalis* is found straightaway fully and definitively established: derived from the ego as its transcendental condition of possibility and taken as a first real truth, it posits the conversion into truth of all absolutely clear and distinct perceptions. (b) Sensible perceptions do not offer this evidence because they intrinsically lack clarity and distinction. Mathematical evidences, intrinsically clear and distinct, are no longer extrinsically so, since the omnipotent God can also submit them to a super-encoding. (c) At no moment does the ego discover itself newly examined, nor confronted by any missing "guarantee" or "veracity" (these terms never appear). (d) To the contrary, the ego reaffirms its evidence and hence its truth after the omnipotent God is mentioned again; it even enlarges its evidence to the temporalization of its existence and restores the truth of simple intellectual natures. (e) The restoration of the simple material natures demands that mathematical evidence be reestablished. This is accomplished already for clarity and intrinsic distinction, but requires the demonstration of the existence of God for validating them extrinsically. (f) Never is it a question of a "circle," nor of a doubling of the "cogito," nor moreover of a "cogito."[65]

But above all, our reading permits us to understand why the *Meditations* displaces and repeats the interventions of the *regula generalis*. In the Third Meditation, it is perfectly and definitively instituted, yet thus far it can only be applied to simple intellectual natures, especially to the *res cogitans* and its modes, just as to the two common simple natures (existence, duration). In the Fourth Meditation (where the *Synopsis* places it), it is reinforced by an articulated doctrine of judgment, even if it does not conquer any new field of application. Finally and above all, in the Fifth Meditation it is applied to simple material natures, whose clarity and intrinsic distinction do not risk any extrinsic questioning. In this way the *regula generalis*, never doubted, does not cease to be deployed, to the point where it appears as the speculative heart of the whole *Meditations*, since it sustains its very ambition — that evidence always shows the truth.

4

Pascal and the "General Rule" of Truth

§1. A Cartesian Point of Departure

"To make light of philosophy is to be a true philosopher" (§513).[1] This formula, which is in itself already hazardous and imprecise, although maybe of Aristotelian origin,[2] has too often been employed as an authorization to dispense with taking seriously the situation in which philosophy is placed by Pascal. One must know philosophy in order to "laugh" at it—and what did Pascal know about philosophy? Is it not necessary for philosophy still to be at stake in such jesting, so that it transcend philosophy to a higher degree? Did Pascal mock philosophy in this sense? As recent works have established, Pascal's tactic in philosophy almost always consisted in subverting the validity of a second order from the point of view of a third order, thus of inverting (generally Cartesian) theses with which Pascal was as familiar as his interlocutors. Thus the *ego cogito* becomes the *moi pensé*, being to know becomes being to love, certainty becomes uselessness, etc.[3] I would like to suggest here that Pascal sometimes follows a different approach: not only does he institute a reversal between second and third order, but he applies one unique conceptual model to both. Put simply, its variation alone is sufficient to move the respective playing out of second and third orders. A remarkable example of this other approach, which implies a continuous differentiation, is found in the case of evidence being erected as the criterion of truth.

Even if the definition literally is taken from Aristotle, Descartes is the first to posit that "all knowledge is certain and evident cognition."[4] He posits it because he bases himself on what since 1637 he had named a "general rule," that of knowing that "the things we conceive very clearly and distinctly are all true" (AT VII:33, 20–22; CSM I:127). In 1641, he will confirm the same equivalence in what he will then call a *regula generalis*: "All the things which I conceive very clearly and distinctly, are true."[5] Considered as a quality of any perception by the ego whatsoever, evidence is thus invested by Descartes with the function of being an index to the truth of what that perception perceives. In no way is this a matter of subjectivizing truth. Is not truth known only from a subject's point of view, and must not any truth *for us* appear in and for subjectivity? More essentially, the respective roles of evidence, which are always determined for and by an ego, and of truth, which necessarily regulates the thing itself, are at stake. Descartes does not doubt that the first can but must not always (or at least a majority of the time)[6] serve as the norm for the second. It follows, of course, that truth remains always (or a majority of the time) that of an object. Truth is known, evidently, because constructed according to the a priori conditions of knowledge itself.

Now Pascal adhered to this Cartesian equivalence, at least when, in October 1647, he refuted the still-Cartesian thesis of subtle matter and negation of the vacuum against Father Étienne Noël, S.J.: "Allow me to quote to you a *universal rule* [my emphasis] which applies to all specific subjects in which it is a matter of recognizing the truth"; he thus employs the same terms as Descartes. To pursue this further: "This is that we should never pass a decisive judgment against or for a proposition without affirming or denying one of the following two conditions. Either, of itself, it seems so clearly and so distinctly evident to the senses or to reason, as the case may be, that the mind has no grounds for doubting its certainty; this is what we call principles [*principes*] or axioms [*axiomes*], such as, for example, *if equals are added to equals, the sums will be equal.* Or it is deduced by infallible and necessary conclusions from such principles or axioms on whose certainty depends the full certainty of the conclusions which are carefully drawn therefrom. An example of this kind is that *the three angles of a triangle are equal to two right angles*; this, though self-evident, is clearly demonstrable by infallible conclusions from such axioms." In short, whether by the short way of definition of axiom and principle, or by the long way of deduction (Descartes had said by *intuitus* or by *deductio*), one must admit nothing unless "an obvious demonstration leads us to regard it as true."[7] Let us hence conclude: in 1647 and in scientific practice, Pascal follows the Cartesian *regula generalis* or *veritatis* to the letter (AT VII:35, 14 or 70, 26): the only thing that is true in itself is what appears as evident to me, evidence and truth corresponding to each other like the two sides of a single phenomenon; they grow or diminish in direct proportion to each other.

About ten years later (that is at least what we would like to demonstrate) this equivalence becomes profoundly modified. To that end, we will consider three texts. (a) First, the fragment *Reflections on Geometry in General: The Geometrical Spirit and the Art of Persuasion*, first its first section, "On the Method of Geometrical Demonstrations, That Is, Scientific and Perfect Demonstration," then its second section, "On the Art of Persuasion." According to L. Lafuma, these two small works date from 1657–58 "or later," and according to J. Mesnard they might even be from "the year 1655."[8] (b) Second, we will examine the fourth letter to Mademoiselle de Roannez, dated the end of October 1656, as well as certain fragments of the *Pensées* that make this equivalence more explicit. It will thus be a matter of following the stages by which Pascal, while preserving the Cartesian thematic of the proportional evidence of truth, succeeds, if not in liberating himself from it, at least in complicating it enough so that it could suggest a new definition of the essence of truth.

§2. Repetition of the Cartesian Model

The fragment called *The Geometrical Spirit* is inscribed openly in the Cartesian horizon of "a method," of "the authentic method," "of correct procedure,"[9] which consists in beginning all reasoning and all knowledge by the most evident terms, following the precepts of the *Discourse on Method*: "never to accept anything as true if I did not have evident knowledge of its truth . . . and to include nothing more in my judgments than what presented itself to my mind so clearly and so distinctly that I had no occasion to doubt it" (AT VI:18, 16–23; CSM I:120); and again: "by beginning with the simplest and most easily known objects" (AT VI:18, 27–29; CSM I:120). But Pascal insists immediately on something that Descartes does not underline: "we necessarily arrive at primitive words which permit of no further definition," hence we must maintain "the proper balance, by not defining those things that are clear and known to all men and by defining all others."[10] A definition certainly depends on evidence, hence respects the equivalence between evidence and truth, but its primitive evidence cannot be defined—and it is for this reason precisely that a definition is at stake. From this emerges the paradox that first evidences, precisely because first, are unveiled as one of the essential characteristics of truth, its discursive rationality. One such evidence, undefinable by its very extremity, haunts the extreme borders of truth: Is this to protect its advances or to transgress its bounds?

To respond to this question demands a more precise examination of the text. (a) This "extreme evidence"[11] first concerns *definitions*. Pascal gives examples of them, which are probably taken from Descartes. "For example, what need is there of explaining what we mean by the term men? Do we not know well enough what the thing is that we want to designate by that term? What advantage did Plato think it would be to us for him to say that man is a two-legged creature without feathers? As if the idea which I naturally have of man and which I cannot express were not clearer and more certain than the one which he gives by his useless and even ridiculous explanation." One thinks here of the Second Meditation: "But what is a man? Shall I say 'a rational animal'? No; for then I should have to inquire what an animal is, what rationality is, and in this way one question would lead me down the slope to harder ones, and I do not now have the time to waste on subtleties of this kind."[12] The criticism of the definition of light, as "a luminary motion of luminous bodies," seems to be directed against that of Descartes: "consider the light in bodies we call 'luminous' to be nothing other than a certain movement, or very rapid and lively action, which passes to our eyes through the medium of the air and other transparent bodies."[13] Yet it nevertheless obeys the same logic as Descartes when he criticizes, for example, the Aristotelian definition of movement.[14]

It is not only an affirmation of the impossibility "to define being without falling into this absurdity: . . . it would be necessary to say *it is*, and in this way to employ the defined word in the definition," which does not allude to the Cartesian refusal to define the difference between *essence* and *existence*, considered as too evidently known by all (*omnibus nota*; Third Replies, AT VII:194, 12; CSM II:136).[15] Nevertheless, Descartes only criticizes his definitions because he believes he can lean on the "simple natures," which are perfectly evident and knowable, although indefinable: thought, will, doubt, extension, figure, movement, existence, nothing, and so on.[16] Pascal does not mention these here as such,[17] leaving the excess of evidence in definitions undetermined, so to speak. They also change their function: henceforth "definitions are made only to designate the things named, and not to set forth their nature."[18] Defining, in the case of first evidences, no longer consists in fixing (or communicating) essence (general or individual, it makes little difference), but in making reference without concepts; from this results a strange situation, namely, that the excess of evidence *deprives* the definitions of first terms of the property of all common definitions. This is to say, it goes back only to "showing the nature"[19] of this thing; for it would not be "just" to "confuse the immutable nature of things with their freely assigned names which depend upon the caprice of men who have made them."[20] Definitions, although linguistic, in fact compensate for "the fault of discourse" by an indication, a purely deictic gesture, "without words."[21] Without doubt, from Pascal's point of view this privation is not a loss: on the contrary, since "the lack of definition is a mark of excellence rather than a defect, because it is not due to any obscurity of these things but rather to their extreme clarity."[22] Yet this excess does not subtract the least evidence from discursive rationality, hence from the form *par excellence* of truth. Leaving evidence, in the case of elementary definitions, as uncontrollable, indisputable, and auto-referential really does limit their truth.

"Extreme evidence," however, also affects (b) *demonstrations*. Indeed, when demonstrations concern infinite objects, such as numbers, space, infinite movements, and time, reasoning is inevitably exposed to paradoxes, all resulting from the possibility of several infinites. Properly speaking, these paradoxes are not objects of demonstration, although it would be a matter of "truths," which assure "the foundation and the principles of geometry." Without doubt, Pascal still maintains them here, "since the quality which makes them incapable of proof is not their obscurity, but rather their extreme obviousness, that lack of proof is not a defect but rather a mark of excellence."[23] Nevertheless, even if one accepts this argument, one must here still conclude from it that evidence does not always coincide with truth, and that extreme evidence can at times forbid the exercise of common discursive rationality. And when Pascal exhorts us that the paradox of "two marvelous infinities" is "not to be conceived but to be admired,"[24] the discursive rationality of truth is indisputably suspended, not reinforced.

(c) In fact, the gap that is widening between evidence and truth in the cases of definitions and the simplest demonstrations must be understood starting from the problem of principles (*principes*). Evoked with effort in the fragment *The Geometrical Spirit* ("in that case, it is a principle or an axiom but never a definition") they receive their explicit treatment in the *Pensées*: "When we are too far or too close we cannot see properly; an argument is obscured by being too long or too short; too much truth bewilders us. I know people who cannot understand that 4 from 0 leaves 0. First principles are too obvious for us."[25] Here again, exemplarily, excessive evidence not only brings about truth without discursivity, but it damages it, or rather, if we follow Pascal here to the letter, it makes truth itself obscure by excess.

Nevertheless, one could refuse to interpret these texts as introducing a very original or even extreme thesis; to do that, it would be sufficient to claim that Pascal here limits himself to a classical position: if the evidence of first principles dazzles (or leads astray) "reason" (here the understanding), it is because it is not directed only to itself, but to another faculty, the one Pascal names the "heart": "We know truth not only by reason but also by the heart. It is of this latter sort that we know the first principles. . . . The principles are sensed, the propositions are concluded."[26] The evidence of principles, excessive or too extreme for "reason," to the contrary conforms perfectly to the "heart." According to this interpretation, Pascal would simply follow Descartes, who names the gaze as a special faculty of principles: "But the first principles themselves are known only through intuition,"[27] which he opposes equally to the discursivity of the *deductio*. But Descartes, for his part, through the intermediary of the medievals, recovers Aristotle's position here: regarding principles, there is noesis and not science, νους αν ειη των αϱχων.[28] Since Pascal confines knowledge of principles to the "heart," as others confine it to the *intuitus* or to the νους, why not simply conclude that the excess of evidence (as much of principles, as of definitions or demonstrations) only affects "reason," hence is inscribed in the normal regimen of rationality taken in the large sense, according to all the faculties it exercises? Why not confine Pascal's pretended originality to a classic metaphysical position, where the distance between evidence and truth would simply reflect the distinction between the faculties of discursive and immediate knowledge? The Cartesian model would then remain the only frame of extremes or of Pascalian excess of evidence.

§3. The Will and Evidence: Inversion of the Cartesian Model

It seems, however, that we must resist this elegant, but without doubt simplistic, solution. First, in consideration of a curious decision in the fragment *On the Art of Persuasion*.[29] Although he has just fixed the eight rules to follow for definitions, axioms, and demonstrations, Pascal immediately posits that there are three "which are not absolutely necessary" that can hence "be neglected without error." Which? Certainly not the five principal ones, which admit as definitions only "things which are so well known in themselves," as axioms only "things which are perfectly self-evident," as demonstrations only those which "are so self-evident that no greater clarity is gained by proving them." One notes easily that all these rules are limited to giving rather clumsily the first Cartesian precept of method, fixed in 1637: "never to accept anything as true if I did not have evident knowledge of its truth" (AT VI:18, 16–18; CSM I:120). Up to this point, Pascal hence validates Descartes without reservation: here evidence offers the unique and univocal index of truth. But immediately he demands or at least permits the elimination of three other rules — and it is a matter precisely of those concerning the case of excessive evidence: "*As regards definitions*: Define no terms that are already perfectly well known. / *As regards axioms*: Do not fail to ask for any axioms which are perfectly evident and simple. / *As regards demonstrations*: Do not demonstrate any things that are very well known in themselves."[30]

Let us remark first that, with definitions, axioms, and demonstrations, as stated above, it is a matter of three rubrics under which evidence can turn to excess and be distinguished from truth. Let us further remark how strange it is that these three rules, which took such effort to formulate, are suspended so quickly. Let us finally remark what a curious motive is advanced for eliminating them: although it is a matter of three rules that demand that one not consider things already very or sufficiently known and evident in themselves, one could think that Pascal wants to dispense with these rules because they are themselves too *easy* and hence superfluous. Now that is not at all the case. Quite the contrary: Pascal dispenses with them, because for us "it is even *difficult* and almost impossible always to observe . . . exactly" what they prescribe. Neither to cede to the fascination of evidence, nor to attempt to define it, nor to admit it or to demand anything from it: this is what appears to be not only a difficulty but an impossibility. We recognize this paradoxical argument clearly in the fact that for Pascal not only is evidence often manifested by excess — but this excess constitutes a "fault" (although certainly "not great"). Yet in this way a "difficulty" is attested to that is almost "impossible" to surmount.[31] In the Pascalian discussion of excess of evidence in the face of truth, it is then not a matter of a serene division of roles between two complementary faculties, "heart" and "reason." Rather, it is a matter of two regimes of rationality: one confronts the excess of evidence, the other treats evidence as indication of truth—following the *regula* [*generalis*] *veritatis* of Descartes.

The ultimate objective of the fragment *On the Art of Persuasion* is to fix a dichotomy between the two regimes of evidence, which cannot absorb any topic of faculties of knowledge.—Pascal is committed to a fundamental distinction: the soul receives its opinions by "two principal faculties, the understanding and the will"; the first demonstrates by truth, the second makes one believe by pleasing; the first, although more "natural," cedes often to the second, "more common, although against nature," "base, unworthy, and alien." The difference between their respective "principles" shows that it is not a matter of two sources of different evidence for the same truths. In this way, principles "are natural verities and are known to everyone, such as that the whole is greater than any of its parts" for the understanding or "mind"; while for the "heart" or "will," it is a matter of "certain natural desires common to all men, such as the desire to be happy which people are bound to have."[32] In this way a desire (the desire for happiness) becomes elevated to the rank of a principle, under the pretext that it would be as universal and natural as a geometrical principle. The practical evidence that "All humans seek happiness"[33] has the same dignity of principle as the evidence of extension does for the geometers. The two "powers" of the soul hence do not amount to the same principle, following the same evidence. Far from one term overlapping the other, as the discursive can always find again the results of immediate apprehension or at least can lean on it, the will and the understanding bring into the light of day two [types of] independent principles that are autonomous and eventually antagonistic: for if humans can desire happiness over truth (above all the truth of geometry), they can also sacrifice their desire for happiness to attain truth. Moreover, the thematic of the two first orders will depend on this irreducible distance.

Thus Pascal clearly marks the limits of the compatibility between understanding and truth, in distinguishing several cases of agreement and of conflict. There is harmony between the faculties and we are easily persuaded by truth when either (a) it is deduced from truths and principles (understanding), or (b) it is "bound up with objects to our satisfaction" (will), or finally (c) it accords to "a double bond, with admitted truths and with the heart's desires," or is accorded neither to one nor the other. But a final hypothesis remains: (d) that the conflict would come up in the case "where things which we should like to make people believe are well founded on known verities, yet at the same time they are contrary to the pleasures which are closest to us."[34] It is no longer a matter of two sources of evidence (discursivity/immediacy) for the same truth, but of two evidences (theoretical/practical) positing two eventually opposed truths. Or if one wants to restrain truth to the theoretical field, it is a matter of two evidences, of which one posits truth and the other is opposed to it. The conflict of evidences succeeds the excess of evidence. In both cases, evidence no longer coincides with truth (or at least not entirely).

This is a matter of a strictly philosophical conflict, not only because Pascal constructs it with concepts, but also because he gives indications that permit the identification of the adversary against whom he constructs the conflict. Far from following the unique evidence proposed by the understanding, the will resists it—and it resists it because it is opposed to a different irreducible evidence (one that is unconditional in the case of the desire for happiness). The second evidence therefore manages to "humble the superb power of reasoning which claims to be the judge of the things that the will chooses."[35] How can one doubt that the adversary here is not still Descartes? The theory of truth and falsity in the Fourth Meditation postulates what Pascal contests here: (a) that evidence only results from the "understanding," from "reasoning" and not also from the will; (b) that evidence in and for understanding brings about (and would be solely qualified to bring about) a great inclination in the will—"a great light in the intellect was followed by a great inclination in the will."[36] By contrast to the restriction of evidence (and first of doubt), the sole theoretical field for Descartes, Pascal discovers, in the opposition not only of the will to the understanding but above all of "pleasure" to "proof," that the naked will encounters its own evidences, those of desire. These evidences, even if (above all if) they do not have any theoretical import, "are received in the soul," and they are received better and more easily by "pleasure" than the evidences of truth are by "proof." In this way, evidence comes as much from desire as from reason. This is what Descartes did not want to know and what Pascal came to recognize.[37]

This discovery disquieted Pascal more than he rejoiced over it. The signs of this confusion are multiplied in the fragment *On the Art of Persuasion*. Let me emphasize the principal signs. (a) Pascal attempts a first response at the first mention of the autonomy of the will in the field of evidence: in the domain of the sciences, one must know in order then to love by the will (Cartesian model), while loving in order then to know would only be suitable in the domain of theology and faith, following the saying of the "saints . . . [who] when speaking of things divine, say that we love them in order to know them." Pascal will illustrate this principle of an evidence proper to the will and to the heart effectively in the project of the *Apology*; but this fact does not prove that the priority of the will (and of its proper evidence) to the understanding would only be valid for theology and for faith, for "the mind believes naturally, and the will loves naturally."[38] Hence if the will loves *naturally*, the agreeableness of these evidences can also impose itself naturally. The distinction between natural and "supernatural" does not hold before the will (this also inscribes Pascal into the tradition that speaks of a natural desire to see God). Furthermore, the conclusion of this tentative attempt fits explicitly: if God established the supernatural order (the will preceding the understanding) to be the inverse of the natural order (the understanding regulating the will), people "have corrupted this [natural] order by making things profane which they should deem holy."[39] In short, although in the natural order humans proceed according to a Cartesian model of true judgment (understanding determining the will by evidence), here they follow the Pascalian model (evidence of the will pleasing despite the understanding). Hence this model in fact has a field of natural application, independent of its theological uses.

Consequently, a new task imposes itself. (b) If the conflict between understanding and will can go all the way to "a doubtful balance between truth and pleasure," this is because the art of persuading is really divided into an art of pleasing and an art of convincing (by proof). At this point Pascal admits the irreducible specificity of the art of pleasing, which goes all the way to granting it the status of a method, in the way in which reasoning by proofs is a method—"these two methods, which are respectively to convince and to please." The method of convincing does not surprise: it merely involves taking up the Cartesian method, from which it draws the requirement of evidence, something followed by the *Logic* of Arnauld and Nicole[40]; this method receives an abundant and relatively banal development, as compared to the *mathesis universalis*, which it would pick up in good logic. In contrast, the method of pleasing does surprise. Pascal barely sketches it, although he suggests that it would fix "as definite rules for pleasing as for demonstrating" or for one to "succeed as surely in making himself loved by kings and all sorts of people" as the other method succeeds in demonstrating.[41]

This promise of infallible certainty confirms that it is definitely a matter of a method in the Cartesian sense; nevertheless, its goal of being loved opens onto an entirely new domain that is unknown to Descartes: it is no longer an issue of objects certified by demonstration, but of other human subjects conquered by a seduction, to which the "delicious objects" would only be the means. A method of pleasing, universalizable to all relations between subjects following "the principles of pleasure," is here added to the Cartesian *mathesis universalis*, which restrains its method radically to the order and measure of objects.[42] To formulate a similar method precisely would in fact permit the exposure of the specificity of evidences proper to the will, to the heart, and to pleasure. Pascal's effort at disassociating evidence from truth in lifting the yoke the understanding has imposed on the will would require going all the way to duplicating the Cartesian method, limited to proofs, with a method absolutely without equivalence—that of the evidence of desires and pleasures, hence of an evidence not directed toward truth.

Yet (c)—and this is the most visible of his embarrassments— Pascal has not attempted to elaborate this new method: "of these two, the art of convincing and the art of pleasing, I shall confine myself here to the rules of the first." He justifies this by repeating it twice, one time before, one time after the refusal. The first time, the impossibility results from the assimilation of this method to the truths of faith: "I am not speaking here of divine verities which I should by no means associate with the art of persuasion, for they have their place infinitely above nature. . . . I am speaking only of those truths within our reach."[43] Here the argument would not know how to convince; first because, between these two denials, Pascal has effectively outlined an inversion of the relationship between the will and the understanding, hence the essence of his discovery; then because, as we have seen, the distinction between nature and the "supernatural" is irrelevant here. The second affirmation enlightens us much more: "But the mode of pleasing is incomparably more difficult, more subtle, more useful, and more admirable. Moreover, if I do not discuss it, it is because of inability to do so; and I feel so utterly unsuited to it that I believe the matter to be absolutely impossible"; or even: "But

I consider, and perhaps my weakness leads me to believe so, that it is impossible to succeed in this." The method of pleasing, precisely because it is the most useful and admirable, appears too difficult and subtle—why, if not because "the principles of pleasure are not firm and not stable"? A fragment of the *Pensées* will make this more explicit: in the intuitive spirit "the principles are so subtle and so numerous, that it is almost impossible but that some escape notice," in the sense that "one must have very clear sight to see all the principles."[44] What is admirable about the anticipated method concerns the new principles (pleasing, pleasure, agreeing, etc.) it implements; its difficulty and its quasi-impossibility depend on their subtlety and their multiplicity. If Pascal stays suspended between the project and the realization of this new method, it is because at this moment he still hesitates between the mathematical spirit [of geometry] and the intuitive spirit. Against Descartes (who only recognized the spirit of geometry) he has seen that the will sometimes follows its own evidence, and not that of the understanding; but he does not yet know when, why, and how the will calls forth its own evidences.

If it is one thing to establish, against Descartes, that the "will is one of the chief organs of belief, not because it creates belief, but because things are true or false according to the aspect by which we judge them,"[45] it is another to view things as the will directs and to attain the evidences that properly belong to it.

§4. Obscure Evidence

Pascal clears the path that leads from one to the other around 1656, without doubt in the course of reflections inspired by the miracle of Saint Épine, since the fourth letter to Mademoiselle de Roannez that we will privilege mentions the sentence of the Grand Vicar of Paris who authenticated the miracle.[46] We will propose reading it as a first real example of what *On the Art of Persuasion* envisioned but did not attain under the title of "the method . . . of pleasing," that is to say, "to cause to love" or to persuade without convincing.

This is a theological hypothesis: God wants to raise up the "faith" of "those whom he wishes to engage in his service"; he is hence not first understood by making himself known by convincing proof, but by making himself agreeable in pleasure [*plaisir*] and wish [*bon plaisir*]. Hence the paradox that he gives himself to be seen only with an obscure evidence, which only the will can see as truth, while it remains obfuscated for the understanding. In short, the more God is "discovered"—and this to the will alone—the more he is dissimulated to the understanding. "All things hide some mystery; all things are veils which hide God." And the more God is made visible, the less he is made easily recognizable: "He was far more recognizable when he was invisible than when he has rendered himself visible." This obscure evidence, which becomes a truth only for the will that it pleases, Pascal specifies in three paradoxes: (i) God "remained hidden under the veil of nature," but even the "infidels" can recognize him there; (ii) "under the veil of human flesh, He was hidden even more than before," but only the Christians can see him there; (iii) finally, he "chose to remain there in the strangest and the most hidden mystery of all, namely, in the Eucharistic species," where only Catholics can contemplate him. Let us focus here on the first paradox, since we are concerned only with Pascal's philosophy.

It is indeed a matter of a philosophical paradox. Certainly, to think God "hidden under the veil of nature" without question goes back to Romans 1:20: "Ever since the creation of the world his eternal power and divine nature, invisible though they are, have been understood and seen through the things he has made. So they are without excuse."[47] But Pascal inverts the sense of the Pauline text entirely. (Visible) "nature" does not make God more visible, but it "conceals" him like a "veil." In place of the Gentiles being, according to Paul, "without excuse" for not recognizing the invisible in the visible, because nature offers evidence of the reality of God, for Pascal it seems almost a miracle that "some infidels" have been able to recognize him in nature at all. Despite or by virtue of this inversion of evidence into veiling, one must underline that Pascal maintains that nature retains a function, but henceforth a negative one, in the knowledge of God: "nature is such, that it points at every turn to a God who has been lost"; "God's conduct is hidden beneath nature"; "There are perfections in nature to show that she is the image of God and imperfections to show that she is no more than his image." Yet he maintains this function of nature only on one condition—that of displacing evidence of conviction (by proof) by agreeableness (by pleasure), of the understanding by the will: "I marvel at the boldness with which these people presume to speak of God. / In addressing their arguments to unbelievers, their first chapter is the proof of the existence of God from the works of nature. Their enterprise would cause me no surprise if they were addressing their arguments to the faithful, for those with living faith in their hearts can certainly see at once that everything which exists is entirely the work of the God they worship. But for those in whom this light has gone out in whom we are trying to rekindle it, people deprived of faith and grace, examining with such light as they have everything they see in nature that might lead them to this knowledge, but finding only obscurity and darkness."[48]

The obscure evidence of God does pass from one regimen to the other, since it is the same nature and the same things that manifest either God or only themselves—according to the "faith" and the "grace" accompanying them or not; or "faith" and "grace" dispose the will to "be pleased" with the evidence of God—or rather the will is disposed by them to this pleasure. Here "faith" and "grace," as theological and supernatural as they might be, exercise a no less strictly epistemological function, making possible the second method of persuading, the pleasure that submits the understanding to the will and proposes an evidence seen only on the condition of really wanting it, hence of wanting it first. Beginning with the general statement that "the secrets of nature are hidden,"[49] one could extricate two parallel hermeneutics of the same nature. (a) The scientific task persuades through convincing by proofs; these proofs produce evidence only for the understanding, which then influences the will. (b) The task of *natural* theology persuades through making agreeable by pleasures; these pleasures produce evidence obscure only to the understanding, but clear to the will (here under the figure of "faith"), which then leads to the understanding. A double meaning of the "secret" contained by this nature also follows: the secrets *in* nature (which take up the scientific task, following the method of the geometrical spirit), and the secrets *of* nature, God (who takes up the method of pleasing).

One would have to show how "faith" in no way monopolizes the method of persuading by pleasure exclusively, but only offers an instance of it. Custom, imagination, and the political community offer other instances.[50] But the recognition of God under the veil of nature has several exemplary characteristics, which make it a privileged case. (a) It is a matter of an evidence submitted to the will that does not remain any less a truth, in contrast to other cases, where it is a matter of "deception" or "injustice." (b) It is a matter of a pleasure that applies not only to a natural object (in contrast to power, passions, and faculties), but in the case of scientific discourse is susceptible to a hermeneutics other than that of pleasure. As Pascal practices both methods on the same object in 1656–57, one can infer that the doubling of the "method of persuading" corresponds to a doubling of Pascal's attitude, as a parallel hermeneutic conversion, condition, or effect of other conversions. (c) The hermeneutic of nature finally marks, as do all other appearances of God, who hides himself, that this God only hides himself (from the understanding) in order to make himself agreeable to the will—"God wishes to move the will rather than the mind. Perfect clarity would help the mind and harm the will." But he only wants to make himself pleasing to the will in order to make himself loved: "Those who do not love truth excuse themselves on the ground that it is disputed and that very many people deny it. Thus their error is solely due to the fact that they love neither truth nor charity, and so they have no excuse."[51]

In this sense, the fourth letter to Mademoiselle de Roannez offers a better complement to the fragment *On the Art of Persuasion*, since it begins to implement what in the fragment remained a program, outlined but quickly abandoned.

§5. Questions

Descartes identifies evidence and truth (*regula veritatis*, in the *Discourse* and the Third Meditation), then subordinates the will to the understanding, whose evidence alone could rule judgment (Fourth Meditation). In contrast, Pascal contests these two presuppositions: first because evidence escapes the truth of discursive reason in certain cases (thus for principles, axioms, definitions); then because evidence of proof for the understanding offers only one of the "two methods" of persuasion, thus extricating evidence. This evidence, which puts pleasure to work for the will, is at times obscure but always difficult and subtle. At the same time, the horizon of truth is enlarged from the objective understanding to the desiring will and becomes complicated, because desire, pleasure, and love obey evidences of a type absolutely irreducible to that of objective rationality. In turn, this new doctrine about the relation between evidence and truth raises a number of new questions. Here are some of them.

(a) The method of pleasure remains more sketched than described; certainly the *Pensées* largely implement what *On the Art of Persuasion* scarcely describes, but nevertheless it does not fix the doctrine. Is it the matter of an anecdotal failure, indeed, as is true of the incompleteness of the Cartesian *Regulae*, a symptom that the method calls forth no more description or foundation than it already works effectively? Or is it rather a matter of a difficulty in principle—for example, that, due to the multiplicity and subtlety of principles that it puts into play, agreeableness can be neither described nor formalized nor assigned? In short, does the redoubling of the *mathesis universalis* in the art of convincing and being convinced not remain an interrupted project? This concerns an interrogation internal to Pascal's work.

(b) But one can also find another, exterior one. The thesis that truth comes as much from the will (ceding to pleasure) as from the understanding (determined by evidence) intervenes against Descartes, for whom the *regula veritatis* identifies truth with evidence as much as possible. This fundamental polemic opens two questions. First is the one of knowing whether Descartes can withstand Pascal here: whether truth has no other sense than evidence, whether evidence itself can do justice to the veritative role of the will (e.g., in the liberty of indifference in its two phases), or whether, finally, Descartes himself outlines an "art of persuasion" (and *The Passions of the Soul* could offer traces of it)—in short, did Descartes already surpass his own *mathesis universalis*? The second question comes down to asking whether the Pascalian art of pleasing has opened a way that others have been able to follow successfully. Asked differently, does the idea of truth for and by the will beyond evidence reappear in the history of metaphysics? We will risk suggesting two names: first Kant, according to the articulation of the second and third *Critiques* by reference to the first; then, Nietzsche, following the reappearance of the will and truth in the will to power. But we plainly admit the difficulty of passing from suggestion to demonstration. Nevertheless, an honest appreciation of the validity of the Pascalian project should not spare itself such tricky investigations.

(c) We must also ask whether such a determination of the essence of truth can pretend to a strictly theoretical status or whether it is a matter only and immediately of a destitution of metaphysics by theology. For the truth of the understanding to be taken down a notch would not really harm theology, which subordinates the evidence of the understanding to grace, hence to the will.[52] Now it is a matter here not only of grace (third order), but also of the principles and definitions of science and the extent of nature (second order). Even more, it is a matter of the body and the world, since the intuitive spirit obeys laws at least analogous to those of grace. The new model of truth tends to apply to all orders and goes from being an exception to becoming the rule. From that moment on, one not only wonders what remains of the distinction between the orders, but can also assert some unexpected suspicions. In leading knowledge in certain occurrences back to the will, hence to desire, hence to the inadequation

of the idea, does not Pascal approach the *conatus* of Spinoza, his contemporary? Also, does he not open already the hazardous path that
Malebranche will follow — interpreting the reign of grace (its distri-
bution, its efficiency, etc.) according to the laws governing the communication of movement or of pleasure? Does he not, finally,
anticipate the harmony that Leibniz will construct between nature
and grace, reducing access to God to one perception among others,
all equally developed according to the complete notion of the monad,
with neither door nor windows? Despite the appearances (and the
indisputable reality) of his intention to offer an apology for Chris-
tianity, it is possible that Pascal maintains such subterranean similar-
ities with his contemporaries that at the very moment he pretends to
set himself free from them, he is prevented from doing so.

Considering Pascal as a philosopher demands distinguishing in his
thought what comes properly from metaphysics (with its limits) from
what arrives at a thought of charity. Given this condition, we will
avoid confusing the two in an ambiguous and ruinous figure of the
"metaphysics of charity." One must choose between metaphysics and
charity, even in Pascal.[53]

5

Substance and Subsistence

Suárez and the Treatise on *Substantia* in the *Principles of Philosophy* 1, §51–§54

§1. The Concept of Substance in Question

Compared to his predecessors and even to his contemporaries, Descartes stands out, among other things, for his sparing and careful use of the concept of substance. It seems as if its definition and diverse properties remain an open question for him, indeed a difficulty left hanging. One could even suggest that Descartes did not succeed in dealing with the concept of substance until—finally, one might say—the developments in §51–§54 of the *Principles of Philosophy* dedicate him to doing so. A quick review of the occurrences of this term in the principal previous works at least seems to suggest as much.

The *Rules for the Direction of the Mind* (*Regulae ad directionem ingenii*) overall make only two marginal and allusive mentions of substance: according to the first, water is "a thinner substance" (*tenioris substantiae*) than earth (Twelfth Rule, AT X:424, 11–12; CSM I:47); according to the other, in the human being "animal" and "living" are merely "different species of substance" (*diversae species substantiae*; Fourteenth Rule, AT X:449, 4; CSM I:63). Moreover, this almost complete absence is quite logical: it follows directly from the decision taken in the Sixth Rule to eliminate the genres of being (*genus entis*) in principle (AT X:381, 11; CSM I:21), that is the categories (*categoriae*) of the philosophers (AT X:381, 12; CSM I:21), in order to substitute for them the simple natures, which organize things "insofar as one thing can be known on the basis of others."[1] Because substance since Aristotle, in the sense of ουσια as well as that of τοδε τι, constitutes the first of all categories, it goes without saying that to eliminate these categories forces one also to eliminate the use of the concept of substance.[2] The two occurrences that we have pointed out in the *Regulae*, far from being surprising by their rarity, rather seem too numerous, given the strict point of view taken by Descartes. Maybe one must simply consider them to be citations or examples taken from adversaries and not authentically Cartesian occurrences.

Without doubt the same thing may be said about the summary of the *monde* proposed by the fifth part of the *Discourse on Method*: "I add here also several things touching on substance, situation, movements and all the diverse qualities of these heavens and stars" (AT VI:43, 25–28; CSM I:133). Subject to an exhaustive lexicographical inventory, we can thus accept in principle the elimination of the concept of substance in the method and in its application following the program that Descartes explicitly sets for himself in 1638: "True, the analogies that are usually employed in the Schools explain intellectual matters by means of physical ones, *substances* by means of accidents, or at any rate one quality by means of a quality of a different kind, and they are not very instructive. But in the analogies which I employ, I compare movements only with other movements, or shapes with other shapes. . . . I maintain, therefore, that analogies of this sort are the most appropriate means available to the human mind for laying bare the truth in problems of physics."[3] Explaining means comparing figures or movements, thus utilizing simple natures (which turn out to be material, presupposing them to be extended). One never refers substance back to accidents, nor does one reason about accidents or about species, etc. The project of a *universal science* (AT I:339, 19; CSMK III:51) or of a *mathesis universalis* (AT X:378, 8–9; CSM I:19) is in no need of the concept of substance; better yet, it excludes it.

Nevertheless, Descartes does not respect the prohibition of substance in metaphysics that he has promulgated following the method. Already from the fourth part of the *Discourse* on he can no longer avoid defining the *I think, therefore I am* as "a substance whose whole essence or nature is simply to think" (AT VI:33, 4–5; CSM I:127). It is not a matter here of a passing imprecision, seeing that the Third Meditation will ratify the substantiality of the finite subject by an explicit but enigmatic claim: "I am myself also a substance" (*ego autem substantia*).[4] In this way, first in 1637 then in 1641, Descartes thinks the *I think* in terms of substance. Consequently, it is a matter of a firm decision and one that concerns an essential truth, namely, the primary one. How should one explain this tactical turnabout? It is not certain that we possess the information that would permit an answer to this question: to the best of my knowledge, Descartes has nowhere commented on this turn nor has he justified it. But, even without being able to explain it, maybe we can take a better measure of its implications and context. From this perspective, two remarks impose themselves.

First remark: if in 1657 the *I think therefore I am* receives the qualification of "substance," it alone receives it: no other thing, be it finite or above all infinite (God), shares this title. Also, Descartes can still ignore or pretend to ignore the difficult question of the univocal, equivocal, or analogical meanings of substance. Thus he shies away from the discussions of the Schools, which, for all their pushing the analysis too far, do have their rigor. On the contrary, in 1641 the declaration "I am a substance" (*ego autem substantia*) no longer enjoys this incomparable solitude. It concludes a demonstration (a fairly laborious one) intended to extend a substantiality to the finite "thinking thing" (*res cogitans*), which since its first appearance — "[the ideas] which represent substances to me" (*[ideae] quae substantias mihi exhibent*; AT VII:40, 12–13; CSM II:28) — extended, indeed, extended particularly, to God, "a supreme God" (*summum aliquem Deum*; 40, 16), as well as to "finite substances" (*finitae substantiae*; 40, 20). Furthermore, the very term "substance" (*substantia*), which is completely missing in the proof of the existence of the ego in the Second Meditation, intervenes in the Third Meditation only finally to demonstrate the existence of God under the figure of "a substance that is infinite" (*substantiam quandam infinitam*; AT VII:45, 11–12; CSM II:31). Substance is described and thought starting from the "infinite substance" (*substantia infinita*).[5] As a result, Descartes inevitably exposes himself to the classic medieval difficulty of the analogy of substance: Is "substance" said in the same sense about the created finite and about the uncreated infinite? And if not, how can the same concept of "substance" allow for this gap without yielding to a pure and simple equivocity? Without a doubt this question still remains implicit in 1641. But precisely its not having been resolved makes it more menacing: if the entire a posteriori demonstration presupposes a comparison between effects (the ideas of accidents, of finite and infinite substances), and if the concept of substance itself turns out to be entirely equivocal, does this comparison between effects still retain any meaning? The Third Meditation hence utilizes a major concept, "substance," that it does not define rigorously enough for the use that it claims to make of it. Consequently, one must pose the question whether §51–§54 of the first part of the *Principles* will finally manage to decide between the univocity or the analogy of the concept of "substance."

A second remark confirms Descartes' indecision. The *Regulae* had eliminated substance from the list of simple natures. And, in fact, most often the *Meditations* reproduces this list without mentioning substance, either in the First Meditation among the "simpler and more universal things [that] are real" (*simplicia et universalia vera*; extension, quantity, greatness, number, place, and time), which are put in doubt by the God who can do everything (AT VII:20, 11, 15–19; CSM II:13), or in the Fifth Meditation among the ideas (quantity, extension, figure, place, movement, duration) that fix the "essences of material things" (63, 16–21; CSM II:44), or in the recovery of the simple intellectual natures by the Second Meditation (28, 20–23; CSM II:19). Nevertheless, the habitual exclusion of substance from the simple natures admits of an exception: the Third Meditation, when it solemnly recapitulates the "ideas of corporeal things," reintroduces it for the first time, as an addition to the simple material natures: "to these may be added substance, duration and number."[6] Although the *Meditations* does not unfold this late reinscription of substance much further, we should not see in this an initiative without sequel or a convention without consequence. Indeed, when the *Principles of Philosophy* finally decides to treat the concept of substance explicitly, it is again within the more comprehensive framework of "all the simple notions which are the basic components of our thoughts."[7] Listed among them, under "things" (*res*), one again finds the sequence already privileged by the Third Meditation: "the most general items are *substance, duration, order, number* and any other items of this kind."[8] Thus, §51–§54 can only be read as explication of one of the common simple natures: the final one to be reinstated, but the first one for what we consider "as things" (*tanquam res*; 22, 31; CSM I:208). Does such a reversal of the status of substance — first excluded from the simple natures, then later included in them — have only a tactical importance (a simple pedagogical concession to the scholastic vocabulary), or does it rest on a real elaboration of its concept? If the latter were the case, would this elaboration allow it to respond to the first question — regarding the univocity or the analogy of the concept of substance?

§2. Substance as Subsistence (§51)

The treatise on substance in the *Principles of Philosophy* 1, §51–§54, opens with a theoretical decision as clear as it is determinative: "By substance we can understand nothing other than a thing which exists in such a way as to depend on no other thing for its existence."[9] According to a reasoning that we will have to reconstitute more precisely, Descartes concludes, in similar words, that all substances are to be understood "under this common concept . . . things that need only the concurrence of God in order to exist."[10] Substance is hence defined by (quasi) nonindigence, hence by its capacity to suffice for its proper needs and to depend on (almost) no one. Not only is substantiality not defined by relation, but by consisting in self-sufficiency it excludes independence and self-identity to itself equal to itself. What does this independence signify in Cartesian terms? Formally, independence implies infinity: "independence being conceived distinctly, comprises in itself infinity."[11] But this independence carries with it right away all the ambiguity of the relation between the finite and the infinite, since it can be understood in two opposing fashions. Is it a matter of the model of the *causa sui*, in the sense that its existence does not depend on any other cause than the power of its essence? Or is it rather a matter of the model of the *res cogitans*, such that its existence only depends on the (spoken or mute) act of its thought?

At first glance Descartes does not resolve the issue. In fact, he is satisfied with two operations. (a) Here, nonindigence recovers a character earlier attributed to substance by Suárez, the most influential of Descartes' masters in scholastics. But Suárez hesitates almost as much as Descartes, and he also maintains that created substance finally remains destitute, at least in respect to God: "The essence of created substance is so imperfect, that it always requires the addition of a different species," that is to say that "the existence of created nature is such that it is essentially dependent on God and on its being effected."[12] Nevertheless, he envisages at least as a possibility what Descartes affirms as a thesis at the beginning of §52: "Indeed, if some created thing incapable of accidents could have existed either possibly or impossibly, and its nature not need any subject in order to exist, it would be a perfect substance."[13] Nonindigence then does not suffice to settle the ambiguity of substantiality, rather it permits it to be formulated clearly.

(b) Nevertheless, is Descartes here concerned only with nonindigent independence? Why does he not resume in *Principles* 1, §51 the definition of substance employed by the Third Meditation: "a stone is a substance, or is a thing capable of existing independently"?[14] Or the one he will mention in *Principles* 1, §64: "subsistent things" (*res subsistentes*)?[15] In fact, at least for Descartes, definition by independence amounts to definition by perseity and by subsistence. The Fourth Replies already mark this double equivalence clearly. First the equivalence between subsistence and perseity: "I find it self-contradictory that they should be substances, that is, things which subsist on their own, and at the same time incomplete, that is, not possessing the power to subsist on their own."[16] Then the equivalence between perseity and nonindigence: "the notion of substance is just this—that it can exist by itself, that is without the aid of any other substance."[17] Thus it is a matter of one and the same concept of substance by three distinct accounts—nonindigence, perseity, and subsistence. This Cartesian concept retains the lexical echo of Suárez and straightaway suffers from an indetermination between univocity and analogy, depending on whether it concerns the finite or the infinite.

Comparison with Suárez will permit us better to measure the originality of Descartes' decision, for the definition of substance goes back precisely to Suárez, first as perseity—"A being, however, constitutes substance through itself; an accident constitutes a being truly in the other"[18]—then as subsistence by itself: "This alone which subsists is said to be a substance most properly and to the highest degree."[19] Consequently, one must conclude that for Suárez (who in this way anticipates Descartes) substance is defined as the *ens per se*, hence by subsistence—the fact of remaining (*immorari*) as a "firm and constant" thing, in the sense in which Descartes defines that "a substance cannot cease to endure without also ceasing to be."[20] In this way the equivalence of the *ens* with permanent presence, persistent in itself, is accomplished. This equivalence will be articulated by Heidegger as the indication without equivocation of a properly metaphysical thought.[21] Yet again, Suárez expresses clearly what metaphysics has always wanted to signify. Must we, for all that, conclude that Descartes follows the position of Suárez here to the letter and in doing so he establishes the metaphysical thematic of the *ens* as persistent presence? The situation will reveal itself to be much more complex.

Indeed, as is often the case, Descartes indisputably only takes up the terms in which Suárez poses the question in order better to invert the solution. If substance amounts to subsistence in itself for Suárez, it follows that God alone merits the title of substance, since he alone persists without any indigence in the direction of exterior help. Statements of this sense are not missing. "The perfect idea of substance is found in God; since God is maximally in Himself and through Himself even if He does not remain in accidents." Or: "For God alone is complete substance without any composition . . . for this God is physically a substance or a substance that is itself completed by things, for through itself it is essentially subsisting, and from itself it does not require anything to be the consummate and absolute perfection of substance." It follows that the creature never accedes, as such, to the rank of subsistent substance without destitution: "But, truly complete substance without real composition is never found in creatures."[22] It is in this context, of course, that one must hear the phrase in *Principles* 1, §51: "And there is only one substance which can be understood to depend on no other thing whatsoever, namely, God."[23] Yet it is precisely at this point that Descartes inverts Suárez instead of following him.

With good logic, Suárez challenges the pretension of finite and/or created substance to subsistence, thus to plain and entire substantiality; it only attains "an imperfect mode of being through itself" (*modus per se essendi . . . imperfectus*), demanding a composition with another term, which is alone subsistent, following a manner of substantiality that subsists accidentally. This can be understood in two fashions. Either as incomplete substance, which "suffers from a lack of the perfect idea of substance, and from itself it neither subsists in act nor in the other, but in the whole; it neither subsists perfectly nor wholly absolutely, but in the order of some whole that must be composed" — and that is the case for primary matter. Or, and this is the case of finite substances, "truly, if there is to be a complete substance, even though it subsists in act, not however by power of its essence subsisting formally and precisely, it is complete through some mode and act of its essence and therefore is a substantial, created nature. . . . It is not essentially a subsisting act, but is by means of something that is apt for it."[24] Here the act of subsistence does not happen to substance by its proper essence, but by an act which is, so to speak, external, of which it does not possess the energy but only the aptitude, and which it does not produce but receives. Suárez, remembering faithfully for once the "real composition" (*compositio realis*) of essence with "being" (*esse*) according to Saint Thomas, maintains that all created substance, even complete substance, still does not remain "simply

and wholly in the idea of substance, for it lacks the ulterior complement of metaphysics."[25] He thus rigorously concludes that, since created substance "always will lack something additional or
complementary for its proper species, so that it would be complete in
it," hence since this complement of subsistence remains for him always exterior—"no created substance is possible that in the thing is
not separable from its subsistence"[26]—no created substance is substance in the full sense of subsistence, which applies only to God.[27]
Descartes acknowledges the same situation, since he admits that following the criterion of (non)indigence, God constitutes the "one substance" (*unica substantia*), while "all other substances . . . can exist
only with the help of God's concurrence."[28] The extraordinary paradox is, however, that he draws from this a conclusion opposite to that
of Suárez: created substances remain no less substances in their own
full right, which in this context signifies subsistence. Without doubt
they do remain indigent (they are in need of the exterior support of
God), but this indigence can be summed up in a condition so commonly conceded that it does not call their subsistence into question.
"Only the concurrence of God" (*solus Dei concursus*; VIIIA:25, 1–2 =
24, 25; CSM I:210) becomes doubly extrinsic: no longer only as a
condition affecting the essence of created substance with an irreducible contingency, but as a condition so transcendent and so universal
that it becomes an external necessity. The ordinary support of God
no more indicates an uncertainty of created substances than the creation of eternal truths affects them with uncertainty: to necessity
under the condition of truths (but under a condition always already
realized), responds subsistence *per se* under the condition of divine
aid of created substances (but under a condition always already accorded). Suárez opposes the two absolutely heterogeneous degrees
of substantiality as subsistence to the simple abstention from subsistence. For Descartes these are superimposed on each other—one becomes the eternal, necessary, and permanent condition for the
second, which suddenly seizes the full and entire subsistence that
was until now reserved for God.

One text at least witnesses this shattering of the Suárezian device
without ambiguity: defending his definition of accident (and hence of
substance), Descartes must confront the formidable problem of real
accidents—accidents that, according to the Thomists, remain the
same if in the Eucharistic transubstantiation the substance of bread
gives way to that of Christ. The Cartesian response contains a dilemma: either accidents are only accidents and have nothing real, or

they are real and then amount to substances: "whatever is real can exist separately from any subject; yet anything that can exist separately in this way is a substance."[29] Even for a supposed accident it suffices that it be in the mode of substance for it to exist in part (hence to subsist). But, one will object, real accidents subsist in the Eucharistic transubstantiation only by the miracle of divine power; hence this substantialization of the nonsubsistent (accident) remains supernatural and therefore philosophically ineffectual. Now—and it is here that Descartes shows the greatest audacity—the gap between the natural and the supernatural does not matter in the least to the question, because the ordinary power of God "in no way differs" (*nullo modo differt*; 435, 3; CSM II:293) from his extraordinary power, since in the two cases it is a matter of a power exercised on the exterior of things. And hence, just as according to *Principles* 1, §51, all finite substances remain marked by accidentality because they depend upon the assistance of God (*concursus Dei*), similarly, according to the Sixth Replies, the truly real accidents would be substantial by their dependence upon the power of God (*potentia Dei*): "Hence if everything which can naturally exist without a subject is a substance, anything that can exist without a substance even through the power of God, however, extraordinary, should also be termed a substance."[30] In short, divine power (even when it is "extraordinary") has nothing extraordinary as long as it assures the subsistence and the permanence of subsistence: under this unique condition, created substance and real accident do not show any difference, since in both cases God's *concursus* guarantees them subsistence, albeit extrinsic. But can one reduce God to the rank of a support of subsistence?

A decisive consequence results from this reversal: Descartes cannot and does not want to establish the least relation of analogy between the total substantiality of God and the conditional substantiality of the created: "The term 'substance' does not apply *univocally* . . . to God and to other things."[31] Indeed, henceforth subsistence no longer inscribes difference in the definition of substance and, indissolubly, the similarity between finite and infinite substantialities, but characterizes the finite univocally, leaving to the infinite only the extrinsic function of a *concursus*. But by proceeding in this fashion, Descartes opposes Suárez explicitly: "Although God, in some manner, belongs to the idea of substance with some created beings, He does so, however, not univocally but analogically."[32] Of subsistent substance, analogically differentiated from created substances missing their subsistence, God simply becomes *concursus*, efficient cause less transcendent than ordinarily arranged by a *conceptus communis* (§52, AT VIIIA:25, 1; CSM I:210). The unification of the concept of substance has as its price the loss of the analogy between the mode of the being of God and that of creatures. Of the *substantia infinita* of the *Meditations*, one must then really say what Descartes specifies to Clerselier: the infinite is not added to substance as an accident, but displays its essence. This means that substance disappears for the infinite. Consequently, substance is associated with the finite alone, but in it blocks all analogical access to the infinite.

§3. Substance as Substrate of the Attribute (§52)

The Cartesian choice in favor of the concept of substance as subsistence by itself is not without violence in §51, but at least it appears to be of a perfect simplicity. (a) Subsistence—reserved by Suarez for God—henceforth characterizes finite substances equally: "a stone is a substance, or is a thing capable of existing independently, and I also think that I am a substance."[33] (b) God, as *substantia infinita*, is characterized in fact more by infinity (which is without analogy to the finite) than by substantiality, which is swallowed up in equivocity. He designates less an infinite substance than a substantial infinity. In this way Descartes recovers a traditional position that thinks God as "ultimate substance" (*ultra substantiam*), "ultra omnem . . . substantiam essentia," which one of his contemporaries, Scipion Dupleix, had maintained as well: "It is however certain that God can be called and is truly substance, or rather (as has said Saint Dionysius) super-substance."[34] Nevertheless, §52 contradicts this simple situation immediately, in juxtaposing a second definition of substantiality to the first: on the *conceptus communis* of substance as that which subsists only with the ordinary aid of God (AT VIIIA:25, 1–3; CSM I:210), follows the *communis notio* (25, 7; CSM I:210) of substance as the substrate known by its attribute(s). This new meaning is not a hazardous or late innovation, because it intervenes since 1641, either by specific definition: "The term substance applies to every thing in which whatever we perceive immediately resides, as in a subject, or to every thing by means of which whatever we perceive exists. By 'whatever we perceive' is meant any property, quality or attribute of which we have a real idea"[35]; or by the functioning of the proof of the existence of material things, which infers beginning from attributes "some substance for them to inhere in" (*aliqua substantia cui insint*; AT VII:79, 1; CSM II:54–55). In fact, at stake is the categorical definition of substance as the subject of attribution of what comes to it ontically by way of attributes, accidents, or modes.

Traditional though it may be, this second definition nevertheless brings up several difficulties in its Cartesian context. (a) It seems perfectly useless, because Descartes already has at his disposal a definition of substance (namely, by subsistence), and he tries to extend the same to the domain of the created finite. (b) It also seems completely inappropriate for restoring a meaning of substantiality that would be suitable for God, since it is precisely the relation of this type of substance to accidents (or accidental attributes) that traditionally forbids applying them to God, in whose essence no accident intervenes.[36] (c) It is, nevertheless, the first definition that can be authorized by a thesis of Suárez. After having defined substance by subsistence and having made it a privilege of the uncreated, Suarez has to introduce a second meaning of substance, so that the created and the finite can also claim it: "substance, which is through itself, is not so much dictated, rather it is that which bears its accidents or is able to make itself a substance. In this way, Aristotle is seen to have taken up and described substance in predicates."[37] But far from alleviating the difficulty, this new identification reinforces it: indeed, for Suárez the categorical definition of substantiality only matters explicitly for the finite created. Hence in taking it up Descartes does not gain any new territory for substance: regarding the finite created, he pretends already to have at his disposal another definition, by subsistence, torn away from divine privilege (contra Suárez); reciprocally, the new meaning of substantiality does not concern God absolutely (here following Suárez). In fact, Descartes mobilizes solely for his finite substance the two definitions that Suárez distributed more clearly between the infinite uncreated and the finite created. Why does he concentrate on finite substance the two definitions proposed by Suárez, since this leaves the possible divine substantiality undetermined?

Without a doubt because he absolutely needs these two definitions in order to think the same and unique finite substance. Why does he have this double need? Doubtless because, at least for Descartes, each of them takes into account a particular version of finite substantiality. The first definition — by subsistence — attains for the finite absolute existence, however conditioned. It assures the finite the privilege of perseity, a privilege that had so far been refused to created substances. This *coup de force* mobilizes one of the two definitions of substance in general. Subsistence by itself then posits finite existence in its strictly isolated, absolute, solitary individuality. Yet such a naked subsistence suffers a patent flaw in the Cartesian theory of knowledge: without a network of relations, it remains for us unknowable as such. Indeed, since the *Regulae*, the knowledge of things deploys itself always due to the "series of objects of investigation" (*series rerum quarendarum*), which embraces them in a network of relations "in so far as some things can be known on the basis of others"[38] and which orders them according to the epistemological exigencies of the ego (*ad acies mentis convertere*; 379, 16; CSM I:20). The definition of substance as absolute subsistence does not satisfy the rules of knowledge: for it remains by itself an "isolated nature" (*natura solitaria*; 381, 19; CSM I:21), inaccessible because separated (*separatim*; 391, 1; CSM I:27). That is also why the *Regulae* had eliminated *substantia* from the list of simple natures: the epistemology of the *mathesis universalis* renders access to separated substances impossible. Consequently, one understands better the difficulty that §52 encounters: the result of §51, an ontic subsistence accorded to the finite, appears straightaway as epistemologically impracticable. From this follows the second phrase of §52, which has the function of an objection to the encounter of the conclusion of §51: "However, we cannot initially become aware of a substance [in the sense of subsistence by itself] merely through its being an existing thing, since this alone does not of itself have any effect on us."[39] Subsistence, hence existence, shies away from all relation; it announces itself no more than it gives itself; it remains in and by itself unknowable. The first definition, precisely because ontically radical, appears epistemologically weak. For this epistemological motive alone, Descartes hence must have recourse to a second definition—by the relation of the substrate to the attribute: following the requirements of the method, it is a matter of reestablishing a *series* between subsistent substance and one or several other terms, in such a way as to know it by relation. Such is the unique function of the attribute and of the recourse to substantiality as substrate.

That the second definition originally has an epistemological function is confirmed by the fact that Suarez (who utilizes it before Descartes) also introduces it with the same motive: substance is known only by its accidents and not at all as subsistent: "from accidents we therefore arrive at the knowledge of substance, and by habit of substance we first understand it."[40] Moreover, Suárez thematizes this thesis explicitly: although in itself substance is more intelligible (because it is more perfect) than accidents, in fact (and for us) accidents are more accessible, hence more intelligible than substance, because they alone affect us in a sensible manner: "Although substance according to itself, may be more perfect or more intelligible, nevertheless, on our view, an accident has greater power to change the intellect, for our intellect is not changed unless by means of certain kinds of sense impressions. Certain kinds of substance are not, however, impressed upon the senses; only accidents alone are impressed upon the senses. Therefore, there are accidents that first alter the intellect. Therefore, they are to be understood as arising first from the intellect rather than from substance." In short, by passing from the point of view of subsistence (existence) to that of substrate (knowledge), the attribute becomes original rather than relative. According to the order of knowledge, substance then becomes an accident of the accident. "We do not, moreover, reach knowledge of substance . . . unless by accidents or properties." One should not object that "the intellect is not able to understand an accident unless it understands a substance,"[41] since it is precisely the argument that establishes that in knowing the accident one must also know the substance. In short, Descartes takes from Suárez not only a second definition of substance, but its epistemological privilege in respect to the first; and through Suárez he inscribes it in a tradition that goes back at least to Duns Scotus: "substance does not immediately change our intellect to some of the intellect's own intellection; only sensible accidents do so."[42]

Several consequences result from this interpretation. First, let us repeat that the passage of §52, "However, we cannot initially become aware of a substance merely through its being an existing thing, since this alone does not of itself have any effect on us,"[43] expresses less a thesis of Descartes than an objection addressed to his first definition of substance: stating that subsistence (existence) remains as such unknowable, he moves on to a second determination—the relation, namely, the relation of substance to attribute. On this point the French text seems clearer than the Latin, because its additions mark the insufficiency and the opposition neatly: "But when it is a question of knowing if any of these substances really exists, that is to say, if it is present in the world, it is not enough that it exists in this fashion [as subsistent by itself] in order to cause us to apperceive it; because that alone does not discover anything for us which excites some particular knowledge of our thought. But beyond that it is required that it have several attributes which we could remark."[44] Here the paradox explodes in all its force: substance as pure existence subsisting in itself without attributes that do not exist in themselves. And literally, presence by *adesse* is recognized first in the attribute ("if we perceive the presence of some attribute"; *aliquod attributum adesse percipiamus*; AT VIIIA:25, 9; CSM I:210) and then solely for substance ("there must also be present an existing thing or substance").[45]

Second, the principal parallel texts, dating from 1641, all mark equally clearly the necessity of this epistemological reversal of the order between substance and attribute. Thus the Third Replies says: "But we do not come to know a substance immediately, through being aware of the substance itself; we come to know it only through its being the subject of certain acts"[46]—it is by itself, not by another, and for all that does not know itself by itself, but by another. Similarly the Fourth Replies: "We do not have immediate knowledge of substances, as I have noted elsewhere. We know them only by perceiving certain forms or attributes which must inhere in something if they are to exist; and we call the thing in which they inhere a 'substance'";[47] the nonimmediacy of substance according to knowledge contradicts the immediacy of the attribute's inherence in it according to existence—"every thing in which whatever we perceive immediately resides, as in a subject, or to every thing by means of which whatever we perceive exists."[48] In this way the Fifth Replies call for "various attributes" (*varia . . . attributa*; CSM II:249) uniquely "to reveal a substance" (*ad manifestandam substantiam*; 360, 3–4)—for rendering manifest a substance that would otherwise remain invisible, since not manifest. In passing from one definition of substance to another, the attribute acquires hence not only an epistemological but, so to speak, a phenomenological primacy. In effect, the attribute "affects us" (*nos . . . afficit*; VIIIA:25, 5; CSM I:210) uniquely because it touches us sensibly: "I will not hide the fact that I am convinced that what affects our senses is simply and solely the surface that constitutes the limit of the dimensions of the body which is perceived by the senses . . . nothing can have an effect on any of our senses except through contact"[49]: the surface is phenomenalized by touch, which affection makes appear. It is a matter of a manner of original impression.

Third, if the absence of affection of the mind by substance does not fix the proper doctrine of Descartes on being, but is an aporia that he must resolve, the celebrated criticism that Heidegger addresses to this text in *Being and Time* is amiss.[50] First, because it is not

Being that would not affect us but only substance; then, because it is not even substance in general that does not affect us but only its first definition as substantiality in itself; finally, because it is a matter here, again, not of Descartes' thesis, but of an objection he attempts to surmount in introducing a second definition of substance, in relation to attributes. Moreover, the simple fact that Descartes clearly sees the difficulty and is not satisfied with having to renounce access — as mediated as one would like — to substance in general, opposes him in advance to his immediate successors (in particular Malebranche) and the proximity of Aristotle (VII:249, 20; CSM II:174).

In conclusion, we will make a remark and pose a question. (a) The remark is obvious: the second definition of substance restores certainly the knowability [*cognoscibilité*] put in danger by the first; but it does so at the price of an inversion of its primacy, since henceforth the attribute (accident, property, etc.) precedes substance instead of depending upon it. This inversion results directly from the substitution of an epistemological order (to manifest, to know, etc.) for the ontic order (being by itself, inherence, etc.). Consequently, does the doctrine of substance in the *Principia*, which maintains the term only in order better to relativize the concept after the exigencies of knowledge, really differ from the silence of the *Regulae*, which excluded the term because it had criticized the concept? Does not the very fact that the *Principia* juxtaposes, indeed opposes dialectically, two definitions that are at root incompatible, without really articulating them, betray how much *substantia* here remains a highly problematic concept? (b) A question follows: Does the second definition make it possible to overcome the aporia of the first one, that is to say, to know substances — to number them, individualize them, characterize them? Only that test would permit us to measure to what extent Descartes could lead inquiry toward a concept of substance. His attempt is played out in §53–§54.

§4. Two Aporias of the Model (§53–§54)

The importance of §53 is due to the fact that it attempts to coordinate the two definitions of substance advanced earlier by §51 and §52. Indeed, it takes up first the epistemological definition of §52, in repeating that substance "may be known through any attribute at all" (*ex quolibet attributo cognoscitur*; AT VIIIA:25, 12; CSM I:210), in the sense in which the Fourth Replies posit that we only know substance inasmuch as "we recognize by form or attribute" (*percipiamus quas-dam formas sive attributa*; AT VII:223, 2–3; CSM II:157, trans. mod.). But §53 immediately adds a major point of precision: if we can know a substance by beginning from any one of its attributes, it remains no less possible and necessary to extricate at the same time one principal one to which all the others refer ("to which all its other properties are referred").[51] How is this choice made? By putting the simple natures in order: in this way imagination, will, and sensation presuppose knowledge of the *cogitatio*, as much as figure and movement presuppose that of the *extensio*: the criterion of hierarchy between the principal attribute and the others still remains epistemological (*intelligi*, 25, 23, 25; CSM I:211). But must one therefore conclude that the doctrine of the principal attribute proposed by §53 is inscribed entirely in the epistemological definition of substance fixed by §52? Precisely not, because the principal attribute also assumes another function, which is resolutely ontic and not at all epistemological, namely, that of constituting substance: "constitutes its nature and essence"; "extension . . . constitutes the nature of corporeal substance; and thought constitutes the nature of thinking substance."[52] This constitution of the nature of substance by the principal attribute must be understood as rigorously as possible—that is to say, as a subsistence by itself of this attribute by itself. It is of the same type as the subsistence by itself of substance according to the first definition that §51 had introduced. One can find at least one Cartesian text to affirm this without ambiguity: "We must take care here not to understand the word 'attribute' to mean simply 'mode.' . . . Thus God has many attributes, but no modes. Again, one of the attributes of any substance is subsisting on its own."[53] Literally translated, this means that it is one of the attributes of any substance that subsists in itself. Properly understood, this means that, among the multiple models, properties, or attributes that are assigned to a substance and make it known, at the same time one is found that is singularized as a principal attribute following its character of "constituting" substance, that is to say, subsisting in itself exactly as itself. The principal attribute hence adds a resolutely ontic character to its epistemological role.

One could surmise that this double characteristic of the principal attribute would permit it to reconcile within itself the two different—indeed concurrent—definitions of substance. One would be right to think so, with the restriction that it is a matter more of a juxtaposition than of a real conciliation. Of course, Descartes does reach a coherent position. But it is precisely this coherence that provokes the difficulty: indeed, if the two rival definitions of *substance* agree in respect to the principal attribute, would it not be the principal attribute that carries the weight of substantiality and could no longer be distinguished from substance? It suffices to recall the celebrated polemic between F. Alquié and M. Gueroult (who will become our support here),[54] for admitting that the question still remains open. Descartes often seems to confine substantiality radically to the attribute, to the point of confusing them; he does so when he posits that "the more attributes we discover in the same thing or substance, the clearer is our knowledge of that substance."[55] But, on the contrary, since the knowledge of substance arises in direct proportion to the knowledge of attributes, and since, moreover, the principal attribute only manifests substance because it first constitutes its nature, should we not say that henceforth substance distinguishes itself neither ontically nor epistemologically from its principal attribute and the others that derive from it? Spinoza certainly takes up this argumentation: "nothing in nature is clearer than that each being must be conceived under some attribute, and the more reality or being it has, the more it has attributes which express necessity or eternity, and infinity."[56] But he will have the double prudence to remove all ontic function from attributes: (a) by substituting "express" (*exprimere*) for the Cartesian "constitute" (*constituere*), and (b) by underlining the "reality" (*realitas*) and the "being" (*esse*) proper to substance, in which existence and essence show themselves without intermediary. Besides, Descartes admits this difficulty when he resorts to the distinction of reason in separating substance from attribute; for, in establishing that without attribute "substance is unintelligible" (*ipsa [substantia] intelligi non potest*) and that "we are unable to form a clear and distinct idea of substance,"[57] he recognizes implicitly that substance is no longer distinguished from attribute, which alone is knowable and also subsists in itself. Without a doubt substance retains a proper role—that of an "active faculty" (*quaedam activa . . . facultas*; AT VII:79, 10; CSM II:55), which produces (79, 11) and sends ideas (79, 11, 24); but this efficiency (*efficere*; 79, 11) does not retain any similarity with its effects, as does every efficient cause. It thus remains anonymous as such. And that is exactly why the Sixth Meditation can separate only with great difficulty the hypothesis of nonmaterial causes from the ideas of material things (God and a faculty unknown to and in the mind).

In this way a difficulty is established that does not cease to attract the attention of Descartes' successors: substance doubles the principal attribute without adding anything intelligible to it, in the sense that extension and thought must assume the functions of substantiality directly—at the risk that matter becomes inaccessible (Malebranche, Kant) or useless (Berkeley) and the soul unknown (Malebranche, indeed Spinoza).

A second aporia, different from though conjoined to the first, is raised by §54: it is no longer a matter of the distinction between each substance and its principal attribute, but of the distinction between substances according to the distinction of their principal attributes. In principle, although we have at our disposal "two clear and distinct notions" (*duas claras et distinctas . . . notiones*; AT VIIIA:25, 28; CSM I:211), we must attain *two* substances, one cognizing, the other extended, according to which we painstakingly distinguish them (*accurate distinguimus*; 26, 1; CSM I:211). Now with these two notions Descartes distinguishes in fact not two, but *three* substances; he "also" (IXB:48, 25; *etiam*, 26, 1; CSM I:211) adds the idea of God to those of the two substances, extended and thinking. By what right? By doubling thinking substance either as "created thinking" (*cogitans creata*),[58] or as "uncreated and independent thinking" (*cogitans increata et indepedens*).[59] But by what rightful measure can this doubling be supported? In principle, it must be a matter of the distinction between the two principal attributes, now that the same principal attribute—the *cogitatio*—is applied to the thinking finite and created substance and to the thinking infinite, independent, and uncreated substance. Therefore this distinction between the two types of substance does not respect the explicit doctrine of the distinction between substances, which §52–§53 have just displayed. This must certainly be conceded, but nevertheless Descartes introduces a new criterion of distinction, which justifies the introduction of an infinite substance—precisely of the infinite. It is to the infinite that he returns to extend the principal attribute of the *cogitatio* indefinitely, all the way to making it applicable to God: "Now everyone surely perceives that there are things he understands. Hence everyone has the form or idea of understanding, and by indefinitely extending this he can form the idea of God's understanding. And a similar procedure applies to the other attributes of God."[60] But this argument inevitably is exposed to two objections, or rather to two faces of the same objection.

(a) Can the *cogitatio* be extended to the infinite and be freed from finitude while still remaining really a *cogitatio*? Do "divine thoughts" (*cogitationes divinae*)[61] still remain thoughts in the sense of those of the ego? And, reciprocally, by what right does the *cogitatio* open out more legitimately in the infinite than in the extended? By what right is the *cogitatio* more suitable for God than for another attribute, for example the extended? Why do we not form an "imaginary idea of God" (*chimerica Dei idea*), indeed "some image" (*aliquod idolum*), when we "comprehend" that in God is found a "wholly perfect power of thought" (*perfectissima vis cogitandi*)?[62] In short, it is far from obvious that the infinite, in supposing that it must intervene in the definition of a third substance, could apply to the *cogitatio* and be appropriate for God.

(b) Above all, in transposing to the infinite a principal attribute originally pinpointed to define a finite substance (the *ego cogito*), Descartes recovers precisely the distance between substance subsistent per se in itself absolutely (God) and that which only subsists by divine aid; he thus recovers not only the ontic definition of substantiality that the intervention of the principal attribute was supposed to have overcome, but the question of analogy. The idea of God, as an infinite and uncreated thought, cannot "adequately represent everything which is to be found in God,"[63] as the end of §54 asserts. In this manner, he repeats the warning and embarrassment that concludes §51: "the term 'substance' does not apply *univocally* to God and to other things."[64] In short, even the name *thinking substance* remains equivocal between the finite and the infinite, not only because the concept of substance as subsistence has nothing univocal (§2), but also because the concept of substance as substrate (§3) is subjected to the equivocity of the principal attribute.

This introduces a difficulty that constantly reappears in Descartes' successors: the distinction between finite thought and infinite thought, indeed, between created understanding and uncreated understanding. The immediate infinite mode (Spinoza), the Word in which truths see themselves (Malebranche), the calculus of possibilities and the analysis of the complete notion (Leibniz), among others, witness that Descartes did not have the means to establish conceptually the nonunivocity and the nonadequation that he had recommended in respect to the divine substance.[65]

The treatise on substance that Descartes finally produced in the *Principles of Philosophy* sets out to provide the doctrine that had been missing since the *Regulae*. To arrive at this, Descartes utilizes the two concepts of substance elaborated by Suárez, not to distribute them between God and creatures, but to describe finite substance alone. From this results a strange and double operation. First, finite substance, for the first time ontically reinforced by subsistence in itself, which it borrows from God, becomes, in a second moment, a strictly epistemological substantiality, that of subsistence consolidating its knowledge in the principal attribute. In this way the *Principles of Philosophy*, with more prudence and information, reproduces the elimination of subsistence, or at least of its subordination to the attribute, that the *Regulae* had already accomplished. It follows, finally, that the determination of substance as the substrate of an attribute, hence its essentially epistemological determination, without a doubt does not already permit a more real and rational distinction: neither of finite substances among each other nor between infinite substance and finite substances. According to this hypothesis, Descartes would be less a new theoretician of substance than the philosopher who marks the beginning of its rapid decline in the history of metaphysics.

It is as if in the sequence *ego autem substantia*, one must choose between the two terms, one of which annihilates the other. And Descartes made that choice.

PART 2

Questions about God

6

God, the Styx, and the Fates

The Letters to Mersenne of 1630

For Jean Deprun

§1. What the Poets Say

Cartesian thought presents the paradox, among others, of pursuing the institution of method for the sciences (or rather, for the first time in Descartes, in *the* science unified by the unique mind) while maintaining a close affinity with poetic speech and theology, indeed, with psychology with regard to the profundity of dreams. In fact, this paradox is easily explained: Descartes cannot be positioned on the frontier demarcating the territory of science, since—for him, if not for us—it still remains to be drawn, and it is he, among others, who is the first to draw it. Consequently, affinities among theology, poetry, philosophy, and the sciences in Descartes no longer surprise us because he is the one to clarify them for us, or, better still, he was the first to identify them, so to speak, before our eyes. What surprises us is hence not so much the remnants of a heritage he would not have mastered, but rather raw material, still in the course of being treated, classified, and separated. In short, Descartes takes his time in becoming Cartesian, and we must follow this labor, without being led astray by the material on which he works.

In the past ten years I have extensively studied the role of theology in the elaboration of Cartesian thought in the case of the creation of the eternal truths,[1] following the heritage of E. Gilson and the recommendation of Marjorie Grene.[2] I have since outlined the role played by the hermeneutics of dreams in the discovery of the unconditioned validity of the *cogitatio*.[3] Today, I would like finally to bring out, very rapidly, the role of a poetic reference in an argument that is properly theoretical—since it is still a matter of the creation of the eternal truths. This is a celebrated declaration in the letter to Mersenne from 15 April 1630, which is formulated twice and in two registers.

First, a strictly conceptual assertion: "The mathematical truths which you call eternal have been laid down by God and depend on him entirely no less than the rest of his creatures."[4] It is this thesis that historians of philosophy have spontaneously privileged in the immense majority of cases; it goes back to the history of the doctrine of the divine ideas, in theology, philosophy, and epistemology. Then comes an imaginative and metaphorical formulation: "Indeed to say that these truths are independent of God is to talk of him as if he were Jupiter or Saturn and to subject him to the Styx and the Fates."[5] This second sequence has received little commentary. F. Alquié himself, although he insisted on this doctrine more than any other, cites this text twice without commenting on it.[6] Rather, in his edition [of Descartes' works], he dramatically weakens its effect: "In truth, nobody has ever said that. But Descartes makes a conception of the divine freedom such that, in his eyes, to declare that mathematical truths are part of the divine understanding comes down to declaring that God notices them passively, as if despite himself, and that he is hence subjected to them."[7] This denial signals that the second sentence (although utilizing the new themes of the pagan gods, Styx, and the Fates) should be understood as a simple doubling of the first (which mobilizes concepts that are rather different: mathematical truths, God, establishment). In this way it is suggested that the first, conceptual pronouncement merely repeats itself in supposedly evocative images with a purely pedagogical intention. It is precisely this interpretation that I want to contest.

The second sequence does not repeat the first; it redoubles it by designating a new target for the creation of the eternal truths. An argument in favor of this interpretation relies on the function that Descartes recognizes for the poets: being himself a "lover of poetry,"[8] he admittedly finds "that poetry has quite ravishing delicacy and sweetness," but above all he reads there "sentences more grave, more sensible and better expressed than those which are found in the writings of the philosophers."[9] And when he speaks in another place of a "chaos as confused as any the poets could invent," we must hear in this more an elegy for poetic power than a reproach of confusion.[10]

In short, for Descartes poetry maintains an attraction strong enough and a status sufficiently serious for its intervention to suffice in itself. And that is why, in other places, he manages to criticize the poets' representations of the gods directly and on their own terms: "those who appear to have had a passion for some divinity without knowing about the mystery of the Incarnation have not loved the true God, but only some idols to which they gave his name; just as, so the poets tell us, Ixion embraced a cloud by mistake for the Queen of the gods."[11] Poetry not only ravishes, it also gives rise to thought. Even for conceptual thought, it is thus necessary to listen to poetry and to examine it for its own sake.

We therefore ask two questions: (a) Which "poets," if any, have put forward the maxim that Descartes condemns? (b) Do such poetic images have a relationship with the theoretical argument?

§2. The Gods and the Fates

To respond to this question—whether God, for Descartes, is subjected to destiny like Jupiter—we must first confirm one fact: Is it true or not that "in truth, no one has said" the hypothesis Descartes denounces? Regarding the properly conceptual assertion that truths can be true independently of God, it is now established that several authors have explicitly "said" that: Suárez and Duns Scotus, at the very least.[12] Is the same true for the assertion of the "poets" regarding Jupiter, the Styx, and the Fates?

A positive response obviously must be given. It grounds itself first on (a) Homer. At least twice in the *Iliad* Zeus wants to save a mortal from the death that fate has imposed on him. First Sarpedon: "Ah, woe is me, since it is fated (μοῖρα) that Sarpedon, dearest of men to me, be vanquished by Patroclus, son of Menoetius! And my heart is divided in counsel as I ponder in my thought whether I shall snatch him up while he yet lives and set him afar from the tearful war . . . or whether I shall let him be vanquished now at the hands of the son of Menoetius." But as a result of Hera's injunctions, Zeus cedes Sarpedon to his destiny, to fate.[13] Then he wants to snatch Hector from death at the hands of Achilles: "Well now! Truly a well-loved man do my eyes look on pursued around the wall; and my heart is grieved for Hector. . . . But come, you gods, consider and take counsel whether we shall save him from death, or now at length shall vanquish him, good man though he is, at the hand of Achilles, son of Peleus." It is here Athena who first convinces the gods to let go of "a mortal man, doomed long since by fate [παλαι πρεπρωμενον αισι]."[14] There is more: the gods must submit their wills to fate not only in the case of mortals but even regarding their own kind. Thus in order to avenge his son Ascalaphus, Ares exposes himself to the hazard of Zeus' lightning, to fate: "even though it be my fate [ει περ μοι και μοιρα] to be struck with the bolt of Zeus and lie low in blood and dust among the dead."[15] Finally, the gods who are subject to the fates (μοιρα) in this way, themselves take an oath by the Styx. Thus Hera: "Now let Earth be my witness and the broad Heaven above, and the down-flowing water of Styx, which is the greatest and most terrible oath for the blessed gods."[16] (b) From this Homeric matrix, the tragedies have drawn exemplary figures. First that of Prometheus, here responding to the coryphaeus: "Who then is the steersman of necessity? / The triple-formed Fates and the remembering Furies. / Is Zeus weaker than these [τουτων ασθενεστερς)? / Yes, for he, too, cannot escape what is fated [ουκουν αν εκφυγοι γε την πεπρωμένην)."[17] (c) The same theme is retained by Herodotus: "None may escape his destined lot, not even a god."[18] (d) Hesiod comes close to it when he attributes to the Fates (Μοιραι) "control [of] the transgressions of both men and divinities."[19]

The Latin poets, whom Descartes without a doubt studied much more closely, inherit this thematic. (e) Thus, Horace underlines the powerlessness of Jupiter: "Tomorrow Jove may blot the sky with cloud. / Or fill it with pure sunshine, yet he cannot / Devalue what has once been held as precious, / Or tarnish or melt back / The gold the visiting hour has left behind"; while "Fortune enjoys her grim work and will never / Give up the cruel game she plays of changing / Her mind and her rewards."[20] (f) But it is perhaps Virgil who corresponds best to the formula utilized by Descartes when he makes Jupiter speak, declaring his neutrality in the supreme battle between Troy and the Rutuli: "What each man does will shape his trail and fortune. / For Jupiter is king of all alike; / The Fates will find their way." He swears this by "his Stygian brother's rivers [Stygii per flumina fratris . . . adnuit]."[21] Submission to the game of the Fates, oath by the Styx: Virgil's Jupiter really does manifest the two traits Descartes rejects in 1630.

From the poets, this theme passes to the prose writers. Plato retrieves it as coming from other authors: "as is said, even a god cannot do violence to necessity."[22] This "as is said" becomes a proverb when the Roman development of Stoicism accentuates the identity of Zeus with the necessity of Zeno and Cleanthes in subordination to destiny.

Thus Cicero insists: "Accordingly Carneades used to say that not even Apollo could tell any future events except those whose causes were so held together by nature that they must necessarily happen."[23] The powerlessness of the gods to predict results in fact from a perfectly rational motive: the majority of futures remains contingent; they do not carry in themselves (by nature) the causes that make them necessary and hence foreseeable. Consequently, they are rational: "And yet from the fact of the gods' existence (assuming that they exist, as they certainly do) it necessarily follows that they are animate beings, and not only animate but possessed of reason. . . . It follows that they possess the same faculty of reason as the human race, and that both have the same apprehension of truth and the same law enjoining what is right and rejecting what is wrong."[24] Cicero's objective is weak: in order to bypass the multitude of popular gods, which he disqualifies with almost the same critical ardor as Augustine shows a little later, he reconstructs a model of divinity that conforms to the portrait of the Stoic wise man; consequently, these new gods conform to the same reason (*eadem ratio*), the same truth (*eadem veritas*), and finally the same law (*eadem lex*) as those of the human race.

For Descartes, this univocity menaces the transcendence of the "incomprehensible power" (AT I:146, 4–5; CSMK III:23 and AT I:150, 22; CSMK III:25) of the true God, especially because it is based on an argument concerning rationality—the univocity of reason, which becomes a law even for God. This "blasphemy" (AT I:149, 26; CSMK III:24) is deepened in passing from the simple irrational fate of the "poets," whose inadequacy appears immediately, to the *eadem ratio*, which can be founded on the univocity of truths as much logical (Suarez, Vasquez) as mathematical (Kepler, Galileo, Mersenne, etc.) or metaphysical (the future *ontologia*). Seneca accomplishes perfectly the synthesis between the gods' and the wise man's submission to fate (voluntary as much as natural): "What, then, is the part of a good man? To offer himself to Fate. It is a great consolation that we are swept along together with the universe; whatever it is that has ordained us to love, so as to die, by the same necessity with which it also binds the gods. One unchangeable course bears along the affairs of men and gods alike. Although the great creator and ruler of the universe himself wrote the decrees of Fate, yet he follows them. He obeys forever, he decreed but once."[25] The popular gods—those of the "poets"—survive the first disenchantment of the ancient world (for he dies early, the "great Pan") only by accepting the "same necessity" (*eadem necessitas*) recognized by the human sages and to which the vulgar submit without knowing that they do so.

But Descartes refuses precisely this "same necessity" in the doctrine of the creation of the eternal truths. This doctrine can certainly be analyzed by identifying scholarly adversaries' views of it—the second scholastic, workers in mathematical physics, indeed, certain "Platonic" theologians—as I have attempted to do elsewhere. But one can also read it as a response to a common Stoicism, which rationalizes the pagan gods by dissolving their transcendence (hence also that of the Christian God) into a univocal wisdom. Although Descartes loved the poets, he nonetheless refuses their theology, even and especially when corrected by Stoicism.

§3. The Origins of the Polemic

In fact, as original as it remains in the epistemological and metaphysical scholarly debate, the firm position taken by Descartes in 1630 is inscribed into a recognized and constant tradition, that of the refusal of all subordination of the Christian God to any superior instance whatsoever: fate, necessity, impassibility, and so on. One must pay attention to this tradition all the more in that it brings together authors who in other respects would be almost entirely opposed.

(a) The most striking critic of God's submission to destiny is Luther. Citing Virgil (as we did above), he emphasizes: "The poet simply seeks to show that in the destruction of Troy and the beginning of the Roman empire Fate did more than all the efforts of men. Indeed, he makes even his immortal gods subject to Fate. Jupiter and Juno themselves must yield to it."[26] Without a doubt Luther here employs Virgil (and those Virgil echoes) ambiguously: on the one hand, he finds in this an argument that allows him to call human free will into question, but on the other hand, he condemns its submission of God to destiny. What matters to us here is that he takes up the ancient theme and gives it pertinence a century before Descartes.

(b) Montaigne echoes this. Against the Protestants (turning Luther's argument on them), he first contests the idea that one can limit God's power to accomplish miracles, as in the Eucharist: "In the disputes which we have at present in our religion, if you press your adversaries too hard, they will tell you quite shamelessly that it is not in God's power to make his body be in paradise and on earth, and in several places at the same time. . . . And, to bind this association of man to God further by comical examples, he cannot make two times ten not be twenty. That is what he says, and what a Christian should avoid having pass out of his mouth. Whereas, on the contrary, men seem to seek out this mad arrogance of speech, to bring God down to their measure." And he cites the same text of Horace, *Odes* 3:29, mentioned above,[27] in order to return the modern error to its ancient origin: "How insolently the Stoics rebuke Epicurus because he holds that to be truly good and happy belongs only to God, and that the wise man has only a shadow and semblance of it! How rashly have they bound God to destiny (I would that none bearing the surname of Christian would still do it!), and Thales, Plato, and Pythagoras have made him a slave to necessity!"[28] If one admits the constancy and force of his influence on Descartes, one can easily recognize in Montaigne one (if not the primary) of the sources of the polemic of 1630.

(c) One should nevertheless not neglect the positions taken by Scipion Dupleix, although he takes up Montaigne's quarrel while still attempting to rely on Homer's authority: "How I cannot endure the impudence of those who make profession of being faithful Christians, who, scorning the [divine] works, cannot be persuaded that God is all-powerful, demanding all the time how it would be possible for him to cause a body to be at the same time in diverse places? How can he cause the bread to be transubstantiated into his flesh and the wine into his blood in the holy sacrament of the Eucharist, the accidents of bread and wine remaining without their abettor? Among Christians, it certainly would be sufficient to say with Homer *that he can do all things*, without entering further into proof of this omnipotence." Or, still identifying the Christian God with the ancient Jupiter, he attempts to draw from this an argument for defending omnipotence in the face of all necessity: "It is to want to revive the ancient quarrel of the Giant sons of the earth, heaping mountains upon mountains in order to claim the heavens and attack Jupiter on his throne like waging war against the omnipotence of God and even attempting to destroy it by opposition to his will, like he who wants to battle the divinity with its own weapons. . . . after all that, see how one wants to tear the lightning and thunder from the hands of the sovereign Jupiter and to take from him the scepter of his omnipotence."[29] Even in reversing the alliances, Dupleix hence anticipates the Cartesian thesis: divine omnipotence (that of the Christian God as much as that of Jupiter) does not suffer any restrictions from destiny or the sons of the earth. This theme is sufficiently widespread that differences in orientation, even among supposed "libertines" and the purportedly "pious," do not prevent its development in any way.

(d) La Mothe Le Vayer proves this in a somewhat curious fashion. He notices first that "the Stoics have made their wise man equal and sometimes superior to God, whom they have submitted to their celebrated Fates." Nevertheless, it is not the arrogance in this ideal that La Mothe Le Vayer contests the most, although he contests it without reservation. Rather it is, in a more surprising fashion, the identification of this God with the Fates, hence the inevitable dilemma that had embarrassed all Stoic theology: "And consequently (they add) establishing a God, he is necessary or one cedes all discretion to the discretion of I do not know which Fates, and that the Jupiter of Homer has had reason to complain of not being able to exempt his own son Sarpedon from the necessity of this celebrated *fatum*; or that fortune alone disposes of all things at its pleasure, albeit that they depend on the fortunate encounter and assistance of the atoms of Democritus or that they result from the contingency of several other purely casual causes."[30]

(e) In order to conclude the genealogy of and parallels to Descartes' refusal to submit God to destiny, and particularly to Stoic destiny, we mention a significant anecdote reported by Mersenne: "saying [of a certain Noël, executed at Metz] that he would rather have preferred to adore a Saturn who eats his children, an adulterous Jupiter, a drunkard Bacchus, a deceiving Mercury, or believe that there is no God at all, than to believe Him to be the author of the ruin of humankind, and of the perdition of reprobates, who surmount the number of the elect by so very much."[31] This man was at heart not as much an "atheist" as Mersenne lets us assume, because the God in whom he refused to believe indeed hardly merits any divinity. Yet a different fact can also hold us back: for contemporary opinion, which Mersenne echoes, "atheism" (the one Descartes combats in 1630), is characterized by a return to "Jupiter" and "Saturn"—as it is for Descartes, stigmatizing "a Jupiter or Saturn." If the thesis concerning the creation of the eternal truths is to keep its profound and powerful originality, one must recognize that it picks up a commonplace that dates back at least to Montaigne, if not to Luther.[32]

§4. The Other Response—Theological

This result raises a question: Descartes (and those around him) think they have to choose—either the Christian God or Stoic destiny. Yet does this alternative really supply the only possible answer to the incompatibility that is evident at first glance between the two terms?

To call this into question, one need only bring up a brief attempt by Scipion Dupleix, who even in the margins of his refusal to submit God to destiny mentions the opinion "of those who have known that destiny is the execution of the counsel of God, that is to say, to speak more Christianly, the effect of divine providence."[33] If the submission of God (as of the gods) to destiny remains unacceptable to a Christian, it remains possible to envision destiny as an instrument of God. Now, not only can this seem legitimate in itself, but in 1630 it is authorized by a long tradition of authorities.

(a) First, Saint Augustine: "But, as to those who call by the name of fate, not the disposition of the stars as it may exist when any creature is conceived, or born, or commences its existence, but the whole connection and train of causes which makes everything become what it does become, there is no need that I should labour and strive with them in a merely verbal controversy, since they attribute so-called order and connection of causes to the will and power of God most high, who is most rightly and most truly believed to know all things before they come to pass, and to leave nothing unordained; from whom are all powers, although the wills of all are not from him."[34] But this conciliation still remains verbal: the same connection of causes, provided that it is extended universally, can call itself either "destiny" [fate] or "God."

(b) It falls to Boethius to articulate the two terms more precisely, by distinguishing between destiny and providence: "Which ways being considered in the purity of God's understanding, are named Providence, but being referred to those things which He moveth and disposeth, they are by the ancients called Fate. . . . For Providence is the very Divine reason itself, seated in the highest Prince, which disposeth all things. But Fate is a disposition inherent in changeable things, by which Providence connecteth all things in their due order. For Providence embraceth all things together, though diverse, though infinite; but Fate putteth every particular thing into motion being distributed by places, forms and time." The distinction between the two terms becomes definitely conceptual: providence is referred to God, destiny to dumb things; providence disposes of the totality that it brings together, taking the destiny of each thing into account. Their relation appears clearly to be a subordination: "Which although they be diverse yet the one dependeth on the other."[35]

(c) As so often, Saint Thomas Aquinas establishes the most pregnant formulation of this subordination. Explicitly taking up Boethius' definition, he illuminates it via an example that has since become classic: the same event — the encounter in the distance by two servants each sent off by their master, who alone knows the place of their crossing — seems to be a fact of destiny to the servants, because they do not refer it to themselves and to inferior causes (the itinerary, the walk, the effort, etc.), while it seems a fact of providence to the master, because he refers it to himself, as superior cause (knowing the time and place of their encounter due to knowledge of the topography etc.).[36] In this way, providence amounts to destiny considered from the viewpoint of the intelligence that knows its causes and what causes them. And this providence would amount to destiny, if it were considered from the point of view of the effects that are subject to a cause without knowing it. The Thomistic solution almost anticipates Spinoza's position.

(d) Even more clearly, Suárez criticizes the thesis of a "necessity absolutely inevitable, even in the view of God," or of "a fatal necessity independent of God,"[37] denouncing it in already Cartesian terms. Relying on the texts of Augustine, Boethius, and Thomas Aquinas that we have examined, among others, he takes up the arguments in order to conclude that "destiny is the disposition of causes, as it is under [the authority] of God, not in the proper sense God himself."[38]

(e) But these reinterpretations of *fatum* in Christian terms rightly remain in a strictly theological field. This is why they do not yet dissolve the Stoic thesis, taken in itself, which they refute without attempting to save it. Precisely the latter undertaking is attempted by a celebrated contemporary of Descartes, Justus Lipsius, whose literary glory could hardly have escaped Descartes, since he exerted his influence from Louvain. His *De Constantia*, which was published in Leiden in 1596, expressly evokes the thesis Descartes contests in 1630: the "genre of the poets" not only admits the primacy of destiny following Homer, but it joins the Stoic philosophers in subjecting God to it: "Submitting God to the chariot of destiny."[39] To excuse the famous declaration of Seneca, Lipsius at first simply identifies God with destiny, which, far from resolving the aporia, emphasizes it: "And our dear Seneca has not submitted God to destiny (because he is not that crazy), but God to God, in a certain manner of speaking";[40] since, what is this in effect but submitting God to God, if not introducing an internal contradiction in God or a hierarchy among different gods? Lipsius also undertakes a more serious differentiation of acceptances of destiny. (i) First, the destiny called "mathematical," which "links or binds firmly all actions and events to the force of the stars and the position of the stars." Of course, this is rejected (as it will be by Descartes). (ii) Then, the destiny called "natural," which, taking up Boethius, is defined as "the order of natural causes which (not being hindered) by their force and their nature produce a certain and identical effect."[41]

Destiny, which from now on will have nothing in common with fortune, is furthermore identified with God on the authority of Paenitius. Even if this position can still seem "unconsidered," it no longer has anything of the "impious."[42] (iii) A final step nevertheless remains to be taken, in order to succeed in bringing the Stoic position back to Christian dogma. Following Boethius and Thomas Aquinas, we must distinguish providence, which is exercised from the viewpoint of God, from destiny, which "seems to come down merely to things themselves." From there the correct definition of destiny is reported of God: "an immovable decree of providence, inherent in movable things, which firmly affects every thing in its order, place, and time."[43] Thus there was a path different from the one pursued by Descartes in 1630: contemporary Stoicism, in the grand figure of Justus Lipsius, had reestablished a Christian acceptance of destiny within the tradition of Seneca itself, by subjecting it to providence. This effort had nothing erratic about it, since it took up a position already defended by Augustine, Boethius, and Thomas Aquinas. Even in the popular philosophy widespread in France (Scipion Dupleix), Descartes would have become familiar with this position, even if (very improbably) he was unaware of Justus Lipsius. Why this refusal to take it into account?

§5. What Descartes Also Said

But it is not evident that Descartes remained a complete stranger to this reconciliation between providence and destiny, on the one hand, and God, on the other. At least two texts of the *Meditations* offer arguments here, because in this new context they take on a different import.

(a) The Sixth Meditation, once it has proven the existence of material things, defines the concept of nature: "For if nature is considered in its general aspect, then I understand by the term nothing other than God himself, or the ordered system of created things established by God."[44] This is a transparent reference to the use of *natura naturans* by Thomas Aquinas (long before Spinoza, who is a simple epigone on this point): "The universal nature is an active force in some universal principle of nature, for instance, in some heavenly body; or again belonging to some superior substance, in which sense God is said by some to be *the Nature Who makes nature* [*nature naturante*]."[45] But one can also reflect on what Boethius names "the very Divine reason itself, seated in the highest Prince, which disposeth all things,"[46] and also on what Justus Lipsius understands in the following formula: "For I consider providence no more than *a power and faculty in God of seeing, knowing and governing all things.*"[47]

(b) Another text attests even more clearly to a utilization of the alternative schema, which is at the same time theological and Stoic: the end of the argument regarding God's omnipotence in the First Meditation. Descartes knows how to maintain his argument of doubt drawn from divine power even for readers who would refuse such hyperbole, calling things into question all the way to material simple natures; he therefore returns to instances of less power in order to arrive *a contrario* at the same result: "According to their supposition, then, I have arrived at my present state by fate or chance or a continuous chain of events, or by some other means."[48] How can we not recognize here the immediate subordination that Thomas Aquinas and Justus Lipsius instituted between God as providence and destiny (*fatum*) as its immediate effect, but with an unknown cause? Descartes' paradoxical argument is indeed clarified perfectly by beginning from this comparison. He says to his supposed adversary: "Even if you refuse the divine omnipotence as providence, you cannot ignore his incomprehensible power as destiny." It is precisely this indissoluble link between providence (God) and destiny that permits the argument to be maintained, even if one refuses God as providence.

But did Descartes then renounce in 1641 his radical rejection of destiny in 1630? One cannot exclude this hypothesis, since in the *Replies* he takes up once more the comparison between the (Christian) God and the Jupiter of the poets, this time to ratify it, no longer to disqualify it. Indeed, one reads in the Fifth Replies the following argument: "But just as the poets suppose that the Fates were originally established by Jupiter, but that after they were established he bound himself to abide by them, so I do not think that the essences of things, and the mathematical truths which we can know concerning them, are independent of God. Nevertheless I do think that they are immutable and eternal, since the will and decree of God willed and decreed that they should be so."[49] Of course, Descartes does not contradict himself doctrinally: the immutability of the mathematical truths had clearly been established in 1630—"'But I understand them [the truths] to be eternal and unchangeable.' — 'But I make the same judgment about God'"[50] — and the eternity of simple material natures, here questioned by Gassendi, depends in the Fifth Meditation on the divine veracity, hence on creation. But Descartes nevertheless inverts his position with respect to the "poets": this time, far from reproaching them with blasphemy, he grants them an authority, since they bear witness to the initial freedom of God in the encounter with the Fates. The rhetoric hence diverges from the conceptualization.[51] It is also possible that in making new arguments, the conceptualization itself admits metaphors, images, and even theological arguments, which it had first rejected or of which it had simply been unaware. The history of the concept of destiny in classical metaphysics still remains to be studied. As does that of the role of poetry in the metaphysics of Descartes.

7

Creation of the Eternal Truths

The Principle of Reason—Spinoza, Malebranche, Leibniz

§1. The Refusal of Refusal

As we know, in his correspondence with Father Mersenne in 1630 Descartes maintains that the eternal truths, whether mathematical or logical, were created and instituted by God, although to our eyes and finite spirit they are immutable and necessary: "the mathematical truths which you call eternal have been laid down by God and depend on him entirely no less than the rest of his creatures. Indeed to say that these truths are independent of God is to talk of him as if he were Jupiter or Saturn and to subject him to the Styx and the Fates. Please do not hesitate to assert and proclaim everywhere that it is God who has laid down these laws in nature just as a king lays down laws in his kingdom."[1] This standpoint contradicts the dominant positions in several domains of knowledge. In theology, Descartes criticized directly the majority of theologians, who inclined either to the univocity of *ens*, of substances and of logical truths (Suárez, Vasquez, etc.), or to an emanation of God's truths in humans according to the Word (Bérulle). In mathematics and physics, he opposed the move of subjecting divine understanding to mathematical truths, which, in this way, benefited from an absolute founding at the price of univocity (Kepler, Mersenne, Galileo, etc.). We will not take these points up again here, since they have been tackled elsewhere.[2] I would like only to emphasize several remarks in which Descartes encountered similar opposition in the properly philosophical domain, although with one difference: in theology and mathematics, he takes the initiative of contradiction, and hence takes it against his predecessors or immediate contemporaries, whereas in philosophy he submits posthumously to the multiform but convergent attack of thinkers who succeed him and are made possible by him. Besides, the triple offensive of Spinoza, Malebranche, and Leibniz against the creation of the eternal truths is parallel to the criticisms that they address in a similar way to two other famous Cartesian theses: the hyperbolic doubt and the *ego sum, ego existo*; without doubt this is due to a direct if dissimulated link. Considering here only the first of these polemics, we attempt to extricate from it a triple coherence, but also to follow its deepening and to fix its metaphysical intention.

§2. Spinoza and Adequation

Spinoza takes up the question of the eternal truths explicitly. In particular, the complexity of his analysis makes his final disagreement with Descartes that much more significant. This essential debate is inaugurated in the *Metaphysical Thoughts* (*Cogitata Metaphysica*) and continues from there. This manner of *compendium* of scholastic vocabulary (certainly already modified) without a doubt goes back via Heerebord to Suárez, among others.[3] Now, one here uncovers a development that Spinoza reproduces and criticizes as not having piety (*non satis pie*), like the reasoning with which Suárez had believed to have been able to overcome Saint Thomas: "That God is all-powerful, one has sufficiently demonstrated. We will now attempt to explain briefly how one must understand this attribute; for many speak about it in lacking either piety or truth [*non satis pie, nec secundum veritatem*]. They actually say that certain things are possible by nature and not by God's decree, others impossible and finally others necessary, in such a way that God's omnipotence has only possible things for its domain. As for us, who have already shown that all depends absolutely upon the decree of God, we say that God is all-powerful; but after having understood that he has decreed certain things by the pure liberty of his will, and then that he is immovable, we say that nothing can go against his decrees, and hence that this is impossible by the sole fact that it contradicts the divine perfection."[4]

The possibles all depend on divine decree, without any privileging of rational truths over contingent truths. And the same text specifies this: if certain people oppose prophecy, which takes its realization "from that which the prophet has announced following the divine decree," to the definition of the triangle (and its property of having three angles, the sum of which equals that of two right angles), the privilege that they want in this way to accord to necessary truth over contingent truth has no consistency at all: it results only from their ignorance. Necessity remains uniform and the same, because it follows always from the unique divine decree, which we do not know or know only partially: "or that he can do all things, and that the necessity we find in things has resulted from the decree of God alone [*a solo Dei decreto*]."[5] Here Spinoza appears here closest to Descartes and to the creation of the eternal truths. This affinity persists all the way to the *Ethics*, as the conclusion of *Ethics* 1, prop. 33, schol. 2 still witnesses, contradicting almost the entirety of its anterior development: "I confess that this opinion, which subjects all things to a certain indifferent will of God, and makes all things depend on his good pleasure [*beneplacitum*], is nearer the truth than that of those who maintain that God does all things for the sake of the good [*sub ratione boni*]. For they seem to place something outside God, which does not depend on God, to which God attends, as a model, in what he does, and at which he aims, as at a certain goal. This is simply to subject God to fate [*Deum fato subjicere*]. Nothing more absurd can be maintained about God, whom we have shown to be the first and only free cause, both of the essence of all things, and of their existence [*tam omnium rerum essentiae quam earum existentiae*]" (*Works* 1:438). The allusions here are obviously to the letters of Descartes in 1630: it would be "to speak of God as a Jupiter or a Saturn, and to subject him to Styx or to the Fates, to say that the truths are independent of him," since "he is as much the author of essence as of the existence of creatures."[6]

In this way Spinoza, like Descartes, thinks God from causality and hence determines causally his relation to truths, as a producing that takes them back to the role of effects. Nevertheless, this relation can itself be understood as the opposite of what Descartes means: in place of a transcendent and transitive cause, Spinoza sees here an "immanent cause" (*causa immanens*; *Ethics* 1, prop. 18; *Works* 1:428). Not only does the divine cause not cease to sustain its effect, as in Descartes, but, in contrast to Descartes, the effect does not cease to remain in the cause, hence leading back to it. Between divine cause and rational effect, the relation no longer manifests transcendence; although the cause is immense (*immensa*), it does not remain incomprehensible (*incomprehensibilis*). Proof is the displacement of the *causa sui.* Mentioned as the first of definitions, it intervenes nonetheless much later in the demonstrative order: "God must be called the cause of all things in the same sense in which he is called the cause of himself" (*Ethics* 1, prop. 25, schol.; *Works* 1:431). The topical displacement of the *causa sui* all the way to finite modes indicates clearly that the internal causality (of God in regard to himself) is understood in the same sense as the external causality (of God in regard to finite modes), is known as pure and simple efficiency: the *causa sui* does not produce any theological analogy, it no longer imposes even the Cartesian reservation of being said "in analogy to an efficient cause" (*per analogiam causae efficienties*), but it is enunciated univocally as a particular case of one unique efficiency. Unique efficiency exercises a unique necessity, so pronounced that, finally, Spinoza repudiates the Cartesian heritage entirely. Three texts make this clear.

(a) *Ethics* 1, prop. 17, schol., considers it straightaway "absurd" to maintain "that God can bring it about that it would not follow from the nature of a triangle that its three angles are equal to two right angles" (*Works* 1:425–26). Why? Because the necessity of causality remains univocal, whether it applies to the connections between the definition of the triangle and its properties or to the connections between the divine essence and its modes: the two necessities produce each other "in the same way" (*eodem modo*): "From God's supreme power, or infinite nature, infinitely many things in infinitely many modes, i.e., all things, have necessarily flowed [*effluxisse*] or always follow, by the same necessity and in the same way [*eodem modo*] as from the nature of a triangle it follows, from eternity and to eternity, that its three angles are equal to two right angles" (*Works* 1:426).

Divine causality exercises itself as and by rational causality. It follows definitions rather than instituting them. The Cartesian argument, that in God understanding and will cannot be distinguished, is inverted: Descartes concludes from it the incomprehensible (and transcendent) omnipotence of God; Spinoza concludes from it the identity of ontic and rational necessities. How? In paying attention solely to the only ambiguous text in Descartes (Sixth Replies, n. 6 and n. 8), where divine indifference only seems to invert human indifference by privileging the will to the detriment of the understanding. The constant thesis from 1630 to 1649 remains in fact masked under an exception, basically in order to enable the double reduction of the will and the understanding to the divine essence. Yet since the divine essence proceeds by the same necessity that is exercised in

every rational definition, the incommensurability of divine understanding and divine will with our own, far from maintaining an equivocity of reason, works to establish a tangential univocity: God's
necessity does not differ from logical and mathematical necessity.[7]

(b) The two scholiae of *Ethics* 1, prop. 33, confirm this destruction
of the creation of the eternal truths. The first identifies the necessity
of definition and essence with the necessity of efficiency: "For a
thing's existence follows necessarily either from its essence and definition or from a given efficient cause" (*Works* 1:436). It results from
this that, barring being logically contradictory, one thing is produced; that this production could seem contingent to us does not result from a lack of necessity, but from our ignorance concerning this
necessity. Necessity remains by right, contingency only subsists as
fact. Already developed in the previous works, this theme only serves
to introduce the major argument of the second note.

(c) If things can arrive otherwise than they do arrive, then, since
the necessity of logical definitions is one with the ontic necessity of
their production, the nature of God must also be able to modify itself:
"If things had been produced by God in another way, we would have
to attribute to God another nature, different from that which we have
been compelled to attribute to him from the consideration of the most
perfect Being" (*Works* 1:437).

Introducing the apparent distance of faculties—understanding
and will—between the essence of God and the eternal truths does
not permit us to evade this consequence: indeed, if God had or could
have wanted nature in another order than the actual one, he would
"necessarily have had an intellect other than he now has, and a will
other than he now has." Can this modification of attributes produce
itself "without any change of his essence and of his perfection"? But
if the divine understanding exercises itself only in act, if the faculties
really distinguish themselves neither *in*, nor *from* God, how can one
not conclude that "if things had been produced by God otherwise
than they now are, God's intellect and his will, i.e. (as is conceded),
his essence, would have to be different"? (*Works* 1:437–38)

Now, that is indisputably "absurd." In Spinoza's eyes this absurdity can only impose itself under one condition: that God's deployment itself is also at issue in God's production of the world, hence
that the necessity of the divine essence persists in the necessity of the
deduction of things from their essences. His criticism of the creation
of the eternal truths results from a decision in favor of univocity.
Without a doubt Spinoza still speaks of eternal truths: "You ask,

next, whether also things or their affections are eternal truths [*aeter-nae veritates*]. I say certainly."[8] He speaks of them even more deliberately when he has established that they do not depend on any creation. Without a doubt the formulations of *decreta Dei* are also not without a reminder of a Cartesian thesis: "But those laws of nature are God's decrees, revealed by the natural light"; "On our minds also the mind of God and His eternal thoughts (*sententiae*) are impressed"; "the universal laws of nature . . . are only another name for the eternal decrees of God, which always involve eternal truth and necessity"; "the laws of nature are eternal decrees and volitions of God"; "universal order of nature, that is to say God's eternal decree unknown to us."[9] But, other than it being here a matter of deliberately esoteric texts (and hence *more* hermeneutic by relation to the authentic text of Spinoza), one must emphasize that the same texts, after having reduced the laws of nature to divine institution, either contest the legitimacy of this reduction (in this way Moses, by ignorance and political sense, has prescribed the divine commandments "not as eternal truths, but as precepts and ordinances, and he ordained them as laws of God"), or reduce divine decrees to a more intimate necessity; in short, Nature is founded on the divine essence, even if the divine decrees have the permanence of a nature "whereas when we know that all things are ordained and ratified by God, that the operations of nature follow from the essence of God, and that the laws of nature are eternal decrees and volitions of God"; "the ordinances of nature are the ordinances of God which God has instituted by the liberty, whereby he exists, and they follow, therefore, from the necessity of the divine nature, and, consequently, are eternal, and cannot be broken."[10] In fact, the eternal truths and the decrees of God only prompt the suspicion of a creation: their truth assumes aspects proper only to God, namely eternity, necessity, infinity, and they follow from a direct emanation.

The disappearance of the created status of the eternal truths accomplishes a first step toward univocity. A second remains to be surmounted: that of an effective practice of knowledge, which would permit the human mind actually to attain divine knowledge of things. The doctrine of knowledge by adequate idea seeks to provide this second step. This knowledge rests its claim on the necessary link that unites the human mind to God as necessarily as all other being is linked to the divine, for "the human mind is a part of the infinite intellect of God. Therefore, when we say, that the human mind perceives this or that, we are saying nothing other but that God, not insofar as he is infinite, but insofar as he is explained through the nature of the human mind, or insofar as he constitutes the essence of the human mind, has this or that idea."[11] This insertion of the human into the divine, as a part into a whole, has an immediate epistemological consequence: "But if it is . . . of the nature of a thinking being [*entis cogitantis*] to form true, or adequate, thoughts [*cogitationes*], it is certain that inadequate ideas arise in us only from the fact that we are a part of a thinking being [*cogitantis*], of which some thoughts wholly constitute our mind, while others do so only in part."[12] The level of adequation of human *cogitationes* hence depends strictly on their relation to "a certain being who knows," in this case not the ego but God. But how can this same idea become true from being false, according to its origin or its point of application? How should we understand that "all ideas, in so far as they are related to God, are true" (*Ethics* 2, prop. 32; *Works* 1:472)? And that "all ideas are in God, and, insofar as they are related to God, are true and adequate. And so there are no inadequate or confused ideas except insofar as they are related to the singular mind of someone" (*Ethics* 2, prop. 36, dem.; *Works* 1:474)?

Does the idea not become adequate precisely through an internal and intrinsic qualification: "A true thought [*cogitatio*] is distinguished from a false one not only by an extrinsic, but chiefly by an intrinsic denomination"[13]? The paradox can be dissipated if one returns to how the adequate idea functions: ideas are adequate only because "all those which contain perfection are adequate [equal] to those which conceive [*conceptum*] without extending beyond it."[14] To affirm an idea that would surpass the *conceptum* to conceive or would remain insufficient, would mean to give only a mutilated idea, hence a confused one. Verification or invalidation of the "adequate (true) idea" (*idea (vera) adequata*) in no way depends on an external referent, but on the possibility that it would offer a deduction of conceivable terms (*conceptus*) to pursue without contradiction by means of a deduction of ideas; deduction without fail or end attests to the adequation of ideas: "When the mind attends to a fictitious thing which is false by its very nature, so that it considers it carefully, and understands it, and deduces from it in good order the things to be deduced, it will easily bring its falsity to light. And if the fictitious thing is true by its nature, then when the mind attends to it, so that it understands it, it will proceed successfully, without any interruption—just as we have seen that, from the false fiction just mentioned, the intellect immediately applies itself to show its absurdity, and the other things deduced from that."[15]

In short, adequation of the idea manifests itself by a deductive series and by its fecundity, without any recourse to the referent. How then could an idea become totally adequate? By producing an infinite deduction, so that no contradiction will come to interrupt it, nor disqualify it. A human idea would be unable to deduce, as the cause produces its effects, an infinity of properties from its proper finite definition. It can certainly be increased by adequate knowledge of other modes (close) to thought, and thus become more and more powerful; but this augmentation of initial capital can only realize itself clearly if the *idea vera* extends to the infinite, that is, if it is related to God: from God's point of view, and from him alone (at least as infinite understanding), the idea becomes true and adequate (*Ethics* 2, prop. 32; *Works* 1:472), for "when we say that there is in us an adequate and perfect idea, we are saying nothing but that there is an adequate and perfect idea in God insofar as he constitutes the essence of our mind [*mens*], and consequently we are saying nothing but that such an idea is true" (*Ethics* 2, prop. 34, dem.; *Works* 1:472). God even takes care of the adequation of human ideas. This is not the place to discuss whether this operation of transfer and achievement is really possible for a given human spirit. It is only important to keep in mind that, for Spinoza, our ideas can be referred to God and this gives us the privilege of knowing as God (infinite understanding) knows: "Insofar as our Mind knows itself and the Body from the viewpoint of eternity [*sub aeternitatis specie*], it necessarily has knowledge of God and knows that it is in God and is conceived through God" (*Ethics* 5, §30; *Works* 1:610). Intellectual love of God becomes possible in this way, because we know that God knows us, that we know in him and, tangentially, like him. The univocity of knowing triumphs, on the condition and the reservation of a *quatenus*: God "insofar [*quatenus*] as he constitutes the mind of some thing" (*Ethics* 2, prop. 12, dem.; *Works* 1:457).

Tangentially, Spinoza ends up with eidetic univocity; the brilliance of this position stands out even more by contrast with that of Descartes, who forbids all adequate knowledge to the finite mind: "no one has this sort of conception either of the infinite or of anything else, however small it may be."[16] Why does Descartes thus refuse any possibility of having an adequate idea of even the smallest thing?

Taken in the strict sense, adequate knowledge must not only cover everything that is a matter of knowing, but also know what it really achieves here: "if a piece of knowledge is to be adequate it must contain absolutely all properties which are in the thing which is the object of knowledge. Hence only God can know that he has adequate knowledge of all things."[17]

Descartes thus anticipates Spinoza: God alone can render an idea absolutely adequate. But he also opposes Spinoza by denying that the human mind can attain the divine point of view: although it is easy for humans to have adequate knowledge, it remains impossible for them to be assured that God could not have understood more properties in the thing than the idea understands: "In order to have adequate knowledge of a thing all that is required is that the power of knowing possessed by the intellect is adequate for the thing in question, and this can easily occur. But in order for the intellect to know it has such knowledge, or that God put nothing in the thing beyond what it is aware of, its power of knowing would have to equal the infinite power of God, and this plainly could not happen on pain of contradiction."[18]

Adequate knowing is possible for the finite human mind because it suffices here to exhaust the thing that is to be thought. But the knowledge that this knowledge is really adequate remains impossible, because the human power of knowing would have to exhaust the divine power of producing. This absolute adequation, for Descartes as for Spinoza, implies the passage to God. But for Descartes, contra Spinoza, such passage is impossible, because the power of God joins incomprehensibility to his infinity. In regard to this, the reply on knowledge says it fully: "When I said that a thing must be understood completely, I did not mean that my understanding must be adequate, but merely that I must understand the thing well enough to know that my understanding is complete."[19]

Knowledge only completely marks the refusal of what adequation could imply about univocity. Adequate knowledge thus breaks on purpose with the Cartesian reservation. The critique of the creation of the eternal truths is achieved by the claim to a univocity of knowledge by the idea. Spinoza is the first to object to Descartes' approach to opening metaphysics to incomprehensibility.[20]

§3. Malebranche and Order

Malebranche addresses a second, even clearer, objection to Descartes. The *Elucidations* (*Éclaircissements*), which in 1676 comes to complete the *Search after Truth* (*Recherche de la vérité*), first delivers the fundamental thesis that links Malebranche explicitly to Mersenne, Kepler, and Galileo, the adversaries of the letters from 1630: "This reason, therefore, is not different from Himself [i.e., God]; it is, therefore, coeternal and consubstantial with Him," "is coeternal with God himself," "there is an order, a law, a sovereign reason that God necessarily loves, which is coeternal with him."[21] In consequence, the ideas "are not at all created," "this wisdom is not at all made," "the truth is uncreated"; uncreated, that is to say submitted to the universal causality that in Descartes (but really already before him) offers the only operative concept of creation: "When we think about order and eternal truths and laws, we do not naturally seek their cause, for they have none."[22] The reversal of the Cartesian position cannot manifest itself more clearly: the eternal truths go back the (transcendent) path of causality and precede it rather than resulting from it. As these truths mark the low-water mark of intelligibility, in a sense power loses both primacy and incomprehensibility; or if Malebranche speaks of an unknown power (that of the Father for the Word) in other places, this incomprehensibility remains, so to speak, parallel to the truths, without dominating them in a rational transcendent instance. Or rather, transcendence will be marked first by its intelligibility (in the Word). But if transcendence becomes, par excellence, intelligible, is it still a matter of transcendence? Be that as it may, Malebranche is opposed to Descartes; but he only sees the creation of the eternal truths in its feeblest enunciation, that of the Sixth Replies, n. 6 and n. 8, as was true of Spinoza and will also be the case with Leibniz.[23]

The refutation invokes two principal arguments: (a) If a free will had instituted mathematical and logical truths, no universality or permanence could have qualified them absolutely: "What assurance would we have that these kinds of truths are not like those that are found only in certain universities, or that last only for a certain time? Do we clearly conceive that God cannot stop willing what He has willed with an entirely free and indifferent will?"[24] The weakness of this argument would appear even more clearly if, instead of confining himself to the Sixth Replies, Malebranche had confronted the letters of 1630, which underline that the immutability of truths does not lose anything (to the contrary) to their eternity (AT I:145, 28 – 146, 3, etc.; CSMK III:23). The distinction of the faculties in God, although expressly rejected by Descartes (AT I:153, 1–3, etc.; CSMK III:25–26), permits the restoration of the creation to the rank of a decision of the divine will and this will to the rank of a simple absence of fluctuating and provisional reason.

(b) In contrast, the second argument pushes much further. If there are really "truths and . . . eternal laws" created and henceforth necessary, if there is hence also a divine "decree," it remains to recognize this decree, hence to know it: "But where do humans see this decree? Has God created some being representative of this decree?" In fact, the creation of the eternal truths cannot be represented by a concept, because it precedes and makes possible any concept; strictly speaking, it can be neither seen nor demonstrated because it conditions all vision and all demonstration. But this characteristic, although entirely correct, does not oppose Descartes, as Malebranche thinks. It recovers a point that the letters of 1630 underline forcefully: the establishment of the eternal truths can be conceived but not comprehended by concepts; the power that institutes them reveals itself through them as incomprehensible ("incomprehensible power," AT I:146, 4–5; CSMK III:23 and AT I:150, 22; CSMK III:25). For Descartes this incomprehensibility identifies the divine creation positively, while for Malebranche it makes the divine decree indiscernible. That is because one does not admit any knowledge without representation, while the other risks putting the human mind outside the representational field. Moreover, Malebranche, in declaring that, if there is one, "the decree may be only in God,"[25] wants not only that the representation suffer no exception at all, but above all that God himself offer himself as the immediate place (and guarantee) of the representation: vision in God signifies that God identifies (and is subjected to) the essence and foundation of the representation. From here he becomes even more decisive than Descartes, because he refuses to think the creation of the eternal truths as a decree susceptible to representation and situates it not "in God" but "in our minds [*in mentibus nostris*], just as a king would imprint his laws on the hearts of all his subjects" (AT I:145, 18–20; CSMK III:23). The creation of the eternal truths coincides with the creation of our mind, and only reveals itself in meditating on its created character, on the finitude that precisely forbids it to see all (and itself) in God.

This double argumentation leads Malebranche to challenge the fundamental thesis of the letters of 1630, that the eternal truths "have been established by God and depend entirely on him" (AT I:145, 9; CSMK III:23), by emphasizing, to the contrary, their absolute independence. Identified with God, reason becomes paradoxically more decisive and, in some manner, more divine than God, as the following passages indicate: "But the reason we consult is not only infinite and universal, it is also independent and necessary, and in one sense, we conceive it as more independent than God Himself. For God can act only according to this reason — He has to consult and follow it"; "necessary and independent"; "the nature of numbers and of intelligible ideas is immutable, necessary, and independent"; "the essences of beings . . . do not depend on a free act of God"; "the geometrical and numerical truths, as two plus two makes four, are eternal and independent, preceding the free decrees of God."[26] As we have seen, for example, in Suárez or in Kepler, as soon as the truths no longer depend upon God, it is God who depends upon them: the compromise of a plain identification remains a diplomatic parody and does not dissimulate (quite the opposite) that a necessity determines God, a necessity stronger than that of the Styx and the Fates because infinitely more rational. God, "obligated to follow the order"[27] and the truths, becomes obligated to them. Malebranche's originality is perhaps due to the extraordinary audacity (if it is not a matter of a brute innocent theological unconsciousness) with which he carries God's rational obligation all the way to its extreme consequences. Where others sidestep the issue, he affirms — more, he underlines to the point of obsession — that the truths are imposed "even on God," an expression emphasized piercingly in practically all his texts, for example, among others: "this law is universal for all minds as well as for God Himself"; "order is in respect to God a law even infinitely more inviolate, than the laws which are established for the construction of his work"; "the order immutable and necessary . . . is, in respect to God himself, an inviolate law, that which is true in respect to humans is true in respect to the angel and in respect to God himself"; "that which is injustice or disturbance in respect to humans is true in respect to the Angel and in respect to God himself"; "what is injustice or disorder in respect to humans is also such for God himself"; "immutable order . . . being the inviolate law of creatures as well as of the Creator"; "this idea [i.e., the intelligible extended] is necessary, eternal, immutable, common to all minds — to humans, to angels, even to God"; "the eternal, immutable and necessary law. God himself is obliged to follow it."[28] God is no exception to reason, to order, and to the eternal truths: like every finite mind, he submits to it; the infinite Word, or rather, the God of power, submits to the rational Word. If God (inasmuch as Father, that is, for Malebranche, inasmuch as power without reason) must be subject to the unique reason of order (that is to say, for Malebranche, to the Word), the human mind, by virtue of the "vision in God," must equally be subject to the reason of the Word. A univocal knowledge of the fundamental truths becomes possible for humans, because it is referred to the same norm as the power of God the Father.

Spinoza's so ambiguous and delicate debate on adequate knowledge becomes, in Malebranche, one of certain, if not extreme, simplicity: by right and by the intermediary of the Word (supposing that the Word could act as intermediary in a quasi-Arian fashion between God's power and human reason!), rational knowledge either will or will not be univocal. Now the choice for univocity is declared without ambiguity, which clearly achieves a decision for the independence of the eternal truths. Decisive texts also abound here: "Thus, when the mind knows the truth, it is united to God, and, to a certain extent, knows and possesses God. But not only might we say that the mind that knows the truth to a certain extent also knows God who contains the truth, we might even say that to a certain extent it knows things as God knows them. Indeed, this mind knows their true relations, which God also knows"; "thus, when the mind perceives the truth, not only is it joined to God, not only does it possess God and to a certain extent see God, but it also in a sense perceives the truth as God perceives it." But soon these restrictions ("in a sense") give way to even more radical identifications: "the most secret of Reason: and how that I knew that you were the Wisdom of the father, I would advise myself not to think that you [i.e., the Word] is also ours and the universal Reason to which all the spirits are united, and by which alone they are reasonable"; "all minds, when contemplating the same intelligible substance, necessarily find therein the same relations of *magnitude*, or the same speculative truths. They also discover therein the same practical truths, the same laws, the same order, when they see the relations of *perfection* existing between the intelligible beings contained in this same substance of the Word, the substance which alone is the immediate object of all our knowledge"; "these relations are the same eternal truths which God sees"; "anyone who sees these relations, sees what God sees"; [in short, the practical consequence of theoretical univocity is that] "there is nothing that God does not do by the same action as that of His creature."[29] That human knowledge becomes adequate does not here depend, as in Spinoza, on a passage to the limit that supposes the (disputable) tour de force of a passage of the finite to the infinite, but leans on the positively immediate evidence of the "vision of God," that is to say, of the unquestioned identification of evidence with the Word, or rather, the identification of the "interior word" with the Trinitarian Word.

Univocity still remains to be conquered: it follows as the condition of the elementary possibility of scientific knowledge. What Descartes did not cease to put at a distance from the incomprehensible infinite, namely, knowing the code (an effective, and hence finite, practice of the human knowledge of intramundane beings), becomes a code for God (founded in the absolute for humans). Malebranche, with a sleepwalking accuracy and that much the more confounding, has the audacity to name this an "eternal code."[30] Without doubt he does not mean exactly what we have attempted to locate in Descartes under the name of the code, the doctrine of perception;[31] but in fact he attains its metaphysical foundations: the code no longer depends on an arbitrary institution and hence on a creation; its rationality emerges immediately, hence divinely, from a Word who, finally, depends more on it than the "eternal" code depends on the Word. The place of intelligibility precedes once again, as for Suárez (and, to a lesser extent, Duns Scotus), the caesura of the finite and the infinite, of the created and the uncreated, of humans and God. The abolition of the creation of eternal truths by their independence before God eliminates Cartesian equivocity, this time directly. A second time the abyss closes, the abyss that the irruption of 1630 had opened in metaphysics as the indelible mark of its modernity. Among other reasons, that is why Descartes remains for us infinitely more contemporary than his chronological successor, Malebranche.

§4. Leibniz and Sufficient Reason

All the same it falls to Leibniz to accord the criticism of the creation of the eternal truths the dignity of elevating and widening the definite refusal by classic metaphysics of its Cartesian opening. Although he really takes up arguments formulated by Spinoza and Malebranche, Leibniz manifests their presuppositions and consequences infinitely better, to the point of recovering Suárez' problematic on essential points. In this way the conclusion of the question rejoins, beyond Descartes alone, its beginning. The refutation of Descartes aims at establishing an explicit thesis: "Necessary or eternal truths . . . do not at all depend on the decrees of God (although the Cartesians say they do)"; "nothing has been more absurd than to affirm the impossibility of knowing the mathematical truths with certainty, at least to know God first; in the sense that certain people, who had learned to know the finesse of Descartes, have here suspected I do not know what unhappy artifice"; "Thus I am far from holding to the opinion of those who maintain that there are no rules of goodness and perfection in the nature of things or in the ideas which God has of them and who say that the works of God are good only for the formal reason that God has made them"; "This is why I find entirely strange, also, the expression of certain other philosophers who say that the eternal truths of metaphysics and geometry, and consequently also the rules of goodness, justice, and perfection, are merely the effects of the will of God; while it seems to me that they are rather the consequences of his understanding, which certainly does not depend upon his will any more than does his essence."[32] Throughout his whole work, Leibniz will not cease to repeat and to reinforce his criticism of the creation of the eternal truths. In retracing one of these attempts in particular, we must follow, beyond the moments of the critique, the modifications it imposes on what it criticizes, precisely in order to criticize it more easily.

In a letter to Philipp of 1680, Leibniz attacks Descartes only by limiting himself, as Spinoza and Malebranche had already done, to the text of the Sixth Replies, n. 6 and n. 8 (not a very Cartesian text, as we have shown elsewhere).[33] This choice not only restricts the corpus to be examined, above all it permits Leibniz to simplify it, hence to make the refutation easier. First moment: Descartes privileges efficient causality to the detriment of all final cause. Leibniz emphasizes that this disappearance, far from reinforcing the dignity of efficient cause, weakens it. In itself, confirmed by final causes, "the efficient cause of things is intelligent," because it aims at an end that its rationality justifies; now, on the contrary, "if things are good or evil only as the result of God's will, the good cannot be a motive of his will, being posterior to his will"; in this way, "Descartes' opinion" strips the will of every motive and, in transforming it into "a certain absolute decree," makes it vain, indeed also "without any reason." [34] Submitting the truths, hence rationality, to an absolute decree seems inadmissible to Leibniz because it implies a double contradiction of what he will name later the "great principle": "there can be found no fact . . . without there being a sufficient reason."

(a) First, because "it seems that every act of will implies some reason for willing and that this reason naturally precedes the act of will itself," and in inverting the relation of the will to the understanding, Descartes deprives the will of all reason, making it strictly unreasonable. Besides, to suppose even that one maintain that the understanding precedes the will if the will already precedes the truth of things, it must be recognized that the divine understanding "will be before the truth of things and consequently will not have truth for its object. Such an understanding is undoubtedly nothing but a chimera." The will, in losing the understanding that enlightens it, loses all reason, "no reason inclines it more to one than to another."

(b) But there is more, or rather, even less: for if orphaned of all understanding, "the will takes the place of reason," not only does it become itself unreasonable, but, as it is a matter of the will *of God*, this unreason disqualifies absolutely all other forms of reason, in the sciences and in morality; it contradicts the principle of reason universally.[35] The radicality of the Leibnizian critique and its superiority over those of Spinoza and Malebranche depend on a decisive metaphysical advance: the creation of the eternal truths contradicts much more than divine immutability (Malebranche) or immanence in its causality (Spinoza); in contrasting one with the other, it contradicts much more fundamentally the universal condition of thought and ontic reality, the principle of sufficient reason. The divine arbitrary forbids the rational arbitration.

Yet because sufficient reason becomes the condition of existence, God, to contradict it, contradicts also the right of existences to exist—or rather, the right of these essences to pretend to existence more than any others. The creation of the eternal truths concerns not only the status of divine knowing, nor even the status of the created universe: it is inscribed (falsely) in the thesis on the Being of beings, as in a scandalous objection to the highest question of metaphysics (for Leibniz, but since him also for us)—"Why is there something rather than nothing?" If God becomes indifferent to truth and to falsity, not only does he himself become unreasonable and hence as incomprehensible as his effects, but above all he makes impossible all satisfying application of the principle of sufficient reason, because he does not hold his role and his rank here; for "the final reason of things must be in a necessary substance . . . it is this substance that we call God"; "this final reason for things is called God."[36] God's indifference demeans his unsurpassable role in the play of sufficient reason. This divine weakness imperils the supreme thesis on the Being of being.

The metaphysical stake of the Cartesian doctrine of 1630 becomes, *a contrario*, that much more massive: Descartes, in thinking God as an "incomprehensible power," shields him from all interrogation on reason (except perhaps by the doctrine of the *causa sui*, which requires even of God a *causa sive ratio*), and relieves him of his sole metaphysical employment as "final *reason* of things." Rather than including him in general metaphysics, and permitting him in this way to be better secured, Descartes even sets God apart from his function among finite beings, who would have been able to involve him in this way, indeed to include him in the same sphere as themselves. In short, the thesis of 1630 would in fact submit the principle of sufficient reason to the divine institution and, by placing the principle of reason in the forefront, would thus also block its clear formulation. Hence, in 1680 Leibniz can only begin to thematize the metaphysical principle par excellence by critiquing the creation of the eternal truths: it is by closing off again the Cartesian opening that he achieves classical metaphysics.

Although Leibniz' opposition to Descartes appears clearly, his formulation remains curiously contorted. Indeed, by focusing on the Sixth Replies, n. 6 and n. 8, Leibniz makes the task easier for himself (as Spinoza and Malebranche did before him), because he confines himself to the only text where Descartes lends (or seems to lend) to God faculties distinct among themselves and from the divine essence. Thanks to this pair [of texts] —where rationality is identified with the understanding and forces the will to irrationality—he can stigmatize a divine unreason in Descartes. One more step is surmounted at this moment: the understanding stripped of reason by the will becomes a "chimera, and consequently it will be necessary to conceive God, after the manner of Spinoza, as a being who has neither understanding nor will."[37] Leibniz contradicts the majority of Cartesian texts, which refuse to distinguish in God any faculties; since it cannot be a matter of ignorance, one must admit that Leibniz privileged this marginal text in Descartes with a precise intention, at the risk of misinterpreting him. Why? Without a doubt with the intention of reproaching him (as a scandalous innovation) for one of his rare points of agreement with Spinoza. Yet why did he not immediately cite the canonical texts on this confusion? Because solely the point of departure of the two faculties can make evident that the Cartesian God contradicts the principle of reason in creating the eternal truths; in this way the "incomprehensible power," stripped of sufficient reason, can seem irrational enough to be reduced "to a certain unmeasurable power from which all emanates, which merits more the name of nature than that of God."[38] The confusion (and even absence) of faculties takes God back to nature: the creation of the eternal truths engenders, in the end, the *Deus sive natura*. This gross amalgamation becomes paradoxical, unless for Leibniz the two doctrines, although so radically opposed, have nothing in common except to pretend to think God without (Spinoza) or outside (Descartes) the principle of reason, that is to say, against his universality. That is what we have demonstrated.

The principle of reason hence demands of "the final reason of things . . . that we call God," that in him understanding determine the will and that the eternal truths make this understanding infinitely rational. To satisfy this double requirement, a single position is suitable: "The eternal truths . . . are in the understanding of God"; "God will be the understanding, and the necessity; that is, the essential nature of things, will be the object of understanding, insofar as this object consists in the eternal truths"; "divine understanding . . . it is the region of the eternal truths"; "the divine understanding is the region of eternal truths"; "[such an] immense region of truths contains all the possibilities [in God, and therefore he submits them to creation]."[39]

As uncreated the truths are thus inscribed in the divine eternity, hence directly in God. Nevertheless, as in Malebranche, this can signify much more than that the truths do not depend on divine creation: namely, knowing that, in a sense, even God himself depends upon them. Leibniz takes several steps in this direction. (a) Their noncreation implies the truths' auto-sufficiency: "The rules of goodness and justice and the eternal truths in general, exist by their nature, and not by an arbitrary choice of God."[40] To what level of self-sufficiency can its nature lead the thing?

(b) It leads all the way to the independence of truths with respect to the will, in the name even of their dependence with respect to understanding: "The will of God is not independent of the rules of Wisdom"; "necessary truths, however, depend solely on his [i.e., God's] understanding"; [it is possible to admit, however, regarding] "truths that are not dependent on the will of God," [that they are] "eternal truths which are in the understanding of God, independently of his will." In the face of God as will, the rational truths, inscribed in God as understanding, remain independent; dependence and independence play in God himself, because "God is incapable of being indeterminate in anything whatsoever . . . his will is always decided, and it can only be decided by the best. God can never have a primitive particular will, that is, independent of laws or general acts of will; such a thing would be unreasonable."[41] In this way the independence of the eternal truths is not exercised except with respect to the will of God, but it would not put into question their radical dependence toward the understanding—their place in God.

(c) All the same, this ultimate dependence seems itself subject to caution. First because, in the response to the question on the origin of evil, the intervention of the eternal truths (and the "ideal nature of the creature, insofar as this nature is contained in the eternal truths") follows exactly the hypothesis of the ancients: matter "which they believed uncreated and independent of God"—which leaves it at least possible to conceive of these truths also as uncreated and independent of God. But another argument confirms the suspicion. The divine understanding certainly dominates the eternal truths in a relation of dependence, but "the essential nature of things will be the object of the understanding insofar as this object consists in the eternal truths. But this object is inward and abides in the divine understanding"; "necessary truths . . . depend solely on his [i.e., God's] understanding, and are its internal object."

A major point: the eternal truths depend certainly on the divine understanding, but in the mode of the object. This signifies not only that the eternal truths do not coincide with the understanding to the point of identification (in contrast to Saint Thomas), but above all that representational distance distinguishes them right away from the understanding. The relation of even internal (above all internal) objectivity imposes a distance from the object to the encounter of what delivers it. Does not this distance already imply some independence of the truths in relation to God, taken as a simple understanding? Without a doubt, seeing that, on the one hand, "God is therefore not the author of essences insofar as they are only possibilities," and that, on the other hand, as these possible essences constitute objectively the divine understanding, "God is not the author of his own understanding."[42] The understanding, as much faculty as ensemble of essences, escapes the authority of God (who is, precisely, not their "author") by remaining at the same time uncreated and independent. This uncreated independence gives to the truths a status comparable to the understanding, which thinks them as its objects: the truths appear in the end as divine as God himself.

(d) From this derives the evocation of an ultimate possibility, namely, that "God would be subjected to a kind of *fatum*" (a hypothesis advanced by Bayle and in which one recognizes the Cartesian admonition; AT I:145, 12; CSMK III:23). Leibniz responds immediately to this: "This so-called *fatum*, which binds even the Divinity, is nothing but God's own nature, his own understanding, which furnishes the rules for his wisdom and his goodness; it is a happy necessity, without which he would be neither good nor wise."[43] Whether this necessity could be qualified as happy (or not) makes little difference, since at issue is acknowledging that a necessity is exercised on God; without a doubt, as understanding, it remains to him as internal as the necessity of the object to the understanding; but, in any case, God is subject to the conditions of certain truths independent of him. The contorted status of this independence does not change anything in the contradiction here brought about by the Cartesian thesis. Even the fact that the Styx and the Fates rise up from God does not prevent this; instead, it reinforces the necessity with which they restrict God. And, in fact, creatures are imposed on God: their essential limitations imply *a priori* (at least) an evil metaphysics, of which the divine architect composes the best of possible worlds, but whose constitutive imperfections he would be unable to modify at root. If these, as truths and eternal essences, do not impose themselves as independent instances even onto God, never would Leibniz have been able to apply to God the celebrated "Mais qui en peut mais?" [But whose fault is that?][44]

If the truths are imposed on God in the same way as an understanding is imposed on objects, then their independence with respect to God even suggests that their evidence can appear equally to God and to finite minds. For independence puts the truths at an equal distance from understandings, whether they be finite or infinite. "For this reason all spirits, whether of men or of higher beings, enter by virtue of reason and the eternal truths into a kind of society with God and are members of the city of God."[45] An at least tangential independence of eternal truths with respect to the divine understanding hence implies at least a tangential univocity, for Leibniz as for Spinoza and Malebranche. Its conquest mobilizes an immense reservoir of research in Leibniz' corpus (primitive notions, calculus of the series, calculus of the best, etc.), which here we cannot treat in detail.

Let it suffice to mention the fundamental stake of the debate that opposes Leibniz to Arnauld, through the intermediary of the Landgrafen E. von Hessen-Rheinfels, from 1686 to 1690. The essential part of the question concerns the definition of the complete notion, such that it permits one to make *a priori* sense of the individual and of the most contingent of its properties in the *Discourse of Metaphysics* (§8 and §13 in particular). Arnauld is surprised that Leibniz pretends that a human mind could never accede to such a complete notion; before the concession of Leibniz, "which you found strange, that 'the individual concept of each person [e.g., of Adam], contains once and for all everything that will ever happen to him' . . . to consider the specific concept . . . by its relation to that which it is represented to be in the divine mind but by the relation to what it is in itself." Arnauld therefore marks neatly that one must choose: either the individual notion is operative but imperfect because taken "in itself" (that is to say, by the human spirit), or it is perfect but operative only for divine understanding. Leibniz will concede this quite voluntarily, although he immediately adds, in an incisive remark that annuls the concession: "I, for my part, have thought that the full and comprehensive concepts are represented in the divine mind as they are in themselves."[46]

Thus he establishes, at least in fact, the equivalence between the notion in God and the notion "possible in itself," as he equates "the nature of things or the ideas God has of them" in the *Discourse of Metaphysics*, without asking himself about the eminently problematic character of the *or* that permits univocity; since he also parallels what "God" and "one" can conceive: "Can one deny that each thing . . . has an accomplished notion, according to which God conceives it, who conceives everything perfectly, that is to say a notion which encloses or comprehends all that which one could say of the thing."[47]

These assimilations would betray a surprising lack of speculative consideration if they did not witness at root—as its indications and consequences—a univocal (tangential) thesis: "For one may say that created spirits differ from God only in degree, or as finite to infinite."[48] What is surprising here certainly consists in the incommensurable relation between finite and infinite being assimilated to the commensurable relation between more and less; it concerns above all that to which the relation between the created and the creator itself is reduced (*ne . . . que*)—to a computation held as practicable, and hence, by right, negligible. The individual complete notion is hence imposed on divine understanding in the same sense in which it is imposed on human understanding. Without a doubt, Leibniz often brings a corrective to bear on this equivalence: the analysis of the predicates, which alone assures their completeness, often if not always outstrips the power of the human mind.[49] This restriction nevertheless must not dissimulate the essential function of the complete notion, the function that insists on (tangential) univocity: satisfying the principle of reason. For if "it is the nature of an individual substance or complete being to have a concept so complete that it is sufficient to make us understand and deduce from it all the predicates of the subject to which the concept is attributed," then "the complete notion of Adam is sufficient to make it possible to deduce from it everything which must happen to him, as far as is necessary to give an explanation of it. It is evident that God can invent, and even does in fact conceive, such a notion, which is sufficient to account for all the phenomena which belong to Adam; but it is no less evident that it is possible in itself."[50] The complete notion has as its function to give an explanation for the individual, precisely in its extreme contingency. It thus satisfies the principle of sufficient reason, as, at the other extreme, it satisfies the uncreated eternity of logical and moral truths. The univocity and the refusal of the creationist thesis acquire an authentic and unique metaphysical status: satisfying the principle of sufficient reason. It is Leibniz' definitive breakthrough to bring together in the same requirement the two theses that Spinoza and Malebranche had advanced only in a disordered polemic. It is not only Descartes who finds himself criticized, it is his entire opening of metaphysics that is closed: the principle of reason closes what the creation of the eternal truths had attempted to open: the unconditioned distance of the infinite (and hence the unrepresentability of the idea of the divine).

§5. The Time of Incubation

Of the three principal instigators of the "parricide" committed against Descartes, the most decided and the only decisive one appears to be Leibniz. He alone links his refusal of the creation of the eternal truths to a conjoined refusal of the hyperbolic doubt and of the infinite will and establishes them all on a counterproposition, comparable in its radicality to Descartes' decision in 1630: the validity of the principle of sufficient reason without exception. Here alone the criticisms that were still dispersed when Spinoza and Malebranche formulated them find their cohesion and their rationality. They find their reason for being [*raison d'être*] only in the principle that being always has a reason [*l'être a toujours une raison*]. In this way, Leibniz achieves a vast and almost unanimous movement of reaction against the Cartesian thesis of 1630, because of its badly perceived and badly accepted origin.[51] One should not be surprised by the dominant role here taken by Leibniz, since this is due only to a very banal motive: formed in a Lutheran university, itself dependent on the *Disputationes metaphysicae*, he naturally assumes the majority of positions that Suarez had formulated at the beginning of the same century, as much regarding the univocity of substance as regarding the independence of the possibles and the distinction of the faculties in God. Leibniz exercises, so to speak, a posthumous revenge of Suárez on Descartes.[52]

Above all one should not be surprised by such a refusal of the greatest of Cartesian theses: the creation of the eternal truths — decisive because it concerns God in his relation to knowing in general, forbidding absolutely the deployment of the principle of reason. Indeed, one cannot emphasize it enough: Descartes himself formulates, or at least outlines, the principle of reason and attempts, in a measure difficult to appreciate exactly, to apply it even to God (AT VII:165, 2; CSM II:116). If he nevertheless does not reach the Leibnizian conclusion of a sufficient reason erected as universal principle, that is because God does not cease to be removed from it, opening metaphysics in this way onto a strange horizon. Missing from the principle of reason is nothing less than the half-century that separates Leibniz (1680, correspondence with Philipp), Malebranche (1678, publication of the *Elucidations*), and Spinoza (1677, posthumous publication of the *Ethics*) from the letters of Descartes to Mersenne (1630), to include God within its empire and to assure in this way, once again, to metaphysics its proper closure, hence its unique goal. This delay could maintain some relation with what Heidegger calls "the time of incubation of the principle of reason."[53] But according to this hypothesis, incubation applies not only to the history of being; it marks rather the embattled and maintained equilibrium of two confronting exigencies: metaphysics in search of its closure weighing against the thought of the infinite petitioning for its opening. The significance of this confrontation remains all the more pertinent today, as its ultimate stake remains concealed from us.[54]

8

The *Causa Sui*

First and Fourth Replies

The one who proves a thing *a priori*, accounts for it by the efficient cause.

—Leibniz, *Theodicy*, §59.

§1. The Singularity

The appearance of the concept of the *causa sui* (assuming there is one) in the First and Fourth Replies raises a considerable number of difficulties. All of them are exceptional. Let us cite three of the principal concerns. (a) First, a historical question: Should the invention of this syntagma be attributed to Descartes? (b) Then, a logical question: How is it not a matter of a simple contradiction in terms? In either case, why did this not suffice for its elimination? (c) Finally, a metaphysical question: What is the relationship between the historical concept of the *causa sui* and, on the one hand, the evolution of what one has named the system of *metaphysica* together with, on the other hand, the onto-theo-logical constitution of metaphysics, which (according to Heidegger) characterizes it essentially?[1] These three questions rely on a preliminary but also formidable question: Supposing, in fact, that Descartes truly does inaugurate the *causa sui*, that he also overcomes its obvious contradiction, and that he thus fixes an inevitable trait for all philosophy that is constituted as metaphysics — supposing, in short, that, with the elaboration of the *causa sui*, Descartes fills his highest metaphysical role, then how could one explain that this concept never appears in the body of the *Meditations*, in the fourth part of the *Discourse on Method*, in the *Principles of Philosophy*, or even in any of the letters concerning metaphysics, but only in two of the *Replies*? Without doubt there is another example of a famous and essential thesis that is equally marginalized outside the major texts: the creation of the eternal truths.[2] But this doubling of the paradox only causes it to be accentuated: how could one not be misled by the textual marginality of these two theses to conclude that they are theoretically secondary? Without doubt one could turn the argument around and find in it the indication of a doctrine that remains esoteric, precisely because it unveils the heart of Cartesian philosophy. Yet, even and above all in this tactic, it remains difficult to establish that the *causa sui* truly designates the center (or one of the foci) of Cartesian metaphysics, exactly as has finally been demonstrated for the creation of the eternal truths.

Our task hence emerges clearly: it is not first a matter of assembling systematically the scattered elements of the *causa sui*,[3] but of establishing it in a situation that is as central as possible in relation to the system (or quasi-system) of Cartesian metaphysics. It is only when its constitutive role is established and thought that the *causa sui* will be able to be evaluated in view of the history of concepts, of logic, and in onto-theology.

§2. An Unthinkable Thesis

Nevertheless, we open our investigation with a double excursus on the history of concepts, since they better permit us to discern the forced strangeness of the thesis of a *causa sui*. Let us begin by asking who first made a positive and dogmatic use of the *causa sui*.

Contrary to an accidental dogma, it cannot have been Spinoza, for at least two reasons. First, the use of the theme in the *Ethics*. Without a doubt, properly speaking, the concept of the *causa sui* constitutes the opening to the whole ensemble: "By cause of itself I understand that whose essence involves existence, or that whose nature cannot be conceived except as existing."[4] But this definition precisely does not define a concept of *causa sui*. It limits itself to positing (evidently without being able to justify) a simple equivalence between what must be thought, on the one hand (the hypothetical concept of *causa sui*), and, on the other hand, the implication of existence in an essence or "nature." But this implication, which is not verified except in the case of the divine essence, intervenes in the argument called "ontological." It is not at all enunciated in terms of cause (or effect) and hence cannot amount to a *causa sui*, at least immediately and with the authority of a definition. In short, for once Spinoza proceeds as one does in algebra, since he establishes an equality between the known (essence encompassing existence) and the unknown (*causa sui*), which, far from signifying that he thinks the *causa sui*, signifies exactly the opposite: he will treat it as an algebraist uses an unknown quantity—as if he knew it, hence in not knowing it. Besides, this assumption of the unknown as if it were known finds a striking confirmation from the only other significant occurrence of the term in the *Ethics*: "In a word, God must be called the cause of all things in the same sense as he is called the cause of himself."[5] In order to explain a known concept—God causes things—Spinoza refers to an unknown and inconceivable concept, that of the *causa sui*. Certainly, the divine causality with respect to "all things" itself offers a difficulty, since formal causality must double efficient causality; but then, it would have been suitable that the principle of explication be that much clearer—which is certainly not at all the case. Meanwhile one should not respond that Spinoza has given a positive definition of the *causa sui* in positing that "a substance cannot be produced by anything else, therefore it will be the cause of itself."[6] Indeed, not being "anything else" (*ab alio*) only leads to being in "itself" (*a se*), in no way to being by itself as by an efficient cause, that is to say to being *causa sui* in the strict sense. If moreover the *causa sui* does not amount to an *a se*, it would certainly become intelligible but also useless. In this way Spinoza only rarely (that much justice must be granted him) utilizes a concept that he never defines.[7]

He does not define it for an excellent reason: he takes it to be already explained and established by others. A phrase of *The Emendation of the Intellect* [*De Intellectus Emendatione*] brings that out without ambiguity: "If the thing is in itself, or, as is commonly said, is the cause of itself, it must be understood through its essence alone."[8] Being in itself hence is understood by its sole essence, what is named habitually the cause of itself. "As is commonly said" (*ut vulgo dicitur*) attributes hence the use of the concept to the common; and this received use supposes its prior invention. In short, Spinoza does not pretend to invent the *causa sui* as he does not pretend to define it—he uses it, that is all.

To what, then, does this common usage, on which Spinoza relies, refer back? The landmarks here can be discovered without effort. First Thomas Aquinas, who, certainly, admits that "free is that which is for its own sake" (*liberum est quod, causa sui est*) but only as a translation of Aristotle: "the man is free, we say, who exists for himself and not for another" (ελευθερος ο αυτου ενεκα και μη αλλου).[9] But when it is a matter of the strict meaning of a cause of itself, his critique does not offer the least ambiguity—"A thing cannot be its own cause"[10]—and is articulated in several clear points. First, a cause of itself would have to precede itself and hence suffer a temporal contradiction: "There is no case known (neither is it, indeed, possible) in which a thing is found to be the efficient cause of itself; for so it would be prior to itself." The cause of itself must precede itself in time.[11] Moreover, Descartes will have to count on this objection, which he is content to outline without seriously resolving it (VII:240, 6–8; CSM II:167). Second, God does not tolerate any cause: "God does not have a cause."[12] Indeed, he cannot exercise the first cause as truly first, inasmuch as he himself is not inscribed in the chain of causes that are in turn performed: "God is the first cause and has no cause."[13] Moreover, the whole second way, which attains the divine being via the chain of causes, would immediately become inoperative if the first cause were to remain inscribed in the causal chain: God is and is first only in being excepted from causality. Indeed, precisely because it links one being to another, the causal relation indicates its relativity, dependence, and hence finitude. In short, causality produces intelligibility less than it stigmatizes finitude. Third, it is notable that Thomas Aquinas does not aim here at causality in general but really at efficient causality: "There is no case known (neither is it, indeed, possible) in which a thing is found to be the efficient cause of itself; for so it would be prior to itself, which is impossible."[14] This point has a particular importance: if Thomas Aquinas refutes as contradictory an expressly efficient causality of self for establishing the *causa sui*, Descartes should have had to justify it first in terms of efficiency, without, for example, escaping toward formal causality. One knows that he has not taken that route. One essential point remains: the hypothesis of the *causa sui* was known and discussed by Thomas Aquinas, but in order to be rejected as contradictory and even harmful to the knowledge of God.

Now, and this is the decisive point, this is not at all a matter of an isolated position or one proper only to Thomism, but of a decision that is in principle ratified by medieval thinkers of all tendencies. (a) Anselm had already emphasized that "the Supreme Nature could not have been [efficiently] caused to exist by itself or by another; nor was it itself or anything else . . . aided."[15] (b) Thomas Aquinas hence ratified it only in more Aristotelian terms. (c) Duns Scotus maintained firmly this thesis: "The first thing effected simply is uncausable. . . . If this first thing is uneffectable, and therefore uncausable, this is the case because it is not able to be finite, material or formal."[16] (d) Ockham, on this point at least, is in accord with his adversary, since he defines God as an "immortal, incorruptible, ungenerated or uncaused being."[17] (e) More impressive even, Suárez, although so often inclined to an adjustment of heaven, remains here formally faithful to the tradition of the first scholasticism: "God is without principle and without cause." He does so to the point that he attaches to the letter the argument that Caterus and Arnauld oppose to the positive aseity introduced by Descartes: "For it is said that being out of itself and from itself, even if this being is viewed as something posited, nevertheless adds only negation to this entity, for a being is not able to be from itself through a posited origin or emanation . . . and some saints proceed with this mode of exposition when they say that God is the cause of His own being or His own substance or His own wisdom."[18] From Anselm to Suárez, there is hence agreement on a received and common principle: "Nothing can cause itself." It is of course the Suárezian formulation of this principle that Descartes considers when he writes to Mersenne: "It is because of the common scholastic axiom 'Nothing can be its own cause' that 'from itself' has not been taken in the appropriate sense."[19] Descartes' predecessors then hold the *causa sui* to be unthinkable; like Spinoza later, they hence do not attempt to think it. Certainly for opposite motives: not because it had already been thought at ground, but because it does not offer any thinkable ground. In short, all the way to Suárez, the *causa sui* remains unthinkable, and after Spinoza, it need no longer be thought. It has hence been thought between Suárez and Spinoza. And only by Descartes. We respond in this way to the first of our initial questions.

To attribute the invention of the *causa sui* to Descartes is to grant him an ambiguous honor. For either the *causa sui* amounts to negative aseity and Descartes would not invent anything except one word for another, or it amounts to a positive cause—which is obviously what Descartes sustains—then it is a matter of a contradiction in terms, since no thing can precede itself. The medievals were not the only ones to formulate this objection and this dilemma; Schopenhauer will take it up again (strangely, with respect to Spinoza): "For my part, I only see in the *causa sui* a *contradictio in adjecto*, a before that really is an after, an insolent claim of authority for tearing the infinite chain of causality." The *causa sui* is suspended by itself as Baron Münchhausen pulls himself up by his own hair. Nietzsche will repeat this comparison and criticism: "The *causa sui* is the best self-contradiction that has been conceived so far, it is a sort of rape and perversion of logic."[20] On this point at least, Anselm and Nietzsche, Thomas Aquinas and Schopenhauer, Duns Scotus and Ockham agree to the letter—the *causa sui* amounts to a logical contradiction. Descartes had, of course, a clear conscience regarding this difficulty, which he recognized as evident: "Who does not know that something cannot be prior to or distinct from itself?"[21] Why then, acknowledging this patent contradiction, does he discard the objection as a "trivial question" (*nugatoria quaestio*; AT VII:108, 12–13; CSM II:78)? Which theoretical requirement leads him to assume, better, to vindicate, what he knows (with the immense majority of his predecessors and his successors) to harbor a patent contradiction? In short, why does Descartes deny the evidence?

Certainly, because another evidence removes the contradiction from the first evidence. But what new evidence comes up here that might invert such a tradition? The question is no longer to inquire if Descartes was the first to think the *causa sui*—that he is, indisputably—but to comprehend why he takes the risk of sustaining such a contradiction in terms. The response to the first question— historical—leads back to the second—logical.

§3. What Reason Dictates

Three times over the *Replies* introduce a universal enunciation, which takes the rank of principle. Let me cite these three texts. (a) First Replies: "However, the light of nature does establish that if anything exists we may always ask why it exists; that is, we may inquire into its efficient cause, or, if it does not have one, we may demand why it does not need one."[22] (b) Second Replies: "Concerning every existing thing it is possible to ask what is the cause of its existence. This question may even be asked concerning God."[23] (c) Fourth Replies: "But I think it is clear to everyone that a consideration of efficient causes is the primary and principal way, if not the only way, that we have of proving the existence of God."[24] These convergent statements receive several common accounts: the character of principle, universality, and the reign of existence.

It is a matter first of universal statements supported by the principle, as the formula "the light of nature does establish" (*dictat autem profecto lumen naturae*; AT VII:108, 18–20; CSM II:78) marks. The natural light says, that is to say, it decrees and formulates a principle. In several French texts of Descartes, it is, moreover, the property of reason to dictate: "reason does not insist that what we thus see or imagine is true. But it does insist that all our ideas or notions must have some foundation of truth."[25]

This edict, indeed this *diktat*, is imposed in virtue of its evidence — "manifest to all" [*omnibus manifestum*]; in consequence, it must render intelligible its universality. That is why Descartes does not extend it to God except by displacing him: in the text (a) the principle either demands the cause of existence or in the case of God, postulates (*postulare*) knowing "why it does not need one" (*cur illa non indigent*; AT IXA:86, 23 = VII:108, 21; CSM II:78); the text (b) specifies that the immensity of his nature is the "cause or reason" (*causa sive ratio*; AT VII:165, 2; CSM II:116) for which no cause is necessary (literally, "why he needs no cause"); finally, the text (c) envisages, once his existence is proven, to "exempt" (*exciperemus*) God from an investigation into his efficient causes (238, 17; CSM II:166). The Cartesian tactic remains the same in all these cases: the essence of God certainly dispenses an efficient cause, but, at the same time, it fulfills its function, thus satisfies the principle.

Causality hence does not intervene universally except as the principle of existence, to the point that causality and existence become interchangeable: "we may always ask why it exists; that is, we may inquire into its efficient cause."[26] The cause is essentially "cause in order to exist" (*causa cur existat*; 164, 29; CSM II:116). All existence is caused; the cause produces existence as its effect: Descartes hence deploys an ontology by this principle. But as this principle must engulf God himself by way of the *causa sui*, it provokes an onto-theology, which we have in another place called an onto-theology of cause (by opposition to a first onto-theology of the *cogitatio*).[27] This comparison also permits the resolution of a formidable difficulty: in imposing the *causa sui*, which is missing from the *Meditations*, does not the *Replies* become incompatible with it? This is not the case. Although the *causa sui* is missing in the *Meditations*, the principle that will provoke it in the *Replies* — all existence results from a cause — appears already in this text with the same abrupt violence. Even more, this principle comes up precisely in the celebrated page of the Third Meditation where Descartes introduces three decisive concepts that have remained absent so far: cause, substance, objective reality (*causa, substantia, realitas objectiva*). In the lexical and conceptual revival of the order of reason that he concedes here, Descartes enunciates the principle in this way: "Now it is manifest by the natural light that there must be at least as much [reality] in the efficient and total cause as in the effect of that cause."[28] Two points common to the formulations are clear: (a) manifest evidence, which is self-justified as a first principle and hence breaks with the previous order of reasons; (b) the direct link between the cause (hence the effect) and the being (*esse*). The significant differences do not appear any less. First, in the Third Meditation it is a matter of the being of the cause or the effect, not directly of the cause of being (or existence) considered as an effect, in the way in which it appears in the *Replies*. But in fact this difference remains unimportant: thinking the being of the cause or the effect presupposes, at least implicitly, that the relation of the cause to the effect is interpreted as ontological, hence that the cause plays the function of the final instance not only for the effect, but for its being in virtue of itself. Where, then, do we find the truly significant difference?

That difference lies in the same principle being found applied in the Third Meditation in the more restrictive manner, while in the *Replies* it deploys all its possibilities. Indeed, only with a double constraint does the Third Meditation introduce the requirement of a cause for all being considered as its effect. (a) The being of the effect can only be understood starting from ideas, since in the regimen of hyperbolic doubt, besides the ego, nothing exists except the ideas of the ego. Properly speaking, the principle of causality cannot yet administer existence, since it is defined as being outside of thought. Besides, on this point the Third Meditation avoids speaking of existence (*existentia*) or of existing (*existere*) in favor of reality (*realitas*) and of being (*esse*). In this way, only a region that is strongly limited by beings (the ideas) falls under the principle of causality. The celebrated formula "also in the case of ideas" (*etiam de ideis*; AT VII:41, 3; CSM II:28) must not be understood as an addition, but, despite the letter, as a residue—what remains to causality when it is divested of it "in the case of effects which possess actual or formal reality."[29]

(b) We can easily infer the second constraint from the first: the Third Meditation exercises the principle of causality on ideas, considered as the privileged effects, and particularly on the idea of God, as a particularly remarkable effect. Does one correctly call this proof a proof by effects, or still an *a posteriori* proof?[30] Yet God, attained as ultimate cause (*causa ultima*; 50, 6; CSM II:54), exercises this last causality without his existence being subjected to it. In the Third

Meditation the principle of causality is exercised only on ideas (then on created and finite being, the ego) but never on God's existence itself. God causes existence, but himself exists without cause: Descartes maintains the position of Thomas Aquinas, in restricting only the second way (*secunda via*) of finite beings in general to the ideas of the ego in particular. On the contrary, the *Replies* pushes the principle of a causality of existence all the way to ultimate possibilities: not only does "no thing" (*nulla res*; AT VII 108, 19 = 164, 28; CSM II:78) exist without cause, or "all things" (*res omnes*; AT VII 238, 16; CSM II:166) exist in virtue of an (ontological) cause, but even and above all "they may even be asked of God"[31]—even for the existence of God (*etiam ipsius Dei*; AT VII 238, 16; CSM II:166), a cause is required (theology). The emergence of the concept of *causa sui* indicates that henceforth the principle of a causality of existence, or even the principle of the cause as (sufficient) reason of all existence, no longer suffers any exception. This principle organizes not only an ontology, but really an onto-theology.

From this moment on, we can respond, although still abstractly, to another of our initial questions: between the Third Meditation and the *Replies*, Descartes maintains coherently the same principle, but he modifies its import radically. From an exception of the divine existence from causality, taken from Thomas Aquinas, he passes to a subjection of God himself to causality, anticipating Leibniz. The sudden and brutal appearance of the *causa sui* in the debate with Caterus (hence, indirectly with Thomas Aquinas) offers an indication of an even more decisive event: the emergence of a principle of sufficient reason in its ontological function, pursued all the way to an onto-theological constitution of metaphysics. Moreover, C. Wolff, who recognizes the principle of sufficient reason in the *diktat* of the Second Replies, seems to confirm this: "That he [i.e., Descartes] will have had a clear idea of reason must not be doubted. And he observes that he even makes clear axiomatically, first, that the distinction of the existence of God and the mind from the body will be demonstrated in a geometric fashion as the subject of the controversial *Meditations on First Philosophy*. . . . And indeed, 'no thing,' he says, 'exists that cannot be asked about its cause, why it exists. And this can be asked about God Himself . . . because the very immensity of His nature is cause or reason on account of the fact that no cause will be required in order to exist.' He confusedly discerned the distinction between cause and reason."[32] By detour through a controversy that

appears to be secondary, a principle then arises: reason in its sufficiency. If Descartes shoulders the patent logical contradiction of the
causa sui, if he risks (himself)—he who is always so prudent, even
and above all in the First and Fourth Replies—explicitly contradicting a well-established tradition, that is because the onto-theological
accomplishment of his metaphysics implies for him incommensurably
more than a polemic even with the greatest medieval thinkers. Hence
we must approach the third question, which is properly metaphysical: What does such a determining onto-theology of the cause accomplish for Descartes to insist here on the *causa sui* to which he submits
God?

§4. Demonstrating God A Priori

Can one confirm, by historical and textual arguments, that the introduction of the concept of the *causa sui* amounts to an onto-theological
institution of the cause as sufficient reason for all existence?

To attempt this, we will choose Suárez as a guide, being the last
scholastic landmark and an indirect master and direct adversary of
Descartes, for it is against the horizon of Suárez that the Cartesian
invention of the *causa sui* (as many other issues in Descartes) becomes
intelligible. In effect, Suárez opens his argument devoted to the
"causes of being in common" with a solemn prologue, which precedes
the discussion itself and fixes his position firmly: "This causality is just
like a certain property of an entity; so it follows: for nothing is a being
that does not participate in some idea of cause"[33]—causality does not
designate a simple relation, but a universal property of being, such
that no being would be without relation to causality. This is resumed
in a laconic alternative: "Nothing, however, is a being that is neither
effect nor cause"[34]—being means here being a cause or an effect. Pascal translates this: "all things are both caused and causing."[35] One can
recognize two Cartesian positions here: the universality of causality
and its ontological status. But Suarez anticipates Descartes even more
when it is a matter of defining the causal status of God. On the one
hand, following the dominant medieval tradition, he formally excludes
God from causality: "God does not have a cause, but all other things,
except him, have a cause"—which prefigures the Third Meditation.[36]
On the other hand, he nevertheless attempts to include God tangentially in the empire of causality: "Although God does not have a true
and real cause, nevertheless certain of his ideas are understood by us
as if they were the causes of others."[37] Indeed, certain reasons of God

can be interpreted "as if" (*ac si*) they had caused others in God. Or even, following another text: "Although we concede, therefore, that a being insofar as it is a being does not have rigorously assumed causes in the prior way, it nevertheless has some ideas of its properties; and even in this way ideas of this sort are able to be found in God, for we return to the cause from the infinite perfection of God."[38] Being, taken logically, has no cause, which does not hinder it from acknowledging reasons justifying its properties. These reasons then take the place of causes. In the same way, reason supplied with its infinite perfection takes the place of a cause for, among other things, the unity of God, who does not have a cause.

One recognizes here without effort three of the most innovative positions of the *Replies*. (a) The enlargement of the cause "also in God" (*etiam in Deo*) anticipates the Cartesian "even concerning God" (*de ipso Dei*; VII:164, 29; CSM II:116), "even God himself" (*etiam ipsius Dei*; 238, 16; CSM II:166); (b) the interpretation of a property in God (infinity) as a reason, and of this reason as a quasi (*ac si*) cause prefigures a similar Cartesian *coup de force*: "not because [God] needs any cause in order to exist, but because the immensity of his nature is the cause or reason why he needs no cause in order to exist";[39] "there is in God such great and inexhaustible power that he never required the assistance of anything in order to exist";[40] "we attend to the immense and incomprehensible power that is contained within the idea of God. . . . it is plainly the cause of his continuing existence, and nothing but this can be the cause."[41]

Finally and above all, (c) in both cases, the divine essence (which, moreover, is characterized equally by infinity) is only found assimilated to a reason then to a cause that dispenses with any exterior cause, inasmuch as it can be interpreted beginning from the supposedly universal empire of causality as supreme trait of the *ens in quantum ens*. Consequently, God is no longer excepted from the causal Being of all being. While in 1630 the "incomprehensible power" exercised an "efficient and total cause" (*causa efficiens et totalis*) without being subjected to it, something the Third Meditation still maintains with the *causa ultima*,[42] the *Replies* inscribes God for the first time completely into the "object of metaphysics." This coherence has a price: God and hence the infinite are interpreted beginning from causality, thus from what will soon be called the principle of sufficient reason. When thought according to sufficient reason, the infinite must be declined as an infinite power. The infinite only explains itself as power: this modification, less visible than the sudden apparition of the *causa sui*, nevertheless delivers truth to it and assures it possibility. If Descartes surpasses Suárez' positions decisively, he certainly owes this to the introduction of the *causa sui*, but above all to the resolute interpretation of God beginning from causality.

But an examination of Suárez can throw an even clearer light on the real import of the Cartesian advance. One must highlight that Suárez, although he excludes the *causa sui* in principle, following the consensus of his predecessors, does not discuss it without repeatedly returning to it and without indulging its impossibility, apparently renouncing it only with regret.[43] Now, one of the most significant appearances of the hypothesis of the *causa sui* occurs in a larger ensemble, *Disputatio* 29, "About God, the First Being and Uncreated Substance, Insofar as He Can by Natural Reason Be Known to Exist,"[44] in short, the discussion concerning the rational knowledge of the existence of God, in which the Third and Fifth Meditations and the First and Fourth Replies also engage. Suárez here proceeds in three stages. The first, examining the possibility of demonstrating the existence of any uncreated being, ends up at such a being—independent, the first cause.[45] The second section examines whether "it can be demonstrated *a posteriori* that God exists"[46] in showing that the uncreated being is unique; it arrives at a being necessary by itself who is "source and efficient cause of created things";[47] one here recognizes without it being forced the trait of the God who is "ultimate cause" (*causa ultima*; AT VII:50, 6; CSM II: 34) and "source of truth" (*fons veritatis*; 22, 23; CSM II: 15) of the *a posteriori* way followed so much by the First and Third Meditations, as well as by the letters of 1630 on the creation of the eternal truths (AT I:151, 1–19; 150, 4; CSMK III: 24). Up to this point Suárez, and Descartes with him, remains in a perfectly Thomist horizon of a knowledge of God by his effects, by way of a cause not itself caused.

There remains the third section, which asks whether "in some way it can be demonstrated *a priori* that God exists."[48] Something surprising emerges here straightaway: Suárez, without even specifying what demands an *a priori* demonstration of the existence of God, undertakes to show its impossibility in the strict sense (*simpliciter loquendo*) in consequence of the fact that God is not *causa sui*. Here is the argument: "God cannot be demonstrated to exist in an *a priori* manner. For God does not have a cause of his being [*causam sui*], through which he might be demonstrated *a priori*. Or if he did have such a cause, God is not known so exactly and perfectly by us that we could follow him (so to speak) from his proper principles. In this sense,

Dionysius, in chapter seven of *On Divine Names*, said that we cannot know God from his proper nature."[49] This absolutely decisive text calls for several remarks.

(a) The *causa sui* plays a part here by being directly linked to *a priori* knowledge, in the same way in which the final cause (*causa ultima*) had permitted *a posteriori* knowledge; in this way the move from the Third Meditation to the *Replies* amounts to a reversal of an *a posteriori* order to an *a priori* order. This is, moreover, what the appendix in the geometrical order of the Second Replies explicitly confirms by placing it in the rank of first axiom, hence of the *a priori* par excellence, the causal determination not only of all existence in general, but even and above all of the divine existence itself. The requirement of a "cause or reason" (*causa sive ratio*; 165, 3; CSM II:116), hence of a causal *a priori*, carries weight first for the existence of God. It follows that the proof of the Fifth Meditation, habitually called "ontological argument," does not merit the fuller title of *a priori* in all rigor, because it is missing causality (and the *causa sui*), which defines the first Cartesian *a priori* on God. Spinoza understood this very well, since he attempted to identify this proof with the *causa sui* (although admittedly by force).[50]

(b) Suárez saw the reversal of the orders perfectly, but he could not accomplish it, doubtless because he persisted in considering the strict *causa sui* to be a contradictory concept (Descartes still thought this), but above all because he refused it the metaphysical presupposition: the interpretation of divine essence beginning from an *a priori* that would precede it. Indeed, even if God had (*si haberet*) a cause of his being (*causa sui esse*), hence, in short, a *causa sui*,[51] God would remain imperfectly known to us,[52] because it would then be necessary to know him by beginning with his proper principles (*ex propriis principiis*). Now, following the normative doctrine of the divine names fixed by Dionysius, the principles and the proper nature of God definitely cannot be known. Suárez sees the possibility of the *a priori* by the *causa sui* and, here at least, he refuses it.

(c) In the guise of *a priori* knowledge, he proposes a weaker substitute: in place of a principle imposed upon God (the causality of existence), one will proceed by beginning with any attribute, provided that it would be common to being in general, in order in this way to reach the divine quiddity, then its existence: "from a particular attribute, which in actuality is the essence of God but is conceived by us as a mode of a non-caused being, another attribute is inferred and in this way it is concluded that that being is God."[53] The attribute, which is inferred in a quasi *a priori* manner, remains the mode of a being resolutely *non causatum*, outside causality. The divine transcendence demands the renunciation of the strict *a priori* of universal causality: for example, from immensity one concludes immutability, hence unity and, finally, necessary existence. One can here venture that the proof of the Fifth Meditation (and maybe also all those of Spinoza) illustrates this method of the attenuated *a priori* exactly.

Descartes' violence toward the conditions of the knowledge of God stands out even more clearly if one pays attention to the repeated admonitions of a good many authors contemporaneous to Descartes. (a) Let us mention first G. Vasquez, the Jesuit rival of Suárez, and firmer than him: "The being of God is not able to be demonstrated *a priori*, for it belongs to God by virtue of the propositions God knows through Himself; it can nevertheless be demonstrated *a posteriori* or by its effects"[54]; as the divine existence remains a proposition not evident for us (*viatores*), its knowledge will remain *a posteriori* and of an inferior evidence to those of mathematical propositions.[55] (b) Neither should one neglect the position taken by Eustache de Saint-Paul, whom Descartes held in esteem: "Let this, therefore, be the first assertion: The being of God cannot be demonstrated *a priori* because the divine being is the same as the essence of God and the fundamental attribute of all things divine, which no cause or idea is able to cause even by our *a priori* mode of understanding." One cannot say it more clearly: the divine being is confused with essence and the attributes which it founds in God, he surpasses hence all cause or reason that we could enunciate before and without it; in consequence, it must remain an *a posteriori* demonstration of it.[56]

(c) But the most significant author, because he is the most explicit, seems to be Scipion Dupleix, whose *Metaphysics* favors without reserve the knowledge "*a posteriori*, that is to say by the proof taken from posterior things. For God does not depend on any superior or preceding cause, also he cannot be known by any preceding cause, that we call in Latin *a priori*." Even more precisely: "one must deny that neither nature, nor reason, nor the human will would be absolute principles and those of God"—and this absence of principles anterior to God hence forbids any knowledge *a priori*: "God is completely unknowable and undemonstrable by antecedent principles, because there are none: that which the Latins call *a priori*, and to the contrary . . . there is nothing more manifest and knowable *a posteriori* than God himself, to be known by his wonders and by his works." This difference between two orders defines even the distance of the creation, more essential than all ontological difference: "Of all other things we can acquire a perfect knowledge, which is named properly *Science*, by principles and preceding causes, that which the Logicians call in Latin *demonstrare a priori*; but of God who is the principle of principles, the first and supreme cause of all other things, one cannot have knowledge . . . if it is not *a posteriori*."[57]

(d) A similar opposition to the Cartesian innovation is confirmed in the United Provinces, in particular in Leiden: under the authority of as declared an anti-Cartesian as J. Revius. Here several theses were sustained that at bottom attempted to criticize the introduction of the *causa sui*. I will cite only one of them, the one sustained by Antoine Dauburgh (d'Alcmar) in February 1647. It affirms very clearly the argument whose exposition we reconstitute: "God cannot be demonstrated *a priori*, because he does not have a cause at all by which he could be demonstrated *a priori*."[58] God does not admit of a demonstration *a priori*, because his being does not admit any cause; an essence or a quiddity (a formal cause, in the Cartesian thematic) cannot be substituted for this missing cause, because the question of essence does not precede that of existence in God, hence quiddity remains inaccessible in it: "And neither is it able to be demonstrated through the essence and quiddity of God just as something that is first according to a reason, for the question Whether something is? is prior to the question What is it? as Thomas rightly [maintains] in Distinction 1"; from there he returns to the classic position: "God can be demonstrated *a posteriori*, by his effects."[59]

(e) The most surprising confirmation, however, comes from Spinoza himself; in effect, the *Short Treatise* (*Korte Verhandeling*) posits the terms of the dilemma confronted (and decided) by Descartes as clearly as possible: "From all this, then, it follows clearly that one can prove God's existence both *a priori* and *a posteriori*. Indeed, the *a priori* proof is better. But, [it will be objected] the things one proves in this way, one must prove through their external causes, which is an evident imperfection in them, since they cannot make themselves known through themselves, but only through external causes. But God, the first cause of all things, and also the cause of himself [*de eerste oorzaak aller dingen, en ook de oorzaak syns zelf*], makes himself known through himself. So what Thomas Aquinas says—that God could not be proved *a priori*, because he supposedly has no cause—is not of much importance."[60] It thus is obvious for Spinoza that an *a priori* proof of the existence of God demands the recourse of a *causa sui*. This is confirmed by another passage from the same treatise: "Moreover, they also say that God can never be proven *a priori* (because he has no cause), but only probably, or through his effects."[61] One would not know how to fix more clearly the frontier that the *Replies* transgresses, nor the rupture that the *causa sui* imposes: to demonstrate the existence of God beginning from causality, Descartes, in consequence, must submit God's essence to an antecedent principle.

Hence, Descartes does not impose the *causa sui* historically, because then he would have surmounted the logical difficulties clearly. Rather, he attempts to attenuate its logical difficulties, because he *must* use it in order to violate the historical prohibition established by the medieval thinkers on the legitimacy of an *a priori* knowledge of the existence and hence of the essence of God. Only the violation of this prohibition permits including God himself (*ipse Deus*) in the onto-theological constitution of metaphysics definitively and for the first time. In this way, I have responded to the third of our initial questions.

§5. The Return of Analogy

The audacity of his advance does not, of course, escape Descartes himself. His customary prudence ceaselessly led him to wish to soften its violence, to the point of almost repudiating it. In 1648, responding to an attack by Revius (in discussing Regius), he pretends never to have written that "*God should be called 'the efficient cause of himself not just in a negative sense but also in a positive sense* . . . as he [Revius] alleges. However carefully he sifts, scans and pores over my writings, he will not find in them anything like this—quite the reverse in fact."[62] Is the positively efficient cause of himself truly a "monster" (*portentum*) for the *Replies*?[63] It is significant that one cannot respond univocally to this question. In one sense, Descartes really did object to the *causa sui* coming strictly from efficient causality: "the phrase 'his own cause' cannot possibly be taken to mean an efficient cause"; "God is not the efficient cause of himself"; "is not an efficient cause in the strict sense."[64] Yet aseity becomes nevertheless as positive (AT VII:110, 7, 21, 31; CSM II:79–80) as divine essence (AT VII:237, 2, 10 and 239, 18; CSM II:165 and 167). To go even further, the principle that leads to the *causa sui* mentions the efficiency of cause at least twice (AT VII:108, 20 and 238, 11; CSM II:78, 166). But above all the discussion begins with an even more ambiguous declaration: "I did not say that it was impossible for something to be the efficient cause of itself."[65] Indeed, against Caterus, who said again that God could not be "from himself . . . as a cause" (*a se . . . ut a causa*; 95, 12; CSM II:68–69), Descartes begins by rejecting this impossibility and by opening the possibility of the opposite. Moreover, in transforming the double negation literally into affirmation, one could almost translate: "I have said that it is possible that something would be the efficient cause of himself."[66] In short, the declaration of opening is already pregnant with all the indecision of the formulations to come from the *causa sui*. Descartes, precisely because he institutes the principle of efficient causality for all existence without reserve (the principle of sufficient reason), develops almost boundlessly the simply polemical concept of the *causa sui*. Besides, one can be surprised that Caterus and Arnauld had almost exclusively concentrated their attention on the consequence (the *causa sui*), without really putting in question the principle that sustains it. In this way they permit Descartes to confirm his innovation, while giving the appearance of extreme accommodation. It is this final ambivalence that must still be specified.

The numerous concessions attempt to make the *causa sui* more acceptable to the objectors. It becomes, for example, a *causa sui* only "in a sense" (*quodammodo*) or *quasi*.[67] Between these concessions, one must privilege those that Descartes takes up again textually in the analyses of causality by Suárez. (a) Descartes must envisage, in God, a "dignity of being a cause" (*causae dignitas*) without nevertheless here importing the "indignity of being an effect" (*effectus indignitas*; 242, 5–6; CSM II:168–69). These strange formulas come directly out of a question of Suarez — "Is every cause more noble by its effect?" — and from his response: "the principal cause can never be less noble."[68] (b) Descartes defends the positive use of the *causa* in God due to the authority of the Greek Fathers, who, contrary to the Latins opposing the *principium* to the *causa*, used the αρχη and the αιτια without distinction (237, 24–238, 6; CSM II:166). In fact, in this way he takes up again to the letter Suárez' exposition of "the manner of speaking of several Greek Fathers, who even among the divine persons named the Father the cause of the Son, in that in which he is the principle."[69] In the same way, Descartes invokes the subtle theological possibility that the Father might be the *principium* without the Son being therefore also *principiatum* (242, 7–14; CSM II:169). Here also he almost copies Suárez: "Therefore, although they [the Theologians] will say that the Father is the principle of the Son, they nevertheless deny that the Son is derived from the principle of the

Father."[70] Descartes hence measures perfectly the implications of the *causa sui* in revealed theology, because Suárez has already opened the dossier for him; none of the theological allusions of the *Replies* is obscure, insignificant, or negligible.

(c) Descartes ends by conceding that the *causa sui* does not come from simple efficiency, but from a "concept of cause that is common to both an efficient and a formal cause"[71]; despite the model of a continued transition between a polygon of an undefined number of corners to a circle, one could legitimately doubt that it would be a matter here of an authentic concept and not of an empty denomination. Now, one finds that Suárez has really examined systematically the reciprocal action of the four causes among each other and their compatibility; in this way formal and material causes, final and efficient, material and final act together and reciprocally. Yet two incompatibilities remain: "the efficient cause cannot have mutual causality with the matter or the form."[72] In short, this stance elaborated by Descartes is certainly not contradictory, devoid of sense—of the sense discussed and elaborated by Suárez—but it is simply false. But once more, even when he is opposed to Suárez, Descartes still speaks in Suárez' own semantics.

Yet, among all the concessions in which Descartes envelops the universal hold of the principle of reason on existence, the most symptomatic consists in the surprising recourse to analogy. In the response to Arnauld's objections, Descartes' final tactic amounts to introducing a distance between the causality of the *causa sui* and strict efficiency. This distance becomes available at times as a "common" concept (AT VII:238, 25; CSM II:166), "intermediary" (239, 17; CSM II:167) between efficiency and formality, but with difficulty, since Suárez explicitly refuses this possibility. The distance also soon exposes itself as an analogy of the *causa sui* with efficient causality. Successively: (a) the *causa positiva* that becomes the divine essence "can be regarded as analogous to an efficient cause"[73] and can refer itself to efficiency by analogy with this; (b) "all the above ways of talking, which are derived by analogy with the notion of efficient causation, are very necessary for guiding the natural light";[74] (c) "using the analogy of an efficient cause to explain features which in fact belong to a formal cause, that is, to the very essence of God";[75] (d) "simply in terms of the essence or formal cause of the thing . . . the formal cause will be strongly analogous to an efficient cause, and hence can be called something close to an efficient cause."[76] Could one not infer of these occurrences of *analogia* that Descartes finds here again, quite naturally, the theological usage of that term when he applies the efficient cause to God *a priori*? Must not one salute the logical coherence and the theological prudence of his move—all existence depends on the principle of sufficient reason that assigns to him an efficient cause but, in the case of God, with the reservation of an analogy? And, moreover, had not Suárez already espoused a similar position?[77]

All the same, this accommodating interpretation does not hold, for several reasons. First, because the analogy with the efficient cause of another cause, supposed suitable for God, would not alleviate any of the difficulties of the *causa sui*: (a) the real difference between cause and effect; (b) the anteriority of a thing (as cause) on itself (as effect); (c) the submission of God to a principle that remains anterior to him, for a proof *a priori*. And Descartes will never go back on his initial refusal of responding—"trivial question" (*nugatoria quaestio*; 108, 12; CSM II:78)—to these aporias.

Second, and above all, the analogy envisaged here would be a counter-analogy, supposing that one could admit it as a new conceptual device. Let us insist on this determining point. In good theological (and Thomistic) rigor, the analogy of *proportio* or of reference is constructed between the analogues and a privileged term, the first analogue; but the first term does not dominate the others as a common reference (like health for the things that are related to it), in the sense of being exercised as an abstract principle. The first analogue remains a member of the series, and it is this one in its entirety that is here related (as the things of medicine to a healthy body). In this way the analogy of *proportio* refers all finite terms of the series to an infinite and uncreated term of this same series.[78] To put it plainly, either efficient causality goes back to God alone and all other beings would exercise it only analogically—and Descartes reasons similarly with respect to substance, which is strict in God but analogical for the finite (*Principles* 1, §51). Or efficient causality belongs strictly to finite beings, and God would be excepted from it—this is what the medievals sustained.

The remaining hypothesis is the one here envisaged by Descartes: efficient causality is said in the strict sense of finite beings and it is said analogically of God. Yet a prodigious reversal results from this: God is said according to and as efficient cause only by analogy, hence by reference to finite causality, alone strictly efficient. In short, following the Cartesian analogy, God (the infinite) is said by analogy and by reference to finite being, while, according to theological analogy, the finite is said with reference to God. The analogy is really exercised, but inverted: God is said to be understood by reference to efficiency, which is not exercised strictly except in the finite, henceforth erected to the rank of principal analogue and center of reference. And, in the same way as the final successors of Thomas Aquinas had reversed the meaning of the analogy of being, in transforming the reference of beings to God (*proportio ad Deum*) into a univocal concept of being that also encompasses God, in the same way the analogy Descartes uses does not, in fact, refer efficiency to God, but God to efficiency. Far from compensating or alleviating the emergence of a principle of sufficient reason in the *causa sui*, analogy, in inverting itself and playing against itself, confirms that even the existence of God comes from the *causa sive ratio*, tangentially but inexorably.

We can conclude. First result: although only the *Replies* introduces the *causa sui*, it does not contradict the *Meditations*, which nevertheless knows nothing of the concept: both obey the same principle *a priori* of causality, even if they diverge on its application either in the restricted domain of the ideas or universally to all existence. In this way, the *causa sui* permits the extrication of a greater internal coherence of the Cartesian metaphysics. Second result: this first and indisputable coherence, however, makes other tensions appear among the Cartesian texts.

(a) Certainly the letters on the creation of the eternal truths define God really as "an incomprehensible power" (AT I:146, 4 and 150, 22; CSMK III:23 and 25), as the First Replies takes up again later (AT VII:110, 26; CSM II:80), because it thinks it straightaway as "efficient and total cause" (*efficiens et totalis causa*; AT I:152, 2; CSMK III:25). But an obvious difference nevertheless forbids accord between these texts: in 1630, incomprehensible power alone defines the divine essence intrinsically, while causality only designates creation *ad extra*; on the other hand, in 1641, causality defines the divine essence in the same way as incomprehensible essence: "But if we have previously inquired into the cause of God's existing or continuing to exist, and we attend to the immense and incomprehensible power that is contained within the idea of God."[79] From a divine attribute, causality has become the divine essence.

(b) The comparison with the letters of 1630 underlines another difficulty: if, in 1641, all existence supposed a *causa sive ratio*, is this a matter of a truth created eternally? A positive response is difficult, because it would limit this truth to finite creatures, leaving divine existence with neither founding nor rationality. But a negative response would come down to admitting that God cannot do without sufficient reason, nor without causality, hence that he does not create absolutely freely, nor is absolutely without condition. In short, either Descartes omitted to mention the equivalence between existence and efficient cause among the created truths in 1630, or he has limited divine transcendence by submitting the divine essence to the principle of sufficient reason in 1641. Following this dilemma, the divergence among his successors on univocity and the principle of reason would take its origin in unresolved tension within Descartes himself.[80]

Third result: the purely historical question (the invention of the *causa sui*) does not receive any justification of a response carried to the logical objection (never is the obvious contradiction of the concept alleviated); it solely obeys a properly metaphysical necessity: the need to constitute an onto-theology without exception by beginning with the *causa*, in this way elevated to the rank of *causa sive ratio*. The principle of sufficient reason hence is not instituted by resolving the objections that the case of God brings up, but by ignoring them. In this way it proves its authority of first reason in making any case of other reasons henceforth relative. One must remark also that the second onto-theology (according to the *causa*) is not accomplished absolutely in the Third Meditation, because, as in 1630, causality here remains distinct from the divine essence; one must surmount a further step in the *Replies* for it to be finally identified. And hence, strangely, recognizing God as the supreme being by way of the *causa sui* will demand a longer path and bolder theological polemic than that of conquering the ego as first supreme being according to the *cogitatio sui*, although the inverse would have appeared more normal: is it not self-evident that God would be supremely, is it not disputable that finite being would be first? Nevertheless, the path of thought was a totally different one for Descartes; to that extent it is true that the rules of the constitution of a metaphysical onto-theology have nothing in common with those of the elaboration of a revealed theology.

Fourth result: the *causa sui* not only introduces an ultimate and late proof of the existence of God, in fact, it constructs the first *a priori* proof of the existence of God ever produced in metaphysics, not only Cartesian, but in general. This reversal of the *a posteriori* (proof by ideas, taken as the effects), to the *a priori* (proof by the *ratio sive causa*) signifies not only that the divine essence will henceforth be supposed to be quasi-known, but above all that it will be subjected to a metaphysical principle that precedes it. From that moment on, God enters decidedly and definitively as the "subject" of metaphysics: far from remaining a principle external to it (according to Thomas Aquinas' formula),[81] it finds itself enclosed within it (according to Suárez' thesis)[82] — in the double sense where a principle precedes it and makes it intelligible.

This final conclusion at once invalidates and confirms the hermeneutics of metaphysics according to Heidegger. The confirmation is obvious: the *causa sui* really does enunciate the name that God must take when he enters into metaphysics, because he enters there to submit himself to the universal *a priori* of the *causa sive ratio*, ceasing at the same time to exercise himself as the *a priori* as such. But what invalidates this confirmation appears equally clearly: perhaps God does not enter truly into metaphysics before Descartes seizes him in it, since it is only with the *causa sui* that a different primacy — onto-theological — subjugates nameless and incomprehensible transcendence. But, if this were the case, one would have to revise fundamentally the question of the metaphysical status of all medieval thought: being unaware not only of the principle of sufficient reason, but above all of its application to the essence of God, hence refusing unanimously the concept of the *causa sui*, the medieval thinkers could, at least partially, be removed from the onto-theological constitution of metaphysics and hence from an idolatrous interpretation of God. Without doubt it does not suffice to ignore the terms of a question in order to respond to it victoriously (even for the medievals); but no question (even those of metaphysics) can be posed seriously without relying on precise concepts. It would not be the least paradox of the Cartesian *causa sui* to liberate those that it pretends to surmount definitively.

9

Outline of a History of Definitions of God in the Cartesian Epoch

For Jean-Robert Armogathe

§1. The Horizon

The seventeenth century marks a significant moment in thought concerning the definition of God.[1] This is the period in which the radical position of subjectivity is replaced by the impersonal recognition of transcendence as a point of departure of philosophical reflection — God is now a term in a demonstration, and no longer the assumed goal of a journey toward him. And philosophy, until this time explicitly constituted by metaphysics (*metaphysica, philosophia prima*, then *ontologia*), has to transpose into the new domain of rationality certain problems and concepts previously treated only by revealed theology (*theologia, sacra scientia*). This twofold transformation is nicely illustrated by the problem of the essence of God: from Descartes on, metaphysical discussions of the characteristics and attributes of God consist in transposing and translating, so to speak, into purely philosophical terms theological debates on the divine names as they arise in the Scriptures, through the intermediation of the formulations given of them by Dionysius the Areopagite (fifth century?) in his celebrated treatise *On the Divine Names* (*De divinis nominibus*).[2]

These innovations can best be understood in their context, a set of themes from Thomas Aquinas. Despite the long gap between the thirteenth and the seventeenth centuries, Thomas' views remained decisive for several reasons. The first was the renewal of the "Thomistic" school: notably through the works of Capreolus, Sylvestre de

Ferrare, and especially Cardinal Thomas de Vio, called Cajetan (1469–1534). These Thomists widely influenced university and ecclesiastical life, in particular the work of the Council of Trent (1545–63), whose sessions were presided over by a copy of the *Summa Theologiae* placed upon the altar.[3] Thomistic views were also diffused in the widely circulated works of Jesuit theologians, both those from the *Collegium Romanum*, like Benedictus Pererius (1535–1610), and those from the great Hispanic universities, like Gabriel Vasquez (1551–1604) and Francisco Suárez (1548–1617). Suárez' *Disputationes metaphysicae*, published in 1597, for example, enjoyed a wide and lasting circulation throughout both Protestant and Catholic Europe.[4] As a notable example of the persistence of this Thomistic influence, Descartes, a former student at the Jesuit school of La Flèche, stated that the only books he carried on his travels were the Bible and a *Summa* of Saint Thomas.[5]

Thomas set three conditions on the adequate construction of a denomination of God. (1) In God, but not in creatures, essence is indistinguishable from the fact of his being: "The essence of God is his very being";[6] "His essence is his being."[7] God is therefore defined as a "pure act,"[8] which subsists through itself and as act.[9] (2) Therefore, we cannot become acquainted with this kind of transcendence directly from created beings, in which there is always a real distinction between essence and being. One can ascend to God only by way of five paths [*viae*], whose very multiplicity marks the gap between the creature and the Creator. These five ways reach God as he is understood under a variety of names, as first mover, as first efficient cause, as necessary cause, as the cause of every perfection, and, finally, as the end of all things.[10] But can we reduce these five ways to one? Or, at the very least, can we reconcile with one another the definitions of God at which they arrive without any logical incompatibility? (3) To address these difficulties, Thomas emphatically states that all our knowledge of God (including that obtained through the *viae*) remains analogical:[11] the gap always remains, even when our knowledge is certain; even if we can know what God is not, we cannot know what he is—he who remains to us "profoundly unknown" (*penitus ignotum*).[12] Although Thomistic interpreters continue to disagree, the debate over the precise type of analogy in question here[13] matters less than Thomas' radical agnosticism: because we can become acquainted with God by several paths, each of which is certain, our knowledge of God terminates in inadequate and relative names, names that only allow God to be known as unknown.

Working within these Thomistic themes, seventeenth-century debates over the idea of God were played out within the space of certain questions that are, strictly speaking, theological: Can the divine names be reduced one to another? Can the divine essence be expressed adequately by any one of these names? Yet something new transforms everything: as regards the divine names, everything becomes a question of ideas, concepts, or definitions of God.

§2. The Analogy of Being and the Progression Toward Univocity

Ironically enough, even though the revival of Thomism was important to sixteenth- and seventeenth-century thought, Thomas' theses were often revived in a weakened form, or even in a form that reversed the original meaning altogether. That was the case with the *Disputationes metaphysicae*. In the *Disputationes*, Suárez filled the analogical gap between the finite and the infinite witih a univocal concept of being (*conceptus univocus entis*), sufficient to represent to the human mind any being whatsoever in a confused and indeterminate way. In the dispute concerning the notion of being that inevitably arises between the univocal concept and traditional analogical conceptions of being, Suárez argued: "If we must deny one of the two, we must deny analogy, which is uncertain, rather than the unity of the concept, which seems to be well demonstrated."[14] Consequently, despite Suárez' apparent restoration of Thomas' analogical theology against its denial (by Duns Scotus) and its distortion (by Cajetan), in the end he recognized that "being is very similar to univocal terms."[15] Thus, being applies in the same sense (logically or intrinsically) to both creatures and God: the ontological gap between the finite and the infinite distinguishes God from his creatures less than the conceptual representation of them as beings joins them.

This theoretical reversal, in essence the victory of Duns Scotus over Thomas, had two consequences. (1) God (existence and essence) was said to derive from the univocal concept of being, of which he constitutes only one among other possible instantiations. Since the concept of being is defined primarily in terms of its internal possibility (noncontradiction), God can be the first being only insofar as he is the greatest possibility, the necessary being par excellence: "A being altogether necessary" (*ens omnimodo necessarium*); "a being with absolute necessity, that is, a necessary being" (*esse absoluta necessita seu ens necessarium*).[16] He achieves all perfection allowed by the possible: "It belongs to his essence to include in some way all the perfection that is possible within the whole dimension of being."[17] Thus "the most perfect of all possible beings" (*ens perfectissimum omnium possibilium*)[18] achieves perfection within the scope permitted by the concept of possibility, a concept connected with the univocal concept of being. (2) The knowledge that God can have of finite essences likewise derives from a univocal concept, since these essences are defined within the scope of possibility and a univocal conception of being. Created essences do not *derive* from God as their exemplar (as in Bonaventure and Thomas), but are *seen* by God under some representation. Furthermore, this representation is true not by virtue of a divine exemplar or God's omnipotence, but by virtue of the intrinsic and independent possibility that pertains to a coherent statement, whether it be a question of logic, mathematics, or morality.[19] God therefore does not create essences but only their existences. Statements concerning what is logically possible, statements that ground what we can say about essences, do not depend upon the creative power of God; indeed, they impose themselves upon his understanding: "These statements are not true because they are known by God, but rather they are known because they are true, otherwise one couldn't give any reason why God would necessarily know that they are true."[20] The univocity of the concept of being thus gives rise to a kind of epistemological univocity; representation governs the knowledge God has with respect to possibilities (creatures) as much as it does the knowledge that finite understandings claim with respect to the infinite. To this extent, at least, God's knowledge is like ours. But one question then arises: Does the definition of God as the most perfect being (*ens perfectissimum*), always imply a tendency toward univocity?

§3. God as Mathematician and Univocal Rationality

This progression toward ontological and epistemological univocity in theology is not an isolated phenomenon and corresponds to the demand of contemporary scientists for univocity. Indeed, to legitimate the mathematical treatment of physics (as opposed to the merely hypothetical status Aristotle granted mathematical statements in the natural sciences), seventeenth-century scientists persistently privileged one argument: humans can interpret the physical world in mathematical language because God first conceived the world that was to be created in accordance with mathematical rationality. Although this argument is certainly powerful, it has one controversial consequence: since mathematical statements are perfectly univocal, God understands them in precisely the same way that humans do. In principle, if not always in fact, God determines the world through calculation in exactly the way humans come to understand it through calculation; the mathematical laws that govern the world are understood univocally for God and for us. This consequence is emphasized by three authors in particular.

1. Johannes Kepler (1571–1630) at first wanted to become a theologian, but dedicated himself to astronomy because in it he found an equal opportunity to know and to praise the Creator.[21] He did not hesitate, therefore, to impose mathematical rationality on God himself: "Mathematical reasons were coeternal with God";[22] "The reasons of geometry are coeternal with God."[23] Indeed, Kepler goes so far as to identify mathematical rationality with God: "Before the creation of the world, geometry [being] coeternal with the mind of God, being God himself (for what is there in God that is not God himself?) supplied God with exemplars for the creation of the world."[24] Therefore God created the world exactly as we understand it: through calculation and the construction of figures, in short, "by practicing an eternal geometry,"[25] for "God practiced geometry in creating."[26] Kepler thus returns to a slogan traditionally attributed to Plato, but in sincerely Christian terms and with a strictly epistemological intention: "What more is needed in order to say with Plato that 'God always practices geometry'?"[27] Kepler formulates nothing less than a new definition of God, a new definition that allows him to free mathematics from any restriction in its application to the interpretation of the physical world; indeed, it goes so far as to guarantee for the human mind a knowledge that is "of the same nature as that of God [*eodem genere cum Deo*]."[28] But an inadequate and relative divine name of the sort that appears in Thomas is already no longer at issue; this epistemological univocity in fact implies that we understand God's divinity to the same extent that we understand mathematical possibilities.

2. Galileo Galilei (1564–1642) takes up the same definition of God for the same epistemological reasons. His famous statement that we must consider the book of nature as "written in mathematical language"[29] meets the requirement that we go beyond the hypothetical status that Aristotle had imposed upon mathematics: for what we read mathematically in nature to have physical significance, the

physical world must receive, from the beginning, a mathematical structure. Hence a second view, which forms the grounds of the first, but with an even greater emphasis, is that "the knowledge [of human understanding] equals [*agguagli*] the divine [knowledge] in objective certitude; . . . to make myself better understood, I say that the truth we know through mathematical demonstrations is the same as the truth divine wisdom knows."[30] Galileo does not affirm the connections between God and mathematics as often as Kepler does, to be sure. However, that is not because of any timidity, but, on the contrary, because of a serene assurance with respect to an already established and indisputable thesis; it is no longer a question of demonstrating it, but rather of exploiting all of its consequences. Nevertheless, the boldness of such an equality between human understanding and divine wisdom might well threaten the creator's omnipotence; one presumes that this played some role in the accusations made against Galileo in his second trial.[31]

3. Marin Mersenne (1588–1648) should not be ignored in this context. A friend of Descartes and the translator of the *Méchaniques de Galilée* (1634), he continually invoked the identity of mathematics and divine understanding, both in his scientific work and in his apologetic writings. Indeed, even atheists must admit mathematical certitude; 2 and 2 makes 4 for both Don Juan and the Prince of Nassau. Now, as Plato held, mathematics constitutes the language and activity of God himself. And so Mersenne argues, "We can raise geometry as an objection [to the atheists], provided that they simply listen to Plato, who discovered God through this science, for he said that . . . God always practices geometry."[32] Furthermore, Mersenne held that the "eternal ideas"[33] of God are to be identified with mathematical statements considered as "the first exemplar and prototype of his reasoning,"[34] to such an extent that eternal truths are "not dependent on anything else and [are] God himself."[35] Thus Mersenne transforms the traditional theological thesis that the divine ideas in the end vanish into the divine essence (as in Augustine, Bonaventure, and Thomas) by identifying God's omnipotence with respect to creation with the requirements of mathematical rationality; mathematical rationality is held to be the only possible and thinkable kind of rationality. In this way divine omnipotence is subordinated to mathematics.

The scientist's univocity of knowing combines with the univocity of being, as held by theologians like Suárez, to constitute an anthropomorphism all the more attractive insofar as it supports, all at the same time, the progress of science, a reasonable apologetic, and a metaphysical account of possibility. Such a view was common even to some who were unsympathetic to mathematics or scholastic theology. Francis Bacon (1561–1626), hardly a mathematician, held that "after the word of God, natural philosophy is the most certain remedy against superstition and the best food for faith. And so one properly sees in it the most faithful and esteemed servant of religion, since the one reveals the will of God, and the other His power."[36] And Pierre Gassendi (1592–1655), no friend of scholasticism, wrote in support of a Suárezian position on univocity: "Is there thus a possibility for abstracting some concept which would be superior to God? And why not, since no one denies that the concept of being is superior to God [*conceptum entis esse Deo superiorem*]."[37]

§4. Transcendence and Unknowability

Widespread as it was, not all seventeenth-century thinkers shared this tendency toward univocity with respect to the question of God. Counterbalancing the trend toward univocity is an exactly contrary orientation, strange but powerful: an insistence upon the radically unknowable transcendence of the divine essence. There were a number of convergent symptoms of this movement, including: (1) the translation of the works of Dionysius the Areopagite, published by Dom J. Goulu (Jean de Saint-François) in Paris in 1608, whose unquestioned success was certainly not due to the quality of the translation; (2) the circulation throughout all of Europe of the writings of John of the Cross (published in Alcalà in 1618), and translated by Father Cyprien de la Nativité;[38] (3) the installation of the Carmelite order in France (Dijon, Poitiers, etc.) by Bérulle; (4) the influence of Madame Acarie's circle; (5) the development of nihilistic [*néantiste*] mysticism under the influence of the Rhenish-Flemish masters (Ruysbroeck, Tauler, Dionysius Carthusianus [Denys le Chartreux], Harphius, etc.); (6) the appropriately named "devout party" in France, whose growing political influence clashed with that of Richelieu, despite the fact that the famous "Gray Eminence" who advised the cardinal, Father Joseph du Tremblay (Joseph of Paris), had at first published several remarkable works of spirituality.[39] There are three decisive figures in this deep, complex, and lasting movement.

1. The most powerful theoretician was no doubt Benoît de Canfeld (1562–1610), whose *Règle de perfection* would leave a strong mark on the age. In it, God is defined by the very impossibility of being defined. Indeed, before God's infinity, the creature must recognize

itself not only as finite, but also as so immeasurably surpassed that its finitude amounts to a pure and simple nothingness; the absence of all proportion between the finite and the infinite reduces the finite to nothing: "Reason tells us that we can only be nothing (compared with the independent being of God) since God is infinite: for if we were something, God would not be infinite; for in that case his being would end where ours began."[40] Insofar as a creature is nothing [néant] before God and acknowledges its "annihilation" [anéantissement], it can only know God through the very characteristics that prevent it from conceiving him: "No speculation by the understanding can apprehend God; but the love that the will offers does. Speculation conceives of God, who is omnipotent, immense, infinite and incomprehensible, in proportion to its own small, weak capacity, while the will, on the contrary, proportions itself to God, enlarging itself in accordance with his immensity, infinity and omnipotence."[41] The will alone can still reach God, since God, beyond every concept and beyond all measure, reveals himself only as a pure Will, in which his entire essence is summed up: "This Essential will is purely spirit and life, totally abstract, purified (of itself) and stripped of all forms and images of created things, bodily or spiritual, temporal or eternal; it is apprehended neither by man's sense nor by his judgment, nor by human reason; but it is outside all human capacity and beyond all human understanding, for it is nothing other than God himself."[42] This is no half-hearted voluntarism; Benoît de Canfeld has rediscovered the Dionysian and patristic "way of eminence," which goes beyond affirmations and negations and reaches God only through the love that the will offers. In this view the names of God can and should all be successively asserted and denied of God, and, in a tension that is never suppressed, they are attributed to God, but as things that we cannot really say of him.[43] When in his treatise *Quinquaginta nomina Dei* (Brussels, 1640) the Jesuit L. Lessius chose infinity as the first name of God, he was following the same tradition.[44]

2. Although less powerful as a thinker, Cardinal Pierre de Bérulle was more accessible, and he was most responsible for popularizing this standpoint, along with its aporias. In his *Discours de l'état et des grandeurs de Jésus Christ* (Paris, 1623) and in the *Opuscules* that complete it, he emphasizes three features of the idea of God. First, following the Thomistic doctrine, Bérulle holds that in God, "his existence is his own essence."[45] Second, following Dionysius the Areopagite, he holds that God's being is, nevertheless, subordinated to his unity: "Unity is the first property that the philosophers attribute to created

being: it is the first perfection that Christians recognize and adore in uncreated being. . . . And the Platonists . . ., the theologians among the philosophers . . . dare to say . . . that God has unity and not being; since the unity, according to their lofty intelligence, is something primary and superior to being."[46] It follows that when he goes beyond being, God also goes beyond logical representation and the realm of possibility. Third, Bérulle is above all inclined to call God infinite: "the infinite being of their [the persons of the Trinity] common essence," "the infinite being of God." And from infinity, incomprehensibility clearly follows for Bérulle.[47] A similar position can be found in the most important Oratorians, Bourgoing (1585–1662), Condren (1588–1641), and Gibieuf (1583–1650).[48]

3. Saint François de Sales (1562–1622) certainly had reservations about this nihilistic mysticism, from which he was separated by his "devout humanism" and Christocentrism. But nonetheless, like Bérulle, he belongs to the Dionysian movement. His fundamental work, the *Traité de l'amour de Dieu*, quite clearly denies that a single name might ever define God: "In order to speak of God in any way at all, we are forced to make use of many names."[49] According to de Sales, one must clearly and immediately recognize God's incomprehensibility, since it flows from an essential infinity, which overdetermines and modifies his other attributes, all the more because it is added to them. Every attribute becomes infinite, and precisely because of this, it loses any claim to univocity: "The Divinity is an incomprehensible abyss of all perfection, infinite in excellence and infinitely sovereign in goodness. . . . O infinite Divinity, O divine Infinity . . . the impotence of this desire comes from the infinite infinity of your perfection, which surpasses any wish and any thought."[50] Infinity thus indicates the incomprehensibility—the "incomprehensible goodness"[51]—in each of the perfections commonly attributed to God: "infinite goodness," "infinite charity," "infinite good will," "infinite good," and so on.[52] Such incomprehensible infinity remains accessible only to love; any attempt to grasp it through other means, through conceptual knowledge in particular, will fail.

Philosophical debate in the seventeenth century would retain several elements from this spiritual movement: the claim that the divine essence is absolutely transcendent, against all claims of univocity, ontological or epistemological—God as incomprehensible; the rational justification of this incomprehensibility by the incommensurable disproportion between God and creature—God as infinite; and the abandonment of all attempts to represent or comprehend God through the understanding, hence the frequent appeal to the will, either love in us, or "essential will" and omnipotence in God.

§5. Descartes: Creation of the Eternal Truths

In three famous letters to Father Mersenne from 1630, Descartes responds clearly with force and originality to the dilemmas posed by the two dominant trends of his time. He first rejects the epistemological univocity of the scientists: "The mathematical truths that you [Mersenne and those like him] call eternal were established by God and depend entirely upon him. To say that these truths are independent of God is in effect to speak of him as a Jupiter or a Saturn, and to subjugate him to Styx and the Fates."[53] Henceforth, 2 plus 2 makes 4 and the radii of a circle are equal only by virtue of a decision God made. Thus God does not reveal his own understanding and rationality through mathematics, which he transcends by virtue of creating it. Next Descartes denies the thesis of ontological univocity, reversing Suárez' doctrine almost word for word: "As for the eternal truths, I say once again that they are only true or possible because God conceived them as true or possible. They are not known as true by God in any way which would imply that they are true independently of him. And if men indeed understood the meaning of their words, they could never say without blasphemy that the truth of something precedes God's knowledge of it, for in God to will and to know are but one."[54]

In this way Descartes the philosopher sets himself against the "blasphemy" of the theologians: logical truths and essences do not preexist eternally in God's understanding, before entering into temporal existence through an act of his will. God's understanding is not a (passive) realm of possibilities; rather, it merges with the will in one single, global act of creation. From this follows a radical consequence: God "is the author as much of the essence as of the existence of creatures."[55] God creates all finite rationality, and in creating it, he stands above it; such transcendent rationality (if it can be so called) cannot be characterized in terms of representation, logical possibility, or calculation. But if that is the case, can we name God at all?

Despite the evident difficulties, Descartes puts forward a name for God in 1630: "incomprehensible power," a formula found also in the *Meditations* of 1641, where Descartes calls God "immense and incomprehensible power."[56] This phrase is to be understood quite literally. First, God is incomprehensible because he acts before any rationality determines or delimits his actions; therefore, from the point of view of our minds, finite and endowed with a limited rationality, the God who creates them remains inaccessible in a sense, even if he is known in another, weaker sense.[57] And second, God is a power, because in the absence of any common rationality and of any analogy of being between the finite and the infinite, only a relation of power remains: even if the understanding does not comprehend it, we are acquainted with that power. In short, as "an infinite and incomprehensible being," God is known only as "a cause whose power surpasses the limits of human understanding."[58] This radical doctrine shapes the debate later in the century; its importance (not to mention its difficulties) cannot be overestimated.[59] This radical and original doctrine clearly reflected the spiritual current and strongly reaffirmed the transcendence and unknowability of God discussed in §4. But in transposing these themes into his metaphysics, Descartes, in fact, finds himself as isolated from the scholastic theologians and philosophers as he is from the scientists.

As original as this doctrine may be, others held similar views. Michel de Montaigne (1533–1592) also recognized God as "an incomprehensible power" and as a "first cause."[60] He therefore consistently held that it is "presumptuous" to reduce the divine power to our understanding, to submit it to the Fates, and to claim "that human reason is in general control of all that is inside and outside the vault of heaven."[61] What is often taken to be a simple skepticism or agnosticism derives primarily from a scrupulous respect for the transcendence of God.

Bérulle, too, agreed with Descartes in defining God in terms of independence: "Just as it is characteristic of and essential to divine and uncreated being to be independent, so is it characteristic of and essential to every created being to be needful of, adhering to, and dependent on its God, its principle, and its origin."[62] A follower of Montaigne, Pierre Charron (1541–1603) anticipated certain Cartesian formulas almost word for word: "belief in a God who is author of all things,"[63] "God primarily sovereign, and absolute Lord and master of the world," "God Himself, or rather the first, original and fundamental law, which is God and the nature of the world, like the King and the law in a state."[64] Among the heirs of Descartes, one of the rare defenders of the creation of eternal truths was Dom Robert Desgabets (1610–78), particularly in his *Traité de l'indéfectabilité des créatures*. There he reaffirms the epistemological transcendence of

God: "It belongs to the nature of the infinite that it cannot be comprehended by a finite understanding; it is always unreasonable to refuse God certain things that should be attributed to Him, under the pretext that that surpasses our knowledge." But Desgabets also defends God's ontological transcendence: "God is the principle of all created things, with respect to both essence and existence."[65]

The Cartesian conception of God as "incomprehensible power" did find some support in 1630. But it was opposed to the dominant trends of contemporary epistemology and theology. Furthermore, the position was not without some pronounced difficulties. It is not surprising, then, that in his first publication, the *Discourse on Method* of 1637, Descartes himself passes over the "incomprehensible power" of God in silence; perhaps he still needed to think it through systematically.[66]

§6. Descartes: The Three Metaphysical Definitions of God

The doctrine of 1630 gave rise to one obvious question: Does the transcendence of an "incomprehensible power" allow one to justify, or even make use of reason? One of the major objectives of the *Meditationes de prima philosophia* (Paris, 1641; Amsterdam, 1642) was to address this problem. The *Meditations* was intended to ground the certainty of the mathematical and empirical sciences. But this goal does not exclude consideration of the nature and existence of God; indeed, the demonstration that God exists (along with the ego) was to become the principal goal of what would later be called the "special metaphysics" (*metaphysica specialis*).

Descartes begins in the First Meditation with an idea of God, "a certain long-standing opinion that there is an omnipotent God."[67] This common and prephilosophical conception of God is the point of departure for Descartes' project; it will be transposed into his metaphysics and given stricter treatment there. On this basis Descartes proposes three ways for demonstrating the existence of God: (1) the so-called *a posteriori* argument, wherein God is considered the cause of his idea in me (Third Meditation, in two formulations); (2) the so-called *a priori* argument, which deduces God's existence from the very idea of the divine essence (the so-called ontological argument, Fifth Meditation); and (3) the argument from the principle of (sufficient) reason, which finds the cause of God in God himself, henceforth named *causa sui* (cause of himself) (First and Fourth Replies). These three demonstrations are examined here not for their logical validity, but for the different conceptions of the essence (and there-fore the idea) of God that they advance, and for their compatibility.

1. The *a posteriori* proof relies on the idea of an infinite substance (*substantis quaedam infinita, Deus infinitus*), indisputably given to an ego. Descartes takes it to be beyond question that we all have such an idea.[68] Insofar as we have such an idea, we are capable of perceiv-ing "the infinite" (*perceptio infiniti*), "the actually infinite" (*actu infini-tum*), "the infinite nature" (*natura infinita*). Indeed, Descartes claims that our perception of the finite is a limitation of the infinite, just as a horizon renders visible that which stands out against its back-ground, and thus, he claims, the perception of the finite presupposes that we have such an idea. The *a posteriori* proof also presupposes that the fact that we have such an idea of the infinite requires a cause, a cause that bears "even upon ideas, in which only objective reality is considered."[69] (This implies a perhaps questionable enlargement of the domain of causality, insofar as God is represented as the cause of his own idea in the ego.) But we still need one last condition for this argument, a condition that many will deny: the finite ego must ac-knowledge that it cannot cause the idea of infinity in itself.[70] For Des-cartes this acknowledgment is self-evident because it follows from the most characteristic property of infinity, its incomprehensibility. Straightaway in the *Meditations*, Descartes recognizes God as incom-prehensible and infinite, as a nature that is "immense, incomprehen-sible, and infinite" (*immensa, incomprehensibilis, et infinita*), as he had since 1630.[71] The basis of Descartes' view here is quite clear. Infinity is excepted from all measure; but through method, understood in the sense of the *mathesis universalis*, we can only learn what can be mea-sured. God therefore becomes unreachable through the method, that is, incomprehensible to objective science.[72] Thus in the first proof for the existence of God in the *Meditations*, Descartes remains strictly consistent with his thesis from 1630.[73] The denomination of God by the idea of infinity, although the clearest and truest idea,[74] neverthe-less escapes all finite representations (as well as all finite causes). Thus the old *via negativa* of theology repeats itself within the domain of Descartes' philosophy.

2. The *a priori* proof relies on the idea of a divine essence that en-compasses all perfections, including existence. This proof, apparently borrowed from Anselm, was criticized by Kant under the name of the "ontological argument." But our concern here is to determine the definition of God that it implies. For the idea of a perfect being (*idea entis perfectissimi*) presupposes that God is identified as the supremely

perfect being (*summe perfectum*).[75] On the one hand, God carries to perfection every quality finite beings possess imperfectly; on the other hand, he embodies in himself, without limit, all possible perfections, diverse as they may be. Thus Descartes does not hesitate to define God as "the aggregation of perfections."[76] This raises two questions. (1) If God is limited to perfecting properties that are already achieved, though imperfectly, in finite beings, does he not remain continuous with them? Does the incommensurable gap between finite and infinite remain intact if God simply accumulates and completes what the finite already possesses? (2) The *a priori* proof claims to deduce the existence of God from his essence "neither more" "nor less" certainly than the sum of the angles of a triangle are deduced from its definition.[77] Does this equivalence not contradict the transcendence of the idea of God with relation to the ideas of the objects of method? Does it not also contradict the original aim of "demonstrating the metaphysical truths in a manner that is clearer than the demonstrations of geometry?"[78] This second conception of God's essence would then be in opposition to the first insofar as it remains within the domain of method (as the geometrical analogy suggests) and denies the complete incomprehensibility of the infinite. In this way it constitutes a return to the affirmative path in theology.

3. The last proof relies on the principle, which Descartes thinks is manifest through natural light and therefore exempt from the order of reasons, that there must be at least as much being in the cause as in the effect.[79] When Descartes moves from the Third Meditation to the First, Second, and Fourth Replies, this principle is made more radical and characterized as a dictate (*dictat*) of reason: "The light of nature dictates that if anything exists we may always ask why it exists; that is, we may inquire into its efficient cause, or, if it does not have one, we may demand why it does not need one."[80] The necessity of having a cause or reason (*causa sive ratio*) allows no exception, since it applies "to God himself."[81] With God, there can be no question of an external cause (God would lose his divinity); so there must be an internal cause. Descartes' view is that God's very essence is the (quasi-)efficient cause of his existence. Far from claiming that God has no cause (the negative sense in which the medieval thinkers characterized God as being "*a se*"), Descartes argues that God in himself is a genuine cause of himself (*causa sui*); God's essence, interpreted at first as an "overabundant power,"[82] ends up playing the role of an efficient cause, though in a somewhat tangential sense. This conception of God as *causa sui* gives rise to three questions. First, Descartes

here establishes the existence of God only by submitting his essence to a principle—soon after called the principle of sufficient reason—that precedes both God's essence and his existence; this third conception of God's essence therefore contradicts the first insofar as it imposes a precondition as to what is possible and what is not upon the supposedly transcendent God. Second, nevertheless, the conception of the divine essence as "overabundant power" still preserves God's infinity: "infinite power" reduces to the "immense and incomprehensible power," which corresponds literally to the definition of the creator of eternal truths from 1630.[83] On this point, therefore, the third conception of God is in agreement with the first (infinity), but in opposition to the second (the aggregate of perfections). In this way it is in accord with the so-called way of eminence. Third, it belongs to Descartes (and not to Spinoza) to have first named God *causa sui;* besides its logical difficulties that are never resolved, this concept carries a profound indecision: is it a matter of a "divine name," or rather of the "metaphysical concept of God" *par excellence*, the one which onto-theo-logy imposes? According to this hypothesis, does the *causa sui* not fix the metaphysical idol *par excellence*, such that it would make possible the "death of God"?[84]

The three conceptions of God Descartes offers in his metaphysics do not mesh with one another; indeed, they seem contradictory for the most part. This apparent inconsistency does not amount to a failure, however. Rather, it attests to the fact that God cannot adequately be conceived within the limited discourse of metaphysics. Descartes here boldly and explicitly confronts the tension between the demand for a conception of God that is intelligible to humans and respect for his transcendence. The fact that Descartes' metaphysical theology remains indeterminate (white) and breaks down into several theses (just as light breaks down when it passes through a prism) makes it, somewhat paradoxically, *the* radical position on the question of God at the beginning of modern thought.[85] This plurality of conceptions of God's essence made it difficult for Descartes' successors, at least up until Berkeley, to decide whether to follow Descartes or to criticize him.

§7. The Indecision of the Cartesian School

Strictly speaking, it is incorrect to talk of a "Cartesian school." Even during Descartes' lifetime, some of his most public disciples (Regius, for example) distanced themselves from him, and there was no single set of doctrines to which one had to subscribe to be a member of the Cartesian school of thought. Nevertheless, after his death, several claimed to follow in his path and took up the defense of his doctrine. Three of these followers in particular demonstrate the tension between Descartes' three conceptions of God's essence: Louis de la Forge, Johann Clauberg, and Dom Robert Desgabets.

(a) Claiming to be a spokesman for Descartes, Louis de La Forge (1632–66) annotated and published *L'homme* and then added his own *Traité de l'esprit de l'homme*, in which he employs the three Cartesian conceptions of God.[86] At times he refers to "the infinite and sovereign spirit," which enables him to attach "the idea that we have of an infinite spirit to this name, God."[87] But then the idea that God is defined as the "most perfect being" (*ens summe perfectum*) (one of whose consequences is God's infinitude) challenges this conception of God defined as infinite: "As for the divine nature, all that we know of it, without the aid of Revelation, is founded upon that great and sublime notion of a very perfect being, whence it follows that it is very simple, necessary, infinite, all-knowing, the first and principal cause of all other beings."[88] La Forge nevertheless adheres to the doctrine of 1630, the creation of the eternal truths: "[God] is the first of all beings, upon which all things depend, both for their essence and for their existence; he is their principal and in some way total cause, the cause which makes them be and be what they are. Thus they are good and true only because he willed, understood, and produced them so. . . . In him there is only a single action which is entirely simple and entirely pure . . . because in God to see and to will [*videre et velle*] are but one thing."[89] However, La Forge's meditation on the creation of eternal truths concentrates almost exclusively on causality, to the detriment of incomprehensibility, in order to prepare the reader for his argument for occasionalism; his account of Descartes' third conception of God (*causa sui*) is concerned with the externally directed causality of creation, and neglects the internal *causa sui*. As La Forge treats it, the "infinite power of God" mainly concerns the "total and proximate cause" at issue in the correspondence between thought and motion; his God is defined as "the first universal, and total cause of motion." In short, "infinite power" creates but is no longer exercised over divine existence.[90]

(b) Johann Clauberg (1622–65) defends Descartes' metaphysical cause with fidelity and intelligence; his equivocations are thus all the more significant.[91] Clauberg begins by reviewing the three traditional theological paths to God, but only in order to dispose of them. The ways of eminence and negation concern only perfection: either the perfection of the Creator or the imperfection of his creatures. From the perspective of the affirmative way, only causality remains.[92] Thus only two of the three Cartesian conceptions remain operative here: perfection and causality. Either God is given as pure act (*actus purus*), "the cause of created things not only with respect to their becoming (*secundum fieri*) but also with respect to their being (*secundum esse*),"[93] or else he is called *ens summe perfectum* or *ens perfectissimum*.[94] As to infinity, it is explicitly reduced to a particular case of perfection: "The idea of an infinite substance, that is, the idea of His substance, which possesses absolutely all thinkable perfections in the most perfect way."[95] Or rather, since "the name 'perfection' . . . is taken to include the contents . . . of all of the attributes,"[96] "infinity" would seem to become the equivalent of any attribute whatsoever. Thus there is at least one exception to Clauberg's Cartesian orthodoxy insofar as in his thought the idea of infinity loses its priority over the other conceptions of the divine essence. This starts a trend that will soon become more general.

(c) Dom Robert Desgabets constitutes a notable exception to this trend. Unlike La Forge and Clauberg, he maintains a strict balance between the three Cartesian conceptions, no doubt because he always privileges the doctrine of the creation of the eternal truths, as earlier noted. God is first defined as the "cause of all existing things, in whatever manner they exist," as their "only cause" and their "only and immediate cause."[97] But in this context, that causality is never reflected back on the existence of God himself; though God is characterized as cause, he is not explicitly characterized as *causa sui*. (It should be remembered, however, when dealing with this Cartesian denomination of God, it is not only a matter of "*causa sui*" taken literally but the interpretation of the essence of God in terms of causality, of which the "*causa sui*" only represents the extreme case.) It remains to determine God in himself. Sometimes Desgabets characterizes him as "a supremely perfect essence, in a word . . . the supreme perfection and reality."[98] But this title remains rare, and does not prevent Desgabets from characterizing God in terms of infinity: "that infinite thing, which is God, exists"; reciprocally, "God . . . by rights has the quality of infinity."[99] Despite having carefully balanced his account, Desgabets is unable to reconcile the three conceptions of the divine essence any better than Descartes does; he simply reproduces Descartes' irresolution.

§8. Metaphysical Attempts at a Unification of the Divine Names

Can the multiplicity of conceptions of the divine essence (divine names), left problematic by Descartes, be reduced to one? To succeed here, one must take a stand against Descartes, and only the greatest thinkers in the seventeenth century risked this. But can such a unification avoid impoverishing the notion of God?

(a) Baruch Spinoza is generally credited with revolutionizing the definition of God. But Spinoza's innovation is probably not as radical as it at first appears. Although Spinoza identified God with nature, his famous formula "God or Nature" (*Deus sive Natura*) in fact appears only rarely in the *Ethics* and never in part 1, which is dedicated to God.[100] Furthermore, Spinoza nowhere elaborates on the phrase or gives it any special attention, especially if we keep in mind here that the distinction between "*natura naturans*" (in fact, God himself) and "*natura naturata*" (in fact, nature in the strict sense) goes back at least to Thomas Aquinas; the provocative novelty of this formula stems less from Spinoza himself than from its later usages.[101] Furthermore, there is nothing novel about the formula that defines God as *causa sui*. The phrase certainly is defined ("that whose essence involves existence"), but here all that Spinoza does is equate these two quite different concepts without any justification; he in no way addresses the obvious logical contradiction in the notion of a *cause of self*.[102] Spinoza has an excellent reason not to enter into this debate: he admits that he is simply appealing to a notion widely known and elaborated previously by others: "If something exists in itself [*in se*], or, *as commonly said*, is a cause of itself [*causa sui*], then it should be understood through its essence alone."[103] From Spinoza's point of view, we are dealing here with a Cartesian concept, assumed to be established and usable without any special precautions.

Therefore, Spinoza added nothing new to the Cartesian conceptions of the divine essence.[104] Indeed, one text seems to imply that he simply juxtaposed Descartes' three conceptions without choosing among them. In proving that "God . . . exists," in *Ethics* 1, prop. 11, Spinoza presents at least three demonstrations, along with a commentary. This profusion of proof and explanation, otherwise rare in the *Ethics*, is difficult to explain if we consider only the geometrical order of the *Ethics*, but it is easily understood if we consider Descartes. The first demonstration relies on the principle that existence is contained in God's essence. Now, this principle arises in the *a priori* demonstration of the Fifth Meditation. Moreover, in prop. 11 Spinoza also evokes, regarding the supreme perfection of God, the conception of God that underlies the same Cartesian argument.[105] The second demonstration relies on the principle of reason ("For every thing there must be assigned some cause or reason [*causa seu ratio*] for either why it exists, or why it does not") to verify that no *causa sive ratio* can prohibit the divine essence from existing. It is, indeed, curious that Spinoza does not mention here the *causa sui*, connected with the principle of reason in Descartes' version of the argument.[106] Nevertheless, it is clear that Spinoza is rehearsing the argument from Descartes' First and Fourth Replies. The third demonstration relies explicitly on the *ens absolute infinitum* and proceeds *a posteriori*, as noted in the scholium (which, strangely enough, then attempts an *a priori* reformulation of the proof from the idea of infinity). Here, then, Spinoza is repeating the Cartesian demonstration from the Third Meditation. Hence he arrives at a somewhat paradoxical conclusion: Spinoza, even more so than Descartes, juxtaposes—without choosing among them—the three metaphysical conceptions of the divine essence; indeed, he goes so far as to merge them into a single statement: "God is absolutely infinite. . . . that is, . . . the nature of God enjoys infinite perfection, accompanied . . . by the idea of Himself, i.e., . . . by the idea of his cause."[107] It seems highly unlikely that such a juxtaposition of infinity, perfection, and cause of self could be justified theoretically. At least, Spinoza never undertook to show their consistency, hiding under the cloak of a deductive system the heterogeneity that Descartes himself did not conceal.

(b) Nicolas Malebranche, on the other hand, did choose among the Cartesian conceptions of God, but it was an extremely difficult and laborious decision, made in several stages. Following Exodus 3:14, Malebranche calls God "He who is." But he immediately adds a gloss that is not very biblical: "the unrestricted being, in a word, *Being*, is the idea of God."[108] The shift from "He who is" to "Being" leads him to define God as "the universal Being [that] contains all beings in itself in an intelligible manner," or rather, that which "is all being."[109] Malebranche must go to this extreme in order to explain how we might see in God not only God himself (in the sense of the Augustinian vision in God), but also "intelligible extension, numbers, infinity, in a word, all the immutable natures that God contains in the immensity of his divine substance."[110] But, in defining God in this way as "universal being, without particular restriction, being in general,"[111] Malebranche opens himself to charges of Spinozism.[112] This difficulty, which Malebranche never resolves, is in fact overshadowed by two other conceptual choices he makes. "Being without restriction," which is suggestive of Spinoza's conception of God, tends little by little to give way to a conception of God as "the vast and immense idea of infinitely perfect Being."[113] Here infinity is lowered to the rank of a simple adverb of perfection in act, that is, the sum of perfections. Thus the Cartesian transcendence of infinity, first reduced to being, then made indeterminate ("Being without restriction"), is finally dissolved into the *summe perfectum*, which itself has become a simple receptacle for the intelligible world (ideas, truths, essences), understood univocally. Even the priority that Malebranche sometimes grants the *a posteriori* proof from infinity should not mislead us: in the end Malebranche weakens it to a proof by intuition, a proof that derives from a vision of the perfect.[114]

In this way, Malebranche does privilege perfection over infinity in characterizing God. But he does not ignore Descartes' third characterization of God in terms of causality. Malebranche's occasionalism requires him to place all actual causality in God, and hence imposes on him, besides the title of *ens summe perfectum*, that of the ultimate and omnipotent cause: "It is not sufficient to consider the infinitely perfect Being without relation to us. On the contrary, one must above all realize that we depend on the power of God."[115] This further distances Malebranche from Spinozism, insofar as his occasionalism would seem to require a transcendent God. But Malebranche's view conceals a radical opposition between wisdom (and hence the love of order) and power (love of the efficient cause). Malebranche asserts that "there are not at all two divinities, Reason and power: that the Omnipotent is essentially Reason, and universal Reason is omnipotence."[116] But this is only to join, without argument, radically different conceptions of God into one. In short, the heterogeneity of the Cartesian conception of God remains.

(c) G. W. Leibniz does not attempt to mask the duality at which Malebranche arrives; indeed, he embraces it. According to Leibniz, there is a preestablished harmony "between God considered as Architect of the Machine of the universe, and God considered as Monarch of the divine City of Spirits."[117] But this harmony is needed precisely because these two distinct kingdoms (nature and grace), hence two different divine causalities (efficient and final), and two different rationalities (mechanical and active), are in fact irreducibly separated. That is why Leibniz recognizes two distinct conceptions of the divine essence; Leibniz' God is both the *ens perfectissimum* or an "infinitely perfect God,"[118] and the "cause of causes" or the "ultimate reason for things."[119] These are not distinguished as mere modalities of the divine essence, but as definitions necessarily inferred from one or the other of Leibniz' "two great principles." (1) Leibniz' first principle is the principle "of contradiction, by virtue of which we judge that that which contains [a contradiction] is false, and that that which is opposed or contradictory to the false is true." This principle presupposes a realm of possibles, whose reality must be grounded in God: "God's understanding is the region of the eternal truths . . . and . . . without him there would be nothing real in possibilities, not only nothing that exists, but nothing even possible."[120] But since Suárez, this aspect of God has been identified with his perfection.[121] God's perfection thus becomes the ground of possibility, hence the foundation of the principle of noncontradiction. In Leibniz' view, the principle of noncontradiction must be applicable to God as well. He therefore rejects—following Spinoza, Malebranche, and many others—the Cartesian doctrine of the creation of the eternal truths.[122] (2) The "great principle . . . that holds that nothing is done without sufficient reason" allows one to "rise to Metaphysics."[123] This principle of sufficient reason presupposes that the causal relation is primary and of universal validity. Because it demands, in the end, "a necessary Being, bearing the reason for its existence within itself,"[124] it leads to a definition of God as the ultimate *causa sive ratio*.

Leibniz thus adopts Malebranche's two conceptions of God and sets them out systematically. But despite his debt to Malebranche, Leibniz makes a decisive step: he offers a justification for this duality in terms of the irreducible duality of the principles of metaphysics; neither the exclusively metaphysical status of the divine names nor their submission to metaphysics ever appeared so clearly.

§9. The Privileging of Causality

We have been following the Cartesian strain in the development of the conception of God.[125] But at the same time, and not unconnected with that Cartesian thematic and its conflicting developments, there is a strong and constant trend toward defining the divine essence in terms of causality among certain other philosophers of the seventeenth century.

(a) Thomas Hobbes, for one, still divides the attributes of God into three classes, but none is any longer intended to make a definite assertion about the nature of God. He writes, "He that will attribute to God, nothing but what is warranted by naturall Reason, must either use such Negative Attributes as *Infinite, Eternal, Incomprehensible*; or Superlatives, as *Most High, most Great*, and the like; or Indefinite, as *Good, Just, Holy, Creator*."[126] The substitution of such indefinite names for affirmative assertions about God destroys the conditions necessary for any analogy whatsoever, either an analogy of names or an analogy of being; the incomprehensibility of the infinity of God becomes in Hobbes a purely negative claim, unbalanced by any positive assertions about him. Hobbes continues: "Whatsoever we imagine, is Finite. Therefore there is no Idea, or conception of any thing we call Infinite. No man can have in his mind an Image of infinite magnitude; nor conceive infinite swiftness, infinite time, or infinite force, or infinite power. When we say any thing is infinite, we signifie onely, that we are not able to conceive the ends, and bounds of the thing named; having no Conception of the thing, but of our inability. And therefore the name of God is used, not to make us conceive Him; (for He is *Incomprehensible*; and his greatness and power are unconceivable;) but that we may honor Him."[127] Consequently, no attribute (name) agrees categorically with God except existence itself, a pure and simple fact without any reason other than itself: "That we may know what worship of God is taught us by the light of Nature, I will begin with his Attributes. Where, First, it is manifest, we ought to attribute to Him Existence: For no man can have the will to honour that, which he thinks not to have any Beeing. . . . For there is but one Name to signifie our Conception of his Nature, and that is, I AM."[128] Despite the appeal to Exodus 3:14, Hobbes does not have a conception of the divine *esse* like the one Thomas advanced, a conception of God as pure act, that which subsists through itself and as act; on the contrary the biblical formula serves to avoid such a conception. Indeed, Hobbes uses only the simplest and most certain argument possible to show that God exists; God is simply posited as cause of the existence of the world. Hobbes writes: "Curiosity, or love of the knowledge of causes, draws a man from consideration of the effect, to seek the cause; and again, the cause of that cause; till of necessity he must come to this thought at last, that there is some cause, whereof there is no former cause, but is eternall: which is it men call God [the] one First Mover; that is, a First, and an Eternall cause of all things; which is that which men mean by the name of God."[129] But Hobbes has nothing of interest to say about the conception of efficient causality on which this argument depends. Perhaps this is less a theoretical argument than a simple account of the beliefs of common people; and in fact, Hobbes often gives the impression of not choosing between a proof in the strict sense, and a sociological description of common belief. But even this indecision is a doctrinal position. It is often argued that Hobbes' talk of God is not to be taken seriously and that Hobbes is really an atheist in disguise. But the ambiguity of Hobbes' theology, often denounced and rightly so,[130] is due less to hidden intentions, or literary ruses, than to the very concept of cause, which Hobbes gives a theological function inversely proportional to the theoretical elaboration he offers. Although he does not put it this way, Hobbes' philosophy actually poses a crucial question: Does the notion of an efficient cause allow one to reach the existence of God? And can the concept of cause be applied univocally both to finite beings and to God, any more than any other concept can? By reducing natural theology to causality and by sacrificing infinity (and even perfection), Hobbes opens a wide path that many will follow. But in this way he exposes metaphysical discourse on God to the danger of collapse, when Hume undermines causality itself.

(b) Although John Locke was opposed to Hobbes' political philosophy, he did follow him in emphasizing causality in his characterization of God. When discussing the idea we have of God, Locke suggests that he is a being that contains all perfections to an infinite degree. But although his view of God may resemble Descartes' in this way, it is at root quite different. Unlike Descartes, Locke is clearly denying that such an idea of God or infinity is innate in us.[131] Rather, he argues, the idea of God is a complex idea, made by us from the same ideas of sensation and reflection that give us our idea of self. Locke writes: "For if we examine the *Idea* we have of the incomprehensible supreme Being, we shall find, that . . . the complex *Ideas* we have both of God, and separate Spirits, are made up of the simple *Ideas* we receive from *Reflection*; *v.g.* having from what we experiment in our selves, got the *Ideas* of Existence and Duration; of Knowledge and Power; of Pleasure and Happiness; and of several other Qualities and Powers, which it is better to have, than to be without; when we would frame an *Idea* the most suitable we can to the supreme Being, we enlarge every one of these with our *Idea* of Infinity; and so putting them together, make our complex *Idea of God*."[132] Because Locke's idea of God is constructed by us from simpler ideas, it is impossible to reach God through the sort of argument Descartes offers in the Third Meditation, where he argues that God must exist as the creator of the idea we have of him. Although he grants that some may find such an argument convincing, he thinks it "an ill way of establishing this Truth, and silencing Atheists, to lay the whole stress of so important a Point, as this, upon that sole Foundation: And take some Men's having that *Idea* of GOD in their Minds, (for 'tis evident, some Men have none, and some worse than none, and the most very different,) for the only proof of a Deity."[133] Although Locke may hold that his God is infinite and perfect, it is a somewhat different conception of God that yields a proof of his existence.

Locke begins his argument for the existence of God by noting that "*Man has a clear Perception of his own Being.*" He continues: "In the next place, Man knows by an intuitive Certainty, that bare *nothing can no more produce any real Being, than it can be equal to two right Angles.* . . . If therefore we know that there is some real Being, and that Non-entity cannot produce any real Being, it is an evident demonstration, that from Eternity there has been something." Since, as Locke argues, an effect can only receive its properties from its cause, "this eternal Source then of all being must also be the Source and Original of all Power; and so *this eternal Being must be also the most powerful.*" Furthermore, since I (the one created thing whose existence Locke grants in this argument) have knowledge and perception, "we are certain now, that there is not only some Being, but some knowing intelligent Being in the World." And so Locke concludes that "from the Consideration of our selves, and what we infallibly find in our own Constitutions, our Reason leads us to the Knowledge of this certain and evident Truth, That *there is an eternal, most powerful, and most knowing Being.*"[134] That is, God exists. Although Locke's argument is more complex than Hobbes', the basic principle is the same: God is established as the ultimate cause of the world. Although Locke gives the appropriate nods to infinity and perfection, it is fair to say that like Hobbes, Locke privileges the conception of causality.

(c) George Berkeley brings to completion this tendency to reduce all rational theology to divine causality. For Berkeley, of course, the concept of matter is contradictory and useless, and sensible things are reduced to collections of perceived ideas. In this context, God's primary role is as the cause of these sensible ideas in the finite spirits which he has created; it is in this way that God creates and sustains the world of sensible things. Hence Berkeley writes, "Everything we see, hear, feel, or any wise perceive by sense, [is] a sign or effect of the Power of God."[135]

Berkeley's conception of God's power is also manifested in his account of the continued existence of objects. An obvious problem for Berkeley's metaphysics is the continued existence of sensible objects when no (finite) mind is sensing them. To solve this problem, he often suggests that God sustains the world of sensible things by perceiving it.[136] But this raises an obvious problem; if God is to sustain objects by sensing them, then God himself must have sensations, something that raises obvious problems for Berkeley.[137] A better account is suggested in his early *Philosophical Commentaries*. According to that account, sensible things exist in God's mind not as collections of sensible ideas, as they do in ours, but as powers, the power to produce particular sensations in finite minds on particular occasions. As Berkeley suggests there, "Bodies etc do exist even wn not perceiv'd they being powers in the active Being."[138] Berkeley seems to have had some doubts about this view; in another entry in the *Philosophical Commentaries* he reminds himself "not to mention the Combination of Powers but to say the things the effects themselves to really exist even wn not actually perceiv'd."[139] But the view still finds a place in the mature writings. One problem Berkeley must face is that of creation: What does it mean to say that God created the world at one specific time? Berkeley's solution is to say that God created the world by decreeing that at one particular time sensible things "should become perceptible to intelligent creatures, in that order and manner which he then established, and we now call the Laws of Nature."[140] In that way, to create a sensible thing is simply for God to decide to cause a sensation in finite minds under appropriate circumstances. An important class of divine ideas thus emerge not as passive objects for divine contemplation but as the potential manifestations of God's power.[141]

Berkeley does not ignore God's wisdom, which is manifested through the order in which we receive these ideas, an order that allows us to frame laws of motion and predict at least certain aspects of the future train of ideas from what has gone before. Indeed, this is what Berkeley emphasizes in the *Principles* when God is first introduced as the cause of all of our ideas of sense: "The ideas of sense are more strong, lively, and distinct than those of the imagination; they have likewise a steadiness, order, and coherence, and are not excited at random, as those which are the effects of human wills often are, but in a regular train or series, the admirable connexion whereof sufficiently testifies the wisdom and benevolence of its Author."[142]

But although God is wise and benevolent, his wisdom and benevolence are manifested primarily in his role as the cause of the sensible world. And so Berkeley writes in his *Philosophical Commentaries*, "One idea not the cause of another, one power not the cause of another. The cause of all natural things is onely God. Hence trifling to enquire after second Causes. This Doctrine gives a most suitable idea of the Divinity."[143]

But there are obvious objections: if we have no more of an idea of God than we have of matter,[144] how can we know what this cause of ideas actually is? In particular, how can one legitimate the claim that the active cause (whatever it may be) coincides with the God of Christian revelation? When the theoretical validity of causality has been challenged (as it will be in Hume), or when the transcendental use of causality applied to the thing-in-itself has been excluded (as it will be in Kant), Berkeley's whole apologetic will become untenable, and along with it, every conception of God deriving from efficient causality.

§10. God and Extension

Seventeenth-century philosophers often defined God as supremely perfect. But what does such supreme perfection actually include? Is it appropriate to integrate *all* the perfections in God's essence? Descartes made at least one exception: for him, the "idea of an uncreated and independent thinking substance, that is, God"[145] excludes extension and therefore all materiality from its definition.[146]

As early as his correspondence with Descartes, Henry More (1614–87) tried to show that "God, in his own way, is extended [*Deus suo modo extenditur*]";[147] in order to communicate motion, God must be able "to touch matter," and if he could touch matter, he must be extended. This view was later elaborated in More's tract *The Immortality of the Soul*. Here, the classic list of the perfections—"*God is a Spirit*, Eternal, Infinite in Essence and Goodness, Omniscient, Omnipotent and of Himself necessarily Existent"—is specified as an "*Essence absolutely Perfect*," which implies "his *Omnipresence or Ubiquity*, which are necessarily included in the *Idea of absolute Perfection*." Therefore, supreme perfection directly implies the ubiquity of God, which More can only conceive of as an extended "Divine amplitude."[148] But there is no confusion between God's extension and the extension of bodies: the two extensions are different. More argues that whereas extended body is divisible and impenetrable, both God (infinite mind) and finite mind are indivisible (*indiscerpible*) and penetrable.[149] Consequently "God is everywhere," present by extension to all extension, without being confused with sensible materiality.

In challenging one of the most important Cartesian strictures on the definition of the divine essence, More opened a radical debate: Is God extended? A number of later British philosophers followed More in holding that God is extended though not corporeal. Most notable in this respect are Ralph Cudworth (1617–88), John Locke, and Sir Isaac Newton. Extension, Cudworth argues, must have a subject; if the space is filled, the subject is body, if not, it is God.[150] Similarly, Locke writes, "GOD, every one easily allows, fills Eternity; and 'tis hard to find a Reason, why any one should doubt, that he likewise fills Immensity: His infinite Being is certainly as boundless one way as another; and methinks it ascribes a little too much to Matter, to say, where there is no Body, there is nothing."[151] And like More, Locke is very careful to argue that although extended, God is not therefore material.[152] Given this context, the position that Newton takes in the *Scholium Generale* of the *Principia* (1687) is not surprising. If one accepts the definition of God as *ens . . . absolute perfectum*, and if one interprets this absolute perfection as pertaining to all God's properties, then one must necessarily apply it even to space, as it is already applied to duration: "He is neither duration or space, but He endures and is present. He always endures and is everywhere present, and existing always and everywhere, He established [*constituit*] duration and space, eternal and infinite. God is one and the same God, always and everywhere. He is omnipresent not only through his power, but also through his substance: for power without substance cannot exist. In Him the very universe is contained and moves."[153] In saying that God is substantially extended, Newton comes close to identifying God with extension. Why does Newton make God substantially extended? Without entering into the complex debate over Newtonian theology, there seems to be a simple explanation: as with Kepler, Galileo, Mersenne, and many others (as discussed above), Newton appeals to an epistemological univocity, here the univocity of space and absolute time, in order to provide a foundation for his science.

More radical was the position of Thomas Hobbes: writing at roughly the same time as More, he held that God is not only extended but also corporeal. The argument Hobbes offers consists of three stages. (1) By "body" must be understood not that which can be sensed ("secondary qualities"), but "that which has determinate magnitude and consequently is understood to be *totum* or *integrum aliquid*."[154] Body is thus defined in terms of the so-called primary qualities. But, Hobbes argues, this concept of body is just the same as our concept of substance. He writes: "The Word *Body*, in the most generall acceptation, signifieth that which filleth, or occupyeth some certain room, or imagined place; and dependeth not on the imagination. . . . The same also, because Bodies are subject to change, that is to say, to variety of apparence to the sense of living creatures, is called *Substance* . . . And according to this acceptation of the word, *Substance* and *Body* signifie the same thing.[155] (2) It follows, therefore, almost trivially and through a stipulative redefinition of terms, that if it is to exist at all, all spirit must be "body" and must thus be extended: "men may put together words of contradictory signification, as *Spirit* and *Incorporeall*; yet they can never have the imagination of anything answering to them." The phrase "incorporeal spirit," which amounts to an admission of incomprehensibility, has only a "pious" sense for Hobbes, not a theoretical one.[156] (3) In particular, God must then be corporeal or not exist at all: "To say that God is an incorporeal substance, is to say in effect there is no God at all." In face of the common dilemma — *either* infinite spirituality *or* finite corporeality — Hobbes responds with a paradox (at least an apparent one): "I deny both, and say He is corporeal and infinite." This presents a second paradox: "God is a spirit, but corporeal."[157] To the "mortal god" (the commonwealth) corresponds an extended and corporeal God.

No doubt under the influence of *Leviathan*, Spinoza too rejects the Cartesian prohibition against attributing extension to God: "Extended substance is one of the infinite attributes of God."[158] For Spinoza, God, the unique substance containing all attributes, is an extended thing (*res extensa*) every bit as much as he is a thinking thing (*res cogitans*). In developing his position, Spinoza considers an obvious objection to this position: while extension is by definition divisible, God cannot be divided. But, Spinoza replies, extension appears divisible only to the extent that we conceive it abstractly and superficially, only to the extent that we imagine extension without thinking of it as a mode of the unique substance; substance, properly conceived in itself, can no more be divided than it can be quantified: "It can be conceived only as one, and only as indivisible."[159] Spinoza can attribute extension to God only because he has certain very strict distinctions at his disposal: real extension (an attribute of substance) is not confused with matter or *materia prima* (as in materialism),[160] nor with substance itself (as in Hobbes' conception of body), nor with the imaginable extension of the mathematicians (which is divisible by abstraction). However, insofar as it is neither corporeal, nor material, nor mathematical, in what sense is Spinoza's extension still extension?

Like Spinoza and Hobbes, Malebranche attempts to integrate extension into the *ens summe perfectum*. But Malebranche completely reverses their strategy. Rather than privileging real extension and criticizing abstract (mathematical) extension, Malebranche places intelligible extension directly in God, while setting aside (in this life, at least) any direct access to the (sensible) extension in which created bodies exist. Transformed from its earlier Augustinian sense, our vision of the ideas in God no longer reveals God and his splendor to the human mind; above all, what we see is the idea of intelligible extension: "God contains in Himself an infinite ideal or intelligible extension"; "the idea of extension is not at all a modification of the mind and it is only found in God"; "infinite intelligible extension is not at all a modification of my mind. . . . Therefore it can only be found in God."[161] This mathematical conception of extension, what Spinoza considered imaginary and abstract, and therefore denied to substance, is the very thing that Malebranche situates in God, under the name of intelligible extension. Despite this tactical reversal, Malebranche is paradoxically closer to Hobbes than even Spinoza is: intelligible extension is not merely *in* God, but rather *is*, in a sense, God himself: "Intelligible extension is eternal, immense, necessary. It is the immensity of divine Being."[162] But since Malebranche holds that this idea of God in terms of intelligible extension is primary, he risks saying that we can only think of the divine essence as extended, and deriving from extension.

The conception of God as extended does not necessarily attest to a new materialism, but rather defends what Descartes, following the greatest medieval thinkers, had attempted to deny: the univocity of knowledge of God and the identification of human and divine science. The position still constitutes theology, even if the very success of the program seems to eliminate one of the fundamental distinctions between the creator and the created and thus render problematic the relation between the God of philosophy and the God of revelation.

§11. The Displacement of the Essence of God

If one grants that the whole debate over the conception of the divine essence played out in the seventeenth century derives from the (not altogether coherent) system of the three Cartesian conceptions of God, one thing stands out: although the *ens summe perfectum* and the *ens causa (sui)* enjoy ample development, either as an admitted duality (as in Spinoza, Malebranche, Leibniz), or under the domination of the notion of causality (as in Hobbes, Locke, Berkeley), the idea of infinity experiences a marked decline.

Although most would agree that God is infinite, the idea of infinity undoubtedly maintains only a few determined, if uninfluential, advocates as a basic characterization of the nature of God. Gassendi still acknowledges the legitimacy of the denomination of infinity.[163] Arnauld and Nicole firmly maintain "infinity as an attribute of God."[164] Desgabets defends the "knowledge of the infinite," in claiming that "God by full right has the quality of infinity."[165] But the most avowed proponent of the Cartesian conception of an infinite God remains Fénelon, who discerns in infinity "the characteristic of divinity itself!"[166] Following Descartes, he specifies that "that being who is through himself, and through whom I am, is infinitely perfect; and this is what we call God"; more radically than Descartes, Fénelon even thinks that he can appeal to an "infinite idea of infinity."[167] Against Spinoza he defends the unity of God through the notion of his infinity: "My conclusion is that everything composite can never be infinite," exclaiming, "O infinite Unity!"[168] If he takes up, with some carelessness, Malebranche's definition of God as "the infinite being who is simply Being, without adding anything,"[169] it is only to criticize the submission of God to order. But the fact remains that these statements appear marginal in the context of the history of these ideas; after Descartes (and Duns Scotus), infinity is not found among the central notions that make up the idea of the divine essence. This demotion can be compared to the parallel and contemporary abandonment of the doctrine of the creation of the eternal truths. One historical factor explains both: the imposition of the principle of sufficient reason as the first metaphysical principle governing essence and existence, and hence all of divine creation. This excludes incomprehensibility from God and his creation. But as "incomprehensibility is contained in the formal definition of infinity,"[170] the requirement of comprehensibility opposes the priority of infinity in the divine nature. The ultimate fulfillment of rationalist metaphysics thus ought to make the infinite God a *persona non grata*.

There remains, however, a final witness to infinity, Blaise Pascal. Pascal acknowledges straightaway "that sovereign being who is infinite by his own definition," for he posits in principle that "if there is a God, He is infinitely incomprehensible."[171] It is obvious here that Pascal is taking up the Cartesian thesis. However, it will give rise to the most radical critique of Descartes imaginable and, in general, the most radical critique of any *metaphysical* conception of God. There are two reasons for this. First, the concept of infinity does not uniquely pick out God, since numbers, motion, speed, space, and even nature can be infinite as well. Second, above all, even if God's infinity did allow the construction of a proof for his existence, it would still be in vain; for "the metaphysical proofs of God are so removed from the reasoning of men and so involved, that they make little impression"; indeed, "this knowledge, without Jesus Christ, is useless and sterile."[172] What is at stake for Pascal is not to *know* God, but to *love* him;[173] the real obstacle to acknowledging him does not rest in the uncertainty of the understanding, but in the arrogance of the will. Within such a perspective, even the doctrine of the creation of the eternal truths, which affirms the absolute transcendence of God, seems illusory: in demonstrating an "author of the geometrical truths," one only satisfies the "pagans"; for even "a God who exercises his providence" is still only suitable for Judaism. In fact, only "the God of Abraham, the God of Isaac, the God of Jacob and the God of the Christians is a God of love and consolation."[174] The project of proving the existence or determining the essence of God must yield to the recognition of a God to be loved, because he himself loves first. Pascal recorded his personal experience of this important shift in the *Mémorial*: "God of Abraham, of Isaac, and of Jacob, not of the philosophers and scholars."[175] He also marked its theoretical status by distinguishing three irreducible orders: bodies, minds, and finally the heart, where God — the God of Jesus Christ — becomes accessible only to the "eyes of the heart and he who sees wisdom."[176]

No doubt, in passing from the question of that which is evident, to the question of charity, Pascal reaches an entirely different transcendence from that which metaphysics (above all Cartesian metaphysics) can envisage. No doubt also, one might object that this new transcendence no longer concerns strictly metaphysical discourse. But was it not the bold and original claim of seventeenth-century metaphysics that we can determine the essence of God through philosophy alone? Its final failure would then become its most useful lesson to modern thought. The continual drift in the determination of the essence of God toward univocity should not be understood primarily or only as a simple failure to perceive God's transcendence, but as an indication of the demands made by the growing empire of metaphysical rationality, making use of its principles, principally that of sufficient reason; here we see quite clearly the importance of the new subjectivity that characterizes philosophy in the seventeenth century, the significance of the Cartesian call to begin philosophy with the *cogito*. From this point of view, the rival projects of Kant and Hegel can well appear as two attempts to restore the rights of the absolute in the face of the limits of the demands of the understanding.[177]

— Translated by Thomas Carlson and Daniel Garber

Notes

Translator's Introduction

1. References are to the standard French and English translations of Descartes; see explanation in the penultimate paragraph of this introduction.

2. For a good summary of Marion's explication of these two metaphysical systems, see his essay "On Descartes' Constitution of Metaphysics," *Graduate Faculty Philosophy Journal* 11, no. 1 (1986): 21–33.

3. Ruud Welten, "Het andere ego van Descartes," *Tijdschrift voor Filosofie* 60, no. 3 (1998): 572–579.

4. Géry Prouvost, "La tension irrésolue: Les *Questions cartésiennes II* de Jean-Luc Marion," *Revue Thomiste* 98, no. 1 (1998): 98.

5. Jean-Luc Marion, *L'idole et la distance* (Paris: Bernard Grasset, 1977), translated by Thomas A. Carlson as *The Idol and Distance* (New York: Fordham University Press, 2001); *Dieu sans l'être* (Paris: Libraire Arthème Fayard, 1982), translated by Thomas A. Carlson as *God Without Being* (Chicago: University of Chicago Press, 1991).

6. He employs this distinction repeatedly in several of his essays on the intersection between philosophy and theology or on the possibility of an exercise of "Christian philosophy." See "Metaphysics and Phenomenology: A Relief for Theology," *Critical Inquiry* 20 (summer 1994): 590–91, and "'Christian Philosophy': Hermeneutic or Heuristic?" in *The Question of Christian Philosophy Today*, ed. Francis J. Ambrosio (New York: Fordham University Press, 1999), 255–56. I have explored this intersection more fully in my article "A New 'Apologia': The Relationship between Theology

and Philosophy in the Work of Jean-Luc Marion," *Heythrop Journal* 46 (2005): 299–313.

7. Jean-Luc Marion, *Etant donné: Essai d'une phénoménologie de la donation* (Paris: Presses Universitaires de France, 1997), translated by Jeffrey L. Kosky as *Being Given: Toward a Phenomenology of Givenness* (Stanford, Calif.: Stanford University Press, 2002); *De surcroît: Études sur les phénomènes saturés* (Paris: Presses Universitaires de France, 2001), translated by Robyn Horner and Vincent Berraud as *In Excess: Studies of Saturated Phenomena* (New York: Fordham University Press, 2002).

8. Jean-Luc Marion, *Le phénomène érotique* (Paris: Grasset, 2003); translated by Stephen E. Lewis as *The Erotic Phenomenon* (Chicago: University of Chicago Press, 2007).

9. Chapter 1 as "The Original Otherness of the Ego: A Rereading of Descartes's *Meditatio II*," in *The Ethical*, ed. Edith Wyschogrod, chapter 2 (Oxford: Blackwell, 2003). Chapter 2 as "The Place of the Objections in the Development of Cartesian Metaphysics," in *Descartes and His Contemporaries: Meditations, Objections and Replies*, ed. Roger Ariew and Marjorie Grene, chapter 1 (Chicago: University of Chicago Press, 1995). Chapter 9 as "The Idea of God," in, *The Cambridge History of Seventeenth-Century Philosophy*, ed. Michael Ayers and Daniel Garber, chapter 10 (Cambridge: Cambridge University Press, 1998). They appear here by permission of the original publishers.

Preface to the French Edition

1. *Questions cartésiennes: Méthode et metaphysique*, collection "Philosophie d'aujourd'hui," under the general editorship of P.-L. Assoun (Paris: Presses Universitaires de France, 1991). [Translated by Daniel Garber as *Cartesian Questions* (Chicago: University of Chicago Press, 1999) — Trans.]

2. I have already noted, in *Cartesian Questions*, "two different solutions to the problem of the 'circle'" (6), of which one does not immediately agree, in fact, with a solution that I had advanced in *Sur la théologie blanche de Descartes* (Paris: Presses Universitaires de France, 1981), 340ff. Now, I propose here (chapter 2, [Chapter 3 in the present volume]) yet a third solution to this same alleged "circle." But here at least this imbalance does not matter much; for the discovery of these hypotheses justify themselves; their harmonization, if it is necessary, will come later.

3. Which hence confirms *Sur le prisme métaphysique de Descartes* (Paris: Presses Universitaires de France, 1986) [translated by Jeffrey L. Kosky as *On the Metaphysical Prism of Descartes* (Chicago: University of Chicago Press, 1999)], chapter 1.

4. I cite Descartes according to the *Œuvres de Descartes*, ed. Charles Adam and Paul Tannery, rev. Bernard Rochot and Pierre Costabel, 11 vols. (Paris: Vrin, CNRS, 1964–74). I cite without the abbreviation "AT," and only give the volume in Roman numerals. ["AT" has been supplied here to

make clearer the distinction from the page numbers of the standard English edition — Trans.]

1. The Originary Otherness of the Ego
A Rereading of Descartes' Second Meditation

1. "Fundamentum, cui omnis humana certitudo niti posse . . . videtur." AT VII:144, 24–25; CSM II:103. See: "I preferred to use my own existence as the basis of my argument"; "malui tui pro fundamento meae rationis existentia meiipsius." AT VII:107, 2–3; CSM II:77.

2. [The French word Marion uses here has connotations of distortion or falsification. — Trans.]

3. I have assumed this in *Questions cartésiennes* (Paris: Presses Universitaires de France, 1991), chapter 6: "L'ego altère-t-il autrui?" [*Cartesian Questions*, trans. Daniel Garber (Chicago: University of Chicago Press, 1999), chapter 6: "Does the *Ego* Alter the Other? The Solitude of the *Cogito* and the Absence of the *Alter Ego*"]. I ask here the same question anew.

4. Malebranche, *De la recherche de la vérité* 6.2.6, in André Robinet, ed. *Œuvres complètes*, 20 vols. (Paris: Vrin), vol. 2, ed. Geneviève Rodis-Lewis (Paris: Vrin, 1974), 369. I follow here the interpretation of Ferdinand Alquié, who maintains on this point a fundamental continuity between Descartes and Malebranche: "Reducing the 'I think, therefore I am' to the affirmation of the existence of my spirit, Malebranche hence retains that which is the most profound and the most indubitable in the *Meditations* of Descartes. The I think remains foundation." Ferdinand Alquié, *Le cartésianisme de Malebranche* (Paris: Vrin, 1974), 103.

5. "Ideoque *cogito, ergo sum*, unica est propositio, quae huic, *ego sum cogitans*, aequivalet." Spinoza in *Ethics* 2, ax. 2 and *Principia Philosophiae Cartesianae* 1, Prolegomenon, ed. Carl Gebhardt (Heidelberg: C. Winter, 1925), 144; trans. Edwin Curley, *The Collected Works of Spinoza* (Princeton: Princeton University Press, 1985), 1:448, 234 (trans. mod.). Henceforth cited as *Works*.

6. Immanuel Kant, *Kritik der reinen Vernunft*, B422, note.

7. Ibid., end of §24, B156.

8. Kant, ibid., A355. See Jocelyn Benoist, *Kant et les limites de la synthèse* (Paris: Presses Universitaires de France, 1996), chapters 4–5.

9. The fortune of this Kantian interpretation of the first Cartesian principle succeeds by way of the Marburg School, in the works of Wolfgang Röd, *Descartes: Die Genese des cartesianischen Rationalismus* (Munich: Beck, 1982), and Franz Bader, *Die Ursprünge der Transzendentalphilosophie bei Descartes* (Bonn: Bouvier, 1983).

10. Fichte's position remains, it seems to us, close enough to that of Kant: "Before him [Kant], Descartes has proposed a similar principle: *cogito, ergo sum*, which is not the result of a different proposition or conclusion of a syllogism of which the major would be *quodcumque cogitat, est*; Descartes can

have considered so voluntarily this principle as an immediate fact of consciousness. In this sense, it would signify: *cogitans sum, ergo sum* (or as we say it, *sum ergo sum*)." *Wissenschaftslehre* 1794–95, §1, in *Gesammelte Werke*, 2:262. But this immediate identity is found also exactly in the terms of Spinoza. See the brilliant analysis of Alexis Philonenko in "Sur Descartes et Fichte" (*Les études philosophique* 2 [1985]), which, moreover, does not hesitate to attribute to the Cartesian proposition a "thetic value . . . in the sense of Fichte; it is neither analytic, nor synthetic [but] existential tautology. *Formaliter spectata*, the formula goes back to the principle of identity A = A, and one knows how Fichte engenders beginning from A = A, formal proposition, the Me = Me, material proposition." Alexis Philonenko, *Relire Descartes: Le génie de la pensée française* (Paris: J. Grancher, 1994), 237ff.

11. Hegel, *Phänomenologie des Geistes*, in *Gesammelte Werke* (Hamburg: F. Meiner, 1980), 9:313. See also Bernard Bourgeois, "Hegel et Descartes," *Les études philosophiques* 2 (1985).

12. Hegel, *Vorlesungen über die Geschichte der Philosophie: Teil 4, Philosophie des Mittelalters und der neueren Philosophie*, ed. Pierre Garniron and Walter Jaeschke (Hamburg: F. Meiner, 1986), 93. Let me note that Hegel cites, to my knowledge, only the following texts: the Latin translation (Pierre de Courcelles, *Specimina*, 1644) of the *Discourse on Method* 4; the *Principia Philosophiae* 1, §7; and—taken as a text of Descartes! Spinoza, *Principia Philosophiae Cartesianae*; the *Meditations* seems entirely ignored—a fact that is even more remarkable since Hegel is without doubt one of the first to devote himself to actually reading the texts of his predecessors. That shows the weight of the canonical interpretation. Moreover, H. G. Hotho, student of Hegel, whose dissertation *De Philosophia Cartesiana* (Berlin, 1826), is cited in the *Encyclopaedia* of 1830 (§64, Zusatz), never mentions anything but the formula "cogito, ergo sum" (11) before concluding that "it cannot be denied that the philosophy of Spinoza is a true consequent and continuation of Cartesian philosophy"; "Spinozae philosophiam veram esse Cartesianae philosophiae et consequentiam et continuationem negari necquaquam potest." (59).

13. Schelling develops a very similar interpretation: "In the *cogito ergo sum*, Descartes believed to have discerned the immediate identity of thought and being." *Sämtliche Werke*, ed. Schröter, 10:9. Here also, the criticism matters less than the interpretation that it presupposes.

14. Friedrich Nietzsche, *Wille zur Macht*, ed. Peter Gast/Elisabeth Förster-Nietzsche, §484 = *Nachgelassene Fragmente* 10 [158], ed. Colli/Montinari, vol. 8:2 (Berlin: W. de Gruyter, 1970), 215. See *Beyond Good and Evil*, §16. See the significant work of Hartmut Brands, *"Cogito ergo sum": Interpretationen von Kant bis Nietzsche* (Freiburg im Breisgau: K. Alber, 1982).

15. Edmund Husserl, *Conférences de Paris*, in *Méditations cartésiennes, Husserliana* 1:4; French translation *Méditations cartésiennes et les conférence de Paris* (Paris: Presses Universitaires de France, 1994), 3.

16. [The paragraph on Heidegger is missing in the existing English translation. — Trans.]

17. Heidegger, *Sein und Zeit*, §82, 433, and *Nietzsche* (Pfullingen, G. Neske, 1961), 2:153. Regarding this issue, see my *Cartesian Questions*, 99ff.

18. Martial Gueroult, *Descartes selon l'ordre des raisons* (Paris: Aubier, 1953), 1:116.

19. Ibid.: "it is further required that it should think that it is thinking, by means of a reflexive act. . . . this is deluded"; "requiri ut actu reflexo cogitet se cogitare, sive habeat cogitationes suae conscientiam. . . . Hallucinatur"; "celui qui exige de penser que l'on se pense, ou que l'on ait conscience de sa pensée par un acte réflexif, celui-là délire." Seventh Replies; see AT VII:559, 5–7; CSM II:382. [Translations in this chapter have been assisted by Thomas McLaughlin (Latin) and Christian DuPont (French).] See Sixth Replies, AT VII:422, 8–14; CSM II:285: "But this does not require reflective knowledge or the kind of knowledge that is acquired by means of demonstrations; still less does it require knowledge of reflective knowledge, i.e. knowing that we know. . . . It is quite sufficient that we should know it by that internal awareness which always precedes reflective knowledge" ("non quod ad hoc [the certainty of being following from thinking] requiratur scienda reflexa vel per demonstrationem acquisita, et multo minus scientia scientiae reflexae, per quam sciat se scire. . . . Sed omnino sufficit ut id sciat cogitadone ilia intema, quae reflexam semper antecedit"). Regarding this awareness, Jean-Marie Beyssade has very nicely shown that it "ought not to be understood here in the sense of reflexive awareness." *La philosophie première de Descartes* (Paris: Flammarion, 1979), 234. Otherwise *reflexio* and *reflectare never* appear in the text of the *Meditations*.

20. In this way, *repraesentare* in AT VII:8, 19, 23; 40, 11, 15; 43, 3, 30; 44, 7; CSM II:7, 28, 29, 30, etc.; these occurrences concern always a *res*, never an *ego* or the *cogitatio*. As for the substantive *repraesentatio*, it simply *never* appears in the *Meditations*. For this double factual motive, the representative interpretation of the *ego cogito, ergo sum* seems, at the very least, highly problematic.

21. Gueroult, *Descartes selon l'ordre des raisons*, 1:116, 95, 94, respectively (see, on reflection, 66, 68, 80, 81, 89, etc.). The reasons to avoid the exclusively reflexive and representative interpretation of the *ego cogito* have often been set out — by, among others, Ferdinand Alquié, *La découverte métaphysique de l'homme chez Descartes* (Paris: Presses Universitaires de France, 1950), chap. 9 (of which "a presence so intimate . . . that no reflection, no doubt . . . would know to prevail against it," 189); Michel Henry, *Généalogie de la psychanalyse* (Paris: Presses Universitaires de France, 1985), chap. 3 [trans. Douglas Brick, *The Genealogy of Psychoanalysis* (Stanford, Calif.: Stanford University Press, 1993)]; and Jean-Luc Marion, *Cartesian Questions*, chap. 5, etc.

22. "Entre ces idées, outre celle qui me représente a moi-même." *Meditationes de prima philosophia / Méditations Métaphysiques, texte latin et traduction du Duc de Luynes* (Paris: Vrin, 1960), 43. AT IXA:34, 3.

23. AT VII:42, 29. *Exhibere* implies in a way something already phenomenological in that he "does nothing at all to go beyond the limits of that which appears to me" and thus remains "in the thought of pure *appearing*" (Beyssade, *La philosophie première de Descartes*, 234–35; my emphasis).

24. "Réflexion envelopée par le processus constitutif du cogito." Gueroult, *Descartes selon l'ordre des raisons*, 60.

25. The most remarkable analytic interpretations always lean on the canonical formulation, even when, in fact, they pass beyond it. In this way, for example, Jaakko Hintikka introduces his so fecund and correct interpretation of the formula of the Second Meditation as performative, not only beginning from the canonical formula, which is precisely missing here, but also as a relation between *cogito* and *sum*: "Their relation is rather comparable to that of a process to its product." Jaakko Hintikka, "*Cogito, ergo sum*: Inference or Performance?," *Philosophical Review* 71 (1962): 3–32. But is there such a "relation" between them? Similarly, Harry Frankfurt concentrates all his effort on the transition between *cogito* (of whom the truth would not be proven) and *sum*: see *Demons, Dreamers, and Madmen: The Defense of Reason in Descartes' Meditations* (Indianapolis: Bobbs-Merrill, 1970). But the question remains of knowing if these are the terms (and not only the modes of their articulation) that permit us to hear what Descartes in fact gains as "first principle."

26. Edwin M. Curley, *Descartes Against the Skeptics* (Cambridge, MA: Harvard University Press, 1978), 72. The same thing is noted by Margaret Wilson: "This passage is widely known as an instance of the '*cogito* reasoning,' despite the fact that the famous formulation 'I think, therefore I am' (*cogito ergo sum*) appears only in cognate passages in other works—not in the *Meditations* itself" (*Descartes* [London: Routledge, 1978], 52), going back to the *Discourse* and to the *Principia Philosophiae*; or also in Beyssade: "The proposition *I am, I exist*, seems indeed to have constituted, in the *Second Meditation*, the fixed and immovable point on which the whole edifice of the first philosophy is built." *La philosophie première de Descartes*, 217. But it is astonishing that on the same page the title of chap. 5 has another formulation, which still remains in accord with the canonical interpretation: "je pense, donc je suis." Also Etienne Balibar: "But the statement in the Meditations is different. It is simply *Ego sum, ego existo*. All immediate, internal reference to *cogitare* and to the *cogitatio* disappears." The designation of this statement as "*cogito*" is then, at best, an interpretation. "Ego sum, ego existo: Descartes au point d'hérésie," *Bulletin de la Société française de Philosophie* 86 (1992): 83.

27. "Denique statuendum sit hoc pronuntiatum, *Ego sum, ego existo* quoties a me profertur vel mente concipiatur, necessario esse verum"; "haec sola [cf. Cogitatio] a me divelli nequit. Ego sum, ego existo." Respectively, AT

VI:32, 19; CSM I:127 (see 33, 17; CSM I:127–28 and AT II:247, 2; not translated in CSMK); AT VII:140, 20–21; CSM II:100 (the addition of *sive existo* is security for the same addition in the French text of *D.M.* in the Latin translation of the *Specimina* by P. de Courcelles, AT VI:588, 25 as remarked by Étienne Gilson, *Descartes, Discours de la méthode, texte et commentaire* [Paris, 1925], 292); then AT VIIIA:7, 7–8 (§7, see §10, 8, 9); AT V:147, 9, 15 (the only occurrence, and marginal at that, of the most habitually used formula, which has then scarcely any legitimacy), AT X:368, 21–2; CSM I:14 (where the logical connective is missing); and, finally, AT VII:25, 11–13 and 27, 8–9; CSMK III:333. I omit here the two formulas that replace *cogito* by *dubito* (*Recherche de la vérité*, AT X:515, 5–6 and 525, 15–18, and *Notae in programma quoddam*, AT VIIIB:354, 18–21; CSM I:301), or that use another antecedent (AT VII:352, 11–12; CSM II:244: *ambulo*; AT VII:37, 26, 38, 9–10; CSM II:26 [both]: *je respire*, etc.). On all these formulas, see Henri Gouhier, *Essais sur Descartes* (Paris: Vrin, 1949), 117–27, and Jean-Marie Beyssade, *Descartes: L'entretien avec Burman* (Paris: Presses Universitaires de France, 1981), 18–19.

28. Jaakko Hintikka, "*Cogito, ergo sum.*" It remains most astonishing nevertheless that here Hintikka still relies on the canonical formulation that, to be precise, *does not* allow to confirm his own, otherwise so remarkable, interpretation. (Although it does not think the ontological dimension to which it lays claim.) See my discussion in *Sur la théologie blanche de Descartes: Analogie, creation des vérités éternelles et fondement* (Paris: Presses Universitaires de France, first ed. 1981, second ed. 1991), §16, "La performance du *cogito.*"

29. Husserl, *First Philosophy* 1, §10, *Husserliana* VII, ed. Ulrich Melle (Dordrecht: Kluwer Academic Publishers, 1988), 64.

30. "Nondum satis intelligo quisnam sim ego ille, qui jam necessario sum" ("mais je ne connais pas encore assez clairement ce que je suis, moi qui suis certain qui je suis"). AT VII:25, 14–15 = AT IXA:21, 39–40; CSM II:17, as commented upon by E. Balibar, "Descartes au point d'hérésie," 92–95. And one should cite a subsequent edition of the French translation, which is even clearer: "This me, that is to say my soul, by which *I am that which I am* is entirely distinct from the body." AT IXA:62, 20–21, my emphasis. See my remarks and criticism in the "Bulletin cartésien 23," *Archives de Philosophie* 57, no. 4 (1995).

31. AT VII:25, 15–18; CSM II:17: the ego finds itself for a time in an anonymous situation: I am, but I ignore what (or who) I am.

32. AT VII:24, 19 – 25, 24; AT IXA:19, 17–38; CSM II:16–17.

33. "Aliquis Deus, vel quocumque nomine illum vocem." AT VII:24, 21–22; CSM II:16.

34. On this necessary indeterminacy, see my remarks in *Sur le prisme métaphysique de Descartes* (Paris: Presses Universitaires de France, 1986) §16, 223ff.; trans. Jeffrey L. Kosky, *On Descartes' Metaphysical Prism: The Constitution and the Limits of Onto-Theo-Logy in Cartesian Thought* (Chicago: University of Chicago Press, 1999), §16, 212ff. [Throughout the rest of the book

Marion's page references have been changed to refer to the English translation of this work. — Trans.]

35. "Me met en l'esprit [d]es pensées" AT IXA:19, 20.

36. Cf. AT VII:39, 10–14; 77, 23–27; 79, 10; CSM II:27, 54, 55. This hypothesis is enough to put up for discussion Descartes' supposed total ignorance of anything unconscious. Cf. Geneviève Rodis-Lewis, *Le problème de l'inconscient et le cartésianisme* (Paris: Presses Universitaires de France, 1950), chap. 1.

37. "Numquid ergo saltem ego aliquid sum?" AT VII:24, 24–25; CSM II:16. "Moi donc à tout le moins ne suis-je pas quelque chose?" AT IXA:19, 23.

38. AT VII:25, 2–4; CSM II:16 actually takes up AT VII:21, 3–7; CSM II:14. The addition of *mentes* (any *spiritsi*, confirming AT IXA:19, 27) matters more here than the omission of the technical list of the simple material (and common) natures. Is it a matter of a simple lapse, or rather of a sophisticated shift, extending the doubt concerning the principal intellectual nature, contrary to the stated doctrine of the *Meditations*? In this second case, must one attribute this shift to Descartes deceiving us (but why?) or, rather, can one attribute it to the ego as still uncertain and deceiving itself? On the major role of the simple natures (especially the material and the common ones) in the performance of doubt, see *Cartesian Questions*, chap, 3, §4 and §5.

39. "Imo certe ego eram, si quid mihi persuasi."

40. "Certe ego [sum], si quid mihi persuasi."

41. [The French can indicate both the passive "I am persuaded" and the reflexive "I have persuaded myself." Throughout this section Marion plays on the two meanings of the construction. — Trans.]

42. Foucault saw this perfectly: "It is true that the *cogito* is the absolute beginning; but one must not forget that the evil genius is anterior to it. . . . And that is not because the truth which takes its illumination in the *cogito* ends by masking the shadow of the evil genius entirely but because one must forget its perpetually menacing power." *Histoire de la folie à l'âge classique* (Paris: Plon, 1961), 196. Further occurrences reestablish, moreover, the real alterity of this persuasion: (a) "Yet when I turn to the things themselves which I think I perceive very clearly, I am so convinced by them that I spontaneously declare" ("quoties vero ad ipsas res, quas valde clare percipere arbitror, me converto, tam plane ab illis [rebus] persuadeor, ut sponte"; AT VII:36, 12–15; CSM II:25) — persuasion by the things themselves, conversion to the things as other than me, in short no solipsism at all; (b) "my intellect has not yet come upon any persuasive reason in favor of one alternative rather than the other" ("nullam adhuc intellectui meo rationem occurrere, quae mihi unum magis quam aliud persuadeat"; AT VII: 59, 10–12; CSM II:41) — the persuasion does not result from a self-conviction, but from the succession (*occurrere*) to the understanding of the ego of a constraining reason; through lack of this advent (hence of alterity), persuasion

is not accomplished; (c) "I am always brought back to the fact that it is only what I clearly and distinctly perceive that completely convinces me" ("semper eo res redit, ut ea me sola plane persuadeant, quae clare et distincte percipio"; AT VII: 68, 22–23; CSM II:47 — persuasion depends on evidence, hence on the immediate presence of the thing inasmuch as it is different from my thought, still of alterity. This is what Francis Jacques has seen perfectly: "One will ask: can anything preserve the privileged experience of the ego? I believe it, still and always the affirmation of an instance is not objectivable, not representable. The *I* does not posit itself without the *you, and in that the solipsism is finished* [my emphasis]. But in the final account, it is neither the ego nor the dyad formed by the *I* and the *you* that signifies, but the relation between them, which will engender them both." *L'espace logique de l'interlocution: Dialogiques II* (Paris: Presses Universitaires de France, 1985), 505, see 550–57.

43. The irreducibility of this *quid* marks maybe one of the rare limits of the interpretation of the *cogito* as auto-affection by Michel Henry, *Genealogy of Psychoanalysis*, chap. 3.

44. Must one understand "igitur ego etiam sum, si me fallit" (AT VII:25, 8; CSM II:17) as *I am, even if he is deceiving me* (concession, as if *etiam si* amounted to *etiamsi*), or as *if he deceives me, I too am*? The translation by De Luynes does not resolve this: "There is hence no doubt that I am, if he deceives me" (IXA:19, 28). I maintain the latter interpretation, because the other occurrences of *etiam* in the Second Meditation go in that direction — in particular, several lines before: "Does it not follow that I too do not exist?" ("nonne igitur etiam me non esse?"; AT VII:25, 4–5 or 29, 1 and 29, 7; CSM VII:16 or 19).

45. AT VII, respectively 7, 20; 18, 1–2; 73, 15–16; CSM II:7, 12, 51.

46. In this way one could respond to the subtle objection of Margaret Wilson against the reading of the *ego sum* as a performative (Hintikka) — the performative supposes "the existence of an audience" ("Performance," 71), now the ego remains alone and pronounces its performative in a private language ("vel mente concipitur"; AT VII:25, 14; CSM II:17). In effect, the ego indisputably has at its disposal an audience, and its performative remains public, because it *responds* to the one who deceives it (eventually in not deceiving it or in not being himself). The ego responds, hears itself *respond*, hears itself speak, hears itself spoken, discovers itself being inasmuch as spoken by or before an other: *cogito me cogitatum, ergo sum*.

47. "Je pris garde que, pendant que *je* voulais ainsi penser que tout était faux, il fallait nécessairement que *moi*, qui le pensais, fusse quelque chose. Et remarquant que cette vérité, *je pense, donc je suis* était si ferme et si assurée, que toutes les extravagantes suppositions des Sceptiques n'étaient pas capables de l'ébranler, *je* trouvais que *je* pouvais la recevoir, sans scrupule, pour le premier principe que *je* cherchais." AT VI:32, 15–23; CSM I:127; my emphasis.

48. "Repugnat enim [there is in effect a contradiction] ut putemus id quod cogitat eo tempore quo cogitat non existere. Atque haec cognitio *ego cogito, ergo sum*, est omnium prima et certissima, quae cuilibet ordine philoso-phanti occurrat." *Principles of Philosophy* 1 §7; AT VIIIA:7, 6–7; CSM I:194–95. The absence of an other then constrains Descartes in (badly) founding the existence of the ego on an uncertain universal principle (§10; AT VIIIA:8, 13), of which discussion is, in fact, lacking.

49. We suppose here, against the majority of critics, that the certitude of the first principle, which remains such even if it turns out to be the highest truth, is here not put into question by any doubt (*post festum*). See Chapter 3, "The General Rule of Truth," in this volume.

50. My emphasis."Yet when I turn to the things themselves which I think I perceive very clearly, I am so convinced by them that I spontane-ously declare: *let whoever can do so deceive me*, he will never bring it about that I am nothing, so long as I continue to think I am something"; "et au con-traire, lorsque je me tourne vers les choses que je pense concevoir fort clairement, je suis tellement persuadé par elles, que moi-même je me laisse emporter a ces paroles: *Me trompe qui* pourra, si est-ce qu'*il* ne saurait jamais faire que je ne sois rien, tandis que je penserai être quelque chose"; "*fallat* me *quisquis* potest, numquam tamen *efficiet* ut nihil sim, quamdiu me aliquid esse cogitabo." AT VII:36, 15; AT IXA:28, 25–30; CSM II:25; my emphasis.

51. "Cogitabo me esse" / "je penserai être quelque chose."

52. "Me trompe qui pourra" / "fallat me quisquis potest."

53. "Je conçois cette ressemblance (dans laquelle l'idée de Dieu se trouve contenue) par la même faculté par laquelle je me conçois moi-même." AT IXA:41, 12–14; CSM II:35.

54. AT VII:51, 21–23: "and that I perceive that likeness . . . by the same faculty which enables me to perceive myself" (literally: "and that likeness to be perceived by me . . . through the same faculty by which I myself am perceived by myself"). CSM II:35.

55. "Je connais aussi en même temps, que celui duquel je depends possède en soi toutes ces grandes choses auxquelles j'aspire." AT IXA:41, 17–19; CSM II:35 (trans. mod.).

56. See AT VII:53, 9–12; CSM II:37: "And when I consider the fact that I have doubts, or that I am a thing that is incomplete and dependent, then there arises in me a clear and distinct idea of a being who is independent and complete, that is, an idea of God" ("Cumque attendo me dubitare, sive esse rem incompletam et dependentem, adeo clara et distincta idea entis in-dependentis et completi, hoc est Dei, mihi occurrit"; 55, 19–21; CSM II:39); "For since I now know that my own nature is very weak and limited, whereas the nature of God is immense, incomprehensible and infinite" ("Cum enim; jam sciam naturam meam esse valde infirmam et limitatam, Dei autem naturam esse immensam, incomprehensibilem, infinitam"); and positively (AT VII:57, 12–15; CSM II:40): "It is only the will, or freedom

of choice, which I experience within me to be so great that the idea of any greater faculty is beyond my grasp; so much so that it is above all in virtue of the will that I understand myself to bear in some way the image and likeness of God" ("Sola est voluntas, sive arbitrii libertas, quam tantam in me experior ut nullius majoris ideam apprehendam; adeo ut illa praecipue sit, ratione cujus imaginem quandam et similtudinem Dei in me referre intelligo"). See already AT VII:9, 15–18; CSM II:8. One could also suggest the hypothesis that the three dreams of *Olympica* (X:179–90) outline already such an original interlocution of a still-undefined subjectivity. See Fernand Hallyn, "Une 'feintise,'" in *Les "Olympiques" de Descartes*, ed. Fernand Hallyn (Geneva: Droz, 1995).

57. "Je vous suis bien obligé de ce que vous m'apprenez les endroits de saint Augustin, qui peuvent servir pour autoriser mes opinions: quelques autres de mes amis avaient déjà fait le semblable; et j'ai très grande satisfaction de ce que mes pensées s'accordent avec celles d'un si saint et excellent personnage." To Mesland, 2 May 1644, AT IV:113, 12–17; CSMK III:232. See AT III:248, 4–7; CSMK III:159: "but I am very glad to find myself in agreement with St. Augustine, if only to hush the little minds who have tried to find fault with the principle" ("mais je ne laisse pas d'être bien aisé d'avoir rencontré avec saint Augustin, quand ce ne serait que pour fermer la bouche aux petits esprits qui ont tache de regabeler sur ce principe").

58. "Je ne m'arrêterai point ici à le [Arnauld] remercier du secours qu'il m'a donné en me fortifiant de l'autorité de saint Augustin, et de ce qu'il a proposé mes raisons de telle sorte qu'il semblait avoir peur que les autres ne les trouvassent pas assez fortes et convaincantes." Fourth Replies, AT IXA:170; AT VII:219, 7; CSM II:154: "for bringing in the authority of St. Augustine to support me" ("quod divi Augustini authoritate adjuvarit").

59. "[Un] passage de saint Augustin." To Mersenne, 25 May 1637, AT I:376, 20; not translated in CSMK. The identification rests on an allusion Descartes subsequently made to this comparison made by Mersenne (and forgotten by him): "Some time ago, you drew my attention to a passage from St. Augustine concerning my *I am thinking therefore I exist*, and I think you have asked me about it again since then. It is in Book Eleven, chapter 26 of *De Civitate Dei*." December 1640, AT III:261, 9–13; CSMK III:161. It is confirmed by his letter of 15 November 1638: "I looked for the letter in which you quote the passage from Saint Augustine, but I have not yet been able to find it; nor have I managed to obtain the works of the Saint, so that I could look up what you told me, for which I am grateful." To Mersenne, AT II:435, 19–23; CSMK III:129. This conclusion is shared by Léon Blanchet, *Les antécédents historiques du Je pense, donc je suis* (1920; Paris: Presses Universitaires de France, 1985), 56.

60. "Nulla in his veris Academicorum argumenta fonnido dicentium: Quid si falleris? Si enim fallor, sum. Nam qui non est, utique nec falli potest: ac per hoc sum, si fallor. Quia ergo sum si tailor, quo modo esse me fallor,

quando certum est me esse, si fallor?"; "En cette triple assurance, je ne re-
doute aucun des arguments des Academiciens me disant: Quoi! et si tu
trompais? Car si je me trompe, je suis. Qui n'est pas, certes ne peut pas non
plus se tromper: par suite, si je me trompe, c'est que je suis. Du moment
donc que je suis, si je me trompe, comment me tromper en croyant que je
suis, quand il est certain que je suis si je me trompe?"

61. "[Le] passage de saint Augustin, parce qu'il ne semble pas s'en servir
a même usage que je fais." To Mersenne, 25 May 1637; AT I:376, 20–21;
not translated in CSMK.

62. "Vous m'avez obligé de m'avertir du passage de saint Augustin, au-
quel mon *je pense, donc je suis* a quelque rapport: je l'ai été lire aujourd'hui
en la bibliothèque de cette ville [Leyde], et je trouve veritablement qu'il s'en
sert pour prouver la certitude de notre être, et ensuite pour faire voir qu'il
y a en nous quelque image de la Trinité, en ce que nous sommes, nous sa-
vons que nous sommes, et aimons cet être et cette science qui est en nous;
au lieu que je m'en sers pour faire connaître que ce *moi*, qui pense, est une
substance immaterielle, et qui n'a rien de corporel; qui sont deux choses fort
differentes." To *X*, November 1640, AT III:247, 1–248, 1; to Colvius, 14
November 1640, CSMK III:159.

63. No occurrence of *immatériel* in 1647 (see André Robinet, *Cogito 75.
René Descartes: Méditations métaphysiques*, Paris: Vrin, 1976) or of *immaterialis*
in 1641.

64. Augustine, *De libero arbitrio* 2.3: "Abs te quaero ut de manifestissimis
capiamus exordium, utrum tu ipse sis, an tu forte metuis ne hac in interro-
gatione falleris, cum utique, si non esses, falli omnino non potes"; "Et, pour
partir des choses les plus manifestes, je te demanderai d'abord si toi-même,
tu existes. Maîs peut-être crains-tu de te tromper en cette question, alors
que tu ne pourrais absolument pas te tromper, si tu n'étais pas du tout."

65. "Sed est deceptor nescio quis, summe potens, summe callidus, qui de
industria me semper fallit. Haud dubie igitur ego etiam sum, si me fallit." AT
VII:25, 5–8; CSM II:17. [Cottingham renders this passage as: "But there is
a deceiver of supreme power and cunning who is deliberately and constantly deceiving me." Haldane's translation reads: "But there is some deceiver or other, very powerful and very cunning, who. . . ."] Arnauld quotes
this and the passage from Augustine above at AT VII:197, 24–198, 8; CSM
II:139.

66. AT VII:219, 6–9; CSM II:154.

67. AT VII:198, 5; CSM II:139.

68. "[Que] c'est une chose qui de soi est si simple et naturelle à inferer,
qu'on est, de ce qu'on doute, qu'elle aurait pu tomber sous la plume de qui
que ce soit." To *X*, November 1640, AT III:248, 1–4; to Colvius, 14 November 1640, CSMK III:159. (The "any writer" happened to be St. Augustine!
It is hard to imagine any greater insolence.) See also AT VII:551, 9; CSM
II:376 (cf. AT VII:130, 20–23; CSM II:94).

69. Arnauld tries once again, several years later (letter to Descartes, 3 June 1648, AT V:186, 11–12), to inscribe Descartes within the Augustinian tradition by invoking this time *De Trinitate* X.14: "But no one can possibly doubt that he lives and remembers, understands, wills, thinks, knows, and judges. For even if he doubts, he lives: if he doubts what has made him doubt, he remembers; if he doubts, he understands that he is doubting; if he doubts, he wishes to be certain; if he doubts, he thinks; if he doubts, he knows that he is ignorant; if he doubts, he judges that he ought not to be hasty in assenting. A man may doubt everything else, but he should not doubt any of these facts; for if they were not so, he could doubt of nothing." Augustine, *Later Works*, ed. John Barnaby (Philadelphia: Westminster, 1955), 85–86. ("Vivere se tamen et meminisse, et intelligere, et velle et cogitare, et scire, et judicare, quis dubitet? Quandoquidem etiam si dubitat, vivit: si dubitat, unde dubitet, meminit; si dubitat, dubitare se intelligit; si dubitat, esse vult; si dubitat, cogitat; si dubitat, scit se nescire; si dubitat, judicat non se temere consentire oportere. Quisquis igitur aliunde dubitat, de his omnibus dubitare neon debet; quae si non essent de ulla re dubitare non posset.") Descartes, in his reply (30 June, AT IV:194ff.) passes over this suggestion in silence insofar as it rests on the development of a similar tautology and therefore contradicts the original formulation. Besides, we see no compelling reason to suppose that Descartes could have known this passage before the redaction of his *Meditations*, despite the authoritative opinions of Léon Blanchet ("the probability . . . very great," *Les antécédents historiques*, 59–61) and Henri Gouhier ("seems therefore," *Cartésianisme et augustinisme au XVIIe siècle* [Paris: Vrin, 1978], 175). See the evidence compiled by G. Rodis-Lewis, "Augustinisme et cartésianisme," *Augustinus Magister* 1 (1954): 1087ff. The work by Gareth B. Matthews, *Thought's Ego in Augustine and Descartes* (Ithaca: Cornell University Press, 1992), is, despite its title, thoroughly useless on account of its misunderstanding of the texts. That, at least, is not the case with Edwin Curley, *Descartes Against the Skeptics*, 173, or Stephen Menn, "Descartes and Augustine," (Ph.D. dissertation, University of Chicago, 1990).

70. Emmanuel Levinas, *Totalité et infini* (The Hague: Martinus Nijhoff, 1961), 66; trans. Alphonso Lingis as *Totality and Infinity: An Essay on Exteriority* (Pittsburgh: Duquesne University Press, 1969), 93. See the texts more specifically dedicated to an interpretation of Descartes: "L'idée d'infini en nous," in *La passion de la raison: Hommage à F. Alquié*, ed. Nicolas Grimaldi and Jean-Luc Marion (Paris: Presses Universitaires de France, 1988), reprinted in Emmanuel Levinas, *Entre nous: Essais sur le penser-à-l'autre* (Paris: Grasset, 1991); trans. Michael B. Smith and Barbara Harshav as "The Idea of the Infinite in Us," in *Entre Nous: On Thinking-of-the-Other* (New York: Columbia University Press, 1998), 219–22. Gilles Deleuze opposes to the *I think* (in fact, to its canonical interpretation) that " the spontaneity of which I have consciousness . . . cannot comprise the attribute of a substantial and

spontaneous being, but only the affection of a passive me, which feels that its own proper thought . . . , that by which it says 'I,' is exercised in it and on it, not by it. . . . he sees it as an Other in him." *Différence et répétition*, 7th ed. (Paris: Presses Universitaires de France, 1993), 116ff. This objection even describes the *ego existo* according to its original alterity.

71. Following, for example, Natalie Depraz, *Transcendance et incarnation: Le statut de l'intersubjectivité comme altérité à soi chez Husserl* (Paris: Vrin, 1995).

2. The Responsorial Status of the *Meditations*

1. "Cum autem ibi [in the *Discourse on Method*] rogassem omnes quibus aliquid in meis scripturis reprehensione dignum occurreret, ut ejus me monere dignarentur, nulla in ea quae de his quaestionibus attigeram notatu digna objecta sunt, praeter duo, ad quae hic paucis, priusquam earumdem accuratiorem explicationem aggrediar, respondeo." AT VII:7, 14–19; CSM II:7.

2. "Cui objectioni respondeo, . . . ordo ad meam perceptionem, . . . ordo ad ipsam rei veritatem."

3. AT VI:75, 19–76, 5; CSM I:149–50.

4. "Tam expresse enim in *Dissertatione de Methodo* rogavi omnes, ut me errorem, quos in meis scriptis invenirent, monere dignarentur, tamque paratum ad illos emendandos me esse testatus sum, ut non crediderim quemquam fore, qui alios erroris condemnare, quam mihimet ipsi errores ostendere, de cujus saltern charitate erga proximum non mihi liceat dubitare." To Mersenne, 30 August 1640, in AT III:169, 2–30; untranslated in CSMK. Unless otherwise noted, translations in this essay are by Marjorie Grene. [References to CSMK have been supplied when available and the translation emended at times.—Trans.] This Latin letter to Mersenne was apparently intended to be read by the Jesuits of Clermont College. Moreover, in it Descartes takes up again his argument in an earlier letter, directly addressed to Father J. Hayneuve, doubtless dated 22 July 1640: "Further, I profess, for myself, to be absolutely free of any obstinacy, and to be no less disposed to learn than another is to give lessons; that is what I already professed in the *Discourse on Method*, which serves as a preface to my *Essays*; for I there expressly asked all those who had anything to say against what I proposed not to refrain from sending me their objections." ("Praeterea profiteor me ab omni pertinacia quam maxime esse alienum, nec minus paratum ad discendum quam ullus alius possit esse ad docendum; quod jam ante etiam professus sum in *Dissertatione de Methodo*, quae meorum *Speciminum* praefatio est; ibique expresse [p. 75] rogavi omnes qui aliquid contra ea quae proponebam dicendum haberent, ne suas ad me objectiones mittere gravarentur"; AT III:99, 9–16; not translated in CSMK).

5. "Quorum ubi fui admonitus, dedi statim litteras ad R. P. Rectorem ejus Collegii [J. Hayneuve], quibus rogabarn 'ut quandoquidem opiniones meae dignae visae fuerunt quae ibi publice refutarentur, me quoque non

indignum judicaret, ad quem refutationes istes mitteret, quique inter vestros discipulos censeri possem' . . . quodque tam expresse in *Dissertatione de Methodo* pag. 75 rogarim omnes, ut me errorum, quos in meis scriptis invenirent, monere dignarentur." Letter to Father Dinet, in AT VII:567, 20–26 and 568, 4–7; trans. Elisabeth S. Haldane and G. R. T. Ross, in *The Philosophical Writings of Descartes* (Cambridge: Cambridge University Press, 1911) 2:150. Cottingham omitted this passage, as did Ferdinand Alquié, *Descartes: Œuvres philosophiques*, 3 vols. (Paris: Garnier, 1963–73), and Jean-Marie Beyssades, *Descartes: Méditations métaphysiques* (Paris: Garnier-Flammarion, 1979).

6. To Mersenne, 29 June 1638, in AT II:192, 9–19; CSMK III:105.

7. On these objections and replies, see, e.g.: Jean-Robert Armogathe, "L'arc-en-ciel dans les *Météores*," in *Le discours et sa méthode*, ed. Nicolas Grimaldi and Jean-Luc Marion (Paris: Presses Universitaires de France, 1987); Pierre Costabel, "La controverse Descartes-Roberval au sujet du centre d'oscillation," in *Démarches originales de Descartes savant* (Paris: Vrin, 1982); Paul Dibon, "La réception du *Discours de la Méthode* dans les Provinces Unies," in *Descartes: il metodo e i saggi*, ed. Giulia Belgioioso et al. (Rome: Instituto della Enciclopedia Italiana, 1990); and Geneviève Rodis-Lewis, "L'accueil fait aux *Météores*," in *Problématique et réception du "Discours" et des "Essais*," ed. Henry Mechoulan (Paris: Vrin, 1988).

8. See Cornelis de Waard, "Les objections de Pierre Petit contre le Discours et les Essais de Descartes," *Revue de métaphysique et de morale* (1927): 53–89.

9. To Mersenne, 27 May 1638, in AT II:144, 16–21; CSMK III:104.

10. Petit, in Waard, "Objections de Pierre Petit," 70–71.

11. To Mersenne, 11 October 1638, in AT II:391, 20–24; not translated in CSMK.

12. Petit, in Waard, "Objections de Pierre Petit," 72.

13. Compare the letter to Mersenne, 15 April 1630, in AT I:144, 15–17; CSMK III:22 and AT VI:36, 29–31; CSM I:129. We can find here confirmation of the difference in standing between the proof from the infinite (where God's existence is demonstrated more certainly than the truths of mathematics) and the so-called ontological proof (where God sees his existence demonstrated neither more nor less certainly than the certainty with which the properties of a triangle result from its essential definition). See my demonstration, "The Essential Incoherence of Descartes' Definition of Divinity," in *Essays on Descartes' Meditations*, ed. Amélie Oksenberg Rorty (Berkeley: University of California Press, 1986), and *Metaphysical Prism*, chapter 5.

14. Petit, in Waard, "Objections de Pierre Petit," 75–79.

15. On this point, see my analysis, "What Is the Metaphysics Within the Method? The Metaphysical Situation of the Discourse on Method," in *Cartesian Questions*, 20–42.

16. To Mersenne, March 1637, in AT I:349, 29–350, 5; 27 February 1637, in CSMK III:53; to Silhon, March 1637, in AT I:352, 2–3; May 1637,

in CSMK III:55; to Vatier, 22 February 1638, in AT I:560, 7–11; CSMK III:85.

17. To Mersenne, 27 August 1639, in AT II:570, 18–20; not translated in CMSK; and 13 November 1639, in AT II:622, 13–16; CSMK III:141. See also the letter to Mersenne of 16 October 1639, in AT II:596, 22–23, CSMK III:139.

18. To Mersenne, March 1637, in AT I:349, 26; 27 February 1637, in CSMK III:53.

19. To Mersenne, 13 November 1639, in AT II:622, 13–20; CSMK III:141.

20. To Mersenne, March 1637, in AT I:350, 5; 27 February 1637, in CSMK III:53; to Vatier, 22 February 1638, in AT I:560, 7; CSMK III:85.

21. To Mersenne, 13 November 1639, in AT II:622, 20–26; CSMK III:141.

22. To Huygens, [31] July 1640, in AT III:102, 5–16; CSMK III:150 (trans. mod.). AT specifies that we have no trace of what was "said last winter."

23. "In April 1640 Descartes had completed the composition of the *Meditations.*" Alquié, *Descartes*, 2:171. He had completed the composition, certainly, but not yet the definitive text, which would integrate many remarks and improvements, both favorable and critical, suggested by readers.

24. "Multum me vobis devixistis, tu et Cl. D. Aemilius, scriptum quod ad vos miseram examinando et emendando. . . . Interpunctiones et orthographiae vitia corrigere." CSMK III:146–47.

25. To Regius, 24 May 1640, in AT III:63, 2–64, 20; CSMK III:146–47. Adrien Baillet gives the following version of this exchange: "He had allowed his manuscript to be read by several friends in Utrecht who had earnestly requested it, and particularly by Messieurs Regius and Emilius, who had been charmed to rapture by it. . . . they proposed to him two difficulties concerning the idea we have of the infinite and infinitely perfect Being, and asked him for a fuller elucidation of what he had written in his Treatise. M. Descartes was pleased to accord them this satisfaction." *Vie de Monsieur Descartes* (Paris, 1692), 2:103. In fact, we will correct three points: (i) it is really here a matter of a manuscript made public before printing, hence susceptible of still integrating corrections suggested by the objections; (ii) it is Descartes who mailed (*miseram*; AT III:63, 3) the manuscript rather than the correspondents, who "solicited" it "eagerly"; (iii) the second objection refers less to God than to the status of evidence as long as God remains unknown.

26. See AT VII:46, 29–48, 2; CSM II:32–33.

27. After the manuscript was sent to Mersenne—that is to say, during the printing—Descartes, however, continued to modify his text. Sometimes, indeed, his changes concerned only style (to Mersenne, 24 December 1640, in AT III:267, 22–268, 8; CSMK III:164). More frequently, however, they

affected the basis of the argumentation (to Mersenne, 31 December 1640, in AT III:271, 9–274, 24; CSMK III:165–66; and 18 March 1641, in AT III:334, 10–335, 10; CSMK III:175). Sometimes he corrected the *Replies* itself (to Mersenne, 4 March 1641, in AT III:329, 7–331, 9; CSMK III:173–75; and 18 March 1641, in AT III:335, 11–338, 5; CSMK III:175–77.

28. As soon as Descartes finished the composition of the *Meditations* and *Replies*, faithful to his argumentative technique (theses, objections, replies), he formed the project from which the *Principles of Philosophy* would eventuate—"comparison between the two philosophies" (to Mersenne, 11 November 1640, in AT III:233, 14–15; CSMK III:157) "in such a way that it will be very easy to see how one compares with the other; and those who have not yet learnt scholastic philosophy will find it much easier to learn from this book than from their teachers, since they will learn to scorn it at the same time" (to Mersenne, December 1640, in AT III:259, 27–260, 4; CSMK III:161). It is only in a letter to Father Charlet in December 1640 that Descartes proves to be somewhat misleading in attributing to "one of my friends" the project of "a full comparison of the philosophy that is taught in our schools with the [philosophy] I have published, in order that by showing what he thinks bad in the one, he will make it so much clearer what he judges to be better in the other." AT III:270, 4–9; not translated in CMSK.

3. The General Rule of Truth in the Third Meditation

1. "Illud omne . . . quod valde clare et distincte percipio" and "esse verum." AT VII:35, 14–15; CSM II:24.

2. J.-M. Beyssade, *La philosophie première de Descartes*, 256.

3. Jean Laporte, moreover, had suspicions about this absence; to the question "in what measure are we authorized to use as a ground this divine veracity?" he responded that "Descartes, quite honestly, never appears to be strongly bothered." *Le rationalisme de Descartes* (Paris: Presses Universitaires de France, 1945), 168. In fact, Descartes was completely unaware of it.

4. "In quarta probatur omnia quae clare et distincte percipimus, esse vera." AT VII:15, 3–4; CSM II:11.

5. "Omnis clara et distincta perceptio proculdubio est aliquid, ac proinde a nihilo esse not potest, sed necessario Deum authorem habet, Deum, inquam, illum summe perfectum quem fallacem esse repugnat; ideoque proculdubio est vera." AT VII:62, 15–20; CSM II:43.

6. "Patet enim illud omne quod verum est esse aliquid; et jam fuse demonstravi illa omnia quae clare cognosco esse vera." AT VII:65, 4–6; CSM II:45.

7. "Sim naturae ut, quamdiu aliquid valde clare et distincte percipio, non possim non credere verum esse." AT VII:69, 16–18; CSM II:48.

8. "At jam scio me in iis, quae perspicue intelligo, falli non posse. . . . Atqui nulla ex iis clare et distincte perceperam, sed hugus regulae veritatis

ignarus ob alias causas forte credideram, quas postea minus firmas esse detexi." AT VII:70, 22–28; CSM II:48–49.

9. AT VII:34, 23 = IXA:27, 16; CSM II:23.

10. Husserl, *Cartesian Meditations*, §8, *Husserliana* 1:60; English translation by Dorion Cairns (The Hague: Martinus Nijhoff, 1960), 21. The irony here is that Descartes accomplishes precisely the reduction (distinguished from doubt, in contrast to the Second Meditation) in the Third Meditation, the one in which, according to Husserl, he has to stigmatize a "fatal . . . turn." *Husserliana* 1:63.

11. "Inasmuch as they are fashions of thought"; "quatenus cogitandi modi tantum sunt"; AT VII:35, 1–2 = AT IXA:27, 17; CSM II:24.

12. To Gibieuf, 19 January 1642, AT III:474, 13–15; CSMK III:201.

13. Plato, *Theaetetus* 263d.

14. . Augustine: "Noli foras ire, in te ipsum redi: in interiore homine habitat veritas" (*De vera religione* 39.72), a text, moreover, cited at the conclusion of the *Cartesian Meditations*, §64, *Husserliana* 1:183; Cairns, 157. The following formulae echo this Augustinian theme even better: "mens humana in se conversa" (AT VII:7, 20; CSM II:7), "solus secedo" (18, 1; CSM II:12), "prudens et sciens meditando" (75, 16–17; CSM II:52), "ex sui ipsius contemplatione reflexa" (X:422, 28; CSM I:47).

15. "An forte adhuc apud *me alia* sunt quae nondum respexi." AT VII:35, 5–6 = IXA:27, 22–24; CSM II:24 (trans. mod.).

16. One should not object that *alia* (AT VII:35, 6; CSM II:24) signifies only "other understandings" (IXA:27, 23) and not different understandings, possibly intentional or transcendent; indeed, the solitary ego disposes so far only of one truth, its isolated existence, and all other/new knowledge would be for it obligatorily, and reciprocally, other/exterior.

17. Husserl, *The Idea of Phenomenology*, lecture 4, *Husserliana* 2:60. Let me underline that it is due to this doctrine that Husserl pretends (rightly) to surpass the Cartesian "circle" (*Husserliana* 2:49, with a transparent reference to the *regula generalis*), but without having envisaged (wrongly) the hypothesis that Descartes was never involved in such a "circle"—as he always defended himself. It is precisely this hypothesis that I want to maintain here, for it is possible that Descartes responded better to Husserl's requirements than the latter thought. The same ambiguity is present in *The Crisis of the European Sciences and Transcendental Phenomenology*, §17–§19, *Husserliana* 6:76.

18. "Sum certus me esse rem cogitantem." AT VII:35, 6–7; CSM II:24.

19. I do not take into account, here, my own interpretation of the ego according to its original alterity, not that I hereby renounce it, but because this alterity remains an alterity of self to self, short of all other externality.

20. "Clara quaedam et distincta perceptio ejus quod affirmo." AT VII:35, 9–10; CSM II:24. The translation of IXA:27, 27 weakens *quod affirmo* into "what I know." In this way, one lacks an anticipation of the doctrine of true judgment in the Fourth Meditation.

21. "Illud omne esse verum, quod valde clare et distincte percipio." AT VII:35, 14–15 = IXA:27, 31–32; CSM II:24.

22. J.-M. Beyssade repeats these: "To begin with, one could say, since the general rule is taken as suspect so long as divine veracity has not guaranteed it, that all evident knowledge, that is to say, clear and distinct, is suspect"—but no part of the Cartesian text speaks of suspicion, or of veracity, or of guarantee. Beyssade also immediately corrects his formulations without any pertinence: "One could also say, in a more subtle manner, which moves closer to the diversity of Cartesian texts, that the general rule remains always perfectly assured, but that we do not yet conceive any other thing with total clarity and distinction so long as we do not know divine veracity, as is the case at the beginning of the Third Meditation." *La philosophie première de Descartes*, 256–57. I will subscribe to this judgment more exactly below, with one reservation: once again, Descartes never mentions divine veracity, neither here nor later.

23. To Clerselier, July 1646, AT IV:444, 4–12; CSMK III:290.

24. On this point, see my earlier analyses in *Metaphysical Prism*, chapter 2.

25. "Hac igitur dectecta veritate [*cogito, ergo sum*] *simul etiam* invenit omnium scientiarum fundamentum; ac *etiam* omnium aliarum veritatum mensuram ac regulam; sc. Quicquid tam claram ac distincte percipitur, quam istud [*cogito, ergo sum*], verum est." Spinoza, *Principia Philosophiae Cartesianae* 1, Prolegomenon, in Gebhardt, 144; *Works* 1:233 (my emphasis).

26. "Ne quidem hoc ipsum indubitatum foret."

27. "Ac proinde jam videor mihi vel ex uno singulari hactenus indubitate cognito, sed cujus ratio nisi ad similia omnia excurreret, ne quidem hoc ipsum indubitatem foret, tuto colligere posse hanc regulam generalem: *illud omne est mihi verum ac certum, quod valde clare distincteque percipio*, vel intelligo." Johannes Clauberg, *Paraphrasis in Renati Cartesii Meditationes* 3, §12 (Duisburg, 1657); taken up again in *Opera omnia philosophica* (Amsterdam, 1691; Hildesheim, 1968), 1:387. I translate supposing that *cujus ratio nisi* stands for [*quod*], *nisi ejus ratio*, conforming to Ernout-Meillet, *Grammaire latine*, 5th ed. (Paris: Klincksieck, 1972), 333.

28. "Verumtamen multa prius ut omnino certa et manifesta admisi, quae tamen postea dubia esse deprehendi." AT VII:35, 16–18 = AT IXA:27, 34–36; CSM II:24.

29. "Statim atque aliquid a nobis recte percipi putamus, sponte nobis persuademus illud esse verum."

30. "Quid curamus istam falsitatem absolutam . . . ? Supponimus enim persuasionem tam firmam ut nullo modo tolli possit." AT VII:144, 24–145, 9; CSM II:103.

31. "Sed dubitari potest an habeatur aliqua talis certitudo, sive firma et immutabilis persuasio." AT VII:145, 10–11; CSM II:103.

32. A text on which J. Laporte comments very well in *Le rationalisme de Descartes*, 151. See VII:192, 19–21; CSM II:135: "As everyone knows, a

'light in the intellect' means transparent clarity of cognition; and while perhaps not everyone who thinks he possesses this does in fact possess it"
("nemo enim nescit per lucem in intellectu intelligi perspicuitatem cogni-
tionis, quam forte non habent omnes qui putant se habere"; AT VII:461, 21;
CSM II:310); *soli prudentes* (462, 2; CSM II:310; 476, 26–28; CSM II:320);
and "There are few people who correctly distinguish between what they in
fact perceive and what they think they perceive; for not many are accus-
tomed to clear and distinct perceptions" ("pauci sint, qui recte distinguant
inter id, quod revera percipitur, et id quod percipi putatur, quia pauci claris
ac distinctis perceptionibus sunt assueti"; 511, 17–20; CSM II:348). The
strongest text comes without a doubt from the Seventh Replies, where the
doubt provoked by ignorance regarding a nondeceiving God only concerns—explicitly—perceptions that are not clear and distinct: "Again, until
we know that God exists, we have reason to doubt everything (i.e. everything such that we do not have *a clear perception of it before our minds, as I have
often explained)*" ("quod antequam quis sciat Deum existere, habeat occasio-
nem dubitandi de omni re [nempe de omni re *cujus claram perceptionem animo
suo praesentem non habet, ut aliquoties exposui*]"; AT VII:546, 22–25; CSM
II:373; my emphasis.

33. "Lumen naturae nobis dictat, nunquam nisi de re cognita esse judi-
candum. In hoc autem frequentissime erramus, quod multa putemus a nobis
olim fuisse percepta, iisque, memoriae mandatis, tanquam omnino perceptis
assentiamur, quae tamen revera nunquam percepimus." CSM I:207.

34. "Quin et permulti homines nihil plane in tota vita percipiunt satis
recte, ad certam de eo judicium ferendum." AT VIIIA:21, 24–29 and 21,
30–22, 1; CSM I:207.

35. "Notandum est hanc regulam, *quicquid possumus concipere, id potest esse*,
quamvis mea sit, et vera, quoties agitur de claro et distincto conceptu, in
quo rei possibilitas continetur, quia Deus potest omnia efficere, quae nos
possibilia esse clare percipimus; non tamen temere ususrpandam, quia facile
sit, ut quis putet se aliquam rem recte intelligere, quam tamen praejudicio
aliquo excaecatus non intelligit." *Notae in programma quoddam*, VIIIB:351,
28–352, 6; CSM I:299.

36. "A conceptu rerum adaeaquato, qualem nemo habet, non modo de
infinito, sed nec forte etiam de ulla alia re quantumvis parva." Fifth Replies,
AT VII:365, 3–5; CSM II:252. See, for a comparison on this point between
Descartes and Spinoza, my study "*Aporias* and the Origin of Spinoza's theory of adequate ideas," in *Spinoza on Knowledge and the Human Mind*, ed. Yirmiahu Yovel (Leiden: Brill, 1994).

37. See below, Chapter 7.

38. AT VII:21, 4–6; CSM II:14. In the same way, Descartes writes in the
Second Meditation: "But I have convinced myself that there is absolutely
nothing in the world, no sky, no earth, no minds, no bodies" ("sed mihi
persuasi nihil plane esse in mundo, nullum caelum, nullam terram . . . nulla

corpora"; AT VII:25, 2–4; CSM II, 16). On the strange addition of the *nullas mentes*, see above, Chapter 1, n. 40. On this difficulty, consult *Cartesian Questions*, chap. 1, §4.

39. "Intellectum a nullo unquam experimento decipi posse, si praecise tantum intueatur rem sibi objectam, prout illam habet vel in se ipso, vel in phantasmate." AT X:423, 1–4; CSM I:47.

40. "Neque praeterea nec denique res externas tales semper esse quales apparent." AT X:423, 4–7; CSM I:47.

41. "Consuetudinem credendi me clare percipere." AT VII:35, 24–25; CSM II:25.

42. "Res quasdam extra me esse, a quibus ideae istae procedebant, et quibus omnino similes erant." AT VII:35, 26–27 = IXA:28, 6–8; CSM II:25. The thesis of the nonsimilitude between object and idea not only has a critical function, it defines positively the entire doctrine of perception from the *Regulae* (AT X:418, 1–419, 5 and 423, 1–30; CSM I:44 and 47) and the *Dioptric/Optics* (AT VI:85, 13ff., 113, 3ff.; CSM I:153, 165). In this context, the definition of the idea by similitude first attempted by the Third Meditation (VII:37, 3–12) and soon abandoned (40, 5ff.) should in no way be taken as the same as that of Descartes; on the contrary, he mentions it only to make the aporia manifest and to impose his own where, since the *Optics*, causality always controls representation. A number of commentators have criticized the first definition, believing to refute Descartes when they thus repeat, often less effectively, the criticism of similitude.

43. See the very enlightening parallel of the Second Replies: AT VII:145, 10–21; CSM II:103–4.

44. "Mentis purae et attentae tam facilem distinctumque conceptum, ut de eo, quod intelligimus, nulla prorsus dubitatio relinquatur." AT X:368, 15–17; CSM I:14.

45. "Haec praeconcepta de summa Dei potentia." AT VII:36, 8–9 = IXA:28, 11–12; CSM II:25.

46. "Infixa quaedam . . . meae mentis vetus opinio, Deum esse qui potest omnia." AT VII:21, 1–2 = IXA:16, 14–15; CSM II:14.

47. It is certainly not a matter here of a cause in the plain sense, of an efficient cause (it only appears in AT VII:40, 22; CSM II:28), but of what the Second Replies names "reason for doubting" (*causam dubitandi*; 144, 29; CSM II:103), a motive of doubting.

48. "Talem mihi naturam indere potuisse, ut etiam circa illa deciperer, quae manifestissima viderentur." AT VII:36, 6–8; CSM II:25.

49. *Théologie blanche*, chapter 14, 324 ff., which I am summarizing.

50. "Fallat me quisquis potest, nunquam tamen efficiet ut nihil sim, quamdiu me aliquid esse cogitabo." AT VII:36, 15–17 = 25, 8–10; CSM II:25.

51. "Sponte erumpam in has voces." AT VII:36, 15; CSM II:25.

52. The confusion and the extrinsic obscurity disappear in this sole case, because it is no longer a matter of a representation (view/object), but of a

pragmatic (acts of deception, of being deceived, of being persuaded, etc.) and even of an interlocution. Hence this confirms the conclusion of Chapter 1.

53. M. Gueroult: "Subjective certainty, that is to say, that of the *cogito*, finding itself put into question, if not by fact, at least in principle, by the subsistence of universal doubt" (*Descartes selon l'ordre des raisons*, 158); a judgment approved by J.-M. Beyssade ("the 'objective' *cogito*, of which he states lucidly that it is called into question"; *La philosophie première de Descartes*, 255), and even by F. Alquié ("it is certain that Descartes neglects here, for some instants, the specificity of the cogito and considers it no more than one evidence among others"; note in *Descartes: Œuvres philosophiques*, 2:432). This common thesis, however, appears unsustainable to me because (a) the text obviously never distinguishes two cogitos, objective or subjective, this having been invented by Gueroult (see the remark of J.-M. Beyssade: "Let us guard here against opposing an actualized *cogito* and an objective *cogito*"; *La philosophie première de Descartes*, 255); (b) never again is the existence of the ego put in question in sections 35, 16–36, 12; when doubt intervenes, it concerns only the sensible [world] and mathematics, exactly as in the First Meditation, but it does not mention the ego; (c) reciprocally, when the ego reappears, it is in a section that no longer mentions doubt (36, 12ff.); (d) and hence the parallel, in the form of an alternative and of a sporadic glance, between the *quoties* referring to omnipotence (36, 8) and the *quoties* referring to evidence (36, 12) suffers an exception: when one regards the reason for doubting, the existence of the ego is *not* mentioned, and when it is mentioned, it is a matter of compiling *certainties*; (e) furthermore, Gueroult himself does not seem to believe his own error, since he affirms "if not in fact, at least by right," but only the (textual) fact matters when it is a matter of understanding a text.

54. Gouhier, *La pensée métaphysique de Descartes* (Paris: Vrin, 1962), 318.

55. "Quod ea, quae semel facta sunt, infecta esse non possint." AT VII:145, 25–26; CSM II:104. For the decisive question of the status of these contradictory statements against the divine omnipotence, see my study *Théologie blanche*, chap. 13, 296ff.

56. *Quamdiu*, VII:36, 16 and 25, 9 or 27, 9–10; *quoties*, 25, 12; see *dum*, 145, 24.

57. Gueroult, *Descartes selon l'ordre des raisons*, 1:157. This position is found also in J.-M. Beyssade, but as a confirmation of Cartesian reasoning: "[The science of my existence] is comparable to mathematical evidences: like a theorem of geometry, it bases itself on primitive notions and on a common notion" (*La philosophie première de Descartes*, 256). To the contrary, I concur with J. Laporte's position: "And why did the defiance have to cede before the *cogito*? Because our effort in doubting maintains our attention fixed on our doubt itself, and in consequence on our thought. But it is a

proper privilege of the *cogito*. For all other truths, the mobility of our attention has made possible a 'hyperbolic' doubt" (*Le rationalisme de Descartes*, 156).

58. Gouhier, *La pensée métaphysique de Descartes*. A perfect judgment in all points, except that in Descartes there is neither "cogito" (see above, Chapter 1), nor "veracity," nor "guarantee."

59. AT VII:36, 18–19; CSM II:25. AT IXA:28, 31 weakens it to "or," which lacks the essential; I follow here with pleasure the translation of Michelle Beyssade, *Descartes: Méditations métaphysiques* (Paris: Librairie Générale Française, 1990), 89.

60. "Et talia, de quibus manifestum est hanc certitudinem haberi." AT VII:145, 26–27; CSM II:104.

61. "Ita uniuscujusque animo potest intueri, se existere, se cogitare, triangulum terminari tribus lineis antum, globum unica superficie, et similia quae longe plura sunt quam plerique animadvertunt." AT X:368, 21–25; CSM I:14.

62. "Ut duo et tria simul juncta plura vel pauciora sint quam quinque."

63. AT VII:36, 19–21; IXA:28, 31–32; CSM II:25; *repugnatia* is not translated by Luynes, but justly reestablished by Michelle Beyssade, *Descartes*, 156.

64. Does not the final sequence—"for if I do not know of this [the existence of God], it seems that I can never be quite certain about anything else" ("hac enim re ignorata, non videor de ulla alia plane certus esse unquam posse"; 36, 28–29; CSM II:25)—suppose that even the ego necessitates the previous consciousness of the existence of God? I will respond by distinguishing the following: (a) The ego attains its existence, in fact, despite its ignorance of that of God and its preliminary deception; Descartes never goes back on this acquisition. (b) The ego, when it ignores the nondeceptive existence of God, does not yet know itself deeply (*plane*), because it must at each instant repeat its act of being by thought. (c) In this sense, its proper idea remains insufficient and demands God to endure without an act of the *cogito* (see n. 35).

65. I join, by other paths, the conclusions of Gilles Olivo, "L'évidence en règle: Descartes, Husserl et la question de la *Mathesis Universalis*," in *Les Études philosophiques* 1–2 (1996): 211.

4. Pascal and the "General Rule" of Truth

1. We cite here according to the numbering of Pascal's *Œuvres complètes*, ed. Louis Lafuma (Paris: Seuil, 1963).

2. "If one must philosophize, one must philosophize, and, if one must not philosophize, one must philosophize." *Fragmenta selecta*, ed. W. D. Ross (Oxford: Oxford University Press, 1964), fgt. 2, 227ff.

3. Among others recently: Michel Le Guern, *Pascal et Descartes* (Paris: A. G. Nizet, 1971); Gregor Sebba, "Descartes and Pascal: A Retrospect,"

Modern Language Notes 87, no. 6 (1972); Pierre Magnard, *Nature et histoire dans l'apologétique de Pascal* (Paris: Société Belles Lettres, 1975 1st ed., 1980 2d ed.); Henri Gouhier, *Blaise Pascal: Conversion et apologétique* (Paris: Vrin, 1986); Marion, *Metaphysical Prism*, chap. 5; above all, Vincent Carraud, *Pascal et la philosophie* (Paris: Presses Universitaires de France, 1992).

4. "Omnis scientia est cognitio certa et evidens." Descartes, *Regulae ad directionem ingenii* 2, AT X:362, 5; CSM I:10; taken up from Aristotle, *Topica* 5.2.130b 16–17.

5. "Illud omne esse verum, quod valde clare et distincte percipio." AT VII:35, 14–15 and IXA:27, 31–33; CSM II:24. We thus take the same point of departure here as in Chapter 3, §1, above.

6. One can consider in effect that the doctrine of the creation of the eternal truths (and its corollaries: the incomprehensible omnipotence of God, hypothetical possibility of impossible contradictories, etc.) constitutes an exception—at least on first analysis. See *Théologie blanche*, in particular §12.

7. *Réponse au Révérend Père Noël, recteur de la Société de Jésus, à Paris*, 29 October 1647, *Œuvres Complètes*, 201a. See also *Œuvres Complètes*, ed. Jean Mesnard, 4 vols. to date (Paris: Desclée De Brouwer, 1964–), 2:519. I will make reference to the Lafuma and Mesnard editions wherever possible (abbreviating L and M). English translation by Emile Cailliet and John C. Blankenagel, *Great Shorter Works of Pascal* (Philadelphia: Westminster Press, 1948), 43.

8. L 348 = M 3:375.

9. Respectively, L 349 (three times "la véritable méthode") = M 3:390–94. *Shorter Works*, 189, 190, 191.

10. Respectively, L 350 = M 3:395. *Shorter Works*, 191 (twice). Here one must not oppose Descartes, who commences straightaway with the most simple evidence, to Pascal, who reaches *in fine* the simplest by beginning with the complex; because, even for Descartes (as later for Leibniz), the simplest is only discovered at the end of a simplification, as the second precept of the method indisputably indicates, [namely the precept found] between the two we have just cited: "To divide each of the difficulties I examined into as many parts as possible and as may be required to resolve them better." AT VI:18, 24–26; CSM I:120. In the *Regulae*, the simple natures result explicitly from a process of simplification, so much more complex that it does not aim precisely at the most simple in itself, but the most simple for the intelligence of evidence (*Regula* 12, AT X:418, 1 – 419, 5 etc.; CSM I:44).

11. L 351b, 352a = M 3:401, 403. *Shorter Works*, 195, 196.

12. "Sed quid est homo? dicamne animal rationale? Non, quia postea quaerendum foret quidnam animal sit, et quid rationale, atque ita ex una questione in plures difficilioresque delaberer." AT VII:25, 29; IXA:20, 11–14; CSM II:17. See *La Recherche de la Vérité* 10:515–16; *Shorter Works*,

192. Descartes follows here, as does Pascal, Montaigne, *Essais* 2:12 and 3:13 (in the Villey-Saulnier edition [Paris: Presses Universitaires de France, 1978], 544 and 1069).

13. *Dioptrique* 1, AT VI:84, 15–19; *Optics* 1, CSM I:153. See parallels and discussion in my *Descartes: Règles utiles et claires pour la direction de l'esprit dans la recherche de la vérité* (The Hague: Martinus Nijhoff, 1977), 198ff, 210ff.

14. *Regula* 12, AT X:42, 3 – 427, 2; CSM I:48–49—as proves the similarity to the Pascalian critique of geometry, which can "define neither the movement, nor the number, nor the space" (L 351b = M 3:401).

15. In regard to the status of *being* and of Being according to Pascal, see *Metaphysical Prism*, §25, 340–41.

16. See my indications in *Sur l'ontologie grise de Descartes*, §22–§24, 131ff.

17. Although he employs these terms of space, time, number, and movement, he does not thematize them as natures or simple terms.

18. L 350b = M 3:398; *Shorter Works*, 193. See "these terms there [space, time, thing, movement, equality, number, etc.] designate so naturally the thing that they signify to those who understand the language, that the enlightenment that one would like to make would bring more obscurity than instruction." L 350a = M 3:396. *Naturally* indicates paradoxically that the defining term never attains the *nature* of the designated (undefined); it is only a matter of the subjective facility of the interlocutors to comprehend themselves without comprehending the object in play, as is the case for Descartes. (See *L'ontologie grise*, 92ff.) Pascal here takes up Descartes: "And I have often noticed that philosophers make the mistake of employing logical definitions in an attempt to explain what was already very simple and self-evident; the result is that they only make matters more obscure" ("et saepe adverti Philosophos in hoc errare, quod ea, quae simplicissima erant ac per se nota, logicis definitionibus, explicere conarentur; ita enim ipsa obscuriora reddebant"; *Principia Philosophiae* 1, §10; AT VIIIA:8; CSM I:195–96). Or: "That the mind, which is incorporeal, can set the body in motion is something which is shown to us not by any reasoning or comparison with other matters, but by the surest and plainest everyday experience. It is one of those self-evident things which we only make obscure when we try to explain them in terms of other things" ("Quod autem mens, quae est incorporea, corpus possit impellere, nulla quidem ratiocinatio vel comparatio ab aliis rebus petita, sed certissima et evidentissima experientia quotidie ostendit; haec enim una est ex rebus per se notis, quas, cum volumus per alias explicare, obscuramus"; Letter to Arnauld, 29 July 1648, AT V:222, 15–20; CSMK III:358).

19. L 350b = M 3:398; *Shorter Works*, 193. One can think here of Hegel criticizing sensible consciousness in the *Phenomenology of Spirit* (*GW* 9:63ff.) and of Husserl's "occasionally significative expressions" (*Logical Investigations* 1, §26), since here "I cannot express" (to which I can hence not fix any signification) what I even so designate (L 350a = M 3:396).

20. L 353b = M 3:407; *Shorter Works*, 199.

21. L 350a/b = M 3:397; *Shorter Works*, 192.

22. L 351b = M 3:401; *Shorter Works*, 195.

23. L 352a = M 3:403; *Shorter Works*, 196. See *Pensées*, §282.

24. L 354b = M 3:410; *Shorter Works*, 201.

25. L 351a = M 3:399; *Shorter Works*, 193; then *Pensées*, §199. English translations by A. J. Krailsheimer (Baltimore: Penguin, 1966), 92. [This seems to be one of the very few translations of the *Pensées* that uses the same paragraph numbering as Lafuma's edition of Pascal's complete works, which Marion almost always cites—Trans.] The passage from "extreme evidence" to bedazzlement ("too much evidence") certainly occurs in §199, not in *The Spirit of Geometry*. Do they remain along the same lines or would a solution of continuity separate them absolutely? V. Carraud has convincingly argued in favor of their irreducibility; but even he hesitates to discard all continuity: "The end of *The Spirit of Geometry* reveals already the rhetorical slipping which amounts to the subversion of [operated by?] §199" (*Pascal et la philosophie*, 432; see 426ff.). Even this simple "slipping" suffices to authorize, it seems to me, the comparison between the extremeness of evidence and its excess. Moreover, one must not underestimate the importance of the recourse to admiration ("not to conceive but to admire," L 354b = M 3:410) at the end of *The Spirit of Geometry*: first, because Descartes himself has recourse to this term in strict metaphysics to mark with an already rather excessive and not merely extreme evidence ("to gaze with wonder and adoration on the beauty of this immense light, so far as the eye of my darkened intellect can bear it"; "quantum caligantis ingenii mei acies ferre potuerit, intueri, admirari, adorare"; Third Meditation, AT VII:52, 14–16; CSM II:36); then, because the *Pensées* make it a privileged operator (sixty-two occurrences, according to Hugh M. Davidson and Pierre H. Dubé, *A Concordance to Pascal's Pensées* [Ithaca: Cornell University Press, 1975]) and, in particular (is it really by chance?), §199: humans finding themselves between "infinity and nothingness," "I believe that with his curiosity changing into wonder, he will be more disposed to contemplate them in silence than investigate them with presumption"; the infinite must be admired, not be "comprehended" (from which derives the criticism of all philosophical research into principles in the same fragment). Hence why not admit that the return of curiosity (or comprehension) in admiration intervenes after *The Spirit of Geometry* and is prolonged to §199 (with the reservation that one passes from an epistemological field to one of anthropology) following a uniform Cartesian meaning of that term?

26. *Pensées*, §110. See §155: "Heart/Instinct/Principles." It is by starting with these two texts that one must understand §423 and 424. See V. Carraud, *Pascal et la philosophie*, 246ff., and H. Gouhier, *Pascal: Conversion et apologétique*, 168ff.

27. "Ipsa autem prima principia per intuitum tantum." AT X:370, 13–15; CSM I:15. See AT X:387, 16; CSM I:25, and Second Replies, AT VII:140, 16 – 141, 2; CSM II:100.

28. Aristotle, *Nicomachean Ethics* 6.6.1141a7. See 6.11.1143a35, and *Posterior Analytic* 2.19.100b5–17.

29. I would be prompted to follow here H. Gouhier, underlining that, contrary to a long tradition of editors, one must consider *The Spirit of Geometry* and *On the Art of Persuasion* as "two separate writings," not only chronologically, but because of their conceptual thematics (*Cartésianisme et augustinisme au XVIIe siècle*, 144, see Appendix 2, 179ff.).

30. *Shorter Works*, 206–7.

31. *On the Art of Persuasion*, L 356b–357a = M 3:419–20. *Shorter Works*, 207. In fact, of the "veritable order, which consists . . . in defining and proving everything," the fragment *The Spirit of Geometry* already clearly realizes that this "splendid" method "is absolutely impossible" (L 349b = M 3:393–95; *Shorter Works*, 191).

32. *On the Art of Persuasion*, L 355b = M 3:415; *Shorter Works*, 202–3.

33. *Pensées*, §148. On the theological origin (desire of beatitude as desire to see God) of this "principle," see Henri de Lubac, *Le mystère du surnaturel* (Paris: Aubier, 1965) and *Augustinisme et théologie moderne* (Paris: Aubier, 1965). Must one oppose to it the desire to know that inaugurates philosophy (*Metaphysics* A1.980a1)?

34. *On the Art of Persuasion*, L 355b = M 3:416; *Shorter Works*, 204.

35. L 355a = M 3:413; *Shorter Works*, 203.

36. "Of a great clarity which was in the understanding, has followed a great inclination in my will"; "ex magna luce in intellectu magna consecuta est propensio in voluntate." AT VII:59, 13; IXA:47, 4–6; CSM II:41.

37. H. Gouhier speaks here judiciously of a "phenomenology of consent" (*Cartésianisme et augustinisme*, 183).

38. Respectively, L 355a = M 3:413–14; *Shorter Works*, 203; and *Pensées*, §661. See, of course, §739: "Truth is so obscured nowadays and lies so well established that unless we love the truth, we shall never recognize it"; and also §377: "What a long way it is between loving God and knowing him." On the pleasure of divine things (in discussion from the beginning of *On the Art of Persuasion*), see V. Carraud, "Évidence et représentation de la mort: Remarques sur l'anthropologie pascalienne du divertissement," *XVIIe siècle* 175, no. 2 (1992): 141–56.

39. L 355a = M 3:413–14; *Shorter Works*, 203.

40. L 356a = M 3:416–17. For the relation to Descartes, see above, §2. The comparison with part 4, "Of the Method," of the *Logic of Port-Royal* follows naturally here; one will remark above all that chap. 11, which cites the Pascalian rules for definitions, axioms, and demonstrations, omits the final ones of each rubric completely, namely, those that concern the things "well known." On the one hand, it is there only a matter of obeying Pascal's

implicit recommendation ("there are three of them which are not absolutely necessary, and which one can neglect without error," L 357a = M 3:420); on the other, it is a matter of a complete evacuation of Pascal's central problem—redoubling the Cartesian method (see the edition of F. Clair and F. Girbal [Paris: Flammarion, 1965], 333ff.). A trace nevertheless remains of this project: the inclusion of the question of miracles in the method (chap. 14).

41. *Shorter Works*, 204.

42. *Shorter Works*, 205. The *mathesis universalis* in fact only appears in the *Regula* 4, AT X:378, 8 and 379:4.

43. L 356a, then 355 a/b = M 3:416, then 3:413–15; *Shorter Works*, 203, then 202.

44. L 356a = M 3:416–17; *Shorter Works*, 205, and *Pensées*, §512.

45. *Pensées*, §539.

46. The miracle took place on 24 March 1656, the opinion of the Grand Vicar was given on 22 October, and the fourth letter to Mademoiselle de Roannez, which refers to both, is logically dated at the end of October. Tetsuya Shiokawa, in *Pascal et les miracles* (Paris: Nizet, 1977; esp. chaps. 4 and 5), links the relation between evidence/obscurity/faith and the question of miracles. I will not insist on this point, because I have made it in another place (*Prolégomènes à la charité* [Paris: Éditions de la Différence, 1986, 1991], 71–88; trans. Stephen E. Lewis as *Prolegomena to Charity* [New York: Fordham University Press, 2002], 53–70) and because I focus here only on Pascal's philosophy. J.-M. Beyssade has recently furnished a good confirmation of this link in his study of the counter-interpretation of Sainte-Beuve, "Images du miracle au XIXe siècle: Du Port-Royal de Sainte-Beuve au Lourdes de Zola," in *Pascal au miroir du XIXe siècle*, ed. Denise Leduc-Fayette (Paris: Éditions Universitaires, 1993), 161–87.

47. Translation by Lemaître de Sacy, in the reprint edition of Philippe Sellier (Paris: Bordas, 1990), 1459. All citations of the fourth letter to Mademoiselle de Roannez in L 267a/b = M 3:1035–37; *Shorter Works*, 146–47. But how can Pascal reconcile this text with the *Pensées*, §463? It is one of the principal merits of the work of P. Magnard, *Nature et histoire dans l'apologétique de Pascal*, in particular of the second part, to have underlined that nature, no less than super-nature, comes from a hermeneutics of obscurity. H. Gouhier spoke already of an "apologetics as hermeneutics" even in "nature" (*Blaise Pascal: Commentaires* [Paris: Vrin, 1966], 200). [English translation of biblical text from the New Revised Standard Version.]

48. *Pensées*, respectively §471, §726, §934, and §781.

49. *Préface au Traité du vide*, L 231b = M 2:780; *Shorter Works*, 53. The comparison with Heraclitus (Fragment 123, Diels/Kranz, *Fragmente der Vorsokratiker* 1 [Dublin and Zürich: Weidmannsche Verlagsbuchhandlung, 1966, 12th ed.], 178) has, moreover, been suggested by Jean Beaufret (*Dialogue avec Heidegger* [Paris: Minuit, 1974], 3:94), unfortunately only in the

mode of mockery; it seems, nevertheless, possible to make a better case for it, in taking account of Romans 1:20 and its biblical parallels on the darkening of the spirit and the hardening of the heart (which even Descartes utilizes: see Second Replies, AT VII:142ff.; CSM II:101ff.).

50. See the works of Gérard Ferreyrolles, *Pascal et la raison du politique* (Paris: Presses Universitaires de France, 1984) and *Les reines du monde: L'imagination et la coutume chez Pascal* (Paris: H. Champion, 1995).

51. *Pensées*, respectively §234 and §176; it is hence found to be a truth attained not through proof but through pleasure, consequently definable not in the second order but in the third. See my analyses in *Metaphysical Prism*, §25, 337–40.

52. At least in the first approximation for theology, precisely because it must confront the excess of the given (and hence the bedazzlement that results from it, at times to the point of obscurity), it must all the more scrupulously be guided "by the level of reason," even if this rationality often takes the figures of paradox. In the end, irrationalism always ruins theology.

53. I wish to thank V. Carraud for the remarks, criticisms, and advice that he was willing to address to me in the process of editing this study.

5. Substance and Subsistence
Suárez and the Treatise on Substantia *in the* Principles of Philosophy *I,* *§51–§54*

1. "In quantum unae ex aliis cognosci possunt." AT X:381, 12–13; CSM I:21 (trans. mod.).

2. See my analysis in *Sur l'ontologie grise de Descartes*, §12–§14.

3. To Morin, 12 September 1638, AT II:367, 21 – 368, 8; CSMK III:122 (my emphasis).

4. Third Meditation, AT VII:45, 7, and French translation by the Duke of Luynes, AT IXA:35, 37; CSM II:31. See also "a doubting or thinking substance" ("substantia dubitans sive cogitans"; Seventh Replies, AT VII:537, 7–8; CSM II:366) and "for these perfections are merely attributes of a substance, whereas I am a substance" ("illae [perfectiones quae mihi desunt] enim sunt tantum attributa substantiae, ego autem sum substantia"; Second Replies, AT VII:168, 7–8; CSM II:118).

5. See: AT VII:45, 11, 21, 22, 27; CSM II:31; but also Second Replies, AT VII:165, 30; 166, 1; CSM II:117; or Third Replies, 185, 26; CSM II:130; and above all the retrospective commentary in AT VII:45, 11; CSM II:31, by Descartes in his letter to Clerselier of 23 April 1649. Here he explicitly specifies about the infinite: "This is not an accident added to the notion of substance, but the very essence of substance taken absolutely and bounded by no defects" ("non est accidens notioni substantiae superadditum, sed ipsa essentia substantiae absolute sumptae, nullisque defectibus terminatae"; AT V:355, 22 – 356, 7; CSMK III:377). In short, substance is essentially (and not accidentally) infinite, from which we can infer that finitude

is here added as an accident. This is enlightened by a more well-known text: "The substance which we understand to be supremely perfect, and in which we conceive absolutely nothing that implies any defect or limitation in that perfection, is called God" ("substantia, quam summe perfectam esse intelligimus et in qua nihil plane concipimus quod aliquem defectum sive perfectionis limitationem involvat, Deus vocatur"; Second Replies, AT VII:162, 4–7; CSM II:114). On this point, see *Metaphysical Prism*, 224ff.

6. "Quibus addi possunt substantia, duratio et numerus." AT VII:43, 20; CSM II:30. Same sequence, beginning this time with the simple intellectual natures, in AT VII:44, 19–21; CSM II:30: "It appears I could have borrowed some of these from my idea of myself, namely substance, duration, number and anything else of this kind" ("quaedam ab ipsa mei ipsius videor mutuari potuisse, nempe substantiam, durationem, numerum, et si quae alia sint ejusmodi"). On these points, see *Cartesian Questions*, chap. 3, §2–§5, or "Metodo et metafisica: le nature semplici," in *Cartesiana*, ed. Giulia Belgioioso (Lecce: Conte, 1992), 3–27.

7. "Simplices omnes notiones, ex quibus cogitationes nostrae componuntur." §47, AT VIIIA:22, 23–25; CSM I:208.

8. "Maxime generalia sunt *substantia, duratio, ordo, numerus*, et si quae alia sunt ejusmodi." §48, AT VIIIA:22, 21–23, 1; CSM I:208.

9. "Per *substantiam* nihil aliud intelligere possumus, quam rem quae ita existit, ut nulla alia re indigeat ad existendum." §51, AT VIIIA:24, 21–23; CSM I:210.

10. "Sub hoc communi conceptu . . . quod sint res, quae solo Dei concursu egent ad existendum." §52, AT VIIIA:25, 1–3; CSM I:210.

11. To Mersenne, 30 September 1640, AT III:191, 15–16; CSMK III:154. For the ambiguity of independence, see several references in *Metaphysical Prism*, §17, 232–34.

12. "Essentia substantiae creatae tam est imperfecta, ut semper indigeat addimento alterius generis . . . existentia naturae creatae talis est, ut sit essentialiter dependens a Deo ut ab efficiente." Suárez, *Disputationes metaphysicae* 34, s. 3, n. 14, in *Opera omnia*, ed. Carolo Berton (Paris: Vivès, 1866ff.), 26:364. [Most translations from the Latin in this chapter are by Antonio Calcagno—Trans.]

13. "Imo, si per possibile vel impossibile fieri posset aliqua res creata incapax accidentium, et natura sua nullo subjecto indigens ad existendum, illa esset perfecta substantia." Suárez, *Disputationes metaphysicae* 33, s. 1, n. 2, *Opera omnia* 26:330.

14. "Lapidem esse substantiam sive esse rem quae per se apta est existere." AT VII:44, 22–23; CSM II:30.

15. AT VIIIA:31, 29; CSM I:216. See letter to Regius, January 1642: "A true substance, or self-subsistent thing" ("vera substantia, sive res subsistens"; AT III:502, 11; CSMK III:207). In the same way "created, self-subsistent matter" ("materia creata et per se subsistens"; *Principles of Philosophy*

2, §17, AT VIIIA:49, 25–26; CSM I:230). To Regius, December 1641, AT III:456, 16 – 457, 2 (on the equivalence between *morbus per se subsistens* and *morbos esse substantias*); not translated in CSMK.

16. "Mihi contradictorium videri, ut sint substantiae, hoc est, res per se subsistentes et simul incompletae, hoc est, per se subsistere non valentes." AT VII:222, 17–20; CSM II:156–57.

17. "Haec ipsa est notio *substantiae*, quod per se, hoc est absque ope ullius alterius substantiae possit existere." AT VII:226, 3–5; CSM II:159.

18. "Ens autem per se constituit substantiam; ens vero in alio constitutit accidens." Suárez, *Disputationes metaphysicae* 32, s. 1, n. 5, *Opera omnia* 26: 313.

19. "Solum id quod subsistit, maxime ac propriissime substantia dicitur." Suárez, *Disputationes metaphysicae* 34, s. 1, n. 7, *Opera omnia* 26:350.

20. "Substantia quaevis, si cessat durare, cessat etiam esse." CSM I:214. "To subsist . . . is nothing other than to have remained" ("subsistere . . . nihil aliud est quam immorari)" and "in this way, being in itself is a firm and constant thing such that it can sustain otherness" ("rem ita esse in se firmam et constantem, ut possit aliam sustinere"). Suárez, *Disputationes metaphysicae* 33, s. 1, n. 3 and 1; *Opera omnia* 26:331 and 330. And *Principles of Philosophy* 1, §62, VIIIA:30, 14–15.

21. On Heidegger's analysis of this Cartesian position and the limits of its pertinence, see *Metaphysical Prism*, §14, 169ff.

22. "In Deo perfectissima ratio substantiae reperitur, quia maxime est in se ac per se, etiamsi accidentibus non substet"; "nam solus Deus est substantia completa sine ulla compositione . . .; est enim hic Deus substantia physice, seu reipsa completa, quia per seipsam est essentialiter subsistens, et ex se non indiget aliquo ad consummatam et absolutam substantiae perfectionem"; "at vero in creaturis nunquam reperitur substantia completa sine reali compositione." Suárez, *Disputationes metaphysicae* 33, s. 1, respectively n. 2 and n. 8 (twice), *Opera omnia* 26:330–32.

23. "Et quidem substantia quae nulla alia re indigeat, unica tantum potest intelligi, nempe Deus." AT VIIIA:24, 23–25; CSM I:210.

24. "Deficit a perfecta ratione substantiae, et ex se vel non subsistit actu nisi in alio, seu in toto, vel non perfecte subsistit, neque omnino absolute, sed in ordine ad componendum aliquod totum"; "si vero sit completa substantia, quamvis subsistit actu, non tamen vi suae essentiae formaliter ac praecise, sed per aliquem modum et actum suae essentiae, et ideo substantialis natura creata . . . non est essentialiter actus subsistens, sed aptitudine." Suárez, *Disputationes metaphysicae* 33, s. 1, n. 7, *Opera omnia* 26:314.

25. "Simpliciter et omnino in ratione sustantiae, quia indiget ulteriori complemento metaphysice." Suárez, *Disputationes metaphysicae* 33, s. 1, n. 18, *Opera omnia* 26:335. See 34, s. 1, n. 7 and 8: "This humanity or this being-Peter is not the first substance, for it means that it is neither subsisting nor the reverse, that it is formally subsisting by the power of its own singular

nature, which has been precisely taken up" ("haec humanitas seu Petreitas, non esse primam substantiam, quia nec significatur ut subsistens, nec revera est formaliter subsistens, ex vi ipsius naturae singularis praecise sumptae"); *Opera omnia* 26:350.

26. "Semper indigebit aliquo addito vel complemento propriis generis, ut in eo complete sit"; "no created substance is possible that in the thing is not separable from its subsistence"; "nulla est possibilis substantia creata, quae in re non sit separabilis a sua subsistentia." Suárez, *Disputationes metaphysicae* 34, s. 3, n. 14 and 15, *Opera omnia* 26:364. See the *vera sententia* of Suárez: "To be given by nature to this personhood so that it gives to it the ultimate complement in the idea of existing or (as I will say) so that it may complete its existence in the idea of subsistence, this is the case so that personhood may not properly be the terminus or the mode of nature according to the being of essence, but rather according to the being of existence" ("personalitatem ad hoc dari naturae, ut illi dat ultimum complementum in ratione existendi, vel [ut ita dicam] ut existentiam ejus compleat in ratione subsistentiae, ita ut personalitas non sit proprie terminus aut modus naturae secundum esse essentiae, sed secundum esse existentiae"; *Disputationes metaphysicae* 34, s. 4, n. 23, *Opera omnia* 26:374). Or again: "The substantial existence of created nature, even though it is complete through itself and by virtue of its rational form, is not a substance because indisputably it does not include that which is spoken by itself" ("existentia substantialis naturae creatae, quamvis completae, per se ipsam et ex vi suae rationis formalis, non sit subsistentia, quia nimirum non includit dictum per se"; *Disputationes metaphysicae* 34, s. 4, n. 28, *Opera omnia* 26:375). On this question, see the remarkable study by Gilles Olivo, "L'homme en personne: Descartes, Suárez et la question de l'*ens per se*," in *Descartes et Regius: Autour de l'explication de l'esprit humain,* ed. Théo Verbeek (Amsterdam: Rodopi, 1993).

27. See the texts of Thomas Aquinas, which do not equivocate: "But to God alone does it belong to be His own subsistent being" ("solius autem Dei proprius modus essendi est ut sit suum esse subsistens"; *Summa Theologiae* 1, q. 12, art. 4c; English translation 1:128) and "It has been shown . . . that God is the essentially self-subsisting being; and also it was shown . . . that subsisting being must be one" ("ostensum est . . . quod Deus est ipsum esse per se subsistens; et iterum ostensum est . . . quod esse subsistens non potest esse nisi unum"; *Summa Theologiae* 1, q. 44, art. 1c; English translation 2:214).

28. "Alias vero omnes, non nisi ope concursu Dei existere posse." AT VIIIA:24, 25–26; CSM I:210.

29. "Quicquid est reale, potest separatim ab omni alio subjecto existere; quicquid autem ita separatim potest existere, est substantia." AT VII:434, 24–25; CSM II:293.

30. "Adeo ut si omne id, quod naturaliter sine subjecto esse potest, sit substantia, quicquid etiam per quantumvis extraordinariam Dei potentiam

potest esse sine subjecto, substantia est dicendum." AT VII:435, 5–8; CSM II:293.

31. "Nomen substantiae non convenit Deo et illis [cf. creatures] *univoce.*" §51, AT VIIIA:24, 27; CSM I:210.

32. "Licet aliquo modo conveniat [Deus] in ratione substantiae cum aliquibus entibus creatis, non tamen univoce, sed analogice." Suárez, *Disputationes metaphysicae* 32, s. 1, n. 9, *Opera omnia* 26:314. See the development of s. 2, in particular, the *Resultio* (n. 11): "Igitur ratio analogiae entis creati respectu accidentis et substantiae sumenda est ex eodem principio, ex quo analogiam entis ad Deum et creaturam declaravimus, nimirum, quia ens per se essentialiter postulat hunc ordinem descendendi prius ad substantiam per se, ad accidens vero propter substantiam et per habitudinem ad ipsam" (*Opera omnia* 26:322). On analogy before and in Suárez, see *Théologie blanche*, 110ff., and Jean-François Courtine, *Suarez et le système de la métaphysique* (Paris: Presses Universitaires de France, 1990), 157ff.

33. "Lapidem esse substantiam, sive esse rem quae per se apta est existere, itemque me esse substantiam." AT VII:44, 22–24; CSM II:30.

34. Respectively: Boethius, *De Trinitate* 4, in *The Theological Tractates*, ed. Stewart, Rand, and Tester (Cambridge: Harvard University Press, 1973), 18; G. de La Porrée, *In Boethii de Trinitate, PL* 64, col. 1283; Scipion Dupleix, *La Métaphysique* (Paris, 1610), 10.6, §12, in the edition by R. Ariew (Paris: Fayard, 1992), 793. To the contrary, Pierre Gassendi, *Exercitationes Paradoxicae adversus Aristoteleos* 2, d. 3, §6, ed. Bernard Rochot (Paris: Vrin, 1959), 325ff.

35. "Omnis res cui inest immediate, ut in subjecto, sive per quam existit aliquid quod percipimus, hoc est aliqua proprietas, sive qualitas, sive attributum, cujus realis idea in nobis est, vocatur *substantia.*" Second Replies, AT VII:161, 14–17; CSM II:114.

36. See: Augustine, *De Trinitate*, 7.5.10; Anselm, *Monologion* 27 and 36; Thomas Aquinas, *Summa Theologiae* 1, q. 29, art. 3; Suárez, *Disputationes Metaphysique* 32, s. 1, n. 6, 26:313ff. On these points, one should consult other contemporaries of Descartes and Suárez (in particular Eustache de Saint-Paul, *Summa Philosophiae quadripartita, Logica* 3, q. 3 [Paris, 1609], 1:91ff.). Some indications can be found in *Metaphysical Prism*, §17, 218ff.

37. "Substantia non tantum dictatur, quae per se est, sed quae accidentibus substat vel substare potest; quomodo videtur Aristoteles sumpsisse et descripsisse substantiam in praedicamentis." Suarez, *Disputationes metaphysicae* 32, s. 1, n. 6, *Opera omnia* 26:314. Allusion to Aristotle, *Categories* 2.1a.20ff. and 5.2a.20ff.

38. "In quantum unae ex aliis cognosci possunt." AT X:381, 13; CSM I:21.

39. "Verumtamen non potest substantia primum animadverti ex hoc solo, quod sit res existens, quia hoc solum per se nos non afficit." AT VIIIA:25, 3–5; CSM I:210.

40. "Nos enim ex accidentibus pervenimus ad cognitionem substantiae, et per habitudinem substandi eam primo concipimus." Suárez, *Disputationes metaphysicae* 33, s. 1, n. 2, *Opera omnia* 26:330.

41. "Licet substantia secundum se sit perfectior et intelligibilior, tamen respectu nostri accidens habet majorem vim ad immutandum intellectum, quia intellectus noster non immutatur nisi mediis speciebus sensibus impressis; sensibus autem non imprimuntur species substantiae, sed accidentium tantum; ergo accidentia sunt, quae primo immutant intellectum; ergo prius concipiuntur ab intellectu quam substantia." "Nos enim non devenimus in cognitionem substantiarum . . ., nisi per accidentia vel proprietates." "Non potest intellectus concipere accidens, nisi concipiendo substantiam." Suárez, *Disputationes metaphysicae* 38, s. 2, n. 8, *Opera omnia* 26:503.

42. "Substantia non immutat immediate intellectum nostrum ad aliquam intellectionem sui, sed tantum accidens sensibile." John Duns Scotus, *Ordinatio* 1, d. 3, p. 1, q. 3, n. 139, in *Opera omnia*, ed. C. Balic (Rome: Typis Pollyglottis Vaticana, 1954), 3:87. In the same way, F. Tolet: "Per accidentia enim et effectus cognosci substantia, omnes fatentur et experiuntur; at quomodo accidentium cognitio substantiae cognitionem inducat, id est valde difficile determinare." *Commentaria . . . in De Anima* 1.1.11, q. 6 (Venice, 1574), cited by E. Gilson, *Index scolastico-cartésien* (1913; rpt. Paris: Vrin, 1979), 280.

43. "Verumtamen non potest substantia animadverti ex hoc solo, quod sit res existens, quia hoc solum non non afficit." CSM I:210.

44. "Mais *lorsqu'il est question de savoir si quelqu'une des ces substances existe véritablement, c'est-à-dire si elle est à présent dans le monde*, ce n'est pas assez qu'elle existe en cette façon [comme subsistant par soi] pour faire que nous l'apercevions; *car cela seul ne nous découvre rien qui exite quelque connaissance particulière en notre pensée.* Mais il faut outre cela, qu'elle ait quelques attributs que nous puissions remarquer." AT IXA:47, 26–30; my emphasis.

45. "Aliquam rem existentem, sive substantiam . . . etiam adesse." AT VIIIA:25, 9–11; CSM I:210.

46. "Cum autem ipsam substantiam non immediate per ipsam cognoscimus, sed per hoc tantum quod sit subjectum quorumdam actuum." AT VII:176, 1–3; CSM II:124.

47. "Neque enim substantias immediate cognoscimus, ut alibi notatum est, sed tantum ex eo quod percipiamus formas sive attributa, quae cum alicui rei debeant inesse ut existant, rem illam cui insunt vocamus *Substantiam.*" AT VII:222, 5–9; CSM II:156.

48. "Res cui inest immediate, ut in subjecto, sive per quam existit aliquid quod percipimus." AT VII:161, 14–15; CSM II:114.

49. "Non dissimulabo me mihi persuadere, nihil plane aliud esse a quo sensus nostri afficiantur praeter solam superficiem . . . nullum sensum affici nisi per contactum." AT VII:249, 15–16, 18–19; CSM II:173. A surprising text reinforces the legitimacy of a phenomenological meaning of the *affici*:

"It makes no difference that these accidents are called corporeal. If 'corporeal' is taken to mean anything which can in any way affect a body, then the mind too must be called corporeal in this sense" ("nec refert quod accidentia illa dicantur esse corporea; si enim per *corporeum* intelligatur id omne quod potest aliquo modo corpus afficere, mens etiam eo sensu corporea erit dicenda"; Letter ad Hyperaspistem, August 1641, AT III:424, 25–29; CSMK III:190). One cannot say better that the *affici* designate originary passivity, like that all attributes exercise on the understanding, than that this attribute arises from thought or extension. The attribute really plays the role of intuitive donation of the phenomenon.

50. Martin Heidegger, *Sein und Zeit*, §20, 94.

51. "Praecipua proprietas . . . ad quam aliae omnes referuntur." AT VIIIA:25, 13–15; CSM I:210.

52. "Ipsius naturam essentiamque constituit. . . . extensio . . . substantiae corporeae naturam constituit; et cogitatio constituit naturam substantiae cogitantis." AT VIIIA:25, 14, 15–18; CSM I:210. See, among other examples, *Principles of Philosophy* 1, §63: "Thought and extension can be regarded as constituting the natures of intelligent substance and corporeal substance" ("cogitatio et extensio spectari possunt ut constituentes naturas substantiae intelligentis et corporeae"; AT VIIIA:30, 26–27; CSM I:215). Or *Notae in programma*: "Is not conceived as a mode, but as an attribute which constitutes the nature of a substance" ("non concipitur ut modus, sed ut attributum, quod constituit naturam alicujus substantiae"; AT VIIIB:349, 6–8; CSM I:298).

53. "Cavendumque est, ne per attributum nihil aliud intelligamus quam modum. . . . Sic multa in Deo sunt attributa, non autem modi. Sic unum ex attributis cujuslibet substantiae est, quod per se subsistat." *Notae in programma*, AT VIIIB:348, 19–25; CSM I:297.

54. See the debate between F. Aliqué and M. Gueroult at length in the *Cahiers de Royaumont, Philosophie* 1, "Descartes" (Paris, 1957 1st ed., New York, 1987 2d ed.).

55. "Quo plures [qualitates] in eadem re sive substantia deprehendimus, tanto clarius nos illam cognoscere." *Principles of Philosophy* 1, §11, AT VIIIA:8, 22–24; CSM I:196. See the parallel of the Fifth Replies: "But as for me, I have never thought that anything more is required to reveal a substance than its various attributes; thus the more attributes of a given substance we know, the more perfectly we understand its nature" ("quantum ad me, nihil unquam aliud requiri putavi ad manifestandam substantiam, praeter varia ejus attributa, adeo ut, quo plura alicujus substantiae attributa cognoscamus, eo perfectius ejus naturam intelligamus"; AT VII:360, 2–6; CSM II:249).

56. "Nihil in natura clarius, quam quod unumquodque ens sub aliquo attributo debeat concipi et, quo plus realitatis aut esse habeat, eo plura attributa [habet], quae et necessitatem, sive aeternitatem et infinitatem exprimunt." Spinoza, *Ethics* 1, prop. 10, schol.; *Works* 1:416.

57. "Non possumus claram et distinctam istius substantiae ideam formare." §62, AT VIIIA:30, 8–9, 11–12; CSM I:214.

58. AT VIIIA:25, 1 and 30; CSM I:210. Note that AT separates *cogitans* and *creata* in the first occurrence with a comma, but not in the second. If this fact goes back to an intention of Descartes (which I doubt), what would this intention be?

59. AT VIIIA:26, 2–3; CSM I:211. This corresponds to the formulation of 1641 "independent substance" (*substantia independens*). AT VII:45, 12 and 185, 26; CSM II:31 and 130.

60. "Quis enim est qui non percipiat se aliquid intelligere? ac proinde qui non habeat istam formam sive ideam intellectionis, quam indefinite extendendo, format ideam intellectionis divinae, et sic de caeteris ejus attributis?" AT VII:188, 16–20; CSM II:132. See, on the divine *cogitatio*, my indications in *Cartesian Questions*, 64ff.

61. To Arnauld, 4 June 1647, AT V:193, 17; not translated in CSMK. See also "sovereign intelligence" (*souveraine intelligence*) in the letter to Chanut, 1 February 1647, AT IV:608, 15; CSMK III:309 or "divine intellect" (*intellectio divina*), AT VII:188, 19; CSM II:132.

62. Respectively, Second Replies, AT VII:138, 15 and 139, 6; CSM II:99; and Fifth Replies, AT VII:373, 4; CSM II:257. In this text, Descartes argues in this way: the extended implies divisibility, hence an imperfection, which is not found in the *cogitatio*. But, apart from the fact that Spinoza contests the divisibility of the extended, the *cogitatio* admits in its mode passivity (sensation, imagination) and indetermination (the will), which are equally imperfections. See below, Chapter 9.

63. "*Adaequate* omnia quae in Deo sunt exhibere." AT VIIIA:26, 4–5; CSM I:211.

64. "Nomen substantiae non convenit Deo et illis [finite things] *univoce*." AT VIIIA:24, 26–27; CSM I:210.

65. See below, Chapter 7.

6. God, the Styx, and the Fates
The Letters to Mersenne of 1630

1. See *Théologie blanche*.

2. "I want to show you, chiefly through adducing some examples, how Gilson's thesis of Descartes' debt to scholasticism has been vindicated by recent scholarship." Marjorie Grene, *Descartes among the Scholastics: The Aquinas Lecture, 1991* (Milwaukee, Wisc: Marquette University Press, 1991).

3. See "La pensée rêve-t-elle? Les trois songes ou l'éveil du philosophe," in *La passion de la raison: Hommage à Ferdinand Alquié*, ed. Jean Deprun and Jean-Luc Marion (Paris: Presses Universitaires de France, 1983), reprinted in *Cartesian Questions*, chap. 1.

4. AT I:145, 7–10; CSMK III:23.

5. AT I:145, 10–13; CSMK III:23.

6. Ferdinand Alquié, *La découverte métaphysique de l'homme*, 88, 92.

7. Ferdinand Alquié, in: *Descartes: Œuvres philosophiques*, 1:260.

8. *Discourse on Method*, AT VI:7, 11–12; CSM I:114. One knows that he studied the anthology of Pierre de la Brosse (Petrus Brossaeus), *Corpus omnium veterum poetarum lationorum*, 2 vols. (Lyon: 1603–11; see the information in V. Carraud and J.-R. Armogathe, *Bulletin cartésien* 15, *Archives de philosophie* 1 [1987]: 4), without doubt recalled in the "anthology of poetries entitled *Corpus poetarum* [marking] in particular and in a more distinct manner philosophy and wisdom as joined together" of the final dream (*Olympica* X:184). Similarly, in 1644 Descartes admits to composing Latin verses — telling Huygens (AT IV:102). This does not hinder him from believing himself to imitate Socrates, who "never made verses except when he was close to his death" (to Huygens, 17 February 1645, AT IV:776, 7–8; not translated in CSMK). On this final point, see the classic study of Jean Deprun, "Descartes et le 'génie' de Socrate," in *La passion de la raison*, 145ff., reprinted in *De Descartes au romantisme: Études historiques et thématiques* (Paris: Vrin, 1987), 21ff.

9. 9. Respectively AT VI:5, 31 – 6, 1; CSM I:113 and AT X:184; not translated in CSM.

10. AT VI:42, 23–24; CSM I:132.

11. To Chanut, 1 February 1647, AT IV:607, 24–30; CSMK III:309.

12. Texts in *Théologie blanche*, 27ff. and 62ff.

13. Homer, *Iliad* 16.433–38. English translation by A.T. Murray in Loeb Classical Library (Cambridge: Harvard University Press, 1919), 2:195. Cicero comments on this episode in *De divinatione* 2.25.

14. *Iliad* 22.168–69, 179; English translation 2:465. See also *Odyssey* 3.231, 236–37: "Easily might a god who willed it bring a man safe home, even from afar. . . . But of a truth death that is common to all the gods themselves cannot ward from a man they love, when the fell fate of grievous death shall strike him down." English translation by A.T. Murray in Loeb Classical Library (Cambridge: Harvard University Press, 1919), 1:85.

15. *Iliad* 15.117–18; English translation 2:115.

16. *Iliad* 15.36–38; English translation 2:109. Similarly Hera in 14.271ff.

17. Aeschylus, *Prometheus* 515–18. English translation by David Grene (Chicago: University of Chicago Press, 1956), 157. See, on all this, Walter Otto, *Die Götter Griechenlands: Das Bild des Göttlichen im Spiegel des griechischen Geistes* (Bonn: F. Cohen, 1929; Frankfurt am Main: G. Schulte-Bulmke, 1947), esp. chap. 7, "Destiny," which emphasizes that the gods can only slow down the death of mortals when their hour, fixed by destiny, arrives.

18. "την πεπρωμενην μοιραν αδυνατα εστι αποφυγειν και Θεω." Herodotus, *Histories* 1.91 (in Hermann Kallenberg's edition [Leipzig, 1884] 1:53). English translation by A. D. Godley in Loeb Classical Library (Cambridge: Harvard University Press, 1920), 117.

19. Hesiod, *Theogony* 220. English translation by Richard Lattimore (Ann Arbor: University of Michigan Press, 1978), 136.

20. Horace, *Odes* 3:29.43–50. English translation by James Michie (New York: Washington Square Press, 1965), 201.

21. Virgil, *Aeneid* 10:111–13. English translation by Allen Mandelbaum (Berkeley: University of California Press, 1981), 257.

22. "αναγκην δε ουδε θεος ειναι λεγεται δυνατος βιαζεσθαι." Plato, *Laws* 5.741a.

23. "Itaque dicebat Carneades ne Apollinem quidem futura posse dicere, nisi quorum causas natura ita contineret ut ea fieri necesse esset." Cicero, *De fato* 32. English translation by Jeffrey Henderson in Loeb Classical Library (Cambridge: Harvard University Press, 1942), 229.

24. "Atqui necesse est cum sint di (si modo sunt, ut profecto sunt) animantes esse, nec solum animantes sed etiam rationis compotes inter seque quasi civili conciliatione et societate conjunctos, unum mundum ut communem rem publicam atque urbem aliquam regentes. Sequitur ut eadem sit in iis quae humano in genere ratio, eadem veritas utrobique sit eademque lex, quae est recti praeceptio pravique depulsio." Cicero, *De natura deorum* 2.31. English translation by H. Rackham, Loeb Classical Library (Cambridge: Harvard University Press, 1933), 199.

25. "Quid est boni viri? Praebere se fato. Grande solatium est cum universo rapi. Quidquid est quod nos sic vivere jussit, sic mori, eadem necessitate et deos alligat; irrevocabilis humana pariter ac divina cursus vehit. Ille ipse omnium conditor ac rector scripsit quidem fata, sed sequitur: semper paret, semel jussit." Seneca, *De providentia* 5.8. English translation by John Basore (London: William Heinemann Ltd., 1928), 39.

26. "Nihil ille Poeta aliud fecit, quam ut Troia vastata et Romano imperio suscitando, fatum plus valere quam omnium hominum studia, significet, atque adeo necessitatem et rebus et hominibus imponere. Denique deos suos immortales fato subjicit, cui necessario caedant et ipse Juppiter et Juno." Martin Luther, *De servo arbitrio*, ed. Otto Clemen (Bonn: Marcus und Weber, 1913), 3:110. English translation by James I. Packer and O. R. Johnston, *The Bondage of the Will* (Grand Rapids, Mich.: Baker Book House, 1957), 83.

27. See text cited above, n. 20.

28. Montaigne, *Essais* 2:12. In the edition by Pierre Villey (Paris: 1988), 2:527–28. English translation by Donald M. Frame, *The Complete Works of Montaigne* (Stanford: Stanford University Press, 1957), 393. I have already used this comparison in *Metaphysical Prism*, 303–4.

29. Scipion Dupleix, *La métaphysique* (Paris, 1610), respectively 11.1.3 and 11.2.3, idem, 818 and 831–32. One should also not neglect the long development that the same author dedicates in the *Physique* (Paris, 1603) to destiny, fortune, and chance (2.9–12); there he denounces "the errors of the pagans touching on destiny" (2.11; in the edition by R. Ariew [Paris, 1991], 159), in particular, of having "believed that fortune was somehow a thing separated from the divine providence" (2.9.2; in Ariew's edition, 148), before reducing it to a name of God. The repeated mention of the "poets" and

the "fabled poetics" (in Ariew's edition, 148, 149, 150, etc.) reinforces the hypothesis of a relation to Descartes.

30. La Mothe Le Vayer, *Dialogues faits à l'imitation des Anciens* (Paris, 1630–32?), "De la divinité," ed. A. Pessel (Paris: Fayard, 1988), respectively 309 and 328–29.

31. Mersenne, *L'impiété des déistes, athées et libertins* (Paris, 1624), 2.15, 280.

32. One can also mention the example of Naudé, because, although attested to in a text later than the letters of 1630, he must have been familiar to Descartes beforehand: he takes up the theme "necessitas Deos ipsos alliget, et irrevocabilis Divina pariter et humana cursus vehat, neque Juppiter ipse fata pervertere, aut immutare possit" and cites Lucian, Philémon, Seneca (see n. 25), and Martial on the death of Sarpedon (see n. 13), *Quaestio iatrophilologica de Fato, et fatali vitae termino*, §6, in J. Beverovicii [Jan van Beverwyck], *Epistolica quaestio de vitae termino, fatali an mobili?*, ed. Gabriel Naudé, vol. 2 (Leiden, 1639) [vol.1, 1634], reprinted by Conte, ed. (Lecce: Conte, 1995), 8–9. In her preface (2–3), Anna-Lisa Schino recalls the historical context in which, as witnesses the bull *Inscrutabilis judicirum Dei* of Urban VIII in April 1631, the question of destiny and of astrological prophecies became crucial.

33. Scipion Dupleix, *La Physique*, 2:9, 9, in Ariew's edition, 151. This thesis of the fates as "execution of the divine providence" is developed in 2:12 and 2:13.

34. "Qui vero non astrorum constitutionem, sicuti est cum quidque concipitur vel nascitur vel inchoatur, sed omnium connexionem seriemque causarum, qua fit omne quod fit, fati nomine appellant: non multum cum eis de verbi controversia laborandum atque certandum est, quando quidem ipsarum causarum ordinem et quandam connexionem Dei summi tribuunt voluntati et potestati, qui optime et veracissime creditur et cuncta scire antequam fiant, et nihil inordinatum relinquere; a quo sunt omnes potestates, quamvis ab illo non sint omnium voluntates."Augustine, *De civitate Dei* 5.8 (BA, 33, 668–69). English translation by Marcus Dods as *City of God* (New York: Modern Library, 1950), 151. A similar argument can be found in 5.1.644ff. Descartes condemns astrology, which pretends to study the influence of the stars on the sublunar world, from the *Regulae* onward (AT X:380, 9–16; CSM I:20–21).

35. "Qui modus cum in ipsa divinae intelligentiae puritate conspicitur, providentia nominatur; cum vero ad ea quae movet atque disponit refertur, fatum a veteribus appellatum est. . . . Nam providentia est ipsa illa divina ratio in summo omnium principe constituta quae cuncta disponit; fatum vero inhaerens rebus mobilibus dispositio per quam providentia suis quaeque nectit ordinibus. Providentia namque cuncta pariter quamvis diversa, quamvis infinita complectitur; fatum vero singula degerit in motum locis, formis ac temporibus distributa . . . Quae licet diversa sint, alterum tamen

pendet ex altero." Boethius, *Consolatio philosophiae* 4 in *The Theological Tract-ates*, 340.

36. Saint Thomas Aquinas: "Now it happens sometimes that something is lucky or chance-like, as compared to inferior causes, which, if compared to some higher cause, is directly intended. For instance, if two servants are sent by their master to the same place; the meeting of the two servants in regard to themselves is by chance; but as compared to the master, who had ordered it, it is directly intended" ("contingit autem quandoque, quod aliquid ad inferiores causas relatum est fortuitum, vel casuale, quod tamen relatum ad causam aliquam superiorem invenitur esse per se intentum: sicut si duo servi alicujus domini mittuntur ab eo ad eundem locum, uno de altero ignorante, concursus duorum servorum, si ad ipsos servos referatur, casualis est; quia accidit praeter utriusque intentionem; si autem referatur ad dominum, qui hoc pareordinavit, non est causale, sed per intentum"; *Summa Theologiae* 1, q. 116, art. 1; Boethius is cited in art. 2, 3, and 4; English translation from *Summa Theologica*, 2d ed. rev. [London: Burns, Oates and Washbourne, 1922], 5:168–69). Descartes remembers this argument, because he transposes it into the encounter of two duelists, fortunate for them and free, but necessary for the king who has provoked them. To Elisabeth, January 1646, AT IV:353, 1–354, 14; CSMK III:282.

37. Suárez, *Disputationes metaphysicae* 19, s. 9, n. 2 ("nihilominus tribuebant necessitatem omnino inevitabilem, etiam respectu Dei"), and n. 5 ("tribuere causis secundis fatalem necessitatem independentem a Deo"; *Opera omnia* 25:738 and 739).

38. "Nam fatum est dispositio causarum, ut est sub Deo, non vero est proprie Deus." *Disputationes Metaphysicae*,19, s. 9, n. 11, *Opera Omnia*, 25:741.

39. *De Constantia* 1:17, "poetarum stirps," and 1:18: "Tribuunt iis duo impia, et Quod subjicem faciunt trigis fati et Quod actiones item internas et nostrae voluntatis" (in Leiden, 1596 edition, 44 and 46). [English translation consulted, but usually emended: *Two Bookes of Constancie, written in Latine by Iustus Lipsius*, englished by Sir John Stradling (New Brunswick: Rutgers University Press, 1939).—Trans.] One should consult also the beautiful work by Jacqueline Lagrée, *Juste Lipse: La restauration du stoïcisme* (Paris: Vrin, 1994), which cites and translates [into French] large extracts from *De Constantia* (as, moreover, from the *Manuductio* and from the *Physiologia Stoïcorum*); we here use 140–43.

40. *De Constantia* 1:18 (*Of Constancie*, 116): "Nec Seneca noster deum Fato subjicit (sanior illi mens), sed genere quodam sermonis deum deo" (Leiden ed., 46 = J. Lagrée, 144), allusion to *De Providentia* 5:8, which we have cited above, n. 25. This will be the position of Leibniz: "This so-called *fatum*, which binds even the Divinity, is nothing but God's own nature, his own understanding." *Theodicy*, §191, *Die philosophischen Schriften* 6:230; English translation by E.M. Huggard (New Haven: Yale University Press, 1952), 246–47.

41. *De Constantia* 1:18 (*Of Constancie*, 114), respectively: "Ac Fatum mathematicum quidem appello *Quod ligat et nectit firmiter actiones omnes eventus ad vim siderum et posituram stellarum*" and "At naturale fatum voco *Ordinem causarum naturalium quae (nisi impediantur) vi et natura sua certum eumdemque producunt effectum.*" Leiden ed., 45 and 46 = J. Lagrée, 140–43.

42. *De Constantia* 1:18, respectively: "Necessity ought not to be called anything else but God" ("Deum ipsum dixite esse Fatum") and "These sayings, if they have any taste of temerity in them, yet not of impiety: and being rightly interpreted differ not much from our true fate or destiny" ("qui sermones, si quid improvidi habent, nihil tamen impii, et apus aequos interpretes haud longe absunt a vero nostroque Fato"; Leiden ed., 49 = J. Lagrée, 144–45 [*Of Constancie*, 117]).

43. *De Constantia* 1:19 (*Of Constancie*, 118), respectively: "Ad Fatum ad res ipsas magis descendere videtur, in iisque singulis descendere videtur" and "*inhaerens rebus mobilibus immobile Providentiae decretum, quod singula suo ordine, loco, tempore firmiter reddit.*" Leiden ed., 50 = J. Lagrée, 146–47. One must translate *reddit* in all its force: render or conduct each thing back to itself following its order, its time, etc.; this is without a doubt a touchstone in awaiting a *principium* reddendae *rationis*.

44. "Per naturam enim, generaliter spectatam, nihil aliud quam vel Deum ipsum, vel rerum creatarum coordinationem a Deo institutam intelligo." AT VII:80, 21–24; CSM II:56. The French version develops this in saying: "Par la nature considérée en général, je n'entends maintenant autre chose que Dieu même, ou bien l'ordre et la disposition que Dieu a établie dans les choses créées" (AT IXA:64, 7–10); the addition of *ordre et disposition* to translate *coordinatio* has a Cartesian legitimacy—see the note in *Règles utiles et claires pour la direction de l'esprit dans la recherche de la vérité* (The Hague: Martinus Nijhoff, 1977), 165–66.

45. Saint Thomas Aquinas, *Summa Theologiae* 1, 2, q. 85, art. 6c.; in the English translation 7:450: "Natura vero universalis est virtus activa in aliquo universali principio naturae, puta in aliquo coelestium corporum, vel alicujus superioris substantiae; secundum quod etiam Deus a quibusdam dicitur *natura naturans*." See *In Dionysii de divinis nominibus* 4:21, *Opuscula omnia*, ed. Pierre Mandonnet (Paris: Lethielleux, 1927), 2:452.

46. "Ipsa illa divina ratio in summo omnium principe constituta, quae cuncta disponit." See n. 35.

47. "Nam providentia non aliter capio aut considero quam ut *in Deo vis sit et potestas omnia videndi, sciendi, gubernandi.*" *De Constantia* 1:19, Leiden ed., 50 (*Of Constancie*, 118).

48. "At seu fato, seu casu, seu continuata rerum serie, seu quovis alio modo me ad id quod sum pervenisse supponant." AT VII:21, 20–22; CSM II:14. Compare the French translation: AT IXA:16, 37–40.

49. "Sed, quemadmodum Poëtae fingunt a Jove quidem fata fuisse condita, sed postquam considta fuere, ipsum se iis servandis obstrinxisse; ita

ego non puto essentias rerum, mathematicasque illas veritates que de ipsis cognosci possunt, esse independentes a Deo; sed puto nihilominus, quia Deus sic voluit, quia sic disposuit, ipsas esse immutabiles et aeternas." AT VII:380, 5–12; CSM II:261.

50. To Mersenne, 15 April 1630, AT I:146, 1–3; CSMK III:23.

51. See Jean Deprun, "Cartésianism et mythologie," in *De Descartes au romantisme*, 35ff. (reprinted in *La mythologie au XVII siècle*, Colloquium of CMR 17, Marseille and Nice, 1981).

7. Creation of the Eternal Truths
The Principle of Reason—Spinoza, Malebranche, Leibniz

1. Letter to Mersenne, 15 April 1630, AT I:145, 7–16; CSMK III:23. See above, Chapter 6, §1ff.

2. In order not to make this development here and in other places too cumbersome, I allow myself to refer to my study *Théologie blanche* and also, in the present work, to Chapter 9, §3–§5.

3. Heerebord depends largely on Suárez, whom he salutes as "the Father of all principles of metaphysics" (*omnium Metaphysicorum princeps ac Papa*; *Meletemata Philosophica*, 1654, 27). See Jacob Freudenthal's old but still valuable study, "Spinoza und die Scholastik," in *Philosophische Aufsätze Ed. Zeller zu seinem 50. jähr. Doktorjub. gewidmet* (Leipzig: Zentral-Antiquariat, 1887/1962); Julius Lewkowitz, *Spinozas "Cogitata Metaphysica" und ihr Verhältnis zu Descartes und zur Scholastik* (Breslau: T. Schatzky, 1902); and Piero di Vona, *Studi sull'ontologia di Spinoza*, 2 vols. (Florence: La nuova Italia, 1960–69).

4. *Disputationes metaphysicae* 31, s. 12, n. 38–40, *Opera omnia* 26:294–95.

5. *Cogitata Metaphysica* 2.9 (*Works* 1:332), which takes up Suárez (see *Théologie blanche*, §4, 44–45, n. 3).

6. Respectively, AT I:145, 10–13, and 152, 2–4; CSMK III:23 and 25. See *Ethics* 1, prop. 25: "God is the efficient cause, not only of the existence of things, but also of their essence" ("Deus non tantum est causa efficiens rerum existentiae, sed etiam essentiae"; *Works* 1:431); and *Ethics* 1, prop. 17, schol.; *Works* 1:425–28.

7. For the celebrated debate underlined by the interpretation of the conclusion of *Ethics* 1, prop. 17, schol., see Alexandre Koyré, "Le chien constellation céleste et le chien animal aboyant," *Revue de métaphysique et de morale* (1950; rpt. in *Études d'histoire de la pensée philosophique* [Paris: A. Colin, 1961], 92–102), and Martial Gueroult, *Spinoza* (Paris: Aubier, 1969), 1:272–84 and 1:562–63.

8. Letter X to de Vries, March 1663, *Works* 1:196. See *Ethics* 1, def. 8: "For such an existence, like the essence of a thing, is conceived as an eternal truth" ("talis enim existentia ut aeterna veritas, sicut rei essentia concipitur," *Works* 1:409); and *Principia Philosophiae Cartesianae* 1, §5: "That his [God's] existence, no less than his essence, is an eternal truth" ("ejusque

[cf. Dei] existentia, non secus atque ejus essentia, sit aeterna veritas"; *Works* 1:246).

9. Respectively, *Cogitata Metaphysica* 2.12, *Works* 1:342. Then *Tractatus theologico-politicus* 1, 3, 6, then 16, etc. English translation by R. H. M. Elwes, *The Chief Works of Benedict de Spinoza* (New York: Dover, 1951), 24, 44, 86, 211.

10. Respectively, *Tractatus theologico-politicus* 4, then 6 (the passage cited in n. 8, put back into context), then *Tractatus politicus* 2, §18; Elwes, 64, 86, 298. See also a symptomatic oscillation: "That He [God] dictates laws like a prince, or that He sets them forth as eternal truths" ("leges tanquam princeps praescribat, vel tanquam aeternas veritates doceat"; *Tractatus theologico-politicus* 14; Elwes, 188).

11. *Ethics* 2, prop. 11, cor., *Works* 1:456. See *Ethics* 3, prop. 3, schol., *Works* 1:498; and 4, appendix 1, *Works* 1:588–94.

12. *De Intellectus Emendatione*, §73, *Works* 1:33.

13. *De Intellectus Emendatione*, §69, *Works* 1:31. See *Cogitata Metaphysica* 1.6, *Works* 1:311–15; and *Koorte Vorhandling* 2.15, *Works* 1:119–21.

14. *De Intellectus Emendatione*, §73. See my analysis, "Le fondement de la cogitatio selon le *De Intellectus Emendatione*, §104–§105," *Les Études philosophiques* 3 (1972).

15. *De Intellectus Emendatione*, §61, *Works* 1:28; see §73, *Works* 1:32–33; and §95, *Works* 1:39. Similarly *Ethics* 2, §35, *Works* 1:472–73.

16. "Conceptu rerum adaequato, qualem nemo habet, non modo de infinito, sed nec forte etiam de ulla alia re quantumvis parva." AT VII:365, 3–5; CSM II:252.

17. "Ut aliqua cognitio sit adaequata, debeant in ea contineri omnes proprietates quae sunt in re cognita; et idcirco solus est Deus qui novit se habere cognitiones rerum omnium adaequatas." AT VII:220, 7–11; CSM II:155.

18. "Ad hoc enim ut [cf. intellectus creatus] habeat adaequatem alicujus rei cognitionem, requiritur tantum ut vis cognoscendi quae de ipso est adaequet istam rem; quod facile fieri potest. Ut autem sciat se illam habere, sive Deum potuisse nihil amplium in illa re, quam id quod cognoscit, oportet ut sua vi cognoscendi adaequet infinitam Dei potestatem; quod plane fieri repugnat." AT VII:220, 14–21; CSM II:155.

19. "Cum dixit rem intelligendam esse complete, sensus non erat intellectionem debere esse adaequatam, sed tantum rem satis debere intelligi, ut scirem esse completam." AT VII:221, 11–14; CSM II:156.

20. [The expression Marion uses here — "fin de non-recevoir" — has legal connotations. Literally, it means something like "putting in a plea at the bar" — Trans.]

21. Respectively, *Recherche de la vérité*, *Éclaircissements* 10 in *Œuvres complètes* 3:131, trans. Thomas M. Lennon, *The Search after Truth* and *Elucidations of the Search after Truth* (Columbus: Ohio State University Press, 1980), 614,

and *Éclaircissements* 8, *Œuvres complètes* 3:86, Lennon, 587. See *Entretiens sur la métaphysique et la religion*, 9.13: "Universal reason is coeternal and consubstantial with him." *Œuvres complètes* 12–13, 220, trans. Willis Doney, *Dialogues on Metaphysics* (New York: Abaris Books, 1980), 219. A similar coeternity has been studied by Auguste LeMoine, *Des vérités éternelles selon Malebranche* (Marseille: Vrin, 1936), 63ff. It coincides sufficiently precisely with the frequent formulas in Kepler and Galileo (see *Théologie blanche*, §10, 181–83, and §11, 210–13).

22. Respectively *Éclaircissements* 8, *Œuvres complètes* 3:85 (twice), Lennon, 587, 586; *Recherche de la vérité* 3.2.6, *Œuvres complètes*, 1:444, Lennon, 233; and, finally, *Éclaircissements* 10, *Œuvres complètes*, 3:133, Lennon, 615. See *Réponses à Regis*, 2.23: "I cannot be persuaded that the ideas depend on God as their efficient cause. For being eternal, immovable and necessary, they are in no need of an efficient cause, although I acknowledge that the perception that I have of these ideas depends on God as their efficient cause" (17–1:308).

23. A text frequently cited, e.g., in the *Éclaircissements* 8 and 10, *Œuvres complètes* 3:85–87 and 136, Lennon, 587 and 618.

24. Lennon, 615.

25. *Éclaircissements* 10, *Œuvres complètes*, 3:132. See *Éclaircissements* 8, *Œuvres complètes*, 3:190–91. For Malebranche's radical opposition to Descartes here, see Martial Gueroult, *Malebranche* (Paris: Aubier, 1955), 1:37–39, 112–13, and F. Alquié, *Le cartésianisme de Malebranche* (Paris: Vrin, 1974), 226–33. André Robinet emphasizes, by contrast, that Malebranche criticizes the Cartesian thesis only beginning in 1677, at the occasion of his polemic with Foucher (2:486–92): here as in other places, it is the *Éclaircissements* that mark the real departure. He remarks also that in 1678 the Congrégation générale de l'Oratoire decided that the "opinions of Descartes for philosophy" were suspect (outlined in *Système et existence dans l'œuvre de Malebranche* [Paris: Vrin, 1965], 237).

26. Respectively, *Éclaircissements* 10, *Œuvres complètes* 3:131, 132, 133, 142, Lennon, 614, 615, 615, 621; then the *Réponses à Regis* 2.23, *Œuvres complètes* 17–1:308.

27. *Éclaircissements* 10, *Œuvres complètes* 3:133. See: "the order . . . has force of law even in respect to God" (*Œuvres complètes* 3:138, Lennon, 619). An obligatory consequence follows from this: "I do not hesitate at all to say that God cannot make that contradictories be true or false at the same time." *Préface contre Foucher*, *Recherche de la vérité* 2:490.

28. *Éclaircissements* 10, *Œuvres complètes* 3:140, Lennon, 620; *Traité de la nature et de la grâce*, *Éclaircissements* 11, *Œuvres complètes* 5:170, *Méditations chrétiennes et métaphysique* 8.10, *Œuvres complètes* 10:86 (see 33, 39, 93, etc.), *Traité de morale* 1.1, §7, *Œuvres complètes* 11.19 and 2.4, §10, 182 (see 27, 228), etc.; trans. Craig Walton, *Treatise on Ethics* (Dordrecht: Kluwer Academic Publishers, 1993), 46 and 160; *Entretiens sur la métaphysique et la religion* 1, §8, *Œuvres complètes* 12:42, Doney, 35; *Entretiens d'un philosophe chrétien*

et d'un philosophe chinois, *Œuvres complètes* 15:25, trans. Dominick A. Iorio, *Dialogue Between a Christian Philosopher and a Chinese Philosopher on the Existence and Nature of God* (Washington: University Press of America, 1980), 90. That "excessive terms" are found here (LeMoine, *Des vérités éternelles*, 57) is not contestable; but essential is the constraining rationality that leads Malebranche here, and that leads him, despite his religious pathos, to the limits of "blasphemy" (AT I:149, 26; CSMK III:24).

29. Respectively, *Recherche de la vérité* 5.5, *Œuvres complètes* 2:168, 169, Lennon, 364; *Méditations chrétiennes et métaphysiques* 2.15, *Œuvres complètes* 10:24, *Traité de morale* 1.1, §7 and §6, *Œuvres complètes* 11:19, Walton, 46; then 1.1, §14, 14, Walton, 46; and finally *Éclaircissements* 15, *Œuvres complètes* 3:243, Lennon, 680.

30. *Entretiens sur la métaphysique et la religion* 12, §19, *Œuvres complètes* 12–13:303, Doney, 305.

31. On the operative concept of the code, insofar as it makes the relation of Cartesian science to the sensible world intelligible, see *Théologie blanche*, §12–§14.

32. Respectively, to Arnauld, 14 July 1686, in Leibniz, 2:49, then 4:327 (French trans.), and, finally, *Discourse on Metaphysics*, §2, 4:427 and 428, trans. Leroy E. Loemker, *Gottfried Wilhelm Leibniz: Philosophical Papers and Letters* (Dordrecht: D. Reidel Publishing Company, 1956/1976), 332 [*Correspondence*] and 304 [*Discourse*], respectively.

33. *Théologie blanche*, 289–96.

34. To Philipp, January 1680, 4:284, Loemker, 273.

35. Respectively, *Monadology*, §32, Loemker, 646 (see *Principles of Nature and of Grace*, §7 and §32); *Discourse on Metaphysics*, §2, 4:428, Loemker, 304; to Philipp, January 1680, 4:285, trans. George Martin Duncan, *The Philosophical Works of Leibnitz* (New Haven, Conn.: Tuttle, 1908), 4; *Discourse on Metaphysics*, ibid, Loemker, 304. Lacking this principle, God would become, properly speaking, unreasonable: "If this opinion were true, it would follow that God had not produced any universe at all: for he is incapable of acting without reason, and that would be even acting against reason." *Theodicy*, §196, 6:232; trans. E. M. Huggard (New Haven: Yale University Press, 1952), 249. [Where the expression "eternal verities" appears in the translation, I have usually emended it to "eternal truths"—Trans.]

36. Respectively, *Monadology*, §38, Loemker, 646 (see *Principles of Nature and of Grace* §8, Loemker, 639). See *Dialogue between Theophilus and Polidor* (October 1679?): "It is hence manifest that the author of things will act with reason, since he acts following the perfections of the ideas of all things. . . . See at present if that which we have just discovered must not be called God," in *Textes inédits*, ed. Gaston Grua (Paris: Presses Universitaires de France, 1948; rpt. New York: Garland, 1985), 1:285–86.

37. To Philipp, January 1680, 4:285, Duncan, 4. On the accusation of Spinozism made against Descartes by Leibniz, see letter to Molanus, "The

God of Descartes has neither will nor understanding, since according to Descartes, he does not have the good as object of the will, nor the true as object of the understanding" (4:299), or letter to Nicaise, 15 February 1697: "One can also say that Spinoza has only cultivated certain seeds in the philosophy of M. Descartes, in such a way that I believe that it matters effectively for religion and for piety that this philosophy be punished for the entrenchment of errors, which are mixed with the truth" (2:563). And, finally, the *Notata quaedam . . . circa vitam et doctrinam Cartesii* (1693), 4:314, etc. Good remarks on the meaning of this assimilation in Georges Friedmann, *Leibniz et Spinoza* (Paris: Gallimard, 1946), 114–130, and above all in Yvon Belaval, *Leibniz, critique de Descartes* (Paris: Gallimard, 1960), in particular 371–449, "Leibniz et Spinoza," *Cahier du Sud* (October 1947), then recently "Leibniz lecteur de Spinoza," *Archives de philosophie* 46, no. 4 (1983), "Leibniz face à Descartes," in *Acta* of the Centre international de synthèse (Paris, 1968).

38. Annex to the *Response to the Reflections . . . Touching the Consequences of Several Places in the Philosophy of Descartes*, 4:344.

39. Respectively, *Monadology*, §38, Loemker, 646; *Theodicy*, §20, 6:114–15 (twice), Huggard, 135, 136; *Monadology*, §43, Loemker, 647. See also *Theodicy*, §184 and §336, 6:226 and 314, Huggard, 243 and 327.

40. *Theodicy*, §185, 6:227, Huggard, 244.

41. Respectively *Theodicy*, §193, 6:231, Huggard, 247; *Monadology*, §46, Loemker, 647; *Theodicy*, §189, 6:229, §20, 6:114–15, and finally §337, 6:315, Huggard, 246, 135, 328.

42. Respectively, *Theodicy*, §20, 6:114, then 115, Huggard, 135, 136; *Monadology*, §46, Loemker, 647; *Theodicy*, §336, 6:314, Huggard, 327; and finally §380:341, Huggard, 353.

43. Respectively, *Theodicy*, §190, 6:229 and §191, 230, Huggard, 246 and 246–47. (See above, Chapter 6, §4, 40). See §339, 315–16, Huggard, 328–29.

44. *Discourse on Metaphysics*, §30, 4:454, Loemker, 322.

45. *Principles of Nature and of Grace*, §15, Loemker, 640.

46. *Correspondence with Arnauld*, respectively 2:28 (see 2:32), 48–49 (this phrase was later crossed out by Leibniz), Loemker, 331–32. [See also translation by Mary Morris, *Leibniz: Philosophical Writings* (London: J. M. Dent & Sons, 1934), 58. Unfortunately, she does not give references to the Gerhardt edition and cuts large portions, which makes references hard to find.—Trans.]

47. *Discourse on Metaphysics*, §2, 4:427, Loemker, 304; and *Correspondence*, 2:131 [not translated in either Loemker or Morris].

48. *Correspondence* 2:125, Loemker, 346.

49. Only an exhaustive analysis would be able to assure the completion of notions; but only "he who would know the things sufficiently" would be able to do so (*Principles of Nature and of Grace*, §7). The univocity of right is

in equilibrium with an equivocity of fact (see 2:62; 7:200; *Textes inédits*, ed. G. Grua, 2:514).

50. Respectively, *Discourse on Metaphysics*, §8, 4:433, Loemker, 307; *Correspondence with Arnauld* 2:44, Morris, 68 (see *Treatise of Nature and of Grace*, §7, and *IV. Writing to Clarke*, n. 4, 7:390).

51. All the same, the refusal of the doctrine of a creation of truths was not complete. In this way, as G. Rodis-Lewis has established, a tradition pursued the thesis of 1630, grouping together P. Cally, Dom Robert Desgabets, Regius, P. Poiret, J.-Robert Chouet, and his student P. Bayle, etc., all authors who knew Leibniz (see "Polémiques sur la création des possibles et sur l'impossible dans l'école cartésiennes," in *Studia Cartesiana* 2 [Amsterdam, 1981]: 105–23; and see below, Chapter 9, §5–§7).

52. On the continuity between Suárez and Leibniz, see P. Mesnard, "Comment Leibniz se trouve placé dans le sillage de Suárez?" *Archives de philosophie* (1949).

53. Heidegger, *Der Satz vom Grund* (Pfullingen: G. Neske, 1957), 96. On Descartes' ambiguity here, see M. Philipps' outline, "La causa sive ratio chez Descartes," in *Les études philosophiques* 1 (1984).

54. I am thinking of Heidegger's insistence on the importance of such a confrontation, e.g, in *Wege zur Aussprache*, in *Gesamtausgabe* (Frankfurt: Klostermann, 1983), 13:15–21.

8. The *Causa Sui*
First and Fourth Replies

1. Heidegger, *Identität und Differenz* (Pfullingen: G. Neske, 1957), 51 and 64; trans. Joan Stambaugh, *Identity and Difference* (New York: Harper Torchbooks, 1969). For an introduction to this comparison, see *Metaphysical Prism*, §7.

2. I have shown elsewhere (*Théologie blanche*) and we see even here (Chapters 5, 7, and 9, §7) that this other marginalization is only apparent.

3. Expositions of the *causa sui* in general are not very numerous (see the article of P. Hadot, s.v., in Joachim Ritter, *Historisches Wörterbuch der Philosophie*, vol. 1 [Basel: Schwabe, 1971], col. 976ff.). For Descartes, see E. Gilson, "Une nouvelle idée de Dieu," in *Études sur le rôle de la pensée médiévale dans la formation du système cartésien* (Paris: Vrin, 1930), and my study *Théologie blanche*, §18, 427ff.

4. "Per causam sui intelligo id, cujus essentia involvit existentiam; sive id cujus natura non potest concipi nisi existens." *Ethics* 1, def. 1; *Works*, 1:408.

5. "Eo sensu, quo Deus dicitur causa sui, etiam omnium rerum causa dicendus est." *Ethics* 1, prop. 25, schol.; *Works*, 1:431.

6. "Substantiam non potest produci ab alio; erit itaque causa sui." *Ethics* 1, prop. 7, dem.; *Works*, 1:412.

7. P. Poiret reproaches Spinoza precisely with *not* having defined the *causa sui* but only necessity: "By *causa sui*, I understand something whose

essence includes existence; or whose nature is not able to be conceived un-less it is existing. . . . This definition is false (that is, Spinoza in this way has falsely conceived the concept of *causa sui*) and captious and has innumerable shortcomings. . . . He defines necessity and not the *causa sui*. It is false, even if such a thing were to exist, that the formal idea of *causa sui* consists in this because essence involves existence. The idea of the *causa sui* consists in this: something is sufficient itself to itself alone. The cause exists in some relation to the effect, that is, there is a reception of the cause. When therefore some-thing in itself possesses what it seeks by itself alone in a most sufficiently manner, it is able to be said that it is *causa sui*. It is not a work in the sense that it receives from somewhere else by means of a different cause" ("per causam sui, intelligo id cujus essentia involvit existentiam; sive id cujus na-tura non potest concipi nisi existens. . . . Haec definitio est falsa (hoc est Spinoza hoc modo falsum habet conceptum causa sui) & captiosa, & defi-ciens enumeratione. . . . Definit necessitatem, non causam sui. Falsum est rationem formalem causae sui in hoc consistere, quod essentia involvat exis-tentiam, quanquam una eademque res sit. Causae sui ratio in hoc consistit, ut aliquid sibi ipsi se solo sufficiat. Causa habet aliquem respectum ad cau-satum dicit receptionem a causa. Quando ergo aliquid in se habet se solo sufficientissime id de quo quaeritur, non opus est ut aliunde recipiat a causa aliena: quare dici potest causa sui"). Poiret distinguishes, to the contrary, the *causa sui* as autosufficiency of the *causa sui* as direction (regimen) free of other things, and finally as an absolute necessity (that from which its nature cannot not exist). *Cogitationes rationales de Deo, anima et malo* (Amsterdam, 1677 1st ed., cited according to second edition, 1685), 842–43. On this po-lemic, see Gianluca Mori, *Tra Descartes e Bayle: Poiret e la Teodicea* (Bologna: Il Mulino, 1990).

8. "Scilicet si res sit in se, sive, ut vulgo dicitur, causa sui, tum per solam suam essentiam debebit intelligi." §92; *Works*, 1:38–39.

9. *Contra Gentes* 2:49, which takes up Aristotle, *Metaphysics* A.2.982b 25ff.; trans. Jonathan Barnes, *The Complete Works of Aristotle* (Princeton: Princeton University Press, 1984), 2:1555. See *Contra Gentes* 1:72: "That is free which is for its own sake" ("liberum est quod sui causa est"; trans. Anton C. Pegis [Notre Dame, Ind.: University of Notre Dame Press, 1975], 1: 241). When he responds to the objection that there is One "who has made himself," being before himself or not being when he is already, Plotinus es-capes immediately from the strict causal relation, by positing that the One "for there are not two, but one" (ου γαρ δυο, αλλ 'εν) hence in metaphoriz-ing the cause of himself (*Ennead*, 6.8.20; trans. A H. Armonstrong, Loeb Classical Library [Cambridge: Harvard University Press, 1988], 6:293). By contrast, Proclus seems to enunciate categorically that "for the cause is of itself" (αιτιον γαρ αυτο εαυτο εστιν). *Elementatio Theologica*, §46, ed. E. R. Dodds, 2d ed. (Oxford: Oxford University Press, 1963), 46. [The entire sentence says: "But the self-constituted, *being its own cause*, never deserts its

cause since it never deserts itself"—Trans.] "As to the thesis *omnis substantia est causa sui ipsius*, it concerns substance as Principle, not as efficient." *Liber de Causis*, §189, ed. P. Magnard et al. (Paris, 1990), 76. One remarks, moreover, that Saint Thomas Aquinas, commenting on this text, only speaks of a *causa formalis* (*In Librum de Causis Expositio*, §414, ed. C. Pera [Rome: Marietti, 1955], 131).

Jean-Marc Narbonne, in an article dedicated to "Plotin, Descartes et la notion de causa sui" (*Archives de Philosophie*, 56, no. 2 [1993]: 177–95, discusses with care our previous analyses of this topic (*Théologie blanche*, §18, and *Metaphysical Prism*, §9), claiming to find in Plotinus and Proclus predecessors to Descartes. Despite the argument he puts forth, I believe all the same that I have to maintain Descartes' absolute originality. To suppose — which still seems very doubtful to me—that the formulae of Plotinus and Proclus can literally anticipate those of Descartes, they would still be missing two decisive points: (i) the character of efficiency of the *causa sui*, (ii) its inclusion in a principle (that of the reason soon [called] efficient). For Descartes' innovation is above all not lexical but conceptual: it is a matter of submitting, albeit only formally, the divine essence and existence to the (efficient) reason of a principle. Moreover, for Plotinus, it is J.-M. Narbonne himself who proves me right: he recognizes not only that if "Plotinus is the inventor of the causa sui" ("Plotin, Descartes," 189), it is "to the close syntagma" ("Plotin, Descartes," 183) —saying as much that he has *not* literally invented it—but also that "curiously . . . the first author at having justified and commented on this proposition is also the first who has placed it into doubt" ("Plotin, Descartes," 189) —saying as much that Plotinus only exposed the cause of self in order to refuse it, as all the medievals did after him. Concerning Proclus, J.-M. Narbonne leans himself, for the essential, on John Whittaker, whose study "The Historical Background of Proclus' Doctrine of the AUYUPOSTATA" (in *De Jamblique à Proclus: Entretiens sur l'Antiquité classique 21*, ed. Heinrich Dörrie, 193–237 [Geneva: Fondation Hardt, 1975]) is effectively the authority. But this work also supports my thesis, because it shows precisely that this formula (i) is nothing but a "philosophical relic" in Proclus, (ii) that it can only be applied to beings already derived, and (iii) it can never be applied to the One, who has "no source either inside or outside" and remains "uncaused" ("Historical Background," 218). J. Whittaker even underlines that on this point Proclus thinks "like the Christians" ("Historical Background," 218), hence anticipates the medieval thinkers, which is what I maintain. In the discussion following this article, two scholars, who approve of its conclusions, add two arguments of importance for our thesis: (i) Jean Trouillard: "The first Principle is not self-constituting because self-constitution implies an (interiorized) procession, a derivation, a dependence. Moreover, the negative theology of Proclus forbids him to attribute to the One a notion of *causa sui*, that Plotinus accords him in *Enn.* 6.8 by the mode of figure. According to

Proclus, all self-constituted is essentially double" ("Historical Background," 234) (ii) Werner Beierwaltes: "*causa sui* as a statement about the absolute being of God cannot be understood as a *causa efficiens sui ipsius* in this context" ("*causa sui* nämlich als Aussage über das absolute Sein Gottes, kann in diesem Kontexte nicht als *causa efficiens sui ipsius* verstanden werden"; "Historical Background," 235).

10. "Idem non est causa sui ipsius." *Summa Theologiae* 1, q. 19, art. 5 ad resp.; 1:269—See q. 45, art. 5, ad 1; 2:233: "For an individual man cannot be the cause of human nature absolutely, because he would then be the cause of himself" ("Non enim hic homo potest esse causa naturae humanae absolute, quia sic esset causa sui ipsius"). Descartes retains an echo of these formulae in 1641: "Finally, I did not say that it was impossible for something to be the efficient cause of itself. This is obviously the case when the term 'efficient' is taken to apply only to causes which are prior in time to their effects, or different from them. But such a restriction does not seem appropriate in the present context" ("denique non dixi impossibile esse ut aliquid sit causa efficiens sui ipsius; etsi enim aperte id verum sit, quando restringuitur efficientis significatio ad illas causas quae sunt effectibus tempore priores, vel quae ab ipsis sunt diversae, non tamen videtur in hac quaestione ita esse restringenda"; AT VII:108, 7–12; CSM II:78). Or also: "Is not an efficient cause in the strict sense, and this I admit" ("non esse causam efficientem proprie dictam, quod concedo"; AT VII:240, 10–11; CSM II:167).

11. "Nec est possibile quod aliquis sit causa efficiens sui ipsius, quia sic esset prius seipso." *Summa Theologiae* 1, q. 2, art. 3 ad resp., second way; 1:25. See *Contra Gentes* 1:18; 1:103–4: "He [God] could not compose Himself, since nothing is its own cause, because it would be prior to itself, which is impossible" ("non enim ipse <Deus> seipsum componere posset, quia nihil est causa suiipsius; esset enim prius seipso, quod est impossibile"); *Contra Gentes* 1:22; in Pegis' English translation, 1:119–20: "It follows that something is the cause of its own being. This is impossible, because, in their notions, the existence of the cause is prior to the effect. If, then, something were its own cause of being, it would be understood to be before it had being—which is impossible" ("sequitur quod aliquid sit sibi ipsi causa essendi. Hoc autem est impossibile, quia prius, secundum intellectum, est causam esse, quam effectum. Si ergo aliquid sibi ipsi esset causa essendi, intelligeretur esse antequam haberet esse; quod est impossibile").

12. "Deus non habet causam." *Summa Theologiae* 1, q. 7, art. 7, ad resp.

13. "Deus est prima causa, non habens causam." *Contra Gentes* 1:22; Pegis, 1:120.

14. "Nec est possibile quod aliquis sit causa efficiens sui ipsius, quia sic esset prius seipso, quod est impossibile." *Summa Theologiae* 1, q. 2, art. 3, ad resp.; 1:25. See *De Ente et essentia* 5: "Now being itself cannot be caused by the form or quiddity of a thing (by 'caused' I mean by an efficient cause),

because that thing would then be its own cause and it would bring itself into being, which is impossible" ("non autem potest esse quod ipsum esse sit causatum ab ipsa forma vel quidditate rei, dico sicut a causa efficiente; quia sic aliqua res causa sui ipsius, et aliqua res seipsam in esse produceret, quod est impossibile"; *Opuscula omnia*, ed. Pierre Mandonnet, 1:157; trans. Armand Maurer, *On Being and Essence* [Toronto: The Pontifical Institute of Mediaeval Studies, 1949], 4, 1.7; 56). Thus the consequence that Thomas Aquinas does not belong, in this precise sense, to metaphysics; see my study "Thomas d'Aquin et l'onto-théo-logie," *Revue Thomiste* 1 (1995); trans. B. Gendreau, R. Rethty, and M. Sweeney, "Saint Thomas Aquinas and Onto-theo-logy," in *Mystic: Presence and Aporia*, ed. M. Kessler and C. Sheppard (Chicago: University of Chicago Press, 2003).

15. "Summa natura nec as se nec ab alio fieri potuit, nec ipsa sibi nec aliud aliquid illi . . . adjuvit." Anselm, *Monologion* 6, ed. Franciscus S. Schmitt (Edinburgh-Rome, 1938–61), 1:19; trans. Jasper Hopkins and Herbert Richardson, *Anselm of Canterbury* (New York: Edwin Mellen Press, 1974), 1:11. Thus: "This essence is not prior to itself"; "haec essentia prior seipsa non est." (ibid.).

16. John Duns Scotus: "Simpliciter primum effectivum est incausabile . . . : si primum illud est ineffectibile, ergo incausabile, quia non est finibile, nec materiabile, nec formabile." *Ordinatio* 1, d. 2, p.1, q. 1–2, n. 57, *Opera omnia* 2:162ff.

17. Ockham: "Ens immortale, incorruptibile, ingenerabile vel incausabile." *In Sententiarum Lib.* 1, d. 3, q. 2, *Opera philosophica et theologica*, ed. S. Brown and G. Gal, (St. Bonaventure, N.Y.: Cura Instituti Franciscani, 1970), 2:405.

18. Suárez: "Deum est sine principio et sine causa." "Nam quod dicitur ex se vel a se esse, licet positivum hoc esse videatur, tamen solam negationem addit ipsi enti, nam ens non potest esse a se per positivam originem et amanationem . . . et hunc modum exponendi sunt aliqui Sancti, cum dicunt Deum sibi causam sui esse, vel substantiae suae aut sapientiae." Suárez, *Disputationes Metaphysicae* 1, s. 1, n. 27, in *Opera omnia*, 25:11. See also 28, s. 1, n. 7: "Moreover, what is said to be from itself or by itself, although it seems to be positive, only adds a negation to being as such, since a being cannot be from itself by way of a positive origin or emanation" ("nam quod dicitur ex se vel a se esse, licet positivum esse videatur, tamen solam negationem addit ipsi enti, nam ens non potest esse a se per positivam originem et emanationem"). Aseity signifies only that "its own essence includes existence itself" ("in se et essentia claudit ipsum existere"). And if the "saints" have been able to speak of a cause of self ("when they say that God is for himself the cause of his own being"; "cum dicunt Deum esse sibi causam sui esse"), nevertheless "all these sayings should be interpreted in a negative way" ("hae omnes locutiones omnes negative interpretandae sunt"; trans. John P. Doyle, *The Metaphysical Demonstration of the Existence of God: Metaphysical*

Disputations 28–29 (South Bend, Ind.: St. Augustine's Press, 2004), 5–6. The examples cited come from the following *sancti*: (i) Lactantius: "But, because it is not possible for anything to become except that which at sometime began to exist; it is a consequence that, since there was nothing before him, he himself was proceeded out of himself before all things . . . "God himself made himself.'" Trans. Sister Mary Francis McDonald (Washington: Catholic University of America Press), 37–38. "It is true, because he cannot become that he is not in himself, at any time he begins to be, is the consequence, when at any time nothing was before him, he himself is before all procreated in himself . . . 'God makes himself'" ("verum quia fieri non potest, quin id quod sit, aliquando esse coeperit, consequens est, ut quando nihil ante illum fuit, ipse ante omnia ex se ipso sit procreatus . . . 'Deus ipse se fecit'"; *Divinae Institutiones* 1, *De falsa religione* 7, *Patrologia Latina* 6, 152a or P. Monat, ed., *Sources Chrétiennes* [Paris: Cerf, 1986], 90); the final formula cites Seneca, ed. Nisard (Paris: 1877), fgt. 3, 521. (ii) Saint Jerome: "How does God lay claim to the common appellation of substance as peculiar to himself? The reason is, as we have said, that other things receive substance by the mediation of God, but God—who always is and does not have his beginning from another source but is himself the origin of himself and the cause of his own substance—cannot be understood to have something which has existence from another source" ("quomodo nomen commune substantiae sibi proprium vindicat Deus? Illa, ut diximus causa: quia caetera ut sint, Dei sumpsere beneficio. Deus vero qui semper est, nec habet aliunde principium, et ipse sui origo est suaeque causa substantiae, non potest intelligi aliunde habere quod subsistit"; *Commentary on the Epistle to the Ephesians*, 2 on 3, 14, PL, 26, 488c–489a; trans. Ronald E. Heine, *The Commentaries of Origen and Jerome on St. Paul's Epistle to the Ephesians* [Oxford: Oxford University Press, 2002], 158; Suárez gives an inexact reference). Finally, (iii) Saint Augustine: "Quapropter quae causa illi est ut sapiens sit, ipsa illi causa est ut sit," *De Trinitate* 7.1.2, ed. Marcellin Mellet and T. Camelot, 514; and also "Igitur sempiternae sapientiae sua causa est [Deus] sempiterna," 83 Questions, c. 16 in *Œuvres de saint Augustin*, ed. Gustave Bardy et al. (Paris: Desclée de Brouwer, 1952), 66. Suárez hence does have reason to see only negative enunciations in these expressions, reducible to the absence of cause in God. It seems probable that Arnauld had these texts in mind in his objection, taken up by Caterus, in VII:208, 12ff. Gilson (*La philosophie au Moyen Age*, vol. 1, 2d ed. [Paris: Payot, 1944], 121ff. and 148) also goes back to an author a bit less "saintly," Candidus the Arian: "What is the cause of God himself? Indeed, he is the first cause and cause of himself" ("qua causa ipsum Deum esse? Etenim prima causa est et sibi causa"); but falsely, for it is a matter of a negative aseity: "Not in that he is different from another but that he is self in itself, for he is the cause of himself as he is" ("non quae altera alterius, sed ipsum hoc quod ipsum est, ad it ut sit, causa est"; *Liber de generatione divina* 3, PL, 8, 1015 b).

19. Respectively Suárez, *Disputationes Metaphysicae* 29, s. 1, n. 20, *Omnia Opera* 26:27; "nihil potest efficere se"; Doyle, *Metaphysical Disputation*, 66; and Descartes to Mersenne, 18 March 1641, AT III:336, 17ff; CSMK III:176.

20. Respectively, Arthur Schopenhauer, *Of the Quadruple Roots of the Principle of Sufficient Reason* 2, §8, in *Werke*, ed. Arthur Hübscher (Wiesbaden: E. Brockhaus, 1972), 1:9. And Nietzsche, *Beyond Good and Evil*, §21, in *Oeuvres philosophiques complètes*, ed. Colli and Montinari (Paris: Gallimard, 1968–97), 6:2, 29ff.; trans. Walter Kaufmann (New York: Random House, 1966), 28.

21. "Quis enim nescit idem nec seipso prius, nec a se ipso diversum esse potest?" AT VII:108, 13–14; CSM II:78, trans. mod.

22. "Dictat autem profecto lumen naturae nullam rem existere, de qua non liceat petere cur existat, sive in ejus causam efficientem inquirere, aut, si non habet, cur illa non indigeat, postulare." AT VII:108, 18–22 = IXA:86, 19–23; CSM II:78.

23. "Nulla res existit de qua non possit quaeri quaenam sit causa cur existat. Hoc enim de ipso Deo quaeri potest." AT VII:164, 28 – 165, 1 = IXA:127, 28–30; CSM II:116.

24. "Atqui considerationem causae efficientis esse praecipuum medium, ne dicam unicum, quod habeamus ad existentiam Dei probandam, puto omnibus esse manifestum." AT VII:238, 11–14 = IXA:184, 20–22; CSM II:166.

25. *Discourse on Method*, AT VI:40, 6–8; CSM I:131. The text continues: "It dictates also to us that our thoughts cannot all be true" (40, 16–17). It is interesting to note that the Latin translation of Etienne de Courcelles recovers the terminology of the *Replies* in 1644: "Ratio enim nobis non dictat ea quae sic vel videmus, vel imaginamur, idcirco revera existere. Sed plane nobis dictat, omnes nostras ideas sive notiones aliquid in se veritatis continere" (VI:563). See, among other occurrences of this syntagma: "For when we do not wonder at the greatness or the insignificance of an object, making no more of it and no less of it than reason deems we ought, then our esteem or contempt for it is dispassionate." *Passions of the Soul*, §150, AT XI:444, 13–16; CSM I:383. In Descartes, it belongs to reason to *dictate*, that is to say to prescribe and to impose.

26. "Petere cur existat sive in ejus causam efficientem inquirere." AT VII:108, 21–21; CSM II:78.

27. See *Metaphysical Prism*, in particular chap. 2 and below, Chapter 9, §6.

28. "Jam vero lumine naturali manifestum est tantumdem ad minimum esse debere in causa efficiente et totali, quantum in ejusdem causae effectu." AT VII:40, 21–23 = IXA:32, 10–12; CSM II:28.

29. "Iis effectibus, quorum realitas est actualis sive formalis." AT VII:41, 2–3; CSM II:28.

30. One can trace the denomination of either *a priori* or *a posteriori* proofs for the existence of God back to Thomas Aquinas: "Demonstration can be

made in two ways: One is through the cause, and is called *a priori*, and this is to argue from what is prior absolutely. The other is through the effect, and is called a demonstration *a posteriori*; this is to argue from what is prior relatively only to us" ("duplex est demonstratio, una, quae est per causam et dicitur propter quid, et haec est priora simpliciter. Alia est per effectum et dicitur demonstratio quia, et haec est par ea, quae sunt priora quoad nos"); it follows, of course, that God cannot be demonstrated except "from those of his effects which are known to us" ("per effectus nobis notos"; *Summa Theologiae* 1, q. 2, art. 2, resp.; English trans., 1:23). This denomination, moreover, does not remain any more fragile. First, because the formula appears (to my knowledge) only in the text of the *Meditations* itself. Then because even the clearest text, the Second Replies, remains imprecise: if it qualifies as *a posteriori* the demonstration by the idea of the infinite, Descartes omits (is it by design?) to qualify reciprocally the *a priori* argument called "ontological" that he nevertheless places in the first rank (AT VII:167, 12, then 166, 20; CSM II:118, then 117); and when these two qualifications intervene explicitly in order to distinguish the analysis from the synthesis, they can still be confused: the synthesis "as it were *a posteriori*" (*tanquam a posteriori*) has, even so, also produced a proof "more *a priori*" (*magis a priori*) than that of the analysis, "discovered . . . as it were *a priori*" (*tanquam a priori inventa*). AT VII:156, 6–7 and 155, 24; CSM II:120 and 111. This embarrassment, nevertheless, does not concern the *a priori* as such, since a different text defines it univocally as a propriety of arguments drawn from metaphysics and (rational) theology: "The reasons . . . against substantial forms . . . are at first those of the metaphysical or theological *a priori*" ("rationes . . . contra formas substantiales . . . sunt in primis haec *a priori* Metaphysica, sive Theologica"; To Regius, January 1642, AT III:505, 8–11; this part of the letter is not translated in CSMK).

31. "Hoc enim de ipso Deo quaeri potest." AT VII:164, 29; CSM II:116.

32. "Rationis notionem claram quin habuerit [cf. Descartes], dubitandum non est. Idem etiam claret ex axiomate primo quod Dei existentiam et animae a corpore distinctionem more geometrico demonstraturus in controversis Meditationibus de prima Philosophia subjunctis . . . praemittit. Dum enim: 'Nulla res, inquit, existit, de qua non possit quaeri, quaenam sit causa, cur existat. Hoc enim de ipso Deo quaeri potest . . . quia ipsa ejus naturae immensitas est causa sive ratio, propter quam nulla causa indigeat ad existendum,' discrimen inter causam et rationem confuse agnovit." C. Wolff, *Philosophia prima sive Ontologia* (Frankfurt and Leipzig, 1730; ed. J. École, Hildesheim: Olms, 1962), §71, 50. Poiret had also insisted on this point: "Therefore in this way God is from Himself, as reason or cause that exists; He is the cause that comes before all others, first and radical, and from where all existences of other things spring forth and even things that spring forth through another cause that is pleasing to God" ("ergo Deus ita est a se, ut ratio sive causa qua existit, sit causa omnes alias antecedens,

prima et radicalis, unde etiam omnes rerum aliarum existentiae, etsi mediante alia causa quae est placiti, pullulant"; *Cogitationes rationales*, 277).

33. "Ipsa causalitas est veluti proprietas quaedam entis, ut sic: nullum enim est ens, quod aliquam rationem causae non participat." Suárez, *Disputationes Metaphysicae* 12, Prologue, *Omnia opera* 25:372–73.

34. "Nullum autem est ens quod non sit vel effectus, vel causa." Suárez, *Disputationes Metaphysicae* 12, Prologue, *Omnia opera* 25:372–73.

35. Pascal, *Pensées*, ed. L. Lafuma (Paris: Seuil, 1962), §199 (B. §72), 525.

36. "Deus causam non habet, tamen omnia alia praeter ipsum, causam habent." Suárez, *Disputationes Metaphysicae* 12, Prologue, *Omnia opera* 25:372–73.

37. "Licet Deus non habet veram et realem causam, quaedam tamen rationes ejus concipiuntur a nobis ac si essent causae aliarum." Suárez, *Disputationes Metaphysicae* 12, Prologue, *Omnia opera* 25:372–73.

38. "Quamvis ergo demus, ens, in quantum ens, non habere causas in rigore sumptas priori modo, habet tamen rationem aliquam suarum proprietatum; et hoc modo etiam in Deo possunt hujusmodi rationes reperiri, nam ex Dei perfectione infinita reddimus causam, cur unus tantum sit, et sic de aliis." Suarez, *Disputatione Metaphysicae* 1, s. 1, n. 29, *Omnia opera* 25:12.

39. "Non quod indigeat [Deus] ulla causa ut existat, sed quia ipsa ejus naturae immensitas est causa sive ratio, propter quam nulla causa indiget ad existendum." AT VII:165, 1–3; CSM II:116.

40. "Inexhausta Dei potentia sit causa sive ratio propter quam causa non indiget." AT VII:236, 9–10; CSM II:165.

41. "Immensam et incomprehensibilem potentiam quae in ejus idea continetur . . . sit plane causa cur ille esse perseveret nec alia praeter ipsam esse possit." AT VII:110, 26–29; CSM II:79–80.

42. Respectively, AT I:150, 22; CSMK III:25, (see I:146, 4; CSMK III:23, and "God is infinite and all-powerful," I:152, 11; CSMK III:25); I:152, 2; CSMK III:25 and AT VII:50, 6; CSM II:34. On the gap between these determinations of the metaphysical essence of God, see my analyses in *Metaphysical Prism*, chap. 4, §19–§20.

43. On the Suárezian temptation to yield to a positive meaning of the *causa sui*, see, e.g., *Disputationes Metaphysicae* 1, s. 1, n. 29, *Omnia opera* 25:12; and 29, s. 1, n. 20, *Omnia opera* 25:27.

44. "De Deo primo ente et substantia increata, quatenus ipsum esse ratione naturali cognosci potest," *Disputationes Metaphysicae* 29, title, *Omnia opera* 26:21; Doyle, *Metaphysical Demonstration*, 51.

45. *Disputationes Metaphysicae* 29, s. 1, *Omnia opera* 26:22–34.

46. "*A posteriori* demonstrari possit Deum esse." Doyle, *Metaphysical Demonstration*, 81.

47. "Fons et causa efficiens rerum creaturum." *Disputationes Metaphysicae* 29, s. 2, n. 4, *Omnia opera* 26:35; Doyle, *Metaphysical Demonstration*, 84.

48. "Aliquo modo possit *a priori* demonstrari, Deum esse." Doyle, *Metaphysical Demonstration*, 113.

49. "Non posse demonstrari *a priori* Deum esse, quia neque Deus habet causam sui esse, per quam *a priori* demonstretur, neque si haberet, ita exacte et perfecte a nobis cognoscitur Deus, ut ex propriis principiis (ut sic dicam) illum assequamur. Quo sensu dixit Dionysius, capite septimo *De Divinis Nominibus*, nos non posse Deum ex propria natura cognoscere." *Disputationes Metaphysicae* 29, s. 3, n. 1, *Omnia opera* 26:47; Doyle, *Metaphysical Demonstration*, 113. The expression "neque Deus habet causam sui esse" ("God does not have a cause of his being") does not differ essentially from the *causa sui*, except in radicalizing its ontological character: it would be a matter of cause not only in itself, but of its being, indeed, of the *esse* inasmuch as it takes the place of the *essentia* of God according to Thomas Aquinas. Dionysius' formula to which Suárez here alludes is found in the *Divine Names* 7.3: "We know God in terms of its nature, for this is unkown" (θεον γινώσκομεν ουχ εκ της αυτου φυσεως [αγνωστον γαρ τουτο]; *Patrologia Graeca*, 3, col. 869d; trans. John D. Jones, *The Divine Names and Mystical Theology* [Milwaukee, Wisc.: Marquette University Press, 980], 178). Let us cite another text of Suárez that also links him to the *a priori* of the demonstration of the use of the *causa* in God: "But I do not see why he [Fonseca] *a priori* articulates an impossible deduction, for it is not from the cause but from the extrinsic medium" ("Sed non video cur deductionem ad impossibile vocet [Fonseca] *a priori*, cum non sit ex causa, sed per extrinsecum medium"; *Disputationes Metaphysicae* 3, s. 3, n. 9, *Omnia opera* 25:114).

50. See my study "Spinoza et les trois noms de Dieu," in *Herméneutique et ontologie: Hommage à Pierre Aubenque*, ed. Rémi Brague and Jean-François Courtine (Paris: Presses Universitaires de France, 1990), or "The Coherence of Spinoza's Definitions of God in *Ethics I*, Proposition 11," in *God and Nature: Spinoza's Metaphysics*, ed. Yirmiahu Yovel (Leiden: Brill, 1991).

51. The equivalence between *causa sui esse* ("cause of its being") and *causa sui* ("cause of itself") cannot alleviate the difficulty: God is his being for Descartes (*Deus est suum esse*, AT VII:383, 15 = AT III:433, 9), as first for Thomas Aquinas (*Summa Theologiae* 1, q. 12, art. 2c), hence also for Suarez; in consequence, to cause oneself or to cause one's being goes back, in each case, to exactly the same thing.

52. "Neque . . . exacte et perfecte a nobis cognoscitur Deus."

53. "Ex quodam attributo quod reipsa est essentia Dei, a nobis autem abstractius concipitur, ut modus entis non causati, colligi aliud attributum, et ita concludi illud ens esse Deum." Suárez, *Disputationes Metaphysicae* 29, s. 3, n. 2, *Omnia opera* 26:47; Doyle, *Metaphysical Disputation*, 114.

54. "Deum esse, non potest *a priori* demonstrari, quod etiam convenit propositioni per se notae; *a posteriori* tamen et per effectus demonstrari potest."

55. G. Vasquez, *Commentatiorum ac disputationum in Primam Partem S. Thomae*, (Ingoldstadt, 1609), respectively d. 19, q. 2 and q. 3, 91, and 95.

56. "Sit igitur prima asssertio. Deum esse *a priori* demonstrari non potest, quia esse divinum est ipsamet essentia Dei et fundamentum omnium attributum divinorum, cujus nulla causa aut ratio *a priori* nostro etiam intelligendi modo afferi potest." Eustache de Saint-Paul, *Summa Philosophiae: Quarta pars quae est Metaphysica*, part 4, d. 3, q. 2: "Utrum Deum esse demonstrari possit et quomodo," (Paris, 1609 1st ed.; citation from 1611 2d ed.), 115.

57. Scipion Dupleix, *La Métaphysique* (Paris, 1610), cited from the 1st ed. R. Ariew, respectively, 4.9.3, 703; 4.9.4, 717; and 4.10.1, 762. See also Justus Lipsius, in a completely different style: "Of this only I am assured, that God's will is a cause above all causes; beyond which, who seeks another, is ignorant of the efficacy and power of the divine nature. For it is necessary, that every cause be of a sort, before and greater than its effect: but nothing is before, nor greater than God and his will, therefore there is no cause thereof" ("hoc tantum scio, causam ante omnes causas esse, voluntatem Dei. A qua qui quaerit aliam, vim et potentiam ignorat naturae divinae. Nam causam omnem necessum est, genere quodam, priorem et majorem esse suo effectu: at Deo et ejus voluntate, nihil prius aut majus. Non ergo ulla ejus causa"; *De Constantia* 2:12; Leiden ed., 91; *Of Constancie*, 159–60).

58. "Deum non potest demonstrari *a priori*, quia ejus esse nullam habet causam per quam *a priori* demonstrari possit."

59. "Neque etiam id potest demonstrari per essentiam et quidditatem Dei, tanquam per aliquod prius secundum rationem, quia quaestio *An est* prior est quaestione *quid est*, ut recte Thomas." *D.[instinctio]* 1 [error: *Summa Theologiae* 1], q. 2, art. 2, ad 2. . . . "Deus potest demonstrari *a posteriori*, ab ejus effectibus." A. Danburgh, *Analectorum Theologicorum Disputatio XXXIII De Cognitione Dei III*, under the presiding of J. Revius, February 1647, respectively chaps. 3 and 4 [pp. 2 and 3]. It is not a matter of an isolated case; indeed, shortly later—March 20, 1647—J. Revius causes Jean d'Appeldorn (of Daventer) to uphold some theses, *De Deo ut est ens a se*, explicitly turned against Descartes: "Concerning this explanation of the Theologians (itself being negative), he did not doubt it at any time. Only Descartes, it was commented, used to think that an [i.e., explanation] other than his Method could be of interest. Truly, the being of God is from Himself not privately but positively" ("de hac explicatione [a se negative] nullus unquam Theologorum [quod sciam] dubitavit. Solus Cartesius aliam [cf. explicationem], quam suae Methodo inservire putabat, commentus est. Nempe, Deum a se esse non negative, . . . sed positive"; *Analectorum Theologicorum Disputatio* 25, *De Deo ut est a se*, 2.9). These judgments, moreover, seem very sure: Descartes really breaks here with all previous theologians, and he actually introduces efficient causality into God in order to apply his method to him. The offensive of J. Revius is still pursued on 27 March 1647 by the intermediary of E. Spiljardus, who concludes his theses *De Attributis Dei* by maintaining that "the being of God is posited from itself and is a

being that must be kept away from the efficient cause as a distinction of Theology" ("Deum esse a se positive et ut a causa efficiente a limine Theologiae arcendum esse"; thesis 17 and final). It is, hence, a matter of a conscious and organized campaign against the contradictory novelty of the Cartesian *causa sui*. I owe my awareness of these very instructive documents to the erudition and friendship of Théo Verbeek (University of Utrecht).

60. Spinoza, *Korte Verhandeling* 1.1, §10; following the [French] translation of Charles Appuhn, *Œuvres de Spinoza* (Paris: Librairie Garnier, 1964), 1:48, but corrected following the critical edition and the Italian translation of Filippo Mignini, *Korte Verhandeling / Breve Trattato* (L'Aquila: L. U. Japadre, 1986), 8 (with an excellent footnote on the authors of our debate, 454ff.). *Works* 1:64–65.

61. Spinoza, *Korte Verhandeling* 1.7, §5, 32; *Works* 1:88–89. Spinoza has applied his program perfectly in *Ethics* 1, §11, where, after having repeated the *a posteriori* proof of Descartes (dem. 3) as if despite himself, he undertakes immediately (scholie) to transpose it into an *a priori* proof, only in conformity with the geometrical order, which he privileges against Descartes: "In this last demonstration I wanted to show God's existence *a posteriori*, so that the demonstration would be perceived more easily—but not because God's existence does not follow *a priori* from the same foundation" ("in hac ultima demonstratione Dei existentiam *a posteriori* ostendere volui, ut demonstratio facilius perciperetur; non autem propterea quod ex hoc eodem fundamento Dei existentia *a priori* non sequatur"; *Works* 1:418). It remains evidently open whether from the "same foundation" one can in a similar fashion draw two proofs in two different orders (see my study cited above, "Spinoza et les trois noms de Dieu").

62. *"Deum non modo negative, sed et positive sui efficientem causam dici debere* . . . ut affirmat. Quaerat, leget, evolvat mea scripta: nihi umquam simile in illis reperiet, sed omnino contrarium." *Nota in programma quoddam*, AT VIIIB:368, 31 – 369, 1; CSM I:310.

63. "Such extravagant views" ("talibus opiniorum portentis"; AT VIIIB:369, 2; CSM I:310). Admittedly, Descartes pushes the denial here as far as honesty permits him, in order to resist the attacks, as numerous as they were heated, coming from the Protestants, more conservative in philosophy and theology than his usual Catholic interlocutors. But Revius could also base himself on the facts; thus the dispute presided over by Adrianus Heereboord in December 1647, *De Notitia Dei naturali*, maintained that "God, not in the negative sense but certainly in the positive sense, is the efficient cause of himself and through his own power conserves his being as cause of himself" ("Deum, non modo negative sed et positive, sui causam efficientem et per potentiam sui ipsius causam conservantem esse"; reported in *Statera Philosophiae Cartesianae* [Leiden, 1650], 245ff., cited in AT V:128). On this debate, see the recent clarification by Théo Verbeek, *Descartes and the Dutch: Early Reactions to Cartesian Philosophy 1637–1650* (Carbondale:

Southern Illinois University Press, 1992), esp. chaps. 3 and 12, 40ff. and 116ff., and "From 'Learned Ignorance' to Scepticism: Descartes and Calvinist Orthodoxy," in *Scepticism and Irreligion in the Seventeenth and Eighteenth Centuries*, ed. Richard Popkin and Arie Vanderjagt (Leiden: Brill, 1993).

64. "Verbum sui causa nullo modo de efficiente potest intelligi," AT VII:236, 8; CSM II:165; "Deum non esse causam efficientem sui ipsius," AT VII:237, 4–5, CSM II:167; "is not an efficient cause in the strict sense" ("non esse causam efficientem proprie dictam." AT VII:240, 10; CSM II:167).

65. "Denique non dixi impossibile esse ut aliquid sit causa efficiens sui ipsius." AT VII:108, 7–8 = IXA:86, 7–9; CSM II:78.

66. We will hence not be as categorical as was F. Alquié, who, all the same, knew Descartes' wily prudence: "On this point, Descartes is not very exact. It suffices to re-read the text of the Fourth Replies to see that it is less far than he claims from the opinion that one attributes to him and that he in no way holds this opinion to be monstrous" (in Descartes, *Œuvres philosophiques*, 3:819, n. 1). Moreover, exceptionally, Alquié does not give here any precise reference, admitting in this manner some embarrassment.

67. "In a sense its own cause" ("quodammodo sui causa"; AT VII:109, 6; CSM II:78). See AT VII:111, 5; CSM II:80, taken up in 235, 18 and 22; CSM II:164–65. "Something close to an efficient cause" ("quasi causa efficiens"; AT VII:243, 26; CSM II:170). See *Théologie blanche*, §18, 432–37.

68. "Utrum omnis causa sit effectu suo nobilior" . . . "causa principalis numquam potest esse ignobilior." Suárez, *Disputationes Metaphysicae* 26, s. 1, title and n. 5, *Opera omnia* 25:916 and 918. Why not recall here the Hugolian version of this thesis? "The effect weeps and without ceasing interrogates the cause" (*Les contemplations*, "Pleurs dans la nuit").

69. "Modus loquendi aliquorum Patrum Graecorum, qui etiam in divinis personis Patrem vocant causam Filii, eo quod sit principium ejus." *Disputationes Metaphysicae* 12, s. 1, n. 1, *Opera omnia* 25:373. See also s. 1, n. 8: "Et ad hanc verborum proprietatem videntur alludere Sancti, cum dicunt Patrem aeternum esse principium, fontem et originem totius deitatis. Non enim ita loquuntur quia Pater sit principium ipsius naturae diviniae, quia juxta fidem Catholicam divina natura non habet principium, quia a nullo procedit." *Opera omnia* 25:375. And Thomas Aquinas, *Summa Theologiae* 1, q. 33, art. 1 (already noted by E. Gilson, *Index scolastico-cartésien*, §74).

70. "Licet igitur dicant [Theologi] Patrem esse principium Filii, negant tamen Filium esse principiatum a Patre." *Disputationes Metaphysicae* 12, s. 1, n. 32, *Opera omnia* 25:383.

71. "Conceptum quemdam causae efficienti et formali communem." AT VII:238, 24–25; CSM II:166.

72. "Causa efficiens non potest habere mutuam causalitatem cum materia vel forma." *Disputationes Metaphysicae* 27, s. 2, n. 19, *Opera omnia* 25:957.

73. "Per analogiam ad efficientem referri posse." AT VII:240, 12; CSM II:167.

74. "Isti omnes modi loquendi, a causae efficientis analogia petiti pernecessarii sunt ad lumen naturale ita dirigendam." AT VII:241, 16–18; CSM II:168.

75. "Analogia causae efficientis usus sim ad ea quae ad causam formalem, hoc est ad ipsam Dei essentiam pertinent, explicanda." AT VII:241, 25–27; CSM II:168.

76. "Ipsam rei essentiam, sive causam formalem . . . magnam habet analogiam cum efficiente, ideoque quasi causa efficiens vocari potest." AT VII:243, 23–26; CSM II:170.

77. A classically analogical interpretation of the concept of principle is still found in Suárez. Thus: "Moreover, this idea of a principle is not only conjoined with causality with respect to creatures but also belongs to God as well as to creatures. And by this reason this can be said about God and creatures according to the analogy of attribution. By the grace of the Word, it can be said analogically about God and creatures that the being of the principle is efficient not according to proportion alone, but according to a real and true relation, which nevertheless includes an analogous attribution, as we will explain below [*Disputationes* 29ff.] on the section on the analogy of being regarding God and creature" ("haec autem ratio principii cum causalitate conjuncta est respectu creaturarum, et convenit tum Deo, tum etiam creaturis. Et hac ratione potest de Deo et creaturis dici secundum analogiam attributionis; verbi gratia, esse principium efficiens analogice dicitur de Deo et de creaturis, non secundum proportionalitatem tantum, sed propter veram et realem convenientiam, analogam tamen et includentem attributionem, ut inferius explicabimus [*Disputationes* 29ff.] in analogia entis ad Deum et creaturam"; *Disputationes Metaphysicae* 12, s. 1, n. 15, *Opera omnia* 25:379.

78. See Thomas Aquinas, *Summa Theologiae* 1, q. 13, art. 5; *Contra Gentes* 1, §29, §34 and 3, §54; *Compendium Theologiae*, §27; "analogy is from God to the creature" ("analogia est creaturae ad Deum") and not the inverse, according to *In Sententiarum* 1, d. 35, q. 1, art. 4. I follow here the conclusions of Bernard Montagnes, *La doctrine de l'analogie de l'Être d'après saint Thomas d'Aquin* (Paris-Louvain: Publications Universitaires de Louvain, 1963).

79. "Si prius de causa cur sit, sive cur esse perseveret, inquisivimus, attendentesque ad immensam et incomprehensibilem potentiam quae in ejus idea continetur." AT VII:110, 24–28 = IXA:87, 39ff.; CSM II:79.

80. See Chapter 7, §7–§8, and Chapter 9, §3–§9, in this volume.

81. In metaphysics (in opposition to revealed theology) "considerantur res divinae non tanquam subjectum scientiae, sed tanquam principium subjecti." *Expositio Boethium De Trinitate*, in *Opuscula Omnia*, ed. Pierre Mandonnet (Paris: Lethielleux, 1927), 3:117.

82. *Comprehendere Deum, Disputationes Metaphysicae* 1, s. 1, n. 13, *Opera omnia* 25:6; n. 19, 25:9; n. 26, *Omnia opera* 25:25, etc. See *Théologie blanche*, 134ff.

9. Outline of a History of Definitions of God in the Cartesian Epoch

1. [Apart from this sentence, the first paragraph in the French version is as follows: "This may be only because it thinks, for the first time, each concept and each idea in the mode of representation, hence by beginning with the requirements of radical subjectivity. The establishment of the representative "I" modifies in this manner, among other questions, that of the names of God, which tends to become henceforth one of ideas and hence of representations of God — Trans.]

2. On the constitution of the concept of *metaphysica* in the sixteenth century, see E. Vollrath, "Die Gliederung der Metaphysik in eine Metaphysica generalis und eine Metaphysica specialis," *Zeitschrift für philosophische Forschung* 16 (1962): 258–84, and Jean-François Courtine, *Suárez et le système de la métaphysique* (Paris: Presses Universitaires de France, 1990).

3. On the revival of Thomas, see Stephen Menn, "The Intellectual Setting," in *The Cambridge History of Seventeenth-Century Philosophy*, ed. Daniel Garber and Michael Ayers (Cambridge: Cambridge University Press, 1998), chap. 2.

4. See: Peter Petersen, *Geschichte der aristotelischen Philosophie im protestantischen Deutschland* (Leipzig: Meiner, 1921 1st ed.; Stuttgart: Frommann, 1962 2d ed.); E. Lewalter, *Spanisch-jesuitische und deutschlutherische Metaphysik des 17. Jahrhunderts* (Hamburg: 1935, 1st ed.; Darmstadt: Wissenschaftliche Buchgesellschaft, 1967 2d ed.); Max Wundt, *Die deutsche Schulmetaphysik des 17. Jahrhunderts* (Tübingen: J. C. B. Mohr, 1939); and John A. Trentman, "Scholasticism in the Seventeenth Century," in *The Cambridge History of Later Medieval Philosophy*, ed. Norman Kretzmann, Anthony Kenny, and Jan Pinborg (Cambridge: Cambridge University Press, 1982), 818–37. For an overall picture of the second Scholasticism, see the summary in Melquiades Andrés Martín, *La teología española en el siglo XVI*, 2 vols. (Madrid: La Editorial Católica, 1976–77). Suárez was chosen by Melanchton to serve as a basis for the philosophical teaching in the Lutheran universities, and J. Revius published, for the Dutch reformed universities, a *Suarez repurgatus* (Leiden, 1643). See Théo Verbeek, *Descartes and the Dutch: Early Reactions to Cartesianism* (Carbondale: Southern Illinois University Press, 1992).

5. To Mersenne, 25 December 1639, AT II:630; CSMK III:141–42.

6. *Summa Theologiae* 1, q. 12, art. 2c. The formula is taken up again by Descartes: "Deus est suum esse" in AT III:433, 9; CSMK III:196, and AT VII:383, 15; CSM II:263.

7. *Summa Theologiae* 1, q. 3, art. 4 ad 2m and art. 5c. Another formula that is also taken up by Descartes: "In the case of God, essence is not distinct from existence"; "in Deo non distinguitur essentia ab existentia." AT VII:243, 17–18; CSM II:169.

8. *Actus purus*: see *Summa Theologiae* 1, q. 3, art. 2c; q. 14, art. 2; q. 12, art. 1c; etc.

9. *Summa Theologiae* 1a, q. 4, art. 2c: "Deus est ipsum esse per se subsistens." See the excellent commentaries by Étienne Gilson in *Le Thomisme*, 5th ed. (Paris: Vrin, 1945). On the historical fate of these formulas, see Gilson, *God and Philosophy* (New Haven: Yale University Press, 1941), Gilson, *L'Être et l'essence* (Paris: Vrin, 1947 lst ed.; 1962 2d ed.), and Gilson, *Being and Some Philosophers* (Toronto: Pontifical Institute of Mediaeval Studies, 1962).

10. *Summa Theologiae* 1, q. 2, art. 3. See *Summa contra gentiles* 1.13.

11. *Summa Theologiae* 1, q. 4, art. 3 ; q. 13, art. 5 and 6. Bernard Montagnes, *La doctrine de l'analogie de l'être d'après saint Thomas d'Aquin* discusses the consistency of this with other texts by Thomas on analogy: mainly *De veritate*, q. 2, art. 3 ad 4 m and art. 11; *In Sententiarum libros* 1, d. 2, q. 1, art. 2; d. 3, q. 1, art. 3; d. 35, q. 1, art. 4; *De Ente et essentia* 2 and 7; etc.

12. "De Deo quid non sit cognoscimus, quid vero sit, penitus manet incognitum" (*Summa contra gentiles* 3, 49). See *Summa Theologiae* 1, q. 2, art. 1c: "Nos non scimus de Deo quid est"; *De potentia*, q. 7, art. 2 ad 1m: "Substantia ejus [cf. Dei] est ignota, ita et esse." See also Étienne Gilson, *Les tribulations de Sophie* (Paris: Vrin, 1967), 22ff. and §7–§8 of my study "Saint Thomas d'Aquin et l'onto-théo-logie," *Revue thomiste* 1 (1995); trans. B. Gendreau, R. Rethty and M. Sweeney, "Saint Thomas Aquinas and Onto-theology," in *Mystic: Presence and Aporia*, ed. M. Kessler and C. Sheppard (Chicago: University of Chicago Press, 2003).

13. The main debate is over whether Thomas has in mind an analogy of attribution or an analogy of proportionality in four terms. See Pierre Aubenque, "Les origines de l'analogie de l'être. Sur l'histoire d'un contresens," *Les Études philosophiques* 1 (Paris, 1978) and "Zur Entstehung der pseudo-aristotelischen Lehre von der Analogie des Seins," in *Aristoteles Werk und Wirkung: Paul Moraux gewidmet*, ed. Jürgen Wiesner (Berlin: de Gruyter, 1987), 2:233–48. For the Thomistic heritage, see my *Théologie blanche*, 27–139. The traditional position is defended in Dominique Dubarle, *Dieu avec l'être: De Parménide à saint Thomas* (Paris: Beauchesne, 1986), chap. 3.

14. *Disputationes metaphysicae* 2, s. 2, n. 36: "Si alterum negandum esset, potius analogia, quae incerta est, quam unitas conceptus, quae certis rationibus videtur demonstrari, esset neganda." Suárez, *Opera omnia* 25:81. Or, put otherwise: "Being is as much univocal as any genus, since a genus, although it is logically univocal, can be physically or metaphysically analogous"; "ens aeque univocum esse ac quodlibet genus, nam genus, licet univocum sit, physice seu metaphysice dici potest analogum." *Disputationes metaphysicae* 28, s. 3, n. 20, 25:14; Doyle, *Metaphysical Disputations*, 48.

15. *Disputationes metaphysicae* 28, s. 3, n. 17: "sine dubio habet ens magnam similitudinem cum terminis univocis, cum medio uno conceptu absolute et since addito de deo et creatura praedicetur." *Omnia opera* 25:19. Similarly, Suárez writes: "a creature is denominated being simply from its own being and not from any proportion which it has to the being of God. . . . the character of being is conceived in a creature in an entirely absolute, intrinsic, and proper way" ("creatura denominatur ens absolute a suo esse et

non ex proportione aliqua, quam servat ad esse Dei. . . . ratio entis omnino absolute et intrinsece ac proprie concipitur in creatura"; *Disputationes metaphysicae* 28, s. 3, n. 4, *Opera omnia* 25:14; Doyle, *Metaphysical Disputations*, 31–32). On the question of univocity in Suárez and his predecessors, see Walter Hoeres, "Francis Suárez and the Teaching of John Duns Scotus on *univocatio entis*," in *John Duns Scotus 1265–1965, Studies in Philosophy*, ed. John K. Ryan and Bernardino Bonensea (Washington: Catholic University of America Press, 1965); *Théologie blanche*, chap. 7, 121ff.; and Montagne, *La doctrine de l'analogie*.

16. *De Divina Substantia* 1, s. 1, n. 1; 1:1.

17. *Disputationes metaphysicae* 30, s. 1, n. 5: "Deus est primum ens . . .; ergo est etiam summum et perfectissimum essentialiter; ergo de essentia ejus est, ut includat aliquo modo omnem perfectionem possibilem in tota latitudine entis." *Opera omnia* 26:61. Suárez also writes: "In the prior way, it is said that the perfect thing, which lacks nothing, owes this to the nature of its integrity. . . . In the posterior way, therefore, it is said that for the perfect thing nothing of its perfection is absolutely absent; And even in this way it is said that this being is, therefore, absolutely perfect, whom all perfection is owed. And, it is necessary that it be there so that no perfection is lacking to it, neither privately nor negatively; and it can be said in both senses that being, and also concerning the essence of God, that they are simply perfect being" ("Priori modo dicitur perfectum, cui nihil deest, quod ei debitum sit natura sua ad suam integritatem. . . . Posteriori ergo modo dicitur perfectum, cui absolute nihil perfectionis deest; atque hoc modum illud ens dicitur absolute perfectum, cui omnis perfectio ita debita est, ac necessario inest, ut nulla ei omnino deesse est, nee privative nee negative, et in utroque sensu dicitur esse, de essentia Dei, esse simpliciter perfectum"; *Opera omnia* 26:60).

18. *Disputationes metaphysicae* 30, s. 1 n. 6; 26:62. See Jean-François Courtine, "Le projet suarézien de la métaphysique," *Archives de philosophie* 42 (1979), and "Le statut ontologique du possible selon Suárez," *Cuadernos Salamantinos de Filosofia* 7 (1980; Salamanca, 1981).

19. *Disputationes metaphysicae* 31, s. 12, n. 40–46, *Opera omnia* 26:294–98.

20. *Disputationes metaphysicae* 31, s. 12, n. 40: "Rursus neque illae enuntiationes sunt verae quia cognoscuntur a Deo, sed potius ideo cognoscuntur, quia verae sunt, alioqui nulla reddi posset ratio, cur Deus necessario cognosceret illas esse veras." *Opera omnia* 26:295. One of the conclusions Suárez draws in s. 12 sufficiently shows that this is, indeed, his thesis: "Even if it is impossible that nothing be such a cause [i.e., God, efficient cause], nonetheless this phrase [i.e., a human is an animal] would be true" ("Unde, si per impossibile, nulla esset talis causa [cf. God, efficient cause], nihilominus illa enunciatio [cf. "Homo est animal"] vera esset"; s. 12, n. 45; *Opera omnia* 26:297). For a contrary view on this question, see Gary Hatfield, "Reason, Nature, and God in Descartes," in *Essays on the Philosophy and Science of René*

Descartes, ed. Stephen Voss (New York: Oxford University Press, 1993). Similar positions can be found in G. Vasquez, *Commentariorum ac disputationum in primam partem s. Thomae tomus primus, disputatio CIV*, chap. 3, n. 9–11 (Ingoldstadt, 1609), 783–84 (= Lyon, 1620; 1:510). Here again divine perfection is measured against the possible: "Since the first being is, it is absolutely perfect in itself and it requires no possible thing. . . . God . . . it is said . . . is therefore perfect, and this whatsoever does not imply a contradiction; it is able to come from it" ("Cum enim sit primum ens, ita in se perfectus absolute est, et nulla re possibili indigeat. . . . Deus . . . dicitur . . . ita perfectus, ut quicquid non implicat contradictionem, ab eo fieri possit"; *Disputatio* 143, 1609, 173). Vasquez' *Opera omnia* appeared from 1598 to 1617 in Alcalà. On the close relation between Suarez and Vasquez on this question, see *Théologie blanche*, 53–57.

21. "Cum Astronomi, sacerdotes Dei altissimi ex parte libri Naturae simus." See letter 91, to Hohenburg, 26 March 1598, Johannes Kepler, *Gesammelte Werke*, ed. Walther von Dyck and Max Caspar (Munich: C. H. Beck, 1938–59; hereafter *GW*), 13:193. See also the autobiographical remarks in letter 23, to Mästlin, 10 March 1595, *GW* 13:40.

22. "Rationes creandorum corporum mathematicae Deo conaeternae fuerunt." *Harmonice Mundi*, 4.1, *GW* 6:219.

23. "Geometriae rationes Deo coaeternae sunt." *Epitome* 4.1.3, *GW* 7:267.

24. "Geometria ante rerum ortum Menti divinae coaeterna, Deus ipse (quid enim in Deo, quod non sit Ipse Deus?), exempla Deo creandi mundi superditavit." *Harmonice Mundi*, 4.1, *GW* 6:31. See also: "Rather, the ideas of quantity are and were coeternal with God, [they are] God himself" ("imo Ideae quantitatum sunt erantque Deo coaeternae, Deus ipse"; *Mysterium cosmographicum*, *GW* 8:30).

25. "Non aberrat enim ab Archetypo suo Creator, Geometriae fons ipsissimus, et, ut Plato scripsit, aeternam exercens Geometricam." *Harmonice Mundi* 5.3, *GW* 6:299.

26. "Si Deus εγεωμετρησεν inter creandum, et animales facultates sunt exemplaria Dei." Letter 357, to P. Heydon, October 1605, *GW* 15:235.

27. "Quid restat amplius, quin dicamus cum Platon θεον αει γεω-μετρειν." *Mysterium cosmographicum* 2, *GW* 1:26. In fact, the phrase "God always practices geometry" is not found in the Platonic corpus; it comes from Plutarch (*Quaestiones conviviales* 8.2.1.718c, in *Moralia*, ed. E. L. Milnar, F. H. Sandback, and W. L. Humboldt [Cambridge: Harvard University Press, 1961], 9:118). On the importance of this theme, see Ernst Cassirer, *Individuum und Cosmos in der Philosophie der Renaissance* (Leipzig and Berlin: B. G. Teubner, 1927), and esp. Jürgen Hübner, *Die Theologie Johannes Keplers zwischen Orthodoxie und Naturwissenschaft* (Tübingen: Mohr, 1975); concerning the univocity that ensues, see Gérard Simon, *Kepler, astronome, astrologue* (Paris: Gallimard, 1979).

28. "Quid enim est in mente hominis praeter numeros et quantitates? Haec sola recte percipimus, et si pie dici potest, eodem genere cum Deo,

quantum in hac mortalitate de iis percipimus." Letter 117, to Hohenburg, 9 September 1599, *GW* 13:309.

29. "La filosofia è scritta in questo grandissimo libro che continuamente ci sta aperto innanzi a gli occhi (io dico l'universo). . . . Egli è scritto in lingua matematica, e i caratteri son triangoli, cerchi, ed altre figure geometriche, senza i quali mezzi è impossibile a inenderne umanamente parola." *Il Saggiatore* 6 in *Opere di Galilei*, Edizione Nazionale, ed. Antonio Favaro (Florence: G. Barbèra, 1890–1909; 1929–39), 6:232. See also the letter to Fortunate Liceti, January 1641, *Opere* 18:295. See: Edwin A. Burtt, *The Metaphysical Foundations of Modern Physical Science* (London: Routledge and Kegan Paul, 1932; rpt., New York: Humanities Press, 1980); Alistair C. Crombie, *Medieval and Early Modern Science*, 2d ed. (Garden City, N.Y.: Doubleday, 1959); Alexandre Koyré, *Études galiléennes* (Paris: Hermann, 1939 1st ed.; 1966 2d ed.), trans. as *Galileo Studies* (Atlantic Highlands, N.J.: Humanities Press, 1978); Maurice Clavelin, *La philosophie naturelle de Galilée* (Paris, 1970 1st ed.; 1995 2d ed.), trans. as *The Natural Philosophy of Galileo* (Cambridge: MIT Press, 1974); and William R. Shea, *Galileo's Intellectual Revolution* (New York: Macmillan, 1972).

30. "Le scienze matematiche pure, cioè la geometria e l'aritmetica . . . di quelle poche intese dall'intelletto umano credo che la cognizione agguagli la divina nella certezza obiettiva, poiché arriva a comprenderne la necessità; . . . Però, per meglio dichiararmi, dico che quanto alla verità di che ci danno cognizione le dimostrazioni matematiche, ella è l'istessa che conosce la sapienza divina." *Dialogo dei Massimi Sistemi* 1, *Opere* 8:128–29. This is confirmed by the letter to G. Gallanzoni, 16 July 1611, *Opere* 11:149. On possible medieval origins of this view, see William A. Wallace, *Galileo and his Sources: The Heritage of the Collegio Romano in Galileo's Science* (Princeton: Princeton University Press, 1984).

31. For the texts and discussion, see Giorgio de Santillana, *The Crime of Galileo* (Chicago: University of Chicago Press, 1955); Guido Morpurgo-Tagliabue, *I processi di Galileo e l'epistemologia* (Milan: Edizioni di Communità, 1963 1st ed.; Rome, 1981 2d ed.); and my *Théologie blanche*, 218–21.

32. "Quibus iterum Geometriam objicis, si forte Platonem audiant, qui ex hac scientia deum agnovit, sic enim dixit ο θεοσ αει γεωμετρει, i.e. Deus semper exercet Geometriam." *Quaestiones celeberrimae in Genesim* 1 (Paris, 1623), art. 2, *ratio* 16, col. 56. My interpretation of this work (*Théologie blanche*, 161–78) is opposed to that found in Robert Lenoble, *Mersenne ou la naissance du mécanisme* (Paris: Vrin, 1943 1st ed., 1971 2d ed.) and Peter Dear, *Mersenne and the Learning of the Schools* (Ithaca: Cornell University Press, 1988); limited exclusively to Mersenne, these studies ignore the parallel theses of Kepler and Galileo, thus misreading Mersenne as a fairly banal positivist and as perfectly anachronistic. See Vincent Carraud, "Mathématiques et métaphysique: les sciences du possible," *Les Études philosophiques* 1–2 (1994).

33. *La vérité des sciences contre les sceptiques* 2.1 (Paris, 1625), 227.

34. Ibid., 2.4, theorem 1, 5, 283.

35. Ibid., 1.9, 108. The formula Mersenne uses here is similar to one in Kepler, given in n. 24 above. There is some interesting information on Mersenne in P. J. S. Whitmore, *The Order of the Minims in Seventeenth-Century France* (The Hague: Martinus Nijhoff, 1967), and on his epistemology in Alistair C. Crombie, "Marin Mersenne and the Seventeenth Century Problem of Scientific Acceptability," *Physis* 17 (1975).

36. "Naturalem enim Philosophiam post verbum Dei certissimam superstitionis medicinam, eandem probatissimum fidei alimentum esse. Itaque merito religioni tanquam fidissimam et acceptissimam ancillam attribui: cum altera voluntatem Dei, altera potestatem manifestet." *Cogitata et Visa*, in *The Works of Francis Bacon*, ed. J. Spedding, R. L. Ellis, D. D. Heath (London: Longmans, 1876), 3:597.

37. Pierre Gassendi: "Urgebis, erit igitur conceptus quispiam abstrahabilis Deo ipso superior? sed quidni sit? cum nemo neget conceptum entis esse Deo superiorem." *Exercitationes paradoxicae adversus Aristoteleos* 2.3, art. 9 (Verdier, 1624 1st ed.; Amsterdam, 1649 2d ed.) rpt. in *Opera Omnia* (Lyon, 1658), 3:170; in the critical edition by Bernard Rochot (Paris: Vrin, 1959), 335. See also Tullio Gregory, *Scetticismo ed empirismo. Studio su Gassendi* (Bari: Laterza, 1961), and Olivier René Bloch, *La philosophie de Gassendi: Nominalisme, matérialisme et métaphysique* (The Hague: Martinus Nijhoff, 1971), chapters 13 and 14.

38. See *Œuvres spirituelles du Bienheureux Père Jean de La Croix*, French trans. Père Cyprien de la Nativité, 2 vols. (Paris, 1645 and 1647).

39. On these authors and the mystical movement, see the still-authoritative L. Cognet, *La spiritualité moderne*, vol. 1: *L'essort* [esp. chapters 7–10], in *Histoire de la spiritualité chrétienne* (Paris: Aubier, 1966), vol. 3, part 2.

40. *Règle de perfection*, ed. Jean Orcibal (Paris: Presses Universitaires de France, 1982), 3.8, 377. The book was originally published in Rouen in 1608 (in English), then in Rouen in 1609 (in French), and twice in Paris in 1610 (both a second French edition, including for the first time the third part, and a Latin edition). My quotations are from the remarkable critical edition of J. Orcibal.

41. *Règle de perfection, L'exercice de la volonté de Dieu*, 7.64. The attributes of incomprehensibility, omnipotence, and infinity here gathered in one definition anticipate the "incomprehensible power" that characterizes God in Descartes (see section 5 of this chapter).

42. *Règle de perfection* 3.1, 333. See also 3.2: "This Essential Will or Essence of God," 339 (and 3.6, 369; 3.8, 377; 3.9, 386, etc.). Similarly: "I think that to the extent one sees this essential will only in God, one sees God, and this [i.e., the will] as something not different [from God himself], for in God there is nothing other than God" (*Lettre contenant le réponse à un doute touchant l'objet de la volonté de Dieu*, 90).

43. See my *L'idole et la distance* (Paris: Grasset, 1977); trans. and introd. Thomas A. Carlson, *The Idol and Distance: Five Studies* (New York: Fordham University Press, 2001), chaps. 13–14.

44. L. Lessius, *Quinquaginta nomina Dei* (Brussels, 1640), chap. 1, 5–8. See also my *Metaphysical Prism*, 209.

45. *Discours* 3.1, col. 189, in Pierre de Bérulle, *Œuvres complètes*, ed. J.-P. Migne (Paris, 1846). See also: "This is why God has among his qualities the following, which is his principal quality and like his motto: *He who is* (Exodus 3:14). It is his proper name uttered by himself." *Discours* 3.1, cols. 251–52.

46. *Discours* 3.4, col. 192. This thesis involves a doctrine of emanation, as much *ad intra* as *ad extra* (3.3; 7.6; 11.6; *Opuscules* 35 and 145, respectively, ibid., col. 191, 273ff., 363ff., 970 and 1200), and allows development toward univocity. See Jean Orcibal, *Le cardinal de Bérulle, évolution d'une spiritualité* (Paris: Cerf, 1965); and my *Théologie blanche*, 140–60.

47. *Discours*, respectively, 4.4; 7.2 (see 2.13); and 6.6 (Bérulle, *Œuvres*, cols. 211, 264, 183, and 251).

48. Gibieuf's treatise, *De libertate Dei et creaturae*, published in Paris in 1630 and read by Descartes, deserves a new examination, according to Étienne Gilson, *La liberté chez Descartes et la théologie* (Paris: Alcan, 1913; rpt., Paris: Vrin, 1982). See also Francis Ferrier, *Un oratorien ami de Descartes: Guillaume Gibieuf* (Paris: Vrin, 1978).

49. *Traité de l'amour de Dieu* (Lyon, 1616), in *Œuvres de Saint François de Sales*, ed. Mackey-Navratel, 27 vols. (Annecy: J. Niérat, 1892–1969), cited according to *Œuvres*, ed. André Ravier and Roger Davos in the Pléiade edition (Paris: Gallimard, 1969), 2.1, 411.

50. *Traité de l'amour de Dieu*, 2.1 and 5.6, 565 and 584. See also 3.15, 523: "Enjoying unreservedly and without any exception whatsoever that whole infinite abyss of the Divinity, nevertheless, they can never make their enjoyment equal to that infinity. The latter always remains infinitely infinite, beyond their capacity." Infinity therefore colors even the final beatitude with incomprehensibility.

51. *Traité de l'amour de Dieu*, 5.7, 587.

52. Ibid., respectively 12.11, 968 (see also 10.14, 853); 10.17, 868; 3.1, 483; and 12.2, 951.

53. To Mersenne, 15 April 1630, AT I:145, 7–13; CSMK III:22–23.

54. To Mersenne, 6 May 1630, AT I:149, 21–28; CSMK III:24. In this last quotation, we have the virtual negation of a passage from Suárez, *Disputationes metaphysicae* 31, s. 12 n. 40, *Opera omnia* 26:295. For further discussion, see Pierre Garin, *Thèses thomistes* (Brussels: Desclée DeBrouwer, 1932); Timothy J. Cronin, *Objective Being in Descartes and Suárez* (Rome: Analecta Gregoriana, 1966); *Théologie blanche*, chap. 1; Geneviève Rodis-Lewis, *Idées et vérités éternelles chez Descartes et ses successeurs* (Paris: Vrin, 1985), 113ff.; and above, Chapter 6, §1 and §3, and Chapter 7, §1.

55. To Mersenne, 27 May 1630, AT I:152, 3–4; CSMK III:25. See also: "But I know that God is the author of all things, and that these truths are something, and consequently that He is their author." AT I:152, 3–9; CSMK III:25.

56. Respectively, to Mersenne, 15 April and 6 May 1630, AT I:146, 4–5 and 150, 22; CSMK III:23 and 25. Then First Replies, AT VII:110, 26–27; CSM II:80. This formula recalls that of Benoît de Canfeld (see n. 41). Efficient causality characterizes God completely (AT I:152, 2; CSMK III:25), that is, without recourse to a distinct formal cause.

57. Hence the distinction Descartes draws in the 1630 letters between what it is to know God [*connaître*] and what it is to comprehend Him [*comprendre*]; see letter to Mersenne, 27 May 1630, AT I:152; CSMK III:25.

58. To Mersenne, 6 May 1630, AT I:150, 6–7 and 18–19; CSMK III:25.

59. On the historical and philosophical significance of Descartes' doctrine here, see Emile Boutroux, *Des vérités éternelles chez Descartes*, French trans. G. Canguilhem from the Latin of 1874 (Paris: Alcan, 1927); A. Boyce Gibson, "The Eternal Verities and the Will of God in the Philosophy of Descartes," *Proceedings of the Aristotelian Society* n.s. 30 (1929–30): 31–54; Ferdinand Alquié, *La découverte métaphysique de l'homme chez Descartes* (Paris: Presses Universitaires de France, 1950); Harry Frankfurt, "Descartes on the Creation of the Eternal Truths," *The Philosophical Review* 86, no. 1 (1977): 36–57; *Théologie blanche*, chap. 13; Jean-Marie Beyssade, "Création des vérités éternelles et doute métaphysique," *Studia Cartesiana* 2 (Amsterdam, 1981): 86–105; Norman J. Wells, "Descartes' Uncreated Truths," *The New Scholasticism* 56, no. 1 (1982): 185–99; Edwin M. Curley, "Descartes on the Creation of the Eternal Truths," *The Philosophical Review* 93, no. 4 (1984): 569–97; G. Rodis-Lewis, *Idées et vérités éternelles*; Sergio Landucci, *La teodicea nell'età cartesiana* (Naples: Bibliopolis, 1986), chapter 3.

60. *Essais* (Bordeaux, 1580 1st ed.; 1582 2d ed.; 1588 3d ed.), quoted from Michel de Montaigne, *Œuvres complètes*, ed. R. Barral and P. Michel (Paris: Seuil, 1967), 2.12.213a and b.

61. Ibid., respectively, 2.12.219a; 2.29.290a (to be compared with Descartes, AT I:145; CSMK III:22–23); then 2.12.225a. See also 1.17.85b; 2.12.218a; 2.32.296a; 2.30.91b; etc. See Richard H. Popkin, *The History of Scepticism from Erasmus to Descartes* (Berkeley: University of California Press, 1979 and 1989), and Michael A. Screech, *Montaigne and Melancholy: The Wisdom of the Essay* (London: Duckworth, 1983).

62. *Discours* 6.6, 253. Compare this with Descartes: "Independence, conceived distinctly, involves [in it] infinity." To Mersenne, 30 October 1640, AT III:191, 15–16; CSMK III:154.

63. *De la sagesse* (Bordeaux, 1580 1st ed.; Paris, 1604 2d ed.); quoted from the edition by Barbara de Negroni (Paris: Fayard, 1986), 2.5, §1, 446 (cf. Descartes, AT I:152; CSMK III:25). Subject to the same skeptical tendencies, Francisco Sanchez (1550–1623) arrives at similar definitions: "God

most excellent, greatest, first of all causes and end of all things . . . inscribed unto infinity, immense, incomprehensible, ineffable, unintelligible"; "Deum optimum, maximum, primam omnium causam, omniumque finem ultimum . . . incidis in infinitum, immensum, incomprehensibilem, indicibile, inintelligibile." *Quod Nihil Scitur*, ed. Andrée Comparot (Paris: Klincksiek, 1984), 50. Sanchez does not go so far as La Mothe Le Vayer (1588–1672), who, violently attacking the Stoics for having "subjugated [God] to their famous Destiny" and Aristotle for having "tied God so much to the Natural necessities," recognizes "his essence which is incomprehensible to everybody other than Himself and calls Him 'All powerful.'" *De la Divinité* in *Cinq autres dialogues* (Paris[?], 1631[?]), rpt. in *Dialogues faits à limitation des anciens*, ed. A. Pessel (Paris: Fayard, 1988), respectively, 309, 320, 325, and 350.

64. *Petit traité de sagesse* (Paris, 1625), respectively §6 and §7, 843 and 844; cf. AT I:145, 13–16; CSMK III:23.

65. *Traité de l'indéfectibilité des créatures* 5 (ca. 1654), published in Robert Desgabets, *Œuvres philosophiques inédites*, ed. Joseph Beaude [introd. G. Rodis-Lewis] (Amsterdam: Quadratures, 1983), 34 and 33. See G. Rodis-Lewis, "Quelques échos de la thèse de Desgabets sur l'indéfectibilité des substances," and "Polémique sur la création des possibles et sur l'impossible dans l'école cartésiennes," in *Studia Cartesiana* 1 and 2 (Amsterdam, 1979 and 1981); rpt. in *Idées et vérités éternelles*.

66. See my "Le statut métaphysique du Discours de la Méthode," in *Le discours et sa méthode*, ed. Jean-Luc Marion and Nicolas Grimaldi (Paris: Presses Universitaires de France, 1987), rpt. as chapter 2 of *Cartesian Questions*.

67. "Infixa quaedam est in me vetus opinio, Deum esse qui potest omnia." AT VII:21, 1–2; CSM II:14; See also "my preconceived belief in the supreme power of God" ("haec praeconcepta de summa Dei potentia opinio"; AT VII:36, 8–9; CSM II:25). Similarly, the *genius aliquis malignus* (22, 5; CSM II:15). On the status of this primitive conception of God, see Henri Gouhier, *La pensée métaphysique de Descartes* (Paris: Vrin, 1962), chap. 7; Tullio Gregory, "Dio ingannatore e genio maligno: Nota in margine alle *Meditationes* di Descartes," *Giornale Critico della Filosofia Italiana* 53 (1974): 477–516, and "La tromperie divine," *Studia Medievali* 23 (1982): 517–27; Harry Frankfurt, *Demons, Dreamers and Madmen: The Defense of Reason in Descartes' Meditations* (Indianapolis: Bobbs-Merrill, 1970); and Richard Kennington, "The Finitude of Descartes' Evil Genius," *Journal of the History of Ideas* 32 (1971): 441–46.

68. AT VII:45, 11–12 and 40, 17; CSM II:31 and 28. This is certainly a reference to the famous phrase "a certain ocean of infinite substance" (*quoddam pelagus infinitae substantiae*), which the medievals borrowed so often from John of Damascus (*De fide orthodoxa* 1.9, ed. P. G. Migne [Paris: 1860], 94, col. 835 A–B).

69. Respectively, AT VII:45, 28–29; 47, 19; 55, 20–21 and 41, 3; CSM II:31, 32, 39 and 28. See Emmanuel Lévinas, "Sur l'idée de l'infini en nous,"

in *La passion de la raison: Hommage à F. Alquié*, ed. Jean Deprun and Jean-Luc Marion (Paris: Presses Universitaires de France, 1983), rpt. in *Entre-nous: Essais sur le penser à l'autre* (Paris: Grasset, 1991); trans. Michael B. Smith and Barbara Harshav, "The Idea of the Infinite in Us," in *Entre Nous: Thinking-of-the-Other* (New York: Columbia University Press, 1998), 219–22. An objective reality is one that exists as represented in something else—an idea, for example. On the notion of objective reality, see Timothy J. Cronin, *Objective Being in Descartes and Suárez* (Rome: Analecta Gregoriana, 1966).

70. On the denial of this claim, see §7 of this chapter.

71. Respectively, AT VII:9, 16–17 and 55, 21–22; CSM II:8 and 39. Infinity is directly characterized in terms of incomprehensibility (AT VII:368, 2–4; CSM II:253).

72. For a fuller discussion, see my *Cartesian Questions*, chap. 3.

73. "Illa omnia tantum, in quibus aliquis ordo vel mensura examinatur, ad Mathesim [Universalem] referri" (*Regula* 4, AT X:377, 23 – 378, 2; CSM I:19). Order and measure are the two conditions for the exercise of method: the idea of infinity eludes at least one of these.

74. AT VII:46, 5–28; CSM II:31–32. Incomprehensibility in no way excludes intelligibility; see Jean-Marie Beyssade's discussion in *La philosophie première de Descartes* (Paris: Flammarion, 1979), 171–81.

75. Respectively, AT VII:51, 3–4 and 54, 13–14; CSM II:35 and 38 (see also VII:66, 12–13; 67, 9–10; CSM II:46 [twice]).

76. *Cumulum perfectionum* (*Notae in programma*, AT VIII–B2:362, 12; CSM I:306) and *perfectionum complementum* (*Principles of Philosophy* 1, §18). For references and discussion, see my *Metaphysical Prism*, 240–44.

77. AT VII:65, 21–22; CSM II:45: *non minus*; AT VII:66, 8 and 12; CSM II:46: *non magis*.

78. To Mersenne, 15 April 1630, AT I:144, 15–17; CSMK III:22. (See also the letters of 25 November 1630, AT I:182, 2, CSMK III:29; March 1637, AT I:350, 27–28; 27 February 1637; CSMK III:53). Even the *Discours de la méthode* weakens "in the same manner" to "at least as certain" (AT VI:36, 24 and 29; CSM I:129). On the relation between the first two proofs, see Alquié, *La découverte métaphysique*, 225ff.; Martial Gueroult, *Descartes selon l'ordre*, chap. 8, and *Nouvelles réflexions sur la preuve ontologique* (Paris: Vrin, 1955); Leslie J. Beck, *The Metaphysics of Descartes: A Study of the Meditations* (Oxford: Oxford University Press, 1965).

79. AT VII:40, 21–23; CSM II:28.

80. AT VII:108, 19–22; CSM II:78: this "dictate" is never justified (no more than the parallel statements in AT VII:164, 26–165, 3 or 238, 11–18; CSM II:116 or 166). The *Discourse* already uses the phrase "reason dictates to us" (AT VI:40, 6, 8, 10; CSM I:131).

81. "Hoc enim de ipso Deo quaeri potest" (AT VII:164, 29 – 165, 1; CSM II:116); see also "we grant . . . to inquire into the efficient cause of all

things, even God himself"; "licentiam . . . in rerum omnium, etiam ipsius Dei, causas efficientes inquirendi." AT VII:238, 15–17; CSM II:166.

82. *Potentia exuperans*, AT VII:110, 27; CSM II:80; *exuperentia potestatis*, AT VII:112, 10; CSM II:80. On the inversion of the negative sense of the term *a se* among the medievals into positive causality, see Gilson, *Études sur le rôle de la pensée médiévale dans la formation du système cartésien* (Paris: Vrin, 1930; rpt., 1967), chap. 5, 224ff.; on analogy and the principle of reason, see my *Théologie blanche*, chap. 18, *Metaphysical Prism*, 256ff., and above, Chapter 5, §5.

83. Descartes speaks of *infinitam Dei potestam* at AT VII:220, 20; CSM II:155; see also *immensitas potentiae* at AT VII:111, 4 = AT IXA 237, 8–9; CSM II:80, and *immensa potestas* at AT VII:119, 13 = AT IXA 188, 23; CSM II:85. He speaks of *immensa et incomprehensibilis potentia* at AT VII:110, 26–27; CSM II:80; see also *puissance incompréhensible* at AT I:146, 4–5 and 150, 22; CSMK III:23, 25.

84. Martin Heidegger, *Identität und Differenz*, 51; and Marion, *Dieu sans l'être* (Paris: Fayard, 1982), trans. Thomas A. Carlson, *God Without Being* (Chicago: University of Chicago Press, 1991).

85. For a fuller development of these themes, see my *Théologie blanche* and *Metaphysical Prism*.

86. Louis de La Forge, *L'homme* (Paris, 1664), and *Traité de l'esprit de l'homme* (Paris, 1666); the latter is reprinted in Louis de La Forge, *Œuvres philosophique*, ed. Pierre Clair (Paris: Presses Universitaires de France, 1974).

87. *Traité de l'esprit de l'homme*, respectively, chaps. 10 and 21, in *Œuvres*, 174 and 301. See also: "God's greatness is infinite" (chap. 11, *Œuvres*, 190).

88. *Traité de l'esprit de l'homme*, chap. 27, *Œuvres*, 335. In fact, this purely philosophical definition agrees perfectly with that of the "theologians [speaking] of God as an infinite and very perfect spirit" (chap. 10, *Œuvres*, 161).

89. *Traité de l'esprit de l'homme*, chap. 11, *Œuvres*, 190. See "general cause," "total cause," chap. 15, *Œuvres*, 226 and 227; "universal cause," chap. 16, *Œuvres*, 242. The passages in question are simply quotations from the 1630 letters to Mersenne discussed earlier (AT I:150, 2–4; 152, 2–4; 149, 21–24 and 28; CSMK III:24, 25).

90. *Traité de l'esprit de l'homme*, respectively, chaps. 11, 15, and 16, *Œuvres*, 193 and 195, 227, and 241.

91. Johann Clauberg, *Opera omnia philosophica*, ed. Joh. T. Schalbruch, 2 vols. (Amsterdam, 1691; Hildesheim: Olms, 1968). The *Defensio cartesiana* originally appeared in 1652, and the first edition of the *Ontosophia* appeared in 1647.

92. *Disputatio physica* 18, n. 32, *Opera omnia*, 1:100.

93. *Metaphysica de ente quae rectius ontosophia*, first 6, n. 96 ("Deus actus dicitur punssimus, ein stets wirkendes Wesen"), then 13, n. 223, *Opera*

omnia, 1:299 and 320. A cause *secundum fieri* is a cause that gives certain already existing materials their properties; in this sense, an architect is the cause of a house. But a cause *secundum esse* is a cause that brings something into existence and sustains it in existence; in this sense the sun was said to be the cause of light, and God was said to be the cause of all creatures. See, e.g., Saint Thomas Aquinas, *Summa Theologiae* 1, q. 104, art. 1; or Descartes' Fifth Replies, AT VII:369; CSM II:254–55.

94. For example, *Ontosophia* 6, n. 81: "ens omnino perfectissimum" (*Opera omnia*, 1:296); *Disputatio physica* 18, n. 32: "ens perfectissimum" (*Opera omnia*, 1:100); *Exercitationes de cognitione Dei et nostri* 6, n. 18: "ens perfectissimum"; 7, n. 20: "ens summe perfectum"; 8, n. 8: "idea Dei, hoc est idea entis perfectissimi"; 20, n. 4, 6, and 11; 31, n. 15, 18, and 19; 37, n. 6, etc. (*Opera omnia*, 2:607, 609, 610, 630ff., 649, and 656). Undoubtedly we are dealing with the essential conception of God for Clauberg.

95. *Exercitationes de cognitione Dei et nostri* 9, n. 5 (*Opera omnia*, 2:611) or else n. 6 and n. 10 (656 ff.).

96. *Ontosophia* 11, n. 193: "Adhaec perfectionis nomen non modo sumitur pro omnium attributorum, vel etiam partium ad rei integritatem pertinentium, comprehensione; sed generali quoque significatione interdum attributum quodvis perfectio rei dicitur." *Opera omnia*, 1:315.

97. Respectively Robert Desgabets, *Traité de l'indéfectabilité des créatures* 1; then, *Le guide de la raison naturelle* 5: "God is not only the universal cause, but . . . He is yet the only cause of all things"; finally *Supplément à la philosophic de Monsieur Descartes*: "God being the efficient cause of all our simple ideas or conceptions, since He alone is the cause of movements in our external and internal senses" In Robert Desgabets, *Œuvres philosophiques*, 19, 123, and 259.

98. *Traité de l'indéfectabilité des créatures* 14 (*Œuvres philosophiques*, 84). See *Supplément à la philosophic de Monsieur Descartes*: "The sovereign perfection that is in God" (*Œuvres philosophiques*, 259). The case of Antoine Arnauld must still be studied. See already Vincent Carraud, "Arnauld: From Ockhamism to Cartesianism," in Ariew, *Descartes and His Contemporaries*, 110–28.

99. Respectively, *Supplément à la philosophie de Monsieur Descartes*, 2.1; and *Le guide de la raison naturelle*, 11 (*Œuvres philosophiques*, 216 and 137). See G. Rodis-Lewis, *Idées et vérités éternelles*, and J. Beaude, "Cartésianisme et anticartésianisme de Desgabets," *Studia Cartesiana* 1 (Amsterdam, 1979): 1–24.

100. *Opera Posthuma* (Amsterdam, 1678), cited according to the *Opera omnia*, ed. C. Gebhardt, 4 vols. (Heidelberg: C. Winter, 1925). The phrase *Deus sive Natura* only appears in *Ethics* 4 (preface, two times) and in Dutch (*de Natuur of God*) in the *Korte Vorhandling*, appendix 2 (Geb. 1:117).

101. On the distinction, see *Ethics* 1, prop. 29, schol.; the parallel passage from *Korte Vorhandling* 1.8 explicitly acknowledges, among others, the Thomistic origin of the theme (*Summa Theologiae* I. II., q. 85, art. 6c, and *In*

Dionysii de divinis nominibus 4.21, in *Opuscula omnia*, 2:452). On these later interpretations, see Paul Vernière, *Spinoza et la pensée française avant la Révolution* (Paris: Presses Universitaires de France, 1952 1st ed.; 1982 2d ed.).

102. *Ethics* 1, def. i., prop. 7, dem., prop. 24, dem., and prop. 25, schol. add further explanation of this concept. See above, Chapter 5, §2.

103. *De intellectus emendatione*, §92; my emphasis.

104. This claim may appear somewhat paradoxical. Spinoza defines God as a substance "consisting of an infinity of attributes, of which each one expresses an eternal and infinite essence" (*Ethics* 1, def. 6). This would seem to be quite different from anything that Descartes offers, particularly insofar as Spinoza holds that a single substance can have multiple attributes. But the infinity of attributes does not directly define God (substance), but every thing whatsoever, substance or mode, finite or infinite. While Spinoza's metaphysics is novel, and differs from Descartes', the innovation is not exactly centered on the conception of God.

105. *Summa Dei perfectione*, *Ethics* 1, prop. 33, schol.; *ens summe perfectum*, prop. 11, dem. 2; *ens absolute perfectum*, prop. 11, schol.; *perfectissima Dei natura*, appendix (Geb. 2:83). This parallel is also noted by Harry A. Wolfson, *The Philosophy of Spinoza*, 2 vols. (Cambridge: Harvard University Press, 1934), 1:179–84. For the equivalence of the Cartesian and Spinozist definitions of God, see Edwin M. Curley, *Behind the Geometrical Method: A Reading of Spinoza's Ethics* (Princeton: Princeton University Press, 1988).

106. The parallel is also noted in Martial Gueroult, *Spinoza*, vol. 1: *Dieu* (Paris: Aubier, 1968), 187, 191.

107. *Ethics* 5, prop. 35, dem. Spinoza's inconsistency here is argued in Ferdinand Alquié, *Le rationalisme de Spinoza* (Paris: Presses Universitaires de France, 1981), 93–117. On all this, see my "The Coherence of Spinoza's Definitions of God in *Ethics* 1, Proposition 11," in *God and Nature: Spinoza's Metaphysics*, ed. Y. Yovel (Leiden: Brill, 1991).

108. *Entretiens sur la métaphysique et la religion* 2, §4, in Malebranche, *Œuvres complètes*, 12:53, Lennon, 47. See also *Recherche de la vérité* 3.2.5; *Œuvres complètes* 1:435, and 3.2.9, §5, *Œuvres complètes* 1:435 and 473, Lennon, 229, 251); Réponses à Arnauld, *Œuvres complètes* 6–7:541; *Entretiens d'un philosophe chrétien et d'un philosophe chinois*, in *Œuvres complètes* 15:3, 4, 43, 44. See also Beatrice K. Rome, *The Philosophy of Malebranche* (Chicago: Regnery, 1963), 120–60, and G. Rodis-Lewis, "L'interprétation malebranchiste d'Exode 3, 14. L'être infini et universel," in *Celui qui est— Interprétations juives et chrétiennes d'Exode 3, 14*, ed. E. Z. Brown (Paris: Cerf, 1986).

109. *Recherche de la vérité*, *Éclaircissement* 10, *Œuvres complètes* 3:137–38 and 3.2.5, *Œuvres complètes* 1:435; Lennon, 618, 229); see 3.2.6: "the place of minds," *Œuvres complètes* 1:437, Lennon, 230. This shift was criticized by Arnauld (Réponses à Arnauld, *OC* 6–7:248ff.) and more recently in Alquié, *Cartésianisme de Malebranche*, 126–28.

110. Réponses à Arnauld, *Œuvres complètes* 6–7, 51–52. For a discussion of Malebranche's doctrine that we see all things in God, see below, n. 162.

111. *Recherche de la vérité* 3.2.8, §1, *Œuvres complètes* 1:456, Lennon, 241 (see also 449 and 473, and *Œuvres complètes* 2:9 and 3:148, etc., Lennon, 236–37, 251, 318, 624). Likewise, *Entretiens sur la métaphysique et la religion*, 2, §4 (*Œuvres complètes* 12–13:53); 8.1 (174); 8.8 (185); etc. (Doney, 47, 171, 181–83). There are also some extremely ambiguous phrases: "The Being of beings" (*Réflexions sur la prémotion physique*, §19, *Œuvres complètes* 16:101 and 103); "God is all being" (*Recherche de la vérité*, 3.2.6, *Œuvres complètes* 1:439, Lennon, 231).

112. "Ens absolute indeterminatum," says Spinoza, *Epistola* 36, Geb. 4:186. The accusation of Spinozism against Malebranche was explicitly formulated by Father Tournemine (*Mémoires de Trévoux*, November 1713, 229ff. = *Œuvres complètes* 19:849ff.), by Dortous de Mairan (letter from 9 November 1713, *Œuvres complètes* 19:858).

113. *Traité de la nature et de la grâce* 1, §11, *Œuvres complètes* 5:26 (see also *Œuvres complètes* V:64, 75, 26; *Éclaircissement* 10, reply to the Second Objection, in *Œuvres complètes* 3:148). See also *Entretiens sur la métaphysique et la religion* (*Œuvres complètes* 12:135, 137, 174, 175, 178, 180, 197, 199, 200, 208, 211, 212, 225, 257, 310, etc. [Doney, 131, 133, 171, 173, 175, 177, 197, 199, 199–201, 207, 209–11, 211, 225, 257, 311]); and the *Entretiens d'un philosophe chrétien et d'un philosophe chinois* (*Œuvres complètes* 15:4, 5, 7, 15, 22, 24, 26, 28, 31, 33, 43, 44, etc.).

114. *Recherche de la vérité*, 3.2.6, *Œuvres complètes* 1:437 (Lennon, 230). On all of these questions, see particularly Alquié, *Malebranche*, part 1, chap. 3, 113–45.

115. *Traité de la morale*, 2, 2, §5, *Œuvres complètes* 11:159 ff. See also *Réponses à Arnauld*, *Œuvres complètes* 6–7:80. And *Traité de la nature et de la grâce* 1, §12; 1, §59; 2, §63; etc. (*Œuvres complètes* 5:27, 64, 116).

116. *Traité de la morale* 2.11, §9, *Œuvres complètes* 11:247. Perhaps there are not "two Divinities," but Malebranche nevertheless admits "two powers" (2.9, §5, 222) claiming "two loves" (2.4, §7, 179). This duality is all the more important to Malebranche's system as it renders intelligible the conflicting relations between the King (cause) and the bishop (wisdom, perfection).

117. Gottfried Wilhelm Leibniz, *Monadology*, §87; see *Principes de la nature et de la grâce fondés en raison*, §15 (according to the edition of A. Robinet [Paris: 1954 1st ed.; 1986 3d ed.]) and *Discours de métaphysique*, §35: "One must not only consider God as the principle and cause of all substances and all beings, but also as the leader of all persons or intelligent substance and as the absolute monarch of the most perfect city." *Die philosophischen Schriften*, ed. Carl Gerhardt, 7 vols. (Berlin: Weidmannsche Buchhandlung, 1875–90), 4:460. See also Jacques Jalabert, *Le Dieu de Leibniz* (Paris: Vrin, 1960); and William E. May, "The God of Leibniz," *New Scholasticism* 36 (1962): 506–28.

118. *Textes inédits d'après les manuscrits de la bibliothèque provinciale de Hanovre*, ed. Gaston Grua, respectively, 16 and 66 (see also 79, 171, 325, etc.). Likewise, see *Discours de métaphysique*, §1, "absolutely perfect being" (4:427); *Principes de la nature et de la grâce*, §10, "the supreme Perfection"; and *Monadology*, §41, "absolutely perfect."

119. *Textes inédits*, 580, and *Monadology*, §38. See *Essais de Théodicée*, part 1, §7–§8, Ger. 6:106–7.

120. *Monadology*, §31, then §43 (see also *Essais de Théodicée*, part 1, §335, Ger. 6:314 and *Principes de la nature et de la grâce*, §10). This thesis obviously goes back to Suárez (see the discussion earlier in the chapter).

121. "God is the first being, and therefore, he is essentially the highest and most perfect; His essence, therefore, will include all perfection of whatever mode of possibility within the entire range of his being"; "Deus est primum ens . . .; ergo est etiam summum et perfectissimum essentialiter; ergo de essentia ejus est, ut includat aliquo modo omnem perfectionem possibilium in tota latitudine entis." *Disputatione metaphysica* 30.1.5, *Opera omnia* 26:62.

122. On this quasi-unanimous rejection, see Gouhier, *Cartésianisme*, 156 ff.; Rodis-Lewis, *Idées et vérités éternelles*, 139ff.; and above, Chapter 6. Even Jacques-Bénigne Bossuet, though of Cartesian inspiration, held that "these eternal truths . . . are something of God, or rather are God himself," that "this reason is in God, or rather, this reason is God himself." *De la connaissance de Dieu et de soi-même* (Paris, 1722), 4, §5 and 5, §2, in *Œuvres complètes de Bossuet*, ed. Guillaume, 10 vols. (Lyon, 1879), 8:115 and 121.

123. *Principes de la nature et de la grâce*, §7. See also *Théodicée*, part 1, §44: "This great principle is found in all events; a contrary example can never be given. . . . Without this great principle, we could never prove the existence of God" (Ger. 6:127). Leibniz uses the very terms Descartes used to announce the *causa sui*; see the discussion earlier in the chapter.

124. *Principes de la nature et de la grâce*, §8. See also *Monadology*, §38–§40, and *Discours de métaphysique*, §16: "God being the true cause of substances" (Ger. 4:441).

125. [This section is significantly longer in the English version of the chapter than the one included in the French book, especially the paragraphs on John Locke. I have therefore in this case left the English version as it was and merely supplied extra references from the French where appropriate—Trans.]

126. *Leviathan* 2.31, *The English Works of Thomas Hobbes of Malmesbury*, ed. Sir William Molesworth, 11 vols. (London, 1839–45; rpt., Darmstadt: Scientia, 1962; hereafter *EW*), 3:352; in Latin, *Opera philosophica quae Latine scripsit omnia*, ed. Sir William Molesworth, 5 vols. (London, 1839–45; reprinted Darmstadt: Scientia, 1966; hereafter *OP*), 3:261.

127. *Leviathan* 1:3 (*EW* 3:17 = *OP* 3:20). See also *Leviathan*, 3:34; 4:45 and 46; *Elements of Law*, 1.5, §3; and *De corpore* 2.7–8.

128. *Leviathan* 2:31 (*EW* 3:350ff. and 352 = *OP* 3:261); see also *De cive*, 15:14: "Ut sciamus autem quern cultum Dei assignet ratio naturalis, incipiamus ab attributis: ubi manifestum est attribuendam ei esse existentiam; . . . Unicum enim ratio dictat *naturae* significativum Dei nomen, *exsistens*, sive simpliciter, *quod est.*" *OP* 2:340 and 342 = *Clarendon Edition of the Philosophical Works of Thomas Hobbes*, ed. Howard Warrender (Oxford: Oxford University Press, 1983), 2:226ff. and 3:190 ff..

129. *Leviathan* 1:11 and 12 (*EW* 3:92 and 96 = *OP*, 2:84 and 86). See *Philosophical Rudiments*, 3:15, §14: "For by the word *God*, we understand the world's cause." *EW* 2:213 ff. The hypothesis of Hobbes' fundamental atheism (Leo Strauss, *Political Philosophy of Hobbes: Its Basis and Genesis* [Oxford: Oxford University Press, 1936; repr., Chicago: University of Chicago Press, 1952]; Raymond Polin, *Hobbes, Dieu et les hommes* [Paris, Presses Universitaires de France, 1981]) is seductive but weak. Hobbes remains traditional; his theology is limited, adopting the Thomist schema, reducing multiple causality to efficient cause alone, following the Cartesian tradition. On this, see Howard Warrender, *The Political Philosophy of Hobbes* (Oxford: Oxford University Press, 1957), and Jean Bernhardt's introduction to Hobbes, *Court traité des premiers principes: Le* Short Tract on First Principles *de 1630–1631. La naissance de Thomas Hobbes à la pensée moderne*, ed. J. Bernhardt (Paris: Presses Universitaires de France, 1988).

130. See, e.g., Strauss, *Political Philosophy*, esp. chapter 5; and Polin, *Hobbes*, chapters 1–3.

131. See *An Essay Concerning Human Understanding*, 1.4.8–17 (London, 1690); *Clarendon Edition of Locke's Works*, ed. P. H. Nidditch (Oxford: Oxford University Press, 1975). Locke was not the only one to deny the innateness of the idea of God. Samuel Clarke also maintains that we have no innate idea of God, and therefore that one must proceed on the basis of causality in order to arrive at "the Being of a supreme independent cause." Clarke, *A Discourse concerning the Being and Attributes of God, the Obligations of Natural Religion, and the Truth and Certainty of the Christian Religion* (London, 1705–06), 19, 21, etc.. We find the same position in the Cartesian Pierre Sylvain Régis, *Cours entier de philosophic ou système générale selon les principes de M. Descartes concernant la logique, la métaphysique, la physique, et la morale*, 3 vols. (Amsterdam, 1691; rpt., New York: Johnson Reprint, 1970), 1:305; see Desmond M. Clarke, "Pierre-Sylvain Régis: A Paradigm of Cartesian Methodology," *Archiv für Geschichte der Philosophie* 62 (1980): 289–310.

132. *Essay Concerning Human Understanding*, 2.23.33. The idea of God is discussed most explicitly in *Essay* 2.23.33–36. The incomprehensibility of God is emphasized in *Essay*, 4.10.19. Here we are dealing with the very thesis which Descartes criticized at length in Gassendi (AT VII:365, 9–26; 370, 6 – 371, 7; AT III:427, 21ff.; etc.; CSM II:252, 255, CSMK III:192).

Although Locke is clear enough that God is infinite in the passage quoted and in others, the proof for the existence of God he offers in 4.10.2 ff. would seem to establish something somewhat weaker, that God is a *most powerful, and most knowing Being*" (4.10.6). The process of enlargement, whereby the idea of infinity in number or space is constructed from the finite ideas given to us in experience is discussed in 2.17. Locke's basic idea is that the idea of infinity arises "from the Power, we observe in our selves, of repeating without end our own *Ideas*" (2.17.6).

133. *Essay*, 4.10.7. Locke characterizes the argument from the idea of God as a "Darling Invention," suggesting that he has the more recent Cartesian argument in mind, rather than the older ontological argument, which also derives from the idea of God, though in a different way.

134. *Essay Concerning Human Understanding*, 4.10.2–6.

135. Berkeley, *A Treatise Concerning the Principles of Human Knowledge*, §148.

136. See, e.g., Berkeley, *Principles of Human Knowledge*, §48, *Three Dialogues Between Hylas and Philonous*, 2, 3, in *The Works of George Berkeley*, ed. Arthur A. Luce and Thomas E. Jessop, 9 vols. (Edinburgh: T. Nelson, 1948–57), 2:214–15, 230–31.

137. Berkeley denies that God has sensations like ours in *Three Dialogues* 3; *Works* 2:240–41. It should, however, be said that he also develops the idea that, since the divine will and understanding are the same, God's causing the sensible world and his sustaining it by (non-passively) perceiving it are two sides of the same coin. In general there is no causality without both will and understanding: "How can that which is *inactive* be a *cause*; or that which is *unthinking* be a *cause of thought*?" *Three Dialogues* 2; *Works* 2:216.

138. Berkeley, *Philosophical Commentaries, generally called the Commonplace Book* B, §52. See also §282, §293, §293a.

139. Berkeley, *Philosophical Commentaries* A, §802. Note also that all the entries in which Berkeley most clearly presents his view of objects in God's mind as powers are preceded by the mark " + ." Although there is still much controversy about the proper interpretation of this symbol, it often seems to indicate entries that Berkeley rejected either because they were wrong, adopted an inappropriate tone, or were simply not useful for the purposes of what he was writing.

140. Berkeley, *Three Dialogues* 3; *Works* 2:253.

141. Cf. Berkeley *Three Dialogues* 2; *Works* 2:213–14.

142. Berkeley, *Principles of Human Knowledge*, §30.

143. Berkeley, *Philosophical Commentaries* A, §433. It should be noted here that this entry is also preceded by the mark " + ." In this case, I suspect that Berkeley felt that he had gone too far in denying causes other than God (Berkeley clearly held that finite spirits were genuine causes too), but that the conception of God as cause remained central in his later works.

144. "Absurd to argue the existence of God from his idea, we have no idea of God. It is impossible," *Philosophical Commentaries* A, §782. The polemic against "Cartesian innatism," common among his contemporaries, is Berkeley's fatal weakness. See Geneviève Brykman, *Berkeley et le voile des mots*

(Paris: Vrin, 1993), and Berkeley, *Philosophie et apologétique* (Paris: Vrin, 1984). On the unknowability of matter, see *Three Dialogues*, in *Works*, 2:231. In fact, it is only by a "reflex act" that I can consider God as an "I" or a mind, hence as an idol of the "I."

145. *Principles of Philosophy* 1, §54. See also letter to Arnauld, 4 June 1648, AT V:193, 17; CSMK III:355: *cogitationes divinae*.

146. Except in the sense that God may contain extension eminently. On the notion of eminent containment, see Thomas M. Lennon, "The Cartesian Dialectic of Creation," in *The Cambridge History of Seventeenth-Century Philosophy*, chap. 12, and Eileen O'Neill, "Mind-Body Interaction and Metaphysical Consistency: A Defense of Descartes," *Journal of the History of Philosophy* 25 (1987): 227–45.

147. To Descartes, 11 December 1648, AT V:238, 21; not translated in CSMK. See also: "Deus suo modo extenditur." AT V 238, 25–26; 239, 2). This correspondence first appeared in 1657, in the first volume of Clerselier's edition of Descartes' correspondence, *Lettres de M. Descartes*, ed. Claude Clerselier, 3 vols. (Paris, 1657–67). This correspondence also appared in part in the volume Henry More, *Henrici Mori Epistolae ad Renatum Descartes* (London, 1662), in *A Collection of Several Philosophical Writings of Dr. Henry More* (London, 1662; rpt., New York: Garland, 1978).

148. More, *The Immortality of the Soul*, ed. Alexander Jacob (London, 1659; rpt., The Hague: Martinus Nijhoff, 1980), respectively, 1.4, §2, 32; 1.4, §3, 33; and 1.4, §4, 33. See also Aharon Lichtenstein, *Henry More: The Rational Theology of a Cambridge Platonist* (Cambridge: Harvard University Press, 1962), 168ff.

149. To Descartes, 11 December 1648, AT V:238, 30 and 240, 6ff.; then 23 July 1649, AT V:379, 16. In addition to the references to More cited in the previous note, see also *Enchiridion metaphysicum* (London, 1679) 8.8: "Divinum quiddam videbitur hoc extensum infinitum ac immobile."

150. Ralph Cudworth, *The True Intellectual System of the Universe* (London, 1678 1st ed.; 1743 2ded.; Latin translation: *Systema intellectuale hujus universi* [Jena, 1733 1st ed.; Leyden, 1773 2d ed.]), ed. John Harrison (London, 1848; rpt., Stuttgart: Frommann, 1964; New York: Garland, 1978) 769–70. Commented on by Serge Hutin, *Henry More: Essai sur les doctrines théosophiques chez les Platoniciens de Cambridge* (Hildesheim: Olms, 1966), 122. See Ralph Cudworth, *A Treatise Concerning Eternal and Immutable Morality* (London, 1731; rpt., New York: Garland, 1976). Cudworth's position is actually somewhat more complicated than this argument might suggest. In general he is agnostic about whether or not spirits are extended. Cudworth's main goal is to refute a position like that of Hobbes, in accordance with which spirit is corporeal, including God. Cudworth's point is that incorporeal substance, *both* extended and unextended, are coherent notions, and whichever we adopt, Hobbes can be answered. And that is what is important. See Cudworth, *True Intellectual System*, preface, v, and 833–34.

151. *Essay Concerning Human Understanding*, 2.15.3.

152. See ibid., 4.10.13–19. It should be mentioned here that Locke is at least agnostic about the question of whether God is the subject of the space or extension in which finite creatures exist and move.

153. "Non est duratio vel spatium, sed durat et adest. Durat semper et adest upique, et existendo semper et ubique durationem et spatium, aeternitatem et infinitatem constitituit." Isaac Newton, *Principia philosophiae naturalis mathematica, Scholium generale*, in *Isaac Newton's* Philosophia Naturalis Principia Mathematica: *The Third Edition with Variant Readings*, ed. Alexandre Koyré, I. Bernard Cohen, and Anne Whitman, 2 vols. (Cambridge: Harvard University Press, 1972), 2:760–62. In the first version of the text, afterward suppressed, Newton wrote: "He is not place nor space, but he is in place and in space and is always and everywhere" ("non est locus, non spatium, sed est in loco et in spatio idque semper et ubique"). In I. Bernard Cohen, *Introduction to Newton's "Principia"* (Cambridge: Harvard University Press, 1971), 250. See also *Unpublished Scientific Papers of Isaac Newton*, ed. C. R. Hall and M. B. Hall (Cambridge: Cambridge University Press, 1962), 98, 99, 103ff.

154. *An Answer to Bishop Bramhall's Book, Called "The Catching of Leviathan"* (1668), in *EW* 4:309. Hobbes also writes "By corporeal, I mean a substance that has magnitude" (*EW* 4:313). Likewise, "Ego per corpus intelligo nunc id de quo vere dici potest, quod existit realiter in seipso, habetque etiam aliquam magnitudinem, non quod sit magnitude ipsa." *Leviathan*, appendix 1, *OP* 3:537.

155. Hobbes, *Leviathan* 1, §34, 428–29.

156. Hobbes, *Leviathan* 1, §12, 171.

157. *An Answer to Bishop Bramhall*, *EW* 4:305, 306, and 383. Hobbes also writes: "Affirmat [author] quidem Deum esse corpus. . . . Magnus est Deus, sed magnitudinem intelligere sine corpore impossibile est." *Leviathan*, appendix 1, *OP* 3:537. Hobbes' textual argument, the claim that the notion of an incorporeal substance does not appear in the Scriptures or in the authoritative writings of Tertullian and Athanasius, does not hide the imprecision of Hobbes' concept of "body," which he treats as a synonym of "substance."

158. *Ethics* 1, prop. 15, schol.

159. *Ethics* 1, prop. 15, schol. See also *Ethics* 2, prop. 2: "Extension is an attribute of God, or God is an extended thing"; "extensio attributum Dei est, sive Deus est res extensa." *Works* 1:449.

160. According to Olivier Bloch, "Sur les premières apparitions du mot 'matérialiste,'" *Raison présente* 47 (1978): 3–16, one must attribute authorship of the term "materialism" to More; More, *Divine Dialogues* (London, 1668), 5–6.

161. Respectively, *Recherche de la vérité, Éclaircissement* 10, Malebranche, *Œuvres complètes* 3:152; Lennon, 626–27; *Conversations chrétiennes* 3, *Œuvres complètes* 4:75; and *Entretiens sur la métaphysique et la religion* 2, §1, *Œuvres*

complètes 12–13, 50ff.; Doney, 43ff.). Leibniz establishes this usage in opposing the "greatest materialists," the Epicurians, to the "greatest idealists," the Platonists (*Réponses aux réflexions . . . de M. Bayle*, 1702; 4:560).

162. *Méditations chrétiennes et métaphysiques* 9, §9, Malebranche, *Œuvres complètes* 10:99.

163. Pierre Gassendi, *Exercitationes paradoxicae adversus Aristoteleos*, ed. Bernard Rochot (Paris: Vrin, 1959), 2.3.8, 331ff.

164. Antoine Arnauld and Pierre Nicole, *La logique ou l'art de penser* (Paris, 1662, 1664, 1668), ed. Pierre Clair and François Girbal (Paris: Presses Universitaires de France, 1965), 1.2, 47. See also Bernard Lamy, *Entretiens sur les sciences* 4 (Grenoble and Paris, 1684); see ed. Clair and Girbal (Paris: Presses Universitaires de France, 1966), 127ff.

165. Desgabets, *Le Guide de la raison naturelle* 9; *Œuvres*, 137.

166. François de Salignac de la Mothe Fénelon, *Traité de l'existence et des attributs de Dieu* 1.2, in *Œuvres de Fénelon*, ed. L. Vivès, 8 vols. (Paris, 1854), 1:62. See also 2.2: "The idea that I have of infinity is neither confused nor negative. . . . The term infinity is infinitely affirmative by its signification, negative as it may appear in its grammatical turn" (*Œuvres* 1:100–101); and "a being that by itself is at the supreme degree of being, and consequently infinitely perfect in its essence" (*Œuvres* 1:98). This last formula brings together the three Cartesian names of God.

167. *Traité de l'existence et des attributs de Dieu*, 2.2, *Œuvres* 1:99; then: "Isn't this infinite idea of infinity in a limited mind the seal of the omnipotent worker, which He stamped upon his work?" *Œuvres* 1:107. It is precisely this last point that Pierre-Daniel Huet disputed: "Certe rei infinitae et infinitionis idea finita est." *Censura philosophiae cartesianae* (Paris, 1689 1st ed.; Kampen, 1690 2d ed.), 4.3; repr., Hildesheim: Olms, 1971, 107.168. *Traité de l'existence et des attributs de Dieu*, 2.3, *Œuvres*, 1:112, 115, respectively. Spinoza, of course, does not exactly deny the unity of God (substance). But God's unity is relative, in a sense, insofar as God has an irreducible plurality of attributes that are genuinely distinct from one another.

169. *Traité de l'existence et des attributs de Dieu* 2.5, *Œuvres* 1:125. Despite a *Réfutation de Spinoza* and a *Lettre sur l'idée d'infini et sur la liberté de Dieu de créer ou de ne pas créer* (*Œuvres*, 1:220 ff. and 224 ff.), Fénelon shared a similar suspicion of Spinozism with Malebranche. Indeed, the definition of God as "Ens ut sic, Ens universalissimum, Ens abstractum, metaphysicum et illimitatum" will be attributed to him not much later by Jean Hardouin as a sign of "quietism" and of "Jansenism." Letter to Gonzalez, 20 November 1697, quoted by Henk Hillenaar, *Fénelon et les Jésuites* (The Hague: Martinus Nijhoff, 1967), 357 ff. On all these points, see also Henri Gouhier, *Fénelon philosophe* (Paris: Vrin, 1977).

170. AT VII:368, 2–4; CSM II:253. We should not forget two defenders of the primacy of the idea of infinity (and also of the creation of the eternal truths): first, Pierre Poiret, whose *Cogitationum rationalium de Deo, anima et*

malo libri quattuor (Amsterdam, 1677) interprets infinity as *Ens sibi sufficient-issimum* (ed. 1715, 6); then J. Fontialis (1630?–1707), whose *De idea mirabilis matheseôs entis* (*Opera posthuma* [Namur, 1740]) carries on the Scotist tradition (see Duns Scotus, *Sur la connaissance de Dieu et l'univocité de l'étant*, ed. Olivier Boulnois [Paris: Presses Universitaires de France, 1988], 423); and Daniel Garber, *Descartes' Metaphysical Physics* (Chicago: University of Chicago Press, 1992), 345.

171. Blaise Pascal, *Entretiens avec Monsieur de Sacy* in *Œuvres complètes*, 294a, and *Pensées*, §418 (see §135, §420, §917, etc.). See P. Courcelle, *L'entretien de Pascal et Sacy: Les sources et ses énigmes* (Paris: Vrin, 1981).

172. Respectively, *Pensées*, §190 (and §191), then §449.

173. *Pensées*, §377: "It is a long way between knowing God and loving Him"; see also §739.

174. *Pensées*, §449. See my *Metaphysical Prism*, chapter 5, and Vincent Carraud, *Pascal et la philosophie* (Paris: Presses Universitaires de France, 1992), chapters 5 and 6.

175. Pascal, *Œuvres complètes*, 618b.

176. *Pensées*, §308; see also §424 and §903.

177. [The final two sentences are not included in the French version of the chapter. — Trans.]

Index

Perspectives in Continental Philosophy Series

John D. Caputo, series editor

1. John D. Caputo, ed., *Deconstruction in a Nutshell: A Conversation with Jacques Derrida.*

2. Michael Strawser, *Both/And: Reading Kierkegaard—From Irony to Edification.*

3. Michael D. Barber, *Ethical Hermeneutics: Rationality in Enrique Dussel's Philosophy of Liberation.*

4. James H. Olthuis, ed., *Knowing* Other-*wise: Philosophy at the Threshold of Spirituality.*

5. James Swindal, *Reflection Revisited: Jürgen Habermas's Discursive Theory of Truth.*

6. Richard Kearney, *Poetics of Imagining: Modern and Postmodern.* Second edition.

7. Thomas W. Busch, *Circulating Being: From Embodiment to Incorporation—Essays on Late Existentialism.*

8. Edith Wyschogrod, *Emmanuel Levinas: The Problem of Ethical Metaphysics.* Second edition.

9. Francis J. Ambrosio, ed., *The Question of Christian Philosophy Today.*

10. Jeffrey Bloechl, ed., *The Face of the Other and the Trace of God: Essays on the Philosophy of Emmanuel Levinas.*

11. Ilse N. Bulhof and Laurens ten Kate, eds., *Flight of the Gods: Philosophical Perspectives on Negative Theology.*

12. Trish Glazebrook, *Heidegger's Philosophy of Science.*

13. Kevin Hart, *The Trespass of the Sign: Deconstruction, Theology, and Philosophy.*